A2
US Government & Politics

Anthony J. Bennett

Philip Allan, an imprint of Hodder Education, an Hachette UK company, Blenheim Court, George Street, Banbury, Oxfordshire OX16 5BH

Orders

Bookpoint Ltd, 130 Milton Park, Abingdon, Oxfordshire, OX14 4SB
tel: 01235 827827
fax: 01235 400401
e-mail: education@bookpoint.co.uk
Lines are open 9.00 a.m.–5.00 p.m., Monday to Saturday, with a 24-hour message answering service. You can also order through the Philip Allan website: www.philipallan.co.uk

ISBN 978-1-4441-8354-2
First published 2004
Second edition 2005
Third edition 2009
Fourth edition 2013

Impression number   5
Year   2017   2016   2015

The publishers would like to thank the following for permission to reproduce photographs:

p.15 Photri/TopFoto; **p.16** imagebroker/Alamy; **p.41** The Image Works/TopFoto; **p.43** The Image Works/TopFoto; **p.68** PixelPro/Alamy; **p.71** The Granger Collection/TopFoto; **p.78** UPP/TopFoto; **p.134** The Image Works/TopFoto; **p.144** M Stock/Alamy; **p.163** The Image Works/TopFoto; **p.164** The Image Works/TopFoto; **p.181** Corel; **p.197** Press Association; **p.214** The Image Works/TopFoto; **p.226** Photri/TopFoto; **p.232** The Granger Collection/TopFoto; **p.237** The Image Works/TopFoto; **p.245** Lightroom Photos/TopFoto; **p.264** AFP/Getty Images; **p.268** The Granger Collection/TopFoto; **p.272** The Granger Collection/TopFoto; **p.287** RIA Novosti/TopFoto; **p.294** James H. Pickerell/Fotolia; **p.305** Kristoffer Tripplaar/Alamy; **p.318** The Granger Collection/TopFoto; **p.346** World History Archive/TopFoto

In all cases we have attempted to trace and credit copyright owners of material used.

Typeset by Integra Software Services Pvt. Ltd., Pondicherry, India
Printed in Dubai

Environmental information
Hachette UK's policy is to use papers that are natural, renewable and recyclable products and made from wood grown in sustainable forests. The logging and manufacturing processes are expected to conform to the environmental regulations of the country of origin.

Contents

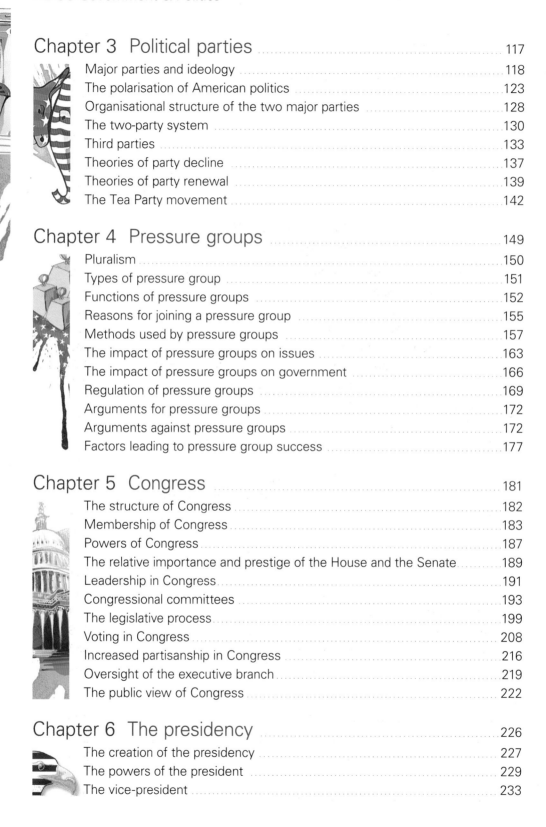

Introduction

About this book

US Government & Politics is a textbook written for students of the A2 specifications offered by Edexcel, OCR and AQA. This fourth edition has been completely revised to include the developments which occurred during President Obama's first term, including the elections of 2012. These 4 years have seen profound changes, such as the Tea Party movement, the 2010 mid-term elections, the evolution of the 'Roberts Court' and another presidential election. All eight chapters have therefore been revised and updated.

Features to help you succeed

Each chapter begins with a short introduction and a series of **key questions** which will be answered during that chapter. These can be used as a revision tool to check your knowledge before the exam.

For those studying the OCR specification, there is a bullet-point section at the end of all relevant chapters, which will help you with your **comparison between US and UK** government and politics. Those students studying other specifications may still find it useful to think through the comparisons so as to better understand the similarities and differences between the two systems they have studied.

At the end of each chapter you will find a **further reading** section with suggestions of up-to-date magazine articles and books on the topic covered in the chapter.

Throughout each chapter, you will find the following features:

Links to follow up

Useful weblinks providing opportunities for further research to extend your knowledge.

Exam focus

Short-answer and long-answer essay questions written in the style of the exam. Use them for homework to consolidate your knowledge or for in-class exam practice.

Key concepts

➢ Key concepts, as identified in the specifications, are explained on the page where they appear.

Activity

Activities designed to stimulate lively debate and discussion.

Key terms

➢ Clear, concise definitions of essential key terms are provided where they appear.

Strengths and weaknesses DEBATE

Learn to assess arguments and use evidence appropriately with these key debate boxes.

Online resources

Exercises to help you with note making are provided online at **www.hodderplus.co.uk/ philipallan**. If you work through all the exercises for each chapter, you will extract the main points of that chapter. Some of these exercise questions may be used for short-answer essay practice too.

Other resources

It is my hope that American politics is a subject in which you will become genuinely interested. This textbook will give you a grounding in the subject, but there are a number of other printed sources which you should try to make use of. Philip Allan, which publishes this textbook, also publishes *Politics Review*, a magazine written exclusively for students of A-level Government and Politics. It is published four times each academic year and includes articles on US and comparative politics as well as on UK politics.

Philip Allan also publishes the *US Government & Politics Annual Update*, which keeps you informed on what has happened in Washington over the previous 12 months. It is full of up-to-date examples, tables and anecdotes for you to use in your essays, and is written exclusively for A-level students.

The Economist magazine, published every Friday and available either through your local newsagent or by subscription, contains an invaluable 'American Survey', a collection of around six short, highly readable articles on matters of topical interest in American politics and society. The main UK newspapers — *The Times*, *Guardian*, *Independent* and *Daily Telegraph* — include articles on US politics too.

Weblinks

In this internet age, students of US politics have unrivalled opportunities to access and read a wealth of material, which just a decade ago would have been unimaginable. You are strongly urged, as much as your own and your school's resources permit, to use this opportunity. If I could make just one recommendation, it would be to get into the habit of logging on daily to the website of the *Washington Post*, **www.washingtonpost.com**, one of the best, frequently updated and freely accessible sites. Click on the 'Politics' button and the world of US politics is there for you to read and browse. True, the *Washington Post* has a liberal perspective on politics, as does the *New York Times* at **www.nytimes.com**. If you want to see things discussed from a conservative perspective, go to the website of the *Washington Times* at **www.washingtontimes.com** and you will get a different slant on events and people. Another site, which comes highly recommended and is now frequently quoted by other highly respected media outlets, is **www.realclearpolitics.com**, which is an amazing source for all things to do with US government and politics, and especially US elections.

You will find more specific website information at the beginning of each chapter.

Exam specifications

The table below shows how you can use this book in conjunction with the specifications of any of three UK awarding bodies — Edexcel, OCR or AQA.

Chapter	Edexcel	OCR	AQA
1 The Constitution	**Unit 4C** The Constitution	**Unit F853** The Constitution	**Unit 4A** The Constitutional framework
2 Elections and voting	**Unit 3C** Elections and voting	**Unit F853** Elections	**Unit 3A** The electoral process Direct democracy Voting behaviour
3 Political parties	**Unit 3C** Political parties	**Unit F853** Political parties	**Unit 3A** Political parties
4 Pressure groups	**Unit 3C** Pressure groups	**Unit F853** Pressure groups	**Unit 3A** Pressure groups
5 Congress	**Unit 4C** Congress	**Unit F853** Congress	**Unit 4A** Congress
6 The presidency	**Unit 4C** The presidency	**Unit F853** The presidency	**Unit 4A** The executive branch
7 The Supreme Court, and the protection of rights and liberties	**Unit 4C** The Supreme Court	**Unit F853** The Supreme Court, civil rights and liberties	**Unit 4A** The Supreme Court
8 Racial and ethnic politics	**Unit 3C** Racial and ethnic politics	**Unit F853** Civil rights and liberties	–

Chapter 1

The Constitution

Most people think they know quite a lot about the USA. Some might have visited part, or parts, of the country, but, for many, their knowledge and experience of the USA will be limited mainly to McDonald's, Coca-Cola, Hollywood, MTV and the Walt Disney Corporation. Of course, they also know something about US politics — they could name the president of the USA.

Students of US politics need to go beyond these superficial images and mere knowledge of names and need to understand more about US society than just what Americans eat and drink and who runs their entertainment industry. They need to realise that US society is still influenced by the principles that led to its establishment over 200 years ago. This will involve learning about some new concepts, such as the separation of powers, federalism and checks and balances. This is not a course in US history; rather, it is a course in contemporary US government and politics. However, it is impossible to appreciate the intricacies of what goes on in Washington today without knowing something about George Washington and the men around him who set up the Republic in 1787.

Key questions answered in this chapter

➤ What are the important characteristics of the USA?

➤ How did the US Constitution come to be written?

➤ What are the key features of the US Constitution?

➤ How are amendments to the US Constitution made?

➤ What are the principal constitutional rights?

➤ What is the doctrine of the separation of powers?

➤ How do the 'checks and balances' of the Constitution work?

➤ What is federalism and how has it changed?

➤ What are the consequences of federalism?

Links to follow up

There are a number of websites you can consult to follow up topics raised in this chapter. To find information on the US Constitution as well as on proposed and failed amendments, the following sites will be useful:

www.constitutioncenter.org

www.usconstitution.net/constam.html

For information on the individual states, you can go to **www.politics1.com/states.htm**. This will give you information on the elected officials, elections etc. within each state.

Other sites of interest are:

www.governing.com

www.usa.gov

www.fedstats.gov

www.nga.org

www.census.gov

www.ncsl.org

As regards the three branches of government — Congress, the president and the Supreme Court — you will find information on links relating to each at the beginning of the respective chapters.

The size and diversity of the USA

The USA is a vast country. The entire UK would fit into the state of Oregon. From coast to coast is over 3,000 miles (4,800 kilometres) and in covering that distance — from, say, New York to San Francisco — the traveller would encounter four different time zones (see Figure 1.1). At midday in London, it is 7 a.m. in New York but still 4 a.m. on the west coast. A non-stop jet takes 6–7 hours to travel across the country — only slightly less than the time to travel across the Atlantic from London to Boston. A train journey from Washington DC to Chicago, across the northern plains of North Dakota and Montana, through the Rockies and on to Portland, Oregon, would take $2\frac{1}{2}$ days. These are sizes and distances unthinkable within the UK.

The USA is also a very diverse country. There is the tropical landscape of Florida but also the frozen Arctic wastes of Alaska. There are the flat prairies of Kansas but also the Rockies of Wyoming and Colorado. There are the deserts of Arizona but also the forests of New Hampshire and Maine. It is diverse in its landscape, its climate, its economy and its people. The USA is also 'the hyphenated society', in which people think of themselves as African-Americans, Irish-Americans, Polish-Americans, Japanese-Americans or even Native-Americans. American society has been described as a 'melting pot' — a great cauldron filled with people from diverse lands, cultures, languages and religions.

This diversity gives rise to Americans' need for symbols of unity — most notably in their attachment to the American flag. While flag waving is regarded as something of an

Figure 1.1 Time zones of the 48 contiguous states of the USA

oddity in the UK — generally associated with football supporters or the Last Night of the Proms — countless families in rural and suburban America go through the daily ritual of raising and lowering the flag outside their homes each morning and evening. Public buildings in the USA display the flag as a matter of course. On 4 July in Washington DC, even the city's buses sport a flag. Each day begins in most American schools with children standing to face the flag at the front of the classroom and reciting the Pledge of Allegiance (see Box 1.1). There is even a day each year designated as 'Flag Day'.

> ## Box 1.1 Pledge of Allegiance
>
> 'I pledge allegiance to the flag of the United States of America and to the Republic for which it stands, one nation, under God, indivisible, with liberty and justice for all.'

These characteristics of size and diversity have important political implications too. Size brings with it the need for decentralisation — for the federal system of government established by the country's Founding Fathers in 1787. Diversity comes in the form of laws that differ between states about such matters as elections, crime and punishment. Different regions of the country (see Figure 1.2) have discernibly different ideological characteristics. The 'conservative' South — the 'Bible Belt' — stretches from Texas to Virginia. The 'liberal' Northeast includes such states as Massachusetts and Rhode Island.

The west coast, too, is liberal-leaning, especially in the Californian cities of Los Angeles and San Francisco. This has implications for political parties. As we shall see, California Democrats are very different from Texas Democrats. And South Carolina Republicans are equally different from Massachusetts Republicans.

Figure 1.2 Regions of the 48 contiguous states of the USA

The events leading to the Philadelphia Convention

How did it all start? Students of US government and politics need to know something of the origins of the country. The 13 original British colonies were strung out along the eastern seaboard of America from Maine in the north to Georgia in the south (see Figure 1.3). Some were the creations of commercial interests, others of religious groups. All had written charters setting out their form of government and the rights of the colonists. Democracy was limited. Although each colony had a governor, a legislature and a judiciary, each also had a property qualification for voting from which women and black people were excluded. And then, of course, there was slavery. Yet, despite their shortcomings, the colonies provided a blueprint of what was to come.

In the view of the British government, the American colonies existed principally for the economic benefit of the mother country. The colonists were obliged to pay tax to Britain, but they had no representation in the British Parliament. This led to a growing resentment. Bostonian patriot James Otis declared: 'Taxation without representation is tyranny!' As Britain tried to tighten its grip of the colonies' economic affairs in the 1770s, revolution became inevitable. The War of Independence began in April 1775.

On 4 July 1776, the colonies issued the Declaration of Independence, declaring themselves 'free and independent states'. The liberties that the colonists were fighting to protect were based not on the generosity of the king, but on a 'higher law' embodying 'natural rights' that were ordained by God and essential to the progress of human

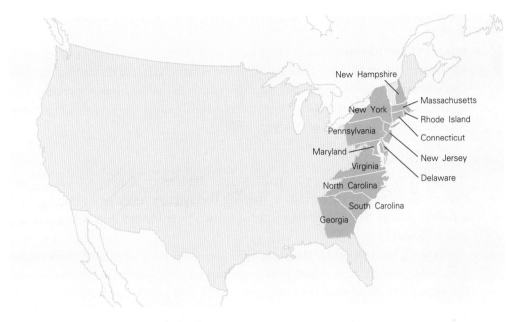

Figure 1.3 The original 13 colonies

society. Thomas Jefferson's glowing words in the opening sentence of the Declaration of Independence (see Box 1.2) became the touchstone of the American colonists' ambitions.

> ## Box 1.2   The Declaration of Independence
>
> 'We hold these truths to be self-evident, that all men are created equal, that they are endowed by their Creator with certain unalienable Rights, that among these are Life, Liberty and the pursuit of Happiness.'

At the same time as Jefferson was announcing high principles, the less well-remembered Richard H. Lee was offering his 'plan of confederation' for post-colonial government. The **Articles of Confederation** were eventually ratified by the 13 independent states by March 1781, although the hostilities with Great Britain were not formally concluded until the Treaty of Paris in 1783. These Articles set up a **confederacy** — a 'league of friendship', a loose collection of independent states — rather than a national government. Having just fought for — and won — their independence from Great Britain, the Virginians, New Yorkers and the rest were not going to give it away again to some new centralised government. Virginians wanted to govern Virginia. New Yorkers wanted to govern New York. The national government was a feeble affair with no executive branch, no judiciary and a legislature that was little more than a talking shop. The most significant fact about

Key terms
- **Articles of Confederation.** The compact made between the 13 original states that formed the basis of their government from 1781 until it was replaced by the US Constitution in 1789.
- **Confederacy.** A league of independent states in which the central government lacks significant powers and resembles more an international organisation — such as the United Nations — than a traditional national government.

the government created by the Articles of Confederation was that it was weak. Thus, the ex-colonists had succeeded in gaining their independence but had failed to form a nation, and by this failure they almost turned their victory into defeat. What ensued was a shambles.

Many of the leaders of the Revolutionary War, such as George Washington and Alexander Hamilton, believed that a strong national government was essential. As the states squabbled over currency, commerce and much else, they began to fear the reappearance of the British and the loss of all they had so remarkably achieved. A small group of men with such fears met at Annapolis, Maryland, in September 1786. Attendance was poor, so another meeting was called in Philadelphia in May 1787 with the declared purpose of strengthening the Articles of Confederation. That might have been their purpose, but 4 months later the attendees had scrapped the Articles, written an entirely new Constitution and become the Founding Fathers of the United States of America.

The writing of the federal Constitution

The **Philadelphia Convention** was made up of 55 delegates representing 12 of the 13 states. (Rhode Island, suspicious of what was planned, refused to send any delegates.) In those four stifling hot months of the summer of 1787 they wrote a new form of government. They quickly concluded that a confederacy was structurally flawed and hopelessly weak, but they saw from political history that stronger forms of government led to the trampling underfoot of the citizens' rights and liberties. Thus they would have to create an entirely new form of government — one that had a strong centre while still preserving states' rights and individual liberties. The answer was a federal constitution,

Key term
- **Philadelphia Convention.** The convention held in Philadelphia from 25 May to 18 September 1787, presided over by George Washington, which framed the Constitution. Its original purpose was merely to revise the Articles of Confederation, but the delegates instead decided to draft an entirely new document.

a bill of rights and an intricate set of checks and balances between the different levels and branches of government.

The convention initially considered two plans: one put forward by New Jersey, the other by Virginia. The New Jersey Plan — favoured by the states with smaller populations — was designed merely to strengthen the Articles of Confederation. The Virginia Plan — favoured by the states with larger populations — was much more radical. But with support equally divided, the convention was deadlocked.

Box 1.3 **The Preamble to the Constitution of the United States of America**

'We the People of the United States, in Order to form a more perfect Union, establish Justice, insure domestic Tranquility, provide for the common defence, promote the general Welfare, and secure the Blessings of Liberty to ourselves and our Posterity, do ordain and establish this Constitution for the United States of America.'

The impasse was broken with what became known as the Connecticut Compromise. The stroke of genius came in the plan's recommendation that the new national legislature should be made up of two chambers. In the lower house (the House of Representatives) the states would be represented proportionally to their population, but in the upper house (the Senate) the states would be represented equally, regardless of population. Other compromises followed, concerning such matters as the method of electing the president.

On 17 September 1787, the task was complete. When the delegates emerged from their self-imposed silence in Independence Hall, it is said that a woman approached delegate Benjamin Franklin and asked: 'Well, Doctor, what have we got — a republic or a monarchy?' Replied Franklin: 'A republic, if you can keep it.' What the US now had was a **codified constitution**.

Key concept
➤ **Codified constitution.**
A constitution that consists of a full and authoritative set of rules written down in a single text.

Article I of the new Constitution established Congress as the national legislature, defining its membership, the qualifications and method of election of its members as well as its powers. Under Article I Section 8 Congress was given specific powers such as those to 'lay and collect taxes', 'coin money' and 'declare war'. It was also given much less specific powers such as those to 'provide for the common defence and general welfare of the United States' and to make all 'necessary and proper laws' — the latter often called the 'elastic clause' of the Constitution.

Article II decided — somewhat surprisingly — on a singular, rather than a plural, executive by vesting all executive power in the hands of 'a President'. The president would be chosen indirectly by an Electoral College.

Box 1.4   What the Constitution provided

Article I   'All legislative Powers herein granted shall be vested in a Congress of the United States, which shall consist of a Senate and House of Representatives.'

Article II   'The executive Power shall be vested in a President of the United States of America.'

Article III   'The judicial Power of the United States shall be vested in one Supreme Court and in such inferior Courts as the Congress may from time to time ordain and establish.'

Article IV   Federal–state and state–state relationships

Article V   Amendment procedures

Article VI   Miscellaneous provisions, including the 'supremacy clause'

Article VII   Ratification procedure of the Constitution

Article III established the United States Supreme Court, though Congress quickly added trial and appeal courts. Although not explicitly granted, the Court was to have the role of umpire of the Constitution, implied in the 'supremacy clause' of Article VI and the provision in Article III itself that the Court's judicial power applies to 'all Cases... arising under this Constitution'. The Court would make this more explicit in its landmark decision of *Marbury v. Madison* in 1803.

Constitutional amendments

The process

The Founding Fathers, while realising the likely need to amend the Constitution, wanted to make doing so a difficult process. Thus, it was to be a two-stage process requiring super-majorities of more than 50%, such as a two-thirds or a three-quarters majority (see Table 1.1). Stage 1 is the proposal and stage 2 is the ratification. Constitutional amendments can be proposed either by Congress or by a national constitutional convention called by Congress at the request of two-thirds of the state legislatures. All constitutional amendments thus far have been proposed by Congress. No national constitutional convention has ever been called, although by 1992, 32 state legislatures had petitioned Congress for a convention to propose a balanced budget amendment — just two states short of the required two-thirds.

Once the amendment has been successfully proposed, it is sent to the states for ratification. An amendment can be ratified either by three-quarters of the state legislatures or by state constitutional conventions in three-quarters of the states. Of the 27 amendments added to the Constitution, only one has been ratified by state constitutional conventions — the 21st Amendment, which repealed the 18th Amendment and thus ended the prohibition of alcohol. Of the 33 amendments passed to them for

Table 1.1 The amendment process

Amendments proposed by:	Amendments ratified by:
Either: **Congress:** two-thirds majority in both houses required	Either: **State legislatures:** three-quarters of the state legislatures must vote to ratify
Or: **National constitutional convention:** called by at least two-thirds of the states (never used)	Or: **State constitutional convention:** three-quarters of the states must hold conventions and vote to ratify

ratification by Congress, the states have ratified 27. Thus, once an amendment has been successfully proposed by Congress, it stands a good chance of finding its way into the Constitution. Only six amendments have failed at the ratification stage in over 220 years. The most recent was the amendment designed to guarantee equal rights for women. Proposed by Congress in 1972, only 35 state legislatures ratified it — three short of the required three-quarters.

The Bill of Rights and later amendments

Of the 27 amendments to the Constitution, the first ten were proposed together by Congress in September 1789 and were ratified together by three-quarters of the states by December 1791. Collectively, they are known as the Bill of Rights. Many states had somewhat reluctantly signed up to the new federal Constitution with its potentially powerful centralised government. The Bill of Rights was designed to sugar the constitutional pill by protecting Americans against an over-powerful federal government.

Seventeen further amendments have been passed since the Bill of Rights, of which we shall come across only around half. The 12th Amendment (1804) revised the process for electing the president and vice-president. The 13th (1865), 14th (1868) and 15th (1870) Amendments were proposed and ratified immediately after the Civil War to end slavery and guarantee rights to the former slaves. The 14th Amendment, as we shall see later, has become increasingly important in American society in any number of areas beyond providing citizenship and civil rights to former slaves through its 'equal protection' and 'due process' clauses. The 16th Amendment (1913) is of crucial importance in understanding how the federal government's power increased during the 20th century. It allowed the federal government to impose an income tax. The 17th Amendment (also 1913) provided for the direct election of the Senate. Previously, senators were appointed by their state legislatures. The 22nd Amendment (1951) limited the president to a maximum of two terms in office. The 25th Amendment (1967) dealt with issues of presidential disability and succession, which had come to the fore following the assassination 4 years earlier of President Kennedy. The 26th Amendment (1971) lowered the voting age to 18.

Recent history of amendments

During the presidency of Bill Clinton (1993–2001), there were 18 votes on proposed constitutional amendments, an unusually high number (see Table 1.2). All these votes occurred during the 6-year period when the Republicans controlled both houses of Congress — 1995–2001. A proposal to amend the Constitution requires a two-thirds majority in both houses to be successful. During this period, the House of Representatives agreed to a Balanced Budget Amendment (1995) and a Flag Desecration Amendment (1995, 1997 and 1999). However, the Senate agreed to none of these, although it was only one vote short of the required two-thirds majority to pass the Balanced Budget Amendment in 1997 and four votes short of passing a Flag Desecration Amendment in 2000. Of the hundreds of amendments debated, Congress has passed only 33.

Table 1.2 Attempts to propose constitutional amendments in Congress, 1995–2012

Date	Chamber	Subject	Vote	Two-thirds majority?
1995				
26 January	House	Balanced budget	300–132	Yes
2 March	Senate	Balanced budget	65–35	No
29 March	House	Term limits	227–204	No
28 June	House	Flag desecration	312–120	Yes
12 December	Senate	Flag desecration	62–36	No
1996				
15 April	House	Tax limitation	243–177	No
6 June	Senate	Balanced budget	64–35	No
1997				
12 February	House	Term limits	217–211	No
4 March	Senate	Balanced budget	66–34	No
18 March	Senate	Campaign finance limitation	38–61	No
15 April	House	Tax limitation	233–190	No
12 June	House	Flag desecration	310–114	Yes
1998				
22 April	House	Tax limitation	238–186	No
4 June	House	School prayers	224–203	No
1999				
15 April	House	Tax limitation	229–199	No
24 June	House	Flag desecration	305–124	Yes
2000				
29 March	Senate	Flag desecration	63–37	No
12 April	House	Tax limitation	234–192	No
2001				
26 March	Senate	Campaign finance limitation	40–56	No
25 April	House	Super-majority to raise taxes	232–189	No
17 July	House	Flag desecration	298–125	Yes
2002				
12 June	House	Super-majority to raise taxes	227–178	No

(Continued)

Table 1.2 *(Continued)*

2003				
3 June	House	Flag desecration	300–125	Yes
2004				
2 June	House	Appointments to fill House vacancies	63–353	No
30 September	House	Marriage protection	227–186	No
2005				
22 June	House	Flag desecration	286–130	Yes
2006				
27 June	Senate	Flag desecration	66–34	No
18 July	House	Marriage protection	236–187	No
2011				
18 November	House	Balanced budget	261–165	No
14 December	Senate	Balanced budget	47–53	No

During the presidency of George W. Bush (2001–09), there were ten further attempts to amend the Constitution. But only three of these ten votes — the three in the House of Representatives to ban the desecration of the American flag — received the required two-thirds majority. This means that the House has now voted on this amendment six times since 1995. Almost every time the number of 'yes' votes has declined: 312 (1995); 310 (1997); 305 (1999); 298 (2001); a slight increase to 300 (2003); but then only 286 in 2005. When the Senate voted on this amendment in June 2006, the vote was 66–34, just one vote short of the required two-thirds majority. But with the Democrats retaking control of both houses of Congress in the 2006 mid-term elections, passage of this amendment seems much less likely as it is the majority of Republicans who vote 'yes' on this amendment. Again, all these votes took place when the respective chambers were controlled by the Republicans. The reason for this is that these issues, such as banning flag desecration and gay marriage, are issues which are supported by Republicans. Democrats tend to vote 'no' on such proposals.

With the Republicans retaking control of the House of Representatives in January 2011, numerous proposals to amend the Constitution further were introduced at the start of the 112th Congress. These included proposed amendments to: balance the federal budget; control federal government spending; prohibit the desecration of the American flag; grant a line-item veto to the president; repeal the 16th Amendment; repeal the 22nd Amendment; and abolish the Electoral College. One can see from this list that these were revisiting many of those issues which Congress had declined to support as constitutional amendments in the previous two decades. In November 2011, the House voted again on a balanced budget amendment but it failed to gain the two-thirds majority required. With 236 Republicans and 25 Democrats voting 'yes' and 161 Democrats and 4 Republicans voting 'no', the final vote was 261–165, which was 23 votes short of the majority required to pass. The Democrat-controlled Senate voted on the same amendment a month later and failed to secure even a simple majority in favour.

Why the Constitution has been amended so rarely

With only 27 amendments passed, and only 17 of those in the last 220 years, the question is raised as to why so few amendments have been passed. There are four significant reasons.

➢ The Founding Fathers created a deliberately difficult process. The need for both Congress and the states to agree, and the need for super-majorities, make the amendment process difficult. Hundreds of amendments have been initiated, but very few have made it successfully through the process.

➢ The Founding Fathers created a document that was, at least in parts, deliberately unspecific. Congress is given the power, for example, 'to provide for the common defence and general welfare' of the United States. This has allowed the document to evolve without the need for formal amendment.

➢ The most important reason, the Supreme Court's power of judicial review, is considered in Chapter 7. Suffice it to say here that this power allows the Court to interpret the Constitution and thereby, in effect, change the meaning of words written over two centuries ago — to make what one might call 'interpretative amendments' rather than formal amendments. Thus, for example, the Court can state what the phrase in Amendment VIII, which forbids 'cruel and unusual punishments', means today.

➢ Americans have become cautious of tampering with their Constitution. They hold it in some degree of veneration. In the early decades of the 20th century, they got themselves into difficulties by amending the Constitution to prohibit the manufacture, sale and importation of alcohol. Fourteen years later, 'prohibition' was discredited and the offending amendment was repealed. This experience proved to be an important lesson for subsequent generations.

Constitutional rights

The Constitution guarantees certain fundamental **constitutional rights**. Just listing rights in a constitution does not, in itself, mean that these rights are fully operative. The government — be it federal, state or local — must take steps to ensure that these rights are effectively protected. As we shall see later, all three branches of the federal (national) government — the legislature (Congress), the executive (the president) and the judiciary (the courts, and especially the Supreme Court) — play an important role in trying to ensure that these constitutional rights are effective for all Americans. So what rights are granted by the Constitution?

Key concept

➢ **Constitutional rights**. The fundamental rights guaranteed by the federal Constitution, principally in the Bill of Rights — the first ten amendments — but also in subsequent amendments.

The 1st Amendment guarantees the most basic and fundamental rights: freedom of religion; freedom of speech; freedom of the press; freedom of assembly. Debates such as those concerning prayers in public (i.e. state) schools, pornography on the internet, flag burning and press censorship all centre upon 1st Amendment rights. The 2nd Amendment guarantees that 'the right of the people to keep and bear arms shall not be infringed'. It is on this amendment that the debate about gun control focuses. The Supreme Court weighed in with a major decision on the meaning of this Amendment in 2008. The 4th Amendment guarantees the right against unreasonable searches — either of your person or of your property. You might well have heard of Americans 'pleading the 5th Amendment' — the right to silence, protecting the individual from self-incrimination. The 8th Amendment, which states that 'cruel and unusual punishments' shall not be inflicted, is the focus of the death penalty debate. The 10th Amendment has become an article of faith of the modern Republican Party in standing up for states' rights over the increasing power of the federal government in Washington DC.

Box 1.5 Amendments to the Constitution

Amendments I–X: the Bill of Rights (1791)

I	Freedom of religion, speech, press and assembly
II	Right to bear arms
III	No quartering of troops in private homes
IV	Unreasonable searches and seizures prohibited
V	Rights of accused persons
VI	Rights when on trial
VII	Common-law suits
VIII	Excessive bail and cruel and unusual punishments prohibited
IX	Unenumerated rights protected
X	Powers reserved to the states and to the people

Some later amendments

XII	(1804) Electoral College process revised for electing president and vice-president
XIII	(1865) Slavery prohibited
XIV	(1868) Ex-slaves made citizens; 'equal protection' and 'due process' clauses
XV	(1870) Blacks given the right to vote
XVI	(1913) Federal government authorised to impose income tax
XVII	(1913) Direct election of the Senate
XXII	(1951) Two-term limit for the president
XXV	(1967) Presidential disability and succession procedures
XXVI	(1971) Voting age lowered to 18

Later amendments have been added to guarantee other fundamental rights and liberties. Three amendments — the 13th, 14th and 15th — were added immediately after the civil war to guarantee rights for former slaves, rights of 'equal protection' and 'due process', about which we shall learn more in later chapters. Voting rights were guaranteed to women by the 19th Amendment in 1920 and to those over 18 years of age by the 26th Amendment in 1971. Voting rights were also guaranteed to minorities who had previously been discriminated against — notably black voters — by the 24th Amendment, passed in 1964. It is largely up to the courts, and most especially the United States Supreme Court, to ensure that these rights are effective. We shall examine this in Chapter 7.

Separation of powers

The Constitution drawn up at the Philadelphia Convention in 1787 divided the national government into three branches based on what is known as the doctrine of the **separation of powers**. This is a theory of government whereby political power is distributed among three branches of government — the legislature, the executive and the judiciary — acting both independently and interdependently (see Figure 1.4).

This framework of government was put in place by the Founding Fathers because of their fear of tyranny. The framers were influenced by the writings of the French political philosopher Baron de Montesquieu (1689–1755). In his book *L'Esprit des Lois* (*The Spirit of the Laws*), published in 1748, Montesquieu argued for a separation of powers into legislative, executive and judicial branches in order to avoid tyranny. 'When the legislative and executive powers are united in the same person...there can be no liberty,' wrote Montesquieu.

Key concept

> **Separation of powers.** A theory of government whereby political power is distributed among three branches of government — the legislature, the executive and the judiciary — acting both independently and interdependently. As applied to the United States government, the theory is better understood as one of 'shared powers'. It is the institutions of government that are separate, while the powers are shared through an elaborate series of checks and balances.

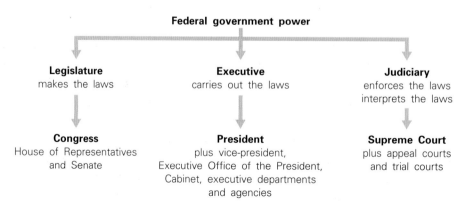

Figure 1.4 Federal government power

The Founding Fathers had the idea that each of these three independent yet co-equal branches should check the power of the others. The framers wanted **limited government**, whereby government would do only what was essential, leaving the citizens' fundamental rights and freedoms as untouched as is possible in an organised and orderly society. James Madison, writing later in *The Federalist Papers*, put it this way:

> If men were angels, no government would be necessary. If angels were to govern men, neither external nor internal controls on government would be necessary. In framing a government which is to be administered by men over men, the great difficulty lies in this: you must first enable the government to control the governed; and in the next place oblige it to control itself.

Key concept

➤ **Limited government.** A principle that the size and scope of the federal government should be limited to that which is necessary only for the common good of the people.

Thus, the three branches were to be separate in terms of their personnel. No person can be in more than one branch of the federal government at the same time — what we might call 'the separation of personnel'. When, in 1992, Senator Al Gore was elected vice-president, he had to resign from the Senate. And similarly in 2008, when Senator Barack Obama was elected president, he too had to resign from the Senate. In this sense the three branches — the institutions of government — are entirely separate.

Barack Obama, the USA's first black president

However, the term 'separation of powers' is misleading, for it is the *institutions* that are separate, not the *powers*. Professor Richard Neustadt was the most helpful in clearing up this potential confusion. Neustadt (1960) wrote: 'The Constitutional Convention of 1787 is supposed to have created a government of "separated powers". It did nothing of the sort. Rather, it created a government of separated institutions *sharing* powers.'

Quite right. So the concept is best thought of as the doctrine of 'shared powers'. And those 'shared powers' are what checks and balances are all about, for the Founding Fathers set up an intricate system whereby each branch of the federal government would check and balance the other two. This is especially important in terms of the legislature and the executive, which Professor S. E. Finer (1970) has described as being 'like two halves of a bank note — each useless without the other'.

Checks and balances

The **checks and balances** exercised by each branch of the federal government — the legislature, the executive and the judiciary — on the other two branches are detailed in Table 1.3. We shall look at each of these in turn.

> **Key concept**
>
> ➤ **Checks and balances.** A system of government in which each branch — legislative, executive and judicial — exercises control over the actions of other branches of government.

Checks by the executive on the legislature

The president is given the power to recommend legislation to the Congress. He (or presumably some day she) does this formally in January of each year in what is known as the **State of the Union Address**. Presidents use this set-piece speech, delivered to a joint session of the House of Representatives and the Senate — as well as cabinet members and the nine justices of the Supreme Court — on primetime television before a nationwide audience. It is the president's main opportunity to lay out his legislative agenda: in effect saying to Congress, 'this is what I want you to debate and pass into law'. President George W. Bush used his State of the Union Address in January 2002 to try to get Congress to focus on his 'war on terrorism' and budget priorities.

In addition, the president has the power to veto bills passed by Congress. During his 8 years in office, President George W. Bush used the regular veto on 11 occasions, including his veto of the State Children's Health Insurance Programme (S-CHIP) in 2007.

George W. Bush — US president 2001–09

> **Key term**
>
> ➤ **State of the Union Address.** An annual speech made by the president — usually in late January — to a joint session of Congress meeting in the chamber of the House of Representatives, in which he lays out his proposed legislative programme for the coming year. The name comes from the phrase in Article II Section 3 of the Constitution which states that the president 'shall from time to time give to the Congress information on the state of the Union, and recommend to their consideration such measures as he shall judge necessary and expedient'.

Table 1.3 Checks and balances

Checks on → Checks by ↓	The legislature	The executive	The judiciary
The legislature		• amend/delay/reject legislation • override president's veto • power of the purse • declare war • ratify treaties (Senate) • confirm appointments Senate) • investigation • impeachment, trial, conviction and removal from office	• impeachment, trial, conviction and removal from office • propose constitutional amendments
The executive	• recommend legislation • veto legislation		• appointment of judges • pardon
The judiciary	• judicial review	• judicial review	

Checks by the executive on the judiciary

Here the president has two significant checks. First, he nominates all federal judges — to the trial court, appeal court and Supreme Court. It is the latter who are the most important. During his first term, President Barack Obama was able to make two appointments to the Supreme Court — Sonia Sotomayor (2009) and Elena Kagan (2010). By choosing justices whose judicial philosophy matches their own, presidents can hope to mould the outlook of the Court for years to come.

Second, the president has the power of pardon. This has become something of a controversy in recent times. In 1974, President Ford pardoned his predecessor — President Nixon — for any crimes that Nixon might have committed in the so-called **Watergate affair**. On the final day of his presidency, President Clinton pardoned 140 people, including Mark Rich, a notorious tax fugitive. In contrast, as of November 2012, President Obama had pardoned only 22 people in just under 4 years.

Key term

➤ **Watergate affair.** A term used to refer to a collection of illegal activities conducted by senior members of the Nixon administration and the subsequent attempted cover-up. The name was drawn from the Watergate building in downtown Washington DC, where the Democratic National Committee had its headquarters during the 1972 presidential election. The building was broken into by people working on behalf of President Nixon's re-election committee. These illegal activities, which included illegal use of the CIA and other government agencies, bugging and bribery, led to Nixon's resignation in August 1974.

Checks by the legislature on the executive

Because the Founding Fathers were most anxious about the possible power of the singular executive they had created — the president — they hedged this branch of government with the most checks. Congress exercises eight significant checks on the president.

➤ Congress can amend, block or even reject items of legislation recommended by the president. In 2010, it passed — but in a significantly amended form — President Obama's healthcare reform bill. In 1993–94, President Clinton found his healthcare reforms blocked by Congress. Similarly, Congress blocked President George W. Bush's attempt at immigration reform in 2007. In 2011, Congress rejected President Obama's proposed job creation legislation.

➤ Congress can override the president's veto. To do this, it needs to gain a two-thirds majority in both houses of Congress. During President George W. Bush's two terms, Congress overrode four of his 11 regular vetoes, including his vetoes of the 2007 Water Resources Development Bill and the 2008 Food Conservation and Energy Bill. President Obama's only two vetoes during his first term were both sustained by Congress.

➤ Congress has the significant power that is referred to as 'the power of the purse'. All the money that the president wants to spend on his policies must be voted for by Congress. Its refusal to vote for this money will significantly curtail what the president can do — be it in domestic or foreign policy. In 2007, the Democrat-controlled Congress attempted to limit President George W. Bush's spending on the military operations in Iraq.

➤ In the field of foreign policy, Congress has two further checks on the president. Although the Constitution confers on the president the power to be 'commander-in-chief' of the armed forces, it confers on Congress the power to declare war. Although this power seems to have fallen into disuse — the last time Congress declared war was on Japan in 1941 — Congress has successfully forced presidents since then to seek specific authorisation before committing troops to situations in which hostilities are likely or inevitable. In October 2002, President George W. Bush gained specific authorisation from Congress to use military force in Iraq. The House approved the use of troops in Iraq by 296–182 while the vote in the Senate was 77–23.

➤ The Senate has the power to ratify treaties negotiated by the president. This requires a two-thirds majority. In 2010, the Senate ratified the new START Treaty with Russia by 71 votes to 26. In 1999, the Senate rejected the Comprehensive Test Ban Treaty by 48 votes to 51 — 18 votes short of the 66 votes required to ratify it. This was the first major treaty to be rejected by the Senate since the rejection of the Versailles Treaty in 1920. Five minor treaties have been rejected in between.

➤ Another check exercised by Congress over the president is an important power held by the Senate alone — the power to confirm many of the appointments that the president makes to the executive branch and all the appointments he makes to the federal judiciary. Executive appointments subject to Senate confirmation include such high-profile posts as cabinet members, ambassadors and heads of important agencies such as the Central Intelligence Agency (CIA) and the Federal Bureau of Investigation (FBI). Only a simple majority is required for confirmation. Rejections are unusual, but only because presidents usually consult informally with key senators before announcing such appointments, naming only those for whom confirmation is a fair certainty. In 1987, the Senate rejected (42–58) President Reagan's nominee, Robert Bork, for a place on the Supreme Court (see Chapter 7). In 1989, the Senate rejected (47–53) John Tower as secretary of defense. In 1997, it refused to confirm William Weld — President Clinton's choice as ambassador to Mexico. In 1999, it rejected (45–54) Ronnie White — President Clinton's nominee to a vacancy on the United States District (trial) Court. In October 2005, Harriet Miers withdrew as a nominee to the Supreme Court following widespread criticism by Republican senators of her lack of qualification and conservative credentials. What was extraordinary about this incident was that it was senators from the President's own party who forced the nominee to withdraw. In all the other examples quoted above, the president had faced opposition from a Senate controlled by the party which was not his own.

➢ Two further important checks on the president are given to Congress. The first is the power of investigation: Congress — usually through its committees — may investigate the actions or policies of any member of the executive branch, including the president. In October 2012, the House Oversight and Government Reform Committee launched an investigation of possible security failures by the Obama administration following the murder of four American diplomats, including the US ambassador, by terrorists in Benghazi, Libya.

➢ Finally, in the most serious circumstances, investigation may lead to **impeachment** — the ultimate check that Congress holds over the executive. Congress may impeach (formally accuse) any member of the executive branch, including the president. Two presidents — Andrew Johnson (1868) and Bill Clinton (1998) — have been impeached by Congress. It is the House of Representatives which has the power of impeachment. In 1998, it passed two articles of impeachment against President Clinton — for perjury (228–206) and obstruction of justice (221–212). Just a simple majority is required. Once the House has impeached, the Senate then conducts the trial. If found guilty by a two-thirds majority, the accused person is removed from office. In President Clinton's case, the Senate found him not guilty on

Key concept

➢ **Impeachment.** A formal accusation of a federal official by a simple majority vote of the House of Representatives. Impeachment is the first step in a two-stage process: it is followed by a trial by the Senate in which a two-thirds majority is required for conviction. If convicted, the federal official is removed from office.

both articles of impeachment — the votes being 45–55 on perjury and 50–50 on obstruction of justice, respectively 22 and 17 votes short of the required two-thirds majority. In the 1860s, President Johnson escaped conviction by the Senate by just one vote. In 1974, President Nixon resigned rather than face near certain impeachment by the House and conviction by the Senate. Thus, through impeachment — what someone has described as 'the political equivalent of the death penalty' — Congress can remove the president. This is the ultimate check. The president holds no similar power — he cannot remove Congress.

Checks by the legislature on the judiciary

Congress has two important checks on the courts. First, there is the power of impeachment by the House of Representatives, trial by the Senate, and — if found guilty by a two-thirds majority — removal from office. In the space of 3 years (1986–89), Congress removed three federal judges from office — Harry Claiborne for tax evasion, Alcee Hastings for bribery and Walter Nixon for perjury. In March 2010, the House of Representatives impeached federal judge Thomas Porteous for corruption, and following guilty verdicts in the Senate on four counts, Judge Porteous was removed from office later that year.

A more subtle but still significant check is that Congress can propose constitutional amendments to — in effect — overturn a decision of the Supreme Court. When in 1896 the Supreme Court declared federal income tax to be unconstitutional, Congress proposed the 16th Amendment granting Congress the power to levy income tax. It was ratified and became operative in 1913. Congress has more recently attempted unsuccessfully to reverse Supreme Court decisions on such issues as flag burning and prayer in public schools.

Checks by the judiciary on the legislature

The judiciary — headed by the Supreme Court — possesses one very significant power over the Congress: the power of judicial review. This is the power of the court to declare Acts of Congress to be unconstitutional and therefore null and void. In the 1997 case of *Reno v. American Civil Liberties Union*, the Supreme Court declared the Communications Decency Act unconstitutional. In 1998, in *Clinton v. New York City*, it declared the Line Item Veto Act unconstitutional. In 2012, the Court declared the Affordable Care Act — President Obama's landmark healthcare reform — constitutional, but at the same time decided that Congress could not require non-insured Americans to buy healthcare insurance by their power under the Commerce Clause of Article I, but only under their taxation powers of that Article. By so doing, the Court clearly put a check on congressional power. We shall discuss this in more detail in Chapter 7.

Checks by the judiciary on the executive

The courts have the same power of judicial review over the executive branch. Here the power of judicial review is the ability to declare actions of any member of the executive branch to be unconstitutional. In *United States v. Richard Nixon* (1974), the Court ordered President Nixon to hand over the so-called White House tapes and thereby stop impeding investigation of the Watergate affair. Nixon obeyed, handed over the tapes and resigned within days once the tapes showed his involvement in an intricate cover-up. In the 2006 case of *Hamdan v. Rumsfeld*, the Supreme Court declared unconstitutional the military commissions set up by the Bush administration to try suspected members of al Qaeda held at Guantánamo Bay in Cuba.

The political importance of checks and balances

The checks and balances between the three branches of the federal government — especially those between the legislature and the executive — have important consequences for US politics. They encourage a spirit of **bipartisanship** and compromise between the president and Congress. Usually, laws are passed, treaties ratified, appointments confirmed and budgets fixed only when both branches work together rather than pursue a partisan approach. In December 2010, President Obama managed to get the Tax Relief and Job Creation Act passed by Congress only because substantial numbers of Republicans in both the House and the Senate were prepared to support it. In the House 139 Democrats were joined by 138 Republicans voting in favour of the legislation, whilst in the Senate the 'yea' votes were cast by 43 Democrats and 37 Republicans.

Key term

➤ **Bipartisanship.** Close cooperation between the two major parties. In the US system of government, where it is possible to have a president of one party and a Congress controlled by the other party, bipartisanship is thought to be crucial to political success.

The trouble is that gridlock can result. Most recent presidents have accused the Senate of either rejecting or blocking their judicial nominations for partisan reasons. As a consequence, a large number of posts in both the federal trial and appeal courts remain unfilled for months, even years, slowing down the work of the courts. In 1995, such a serious impasse developed between the Republican-controlled Congress and Democrat President Clinton over the passage of the federal budget that parts of the federal government had to close when they ran out of money.

Divided government

This raises the issue of 'divided government', a term used to refer to the situation in which one party controls the presidency and the other party controls Congress. Of late, this has indeed become the norm. The 44 years between 1969 and the end of 2012 have seen 22 years of divided government when both houses of Congress were controlled by the party which did not control the White House. As Figure 1.5 shows, for only 12½ years of this period did one party control the presidency and both houses of Congress:

1977–80 (Jimmy Carter) and 1993–94 (Bill Clinton) for the Democrats; January–June of 2001 and 2003–06 (George W. Bush) for the Republicans; and 2009–10 (Barack Obama) for the Democrats. For the remaining 9½ years, the president controlled one house of the Congress but not the other. This was the case between January 2011 and December 2012 when Barack Obama's Democratic Party controlled the Senate but not the House of Representatives. It is worth noting, too, that divided government has not always been the norm. In the previous 44 years — from 1925 to 1968 — there was divided government for only 8 years.

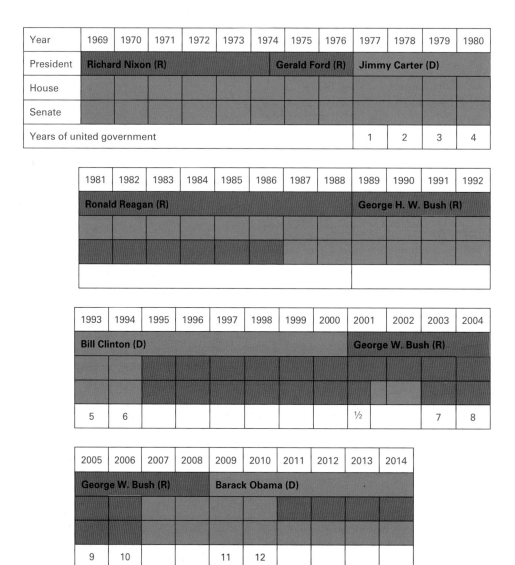

Figure 1.5 Divided and united government: 1969–2014

Does divided government make the checks and balances between Congress and the president more or less effective?

There are arguments on both sides. Some think that divided government leads to *more* effective government. Bills are scrutinised more closely, treaties checked more carefully and nominees questioned more rigorously in the confirmation process. There is some evidence that when Congress and the president are of the same party, legislation, nominations, budgets, treaties and the like are nodded through without as much careful scrutiny as there should be. Not since 1935 has the Senate rejected a treaty of a president of its own party. Only twice in the last 50 years has Congress overridden a veto of a president of its party. In 1964, Democrat President Johnson managed to persuade a Congress with Democrat majorities in both houses to pass the Tonkin Gulf Resolution which authorised the President to take whatever action was deemed appropriate in South Vietnam. During the years of Republican control from 2003 to 2006, Congress was fairly feeble in exercising its oversight function of Republican President George W. Bush's war in Iraq.

Others, however, think that divided government leads to *less* effective government. Examples such as the treatment of Republican Supreme Court nominees Robert Bork (1987) and Clarence Thomas (1991) by a Democrat-controlled Senate, and the impeachment proceedings conducted against Democrat President Bill Clinton by a Republican-controlled Congress (1998–99), seem poor advertisements for effective checks and balances.

Does the US Constitution still work? DEBATE

Yes

➤ Federalism has proved to be an excellent compromise between strong national government and state government diversity.

➤ The text has proved very adaptable to the changes in American society.

➤ The demanding amendment process has usually prevented frequent and ill-conceived amendments.

➤ Rights and liberties of Americans have been protected.

➤ Supreme Court's power of judicial review has made the Constitution even more adaptable to change through 'interpretative amendment'.

No

➤ The amendment process is too difficult, thereby making it well nigh impossible to remove parts no longer applicable or add parts which a majority desires.

➤ The power of judicial review gives the Supreme Court too much power to 'amend' the meaning of the Constitution.

➤ The Constitution is too negative, giving too much power to those who oppose change and causing gridlock.

➤ Some parts make no sense in today's society (e.g. the Second Amendment, the Electoral College).

➤ Some parts don't work as the Framers would have envisaged (e.g. war-making power, confirmation process of Supreme Court justices).

Source: based on Kay Moxon and Tom Murphy, 'Does the US Constitution work?', *Politics Review*, Vol. 21, No. 3, February 2012

There are specific checks and balances that have proved problematic in modern times. Congress's power to declare war is one obvious example. Modern presidents have managed to conduct overt wars in Korea, Vietnam and the Persian Gulf, to name but three, with no congressional declarations of war. Impeachment used against Presidents Andrew Johnson and Bill Clinton seems to have become overtly political. Analysts suggest, with considerable evidence, that the confirmation process of federal judges has become overly politicised. 'Innocent until nominated' is how one US political figure has described the situation.

That said, the checks and balances of the Constitution have stood the test of time remarkably well. The Founding Fathers would be pleased with how well their creation has survived. Few back wholesale constitutional reform — and certainly those who do are likely to be disappointed.

Federalism and the changing federal–state relationship

Federalism and the Constitution

'We the People of the United States, *in order to form a more perfect Union...*' So began the preamble to the new Constitution. Certainly, the first attempt at union was weak and almost disastrous. The Articles of Confederation showed just about how far the newly independent peoples of America were prepared to go in the formation of a national government — not very far; but the experience of confederacy had been educative. The compromise between a strong central government and states' rights was to be **federalism**. It was what James Madison called 'a middle ground'.

Key concept

➤ **Federalism.** A theory of government by which political power is divided between a national government and state governments, each having their own area of substantive jurisdiction.

Federalism involves a degree of **decentralisation**, which has proved suitable for a country as large and diverse as the USA has become. As Benjamin Franklin knew at the signing of the Declaration of Independence, a certain level of national unity was vital: 'We must all hang together, or, most assuredly, we shall all hang separately.' Thus, out of the disunity of the Articles of Confederation came the *United* States of America — *e pluribus unum* — 'out of many, one'.

Key concept

➤ **Decentralisation.** The principle by which governmental and political power is vested not only in the federal government, but also in the state governments.

Nowhere is the word 'federal' or 'federalism' mentioned in the Constitution. How, then, was it written into the document? First, it was written into the enumerated powers of the three branches of the federal government — Congress was 'to coin money', the president was to 'be commander-in-chief' and so on. Second, it was included in the implied powers of the federal government. These are the powers that flow from, for example, the 'elastic clause' of the Constitution — Congress's power to 'make all laws necessary and proper for carrying into execution the foregoing powers'. Third, the federal government and the states were given certain concurrent powers: for example, the power to tax. Fourth, the 10th Amendment reserved all remaining powers 'to the states and to the people'. Finally, the Supreme Court was to be the umpire of all disagreements between the federal and state governments. As Chief Justice Charles Evans Hughes wrote in 1907: 'We are under a Constitution, but the Constitution is what the judges say it is.'

The changing federal–state relationship

Federalism is not, however, a fixed concept. It is ever changing. As America has changed, so has the concept of federalism.

During the latter part of the 19th century and the first two-thirds of the 20th century, a number of factors led to an increased role for the federal government.

➤ **Westward expansion.** From 13 colonies clustered up and down the Atlantic coast, settlement spread westwards across the Appalachian mountains, over the plains of the Midwest, across the Rockies and all the way to the Pacific coast.

➤ **The growth of population.** Simultaneously, the population grew from just under 4 million in 1790 to 76 million by 1900 and 275 million by 2000. A growing nation required management by a growing government.

➤ **Industrialisation.** This brought the need for government regulation — federal executive departments of Commerce and Labor were formed in 1903.

➤ **Improvements in communication.** While the nation grew in size, it shrank in terms of accessibility as modern methods of communication gradually developed. Journeys that took weeks eventually took only days or hours as roads, railways and aircraft opened up the nation. Radio, followed by television, brought instant communication and a feeling of national identity. People could communicate with others thousands of miles away, first by telephone and then by fax and e-mail.

➤ **The Great Depression.** Events influenced the federal–state relationship, too. When the Great Depression hit the USA in 1929, the states looked to the federal government to cure their ills. The state governments did not possess the necessary resources to reverse the huge levels of unemployment, launch vast public works schemes or rescue agriculture from the effects of the dust bowl conditions. It was Franklin Roosevelt's New Deal, with its ambitious schemes to build roads and schools and provide hydroelectric power, which helped get the USA back to work.

➤ **Foreign policy.** With the onset of the Second World War, the USA stepped out as a world superpower and the federal government — with exclusive jurisdiction over foreign policy — found its role enhanced significantly.

➤ **Supreme Court decisions.** Political changes occurred to alter the federal–state relationship. Decisions made by the Supreme Court — especially between 1937 and the 1970s — further enhanced the power of the federal government through their interpretation of the implied powers of the Constitution. This was possible through the Court adopting a more expansive meaning to the powers allocated to Congress in Article I Section 8 of the Constitution, especially the 'necessary and proper clause', the 'common defense and general welfare clause' and the 'commerce clause'. From the mid-1980s, under the chief justiceships of William Rehnquist (1986–2005) and more recently John Roberts (2005–), the Court sometimes took a more restrictive view of these clauses, thereby limiting the role of Congress in particular and the federal government as a whole. This was most clearly seen in the 2012 decision of *National Federation of Independent Business v. Sebelius* in which the Court declared that President Obama's healthcare reform act could not be justified under the commerce clause, but only under Congress's power to levy taxes.

➢ **Constitutional amendments.** One of the three post-Civil War amendments, the 14th, changed dramatically — although not immediately — the federal government's relationship with the states. For the first time, the Constitution had been amended to impose prohibitions directly on state governments. Two requirements of the 14th Amendment in particular have, over time, revolutionised the federal–state government relationship. These requirements — referred to as the 'due process' and the 'equal protection' provisions — are found toward the end of Section 1 of the 14th Amendment. They read:

Nor shall any State deprive any person of life, liberty, or property, without due process of law; nor deny to any person within its jurisdiction the equal protection of the laws.

➢ These 14th Amendment provisions have been used by the Supreme Court to invalidate state laws requiring public (i.e. state) school segregation and other forms of racial discrimination. Moreover, the Supreme Court has employed them to outlaw a wide array of other state determinations, ranging from certain restrictions on abortion, to Florida's attempt to order a recount in the 2000 presidential election between George W. Bush and Al Gore.

➢ Equally importantly, the passage of the 16th Amendment (1913) allowed the federal government to impose an income tax. This gave the federal government the means to launch all the grand programmes that would flourish from Roosevelt's New Deal through the presidencies of Truman, Kennedy and Johnson to the late 1960s.

Phases of federalism

In the period between the 1780s and the 1920s, the individual state governments exercised most political power. The focus was very much on **states' rights**. But following the devastating effects of the Wall Street Crash and the Great Depression, the period from the 1930s to the 1960s saw a significant increase in the power and scope of the federal government. During this period, the federal government made increasing use of categorical grants — schemes by which it was able to stipulate how federal tax dollars were used by the states. By the Clinton era, the federal government was giving over $200 billion to the states, over 90% of which went in the form of categorical grants. So by now the federal government was involved in a number of policy areas where previously only the state governments had operated — such as education, transport and welfare.

Key concept

> **States' rights.** Literally, the rights, powers and duties of the state governments. But it is used as a term to denote opposition to increasing the national government's power at the expense of that of the states. States' rights advocates call for an interpretation of the Constitution that places limits on the implied powers of the federal government and gives expansive interpretation to the reserved powers of the states.

During the final three decades of the 20th century, however, there was a discernible movement towards decentralisation — what President Nixon called **new federalism**. This era saw the rise of block grants — money given to states by the federal government to be used at their discretion within broad policy areas. This change in the federal–state relationship coincides with the administrations of four Republican presidents: Richard Nixon, Gerald Ford, Ronald Reagan and George H. W. Bush.

Key concept

> **New federalism.** An approach to federalism characterised by a return of certain powers and responsibilities from the federal government to state governments. Seen as an attempt to reverse the growth of the federal government under successive Democrat presidents (from FDR to Johnson), it is closely associated with the Republican presidents Richard Nixon and Ronald Reagan.

Even Democrat President Bill Clinton recognised that Americans' view of the federal–state relationship had changed, when he stated in his 1996 State of the Union Address: 'The era of big government is over.'

Federalism under George W. Bush

When George W. Bush arrived in Washington in January 2001, one would have presumed that as a Republican president he would continue the moves towards shrinking the size of the federal government and decentralisation. But one of the most unexpected facts about the administration of George W. Bush was that he presided over the largest overall increase in inflation-adjusted federal government spending since Lyndon Johnson's Great Society programme of the mid-1960s. As Andrew Cline commented somewhat waspishly in *The American Spectator* (2 June 2006):

When Americans handed Republicans the reins of government [in 2001], they thought they were getting a conservative regime, one that would be honest, frugal and competent. Instead, they got a big government regime that has been dishonest, profligate and incompetent.

Total federal government spending grew by 33% during Bush's first term (2001–05). The federal budget as a share of the economy grew from 18.4% of gross domestic product (GDP) in 2000, Clinton's last full year in office, to 20.5% in 2008 — Bush's last full year in office. As Figure 1.6 shows, the total dollar increases in the federal budget grew dramatically during the George W. Bush administration. Whereas Ronald Reagan had arrived in Washington pledging to abolish federal government departments, Bush oversaw and supported the creation of a new one — the Department of Homeland Security.

In an article in the 3 May 2005 edition of *Policy Analysis*, entitled 'The Grand Old Party: how Republicans became big spenders,' Stephen Slivinski wrote:

Once upon a time, the Republican Party frequently made the case for smaller government and occasionally backed up the rhetoric with action. Republicans won a historic electoral victory in 1994 partly by trumpeting their opposition to the big-spending [Democrat] congressional leadership and offering the alternative of balancing the budget by cutting spending. The first budget proposed by the Republican majority in 1995 eliminated three cabinet agencies and more than 200 federal programmes. Ten years later, the Republicans in Congress and the White House have become defenders of big government.

There were four policy areas which accounted for this expansion of the federal government under George W. Bush — education, Medicare, homeland security and national defence, and the economy and jobs following the Wall Street and banking collapse of 2008.

Education

The first policy area which saw a huge increase in federal spending was education. As governor of Texas, George W. Bush had focused on education as one of the most important areas of policy and he brought the same focus to Washington in 2001. This was a dramatic turnaround from the days of previous Republican presidents — Ronald Reagan (1981–89) and Bush's father (1989–93). Twenty years earlier, Ronald Reagan had arrived in Washington with a pledge not to expand federal government involvement in education but to abolish the federal Department of Education. Not so in the George W. Bush administration when Department of Education spending rose from $35.5 million in 2001 to $46.3 million in 2002, and to $57.1 million in 2003. By 2006, the department was spending $93.4 million, a 165% increase in 5 years.

Education had been a cornerstone of George W. Bush's 2000 election campaign with its slogan of 'no child left behind'. Now, as president, Bush wanted to use the re-authorisation of the 1965 Elementary and Secondary Education Act (ESEA) as a

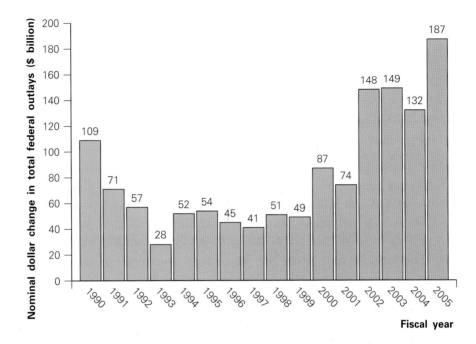

Figure 1.6 Growth in federal government spending: 1990–2005

vehicle for his education reforms. The No Child Left Behind Act, signed into law by President Bush in January 2002, ushered in the most sweeping changes in federal education policy since the 1960s. In what was a major expansion of the federal government's role in education, the new law mandated that the states test children annually in grades 4 to 8 using, in part, a uniform national test. It required that children in failing schools be moved to successful ones and provided for a 20% increase in funding for the poorest, inner city schools. It tripled the amount of federal funding for scientifically based reading programmes. For Bush, this was the federal government as enabler. At the bill signing ceremony at the White House, he declared:

> The federal government will not micromanage how schools are run. We believe strongly the best path to education reform is to trust the local people. And so the new role of the federal government is to set high standards, provide resources, hold people accountable, and liberate school districts to meet these standards.

Significant questions remain as to the effectiveness of Bush's much-trumpeted education reforms. But whatever else the No Child Left Behind Act was, it signalled a whole new approach to federal–state relations for a Republican president.

Medicare

In December 2003, George W. Bush signed a major Medicare expansion bill into law which included a new prescription drug benefit. The measure was estimated to cost

$400 billion in its first 10 years and was written to benefit American seniors. Medicare is a federal government healthcare programme for the elderly introduced in 1965 by Democrat President Lyndon Johnson. That a Republican president should preside over its modernisation and expansion was certainly something of an irony. But a number of conservative Republicans were critical of the price tag of the reforms as well as of the fact that a Republican president was supporting such a huge expansion of a federal government programme. In the House, 25 Republicans voted 'no' on its final passage, as did nine Republicans in the Senate.

Homeland security and defence

Between 2001 and 2009, spending by the Department of Defense increased from $290 million to $651 million, an increase of 125%. Between 2001 and 2006, spending on homeland security increased from just $13 million to $69 million — more than a five-fold increase in 5 years. Both these increases were, of course, the direct result of the events of 11 September 2001, and the subsequent military operations in both Afghanistan and Iraq, as well as the 'War on Terror' and the push to significantly increase homeland security. Defence spending rose during the George W. Bush years from 15% of the federal budget to 21%; homeland security increased from less than 1% to just shy of 3%.

Economy and jobs

There was yet another extraordinary example of big-government Republicanism in September 2008 when President Bush authorised the Secretary of the Treasury Henry Paulson to take control of the two troubled privately owned but government-sponsored mortgage companies — the Federal National Mortgage Association, known as Fannie Mae, and the Federal Home Loan Mortgage Corporation, known as Freddie Mac. Together Fannie Mae and Freddie Mac owned or guaranteed about half of the $12 trillion US mortgage market and had suffered huge losses with the collapse of the housing market. 'In Crisis, Paulson's Stunning Use of Federal Power', headlined the *Washington Post*'s front page the day after Paulson's announcement. 'Not since the early days of the [Franklin D.] Roosevelt administration, at the depth of the Great Depression, has the federal government taken such a direct role in the workings of the financial system,' wrote the *Post*'s Steven Pearlstein in the related article. This was followed by the Bush administration's sponsorship of a $700 billion so-called 'bail-out' package for Wall Street to alleviate the effects of the credit crunch. Again, this looked more like the policies of a New Deal Democrat than a conservative Republican. The package was passed through Congress by mostly Democrat votes.

With the White House having been run by ex-state governors for 24 of the 28 years between 1981 and 2009 — Reagan (1981–89), Clinton (1993–2001) and Bush (2001–09) — state governments had been hopeful of a more cooperative relationship between themselves and Washington. But they were mostly disappointed. Many see the way forward in returning to the view that states can act once again as policy laboratories.

Massachusetts, Vermont and Maine are offering model attempts at providing or requiring universal health insurance. More than 700 local governments have agreed to abide by the Kyoto Treaty on climate change despite its failure to be ratified by the United States Senate. States as laboratories is maybe a better picture of federalism than states with begging bowls.

The 25 June 2007 front cover of *Time* magazine showed a smiling New York Mayor Michael Bloomberg and California Governor Arnold Schwarzenegger posing arm in arm under the headline, 'Who Needs Washington?' Writing in the *Congressional Quarterly* magazine in October 2008, Peter Harkness concluded that in the more challenging economic climate, 'we all need Washington'. His prescription was not federal–state rivalry, but federal–state cooperation, 'to work as true partners to solve our most pressing problems'.

Federalism under Barack Obama

Whereas the Bush administration concentrated mainly on war and terrorism, the Obama White House between 2009 and 2012 was clearly much more focused on domestic policy as a way of delivering the 'change' agenda announced during Obama's 2008 campaign. This has had a profound effect on the relationship between Washington and the states. War and security against terrorism are conducted exclusively by the federal government; domestic policy is increasingly the domain of the states. As a result of Obama's first-term policies, a number of changes in the federal–state relationship were observed.

By 2012 the ratio of state and local government employees to federal employees was the highest since before President Roosevelt's New Deal in the 1930s. Federal government assistance to the states increased from 3.7% of GDP in the last year of the Bush administration (2008) to 4.6% of GDP in the first year of the Obama administration (2009). Similarly, money from the federal government, which accounted for 25% of state government spending in 2008, accounted for 30% of such spending in 2009. Whereas under Bush's economic stimulus package (2003) just $20 billion went to the states, under Obama's stimulus package (2009) $246 billion went to or through the state governments. This significant increase in federal money going to the states during Obama's first term came partly as a result of the re-authorisation of the State Children's Health Insurance Programme (S-CHIP) in 2009; the expansion of Medicaid; and over $4 billion invested in the Race to the Top programme to boost education in the states as well as programmes like the Pell Grants for university education.

But the aspect of Obama's legislative programme which came in for most criticism regarding its implications for the federal–state relationship was his healthcare reform legislation. Many Republicans saw the passage of this programme in 2010 as 'the end of federalism' and there were those in the Tea Party movement who accused Obama of being more of a socialist than a federalist. In exit polls in the 2010 mid-term elections, 74% of Republicans and 60% of independents agreed with the statement that the 'federal government is doing too many things better left to business and individuals'. Obama's expansive view of the federal government was somewhat curbed by the Supreme Court's refusal to allow this legislation to stand under an expansive reading of the commerce clause, but only under Congress's power to levy taxes. Although most of the Affordable Care Act was allowed to stand by the decision, the philosophical argument underpinning the decision was clearly based on a more limited role of the federal government than President Obama and Democrats in Congress had claimed.

Consequences of federalism

Federalism has consequences throughout US government and politics.

➤ **Legal consequences.** There is tremendous variety in state laws on such matters as the age at which people can marry, or drive a car, or have to attend school. Laws vary on drugs and whether the death penalty is used. Oregon allows doctor-assisted suicide. There are both federal and state courts.

➤ **Policy consequences.** The states can act as policy laboratories, experimenting with new solutions to old problems. Of late we have seen this in such areas as healthcare provision, immigration reform, affirmative action programmes and environmental policies. This state-based policy development often comes through, or as result of, statewide propositions (or initiatives). In 2010, for example, Arizona voters approved Proposition 107, which prohibited the state from discriminating for or against individuals on the basis of race or ethnicity, effectively banning any form of affirmative action. California, Michigan, Nebraska and Washington State had previously passed similar measures. Healthcare reform in Massachusetts and immigration reform in Arizona have both received considerable national attention, though much of the latter was declared unconstitutional by the Supreme Court in 2012.

➤ **Political consequences.** All elections in the United States are state-based and run under state law. Even the presidential election is really 50 separate state-based elections with the outcome decided by a state-based Electoral College. Each state decides such matters as: how candidates will be chosen for elections in their state; the procedures for getting a candidate's name on the ballot paper; and what mechanisms are used in polling stations — punch cards or touch-screen computers. Arizona has experimented with on-line voting and Montana with an entirely postal ballot.

➤ **Consequences for political parties.** It is important to realise that political parties in America are essentially de-centralised, state-based parties. Texas Democrats are more conservative than Massachusetts Democrats; Vermont Republicans more liberal than South Carolina Republicans. One can see the effects of federalism in the United States Congress with its state-based representation.

➤ **Economic consequences.** These are seen not only in the huge federal grants going to the states, but also in the complexity of the tax system in America. Income tax is levied by both the federal government and some state governments, different property taxes are levied by the state governments, and sales taxes vary between cities.

➤ **Regionalism.** The regions of the South, the Midwest, the Northeast and the West have distinct cultures and accents, as well as racial, religious and ideological differences. There is a distinct difference between the conservatism of the Deep South and the liberalism of the Northeast. What plays well in 'the Bible Belt' may not be popular in 'New England'.

When all is said and done, federalism has proved to be an appropriate system of government for the United States. It has adapted itself to the ever-changing nation. Despite its frustrations, there are few who question its future. Some Americans may think the federal–state relationship has at times got out of kilter, but most believe that its strengths far outweigh its weaknesses.

Pros and cons of federalism
DEBATE

Pros
➤ permits diversity
➤ creates more access points in government
➤ better protection of individual rights
➤ states become 'policy laboratories', experimenting with new solutions to old problems
➤ well suited to a geographically large nation

Cons
➤ can mask economic and racial inequalities
➤ frustrates the 'national will', making solving problems more complex
➤ the federal–state government relationship is a continual source of conflict and controversy
➤ overly bureaucratic — therefore costly to run and resistant to change

---

Activity

Using the information covered in this chapter and any of the further reading suggested below, write a 500-word piece (250 words on each side of the argument) in which you debate the proposition: 'The US Constitution is past its use-by date and is therefore no longer suitable for 21st-century America.' Alternatively, you could present your arguments in a class debate using the same proposition.

UK/US comparison

The US and UK constitutions

There are six basic characteristics of the US Constitution:
➤ It is codified, a single document, running to more than 7,000 words — under 20 printed pages — which contains the nation's constitutional arrangements.
➤ It is based on the principle of the federal division of powers with some significant powers being vested in the national (federal) government and other significant powers being vested in the state governments.

> It is based upon a strict separation of powers — or rather 'separate institutions, sharing powers'. The three branches of government are clearly separate in terms of their personnel.
> It is a presidential system.
> It is based on the principle of popular sovereignty, a system of government in which the people's voice is given great importance.
> It is characterised by high levels of democratic participation.

The six basic characteristics of the UK Constitution stand in sharp contrast to all of this:

> It is uncodified — it is not written down and collected together into one document.
> It has traditionally been seen as a unitary — rather than a federal — system of government, in which power is centralised in the hands of the national government.
> It has a system of government characterised by a fusion of powers with, for example, members of the executive being also members of the legislature.
> It is a parliamentary, rather than a presidential, form of government.
> It is characterised by parliamentary — rather than popular — sovereignty. Emphasis is on representative, rather than direct, democracy.
> There are low levels of democratic participation. In the UK, only party members can participate in the selection of parliamentary candidates, and that only for the lower chamber. The upper chamber remains entirely unelected; the chief executive is indirectly elected; and there is a hereditary monarch.

But the differences between the two constitutions may not be as sharp as they first appear:

> There are important elements of US government and politics which are nowhere to be found in the codified Constitution — the Supreme Court's power of judicial review, primary elections, the Executive Office of the President and congressional committees, to name but four.
> The extent to which the UK has a unitary system of government is debatable following Britain's membership of the EU and devolution within the UK.
> Constitutional reform is debated in both the USA and the UK. However, the debate is often in different areas.
> In the USA, constitutional reform usually comes in the shape of calls for further amendments to the Constitution. These have included proposals to balance the federal budget, ban flag desecration, permit prayers in state-run schools and preserve the traditional concept of marriage. But these are all policy matters. In terms of reform of the workings of government, the most frequently talked about proposals for reform have concerned term limits for members of Congress, a line-item veto power for the president, and reform or abolition of the Electoral College as a means of electing the president.
> One area of constitutional reform common to both countries is that of decentralisation in the USA and devolution in the UK. The debate in the USA, however, is strictly within the limits of a federal system. In addition, moves towards devolution within the UK are no more than that. Devolution within a unitary system of government is not the same as decentralisation within

a federal system of government. Devolution is simply the transfer of power from central government to *subordinate* regional governments. Sovereignty remains with the central government. To 'devolve' is to 'pass powers *down*', from a higher to a lower authority.

Exam focus

Short-answer questions

1 Explain the advantages and disadvantages of the process of amending the Constitution.
2 What is the Bill of Rights and how important is it?
3 How effectively do the three branches of the federal government check each other?
4 How and why is federalism enshrined in the Constitution?

Essay questions

1 To what extent is the constitutional system of checks and balances an obstacle to effective government?
2 Which is the most accurate description of US government: 'separated powers' or 'shared powers'?
3 What are the merits and demerits of federalism for US government and politics?
4 'The federal government increasingly dominates state governments in the USA.' Discuss.

Further reading

Ashbee, E., 'Federalism in the USA', *Politics Review*, Vol. 17, No. 3, February 2008.

Bennett, A. J., 'Does the US Constitution work?', *Politics Review*, Vol. 18, No. 4, April 2009.

Bennett, A. J., 'Divided government: strength or weakness of US politics?', *Politics Review*, Vol. 21, No. 2, November 2011.

Fletcher, R., 'Federalism under George W. Bush', *Politics Review*, Vol. 19, No. 4, April 2010.

Moxon, K. and Murphy, T., 'Debate: Does the US Constitution work?', *Politics Review*, Vol. 21, No. 3, February 2012.

Chapter 2

Elections and voting

Presidential elections

The aspect of US politics that is most thoroughly covered by the British media is presidential elections. Maybe because the election of the US president is seen as the election of the leader of the world's only superpower, this event is deemed to be of significance even 3,000 miles (5,000 kilometres) from Washington DC. Yet the presidential election is much more than what happens on Election Day. It is a more than year-long event in which ordinary voters are given a chance to say whom they would like to see as the major parties' candidates. Important issues concerning democracy, campaign finance and the role of the media are raised. There is also the question of how an electoral system devised more than two centuries ago as an indirect election has been adapted to become a direct election. Finally, there are issues concerning voting behaviour: who votes for whom, and why? It is easy to criticise a process that lasts so long, costs so much, seems at times to be more about style than substance, and sometimes, as in 2000, allows into the White House the candidate with fewer votes than his major rival. But presidential elections are only part of the electoral scene in the United States. In the following chapter we shall consider congressional elections, as well as the propositions, initiatives, referenda and recall elections which are used in some states.

Key questions answered in this section

➤ When do presidential elections occur?

➤ What are the requirements for presidential candidates?

➤ What is the 'invisible primary'?

➤ How are presidential candidates selected?

➤ How and when are vice-presidential candidates selected?

➤ What functions do modern-day National Party Conventions have?

➤ What roles do money and television play in the general election campaign?

➤ What factors explain voting behaviour?

➤ How does the Electoral College system work?

Links to follow up

There is a significant amount of electronic information available on the subject of presidential elections, almost too much, and you need to be careful that you don't get overwhelmed.

When election campaigns — either presidential or congressional — are in progress (which seems to be pretty much all the time!) the following sites will keep you updated on a daily basis:

www.realclearpolitics.com — an extraordinarily comprehensive collection of news, articles, polling data and videos with a very comprehensive archive

www.thegreenpapers.com — very detailed information on candidate selection, primaries and general election data

www.washingtonpost.com — probably the best collection of material from a media website, closely followed by **www.nytimes.com** and **www.cnn.com/politics**

If you want to follow up details on possible reforms to the presidential primary calendar, you can view the proposal put forward by the National Association of Secretaries of State at **www.nass.org**

If you are seeking opinion poll data, not only will the above-named sites give you lots of information but the following specific sites are well worth looking at:

> **www.gallup.com**
> **www.rasmussenreports.com**
> **www.pollingreport.com**

The best site to visit for data on campaign finance is **www.opensecrets.org**

To follow up issues relating to the conduct of campaigns and voter turnout you can visit **http://elections.gmu.edu**

Maps and state-by-state results of previous presidential elections can be found at two sites. Probably the best one, with every presidential election since 1788, is **www.presidency.ucsb.edu** then click on 'Election Resources'. The other is **www.uselectionatlas.org** but the trouble with this site is that the now traditional red (Republican) and blue (Democrat) colours are reversed.

To watch some of the most iconic television commercials of presidential campaigns from 1952 to 2012 go to **www.livingroomcandidate.org**

On the Electoral College, the Real Clear Politics site mentioned above allows you to compile your own forecast of an upcoming presidential election. You can also try: **www.270towin.com** and **www.electoral-vote.com**

Many of these sites will also carry information on congressional elections.

On initiatives and referendums, the two best websites are those of the National Conference of State Legislatures at **www.ncsl.org** and the Initiative and Referendum Institute at **www.iandrinstitute.org**

When presidential elections occur

America has fixed-term elections that occur every 4 years. The first presidential election was held in 1788. Since then, a presidential election has been held every 4 years, even during wartime. If the president dies in office, there is still no special election. When President John Kennedy was assassinated in November 1963, Vice-President Lyndon Johnson automatically became president and completed the remaining months of Kennedy's term. The next presidential election was not until 1964.

The fact that these elections occur every 4 years is laid down in Article II of the Constitution. But federal law goes even further, stating that the election shall be held on the Tuesday after the first Monday in November of every fourth year. In practice, that means that the election occurs between 2 and 8 November.

Presidential elections can best be thought of as occurring in seven distinct stages (see Table 2.1). The first four are concerned with choosing the candidates. The last three are concerned with electing the president.

Table 2.1 Presidential elections: a seven-stage process

Stage	Functions	Occurs
(1) Invisible primary	Announcement of candidacy Increasing name recognition Money-raising Organisation Intra-party TV debates	Calendar year before the election
(2) Primaries and caucuses	Show popular support for candidates Choose delegates to attend National Party Conventions	January–early June
(3) Choosing the vice-presidential candidate	Presidential candidate announces choice of running-mate	Some days/weeks before the convention (July/August)
(4) National Party Conventions	Confirm presidential and vice-presidential candidates Approve the party platform Acceptance speech delivered by presidential candidate	August–early September (each lasts about 3 or 4 days)
(5) General election campaign	The campaign between the candidates of various parties	September, October, first week of November
(6) Election Day	Registered voters go to the polls	Tuesday after the first Monday in November
(7) The Electoral College	Electors vote in their state capitals to choose the president and vice-president	Monday after the second Wednesday in December

Requirements for a presidential candidate

What does a person need to become a candidate for the presidency? In answering such a question, consider carefully the word 'need'. There are two possible meanings: first, what is *absolutely essential* — the constitutional requirements; and second, what is *very helpful* — things without which your candidacy either won't be taken very seriously or won't get very far.

Constitutional requirements

Several constitutional qualifications are necessary in order to be president:

➢ One must be a natural-born American citizen.
➢ One must be at least 35 years old. The youngest ever president was Theodore Roosevelt, who was just 42 when he became president following the assassination of President William McKinley in 1901. The youngest ever *elected* president was John Kennedy, who was 43.
➢ There is a residency qualification of 14 years.

In 1951, the Constitution was amended to limit presidents to two terms in office. The first president to feel the effect of this two-term limit was Dwight Eisenhower in 1960. Subsequently, three more presidents have been term limited: Ronald Reagan (elected 1980; re-elected 1984), Bill Clinton (elected 1992; re-elected 1996) and George W. Bush (elected 2000; re-elected 2004). So a fourth constitutional requirement could be added — not to have already served two terms as president.

Extra-constitutional requirements

In addition to the constitutional requirements, there are a number of other elements which candidates need to stand a chance of making a serious bid for the presidency. They are not mentioned in the Constitution, hence they are 'extra-constitutional' requirements. They fall into seven areas.

Political experience

Conventional wisdom would tell us that probably the most important of these extra-constitutional requirements is political experience. Three groups of politicians are good pools of recruitment for the presidency: vice-presidents, state governors and senators. One could add a fourth — members of the House of Representatives. However, very few serving members of the House manage to get themselves regarded as leading presidential candidates. The most recent political office of six of the 11 candidates for the Republican presidential nomination in 2012 was state governor (see Table 2.2) with four coming from Congress — three from the House and one from the Senate.

Of the 17 politicians who were nominated as presidential candidates in the last 12 elections to 2012, nine were or had been senators, six had been vice-president and six had been governors. The last time either the Democrats or the Republicans

Table 2.2 Most recent political office of Republican presidential candidates, 2012

Candidates	Most recent political office
Gary Johnson	Governor
Newt Gingrich	Congressman
Ron Paul	Congressman
Herman Cain	[None]
Tim Pawlenty	Governor
Mitt Romney	Governor
Rick Santorum	Senator
Michele Bachmann	Congresswoman
Jon Huntsman	Governor
Buddy Roemer	Governor
Rick Perry	Governor

Table 2.3 Winning and losing candidates in presidential elections, 1980–2012

Year	Winning candidate	Losing candidate
1980	Ronald Reagan (R)	Jimmy Carter (D)
1984	Ronald Reagan (R)	Walter Mondale (D)
1988	George H. W. Bush (R)	Michael Dukakis (D)
1992	Bill Clinton (D)	George H. W. Bush (R)
1996	Bill Clinton (D)	Bob Dole (R)
2000	George W. Bush (R)	Al Gore (D)
2004	George W. Bush (R)	John Kerry (D)
2008	Barack Obama (D)	John McCain (R)
2012	Barack Obama (D)	Mitt Romney (R)

nominated someone for the presidency who did not have this political background was in 1952, when the Republicans nominated the former Second World War general, Dwight Eisenhower. The only person who has recently been mentioned as a serious presidential candidate without such political experience is ex-army general Colin Powell. Businessman Herman Cain had a brief moment of glory before the 2012 Republican primaries but never looked like becoming the party's nominee.

What was so noteworthy in the 2008 Democratic presidential nomination contest was that the candidate with the most political experience, Hillary Clinton — 8 years as first lady and 7 years in the Senate — was defeated by a candidate with the least experience, Barack Obama, who had been in the Senate for just 3 years at the start of the election year.

Major party endorsement

If someone is serious about becoming president, it is vital to be chosen as the candidate for one of the two major parties. Even Eisenhower in 1952 had to become a Republican. The political endeavours of George Wallace (1968), John Anderson (1980), Ross Perot (1992 and 1996) and Pat Buchanan (2000) show that third-party or independent candidacies do not lead to the White House.

Personal characteristics

One has traditionally begun this discussion by pointing out that all presidential candidates for major parties have been white males. No longer. Another remarkable fact of the 2008 Democratic presidential nomination race was that it came down to a choice between a white woman (Hillary Clinton) and a black man (Barack Obama). Given the pools of recruitment — the vice-presidency, state governors and US senators — it had hardly been surprising that until 2004, major party

Hillary Clinton — defeated by Barack Obama in the race for the Democratic nomination in 2008

presidential candidates had all been white males. Even by January 2013 there were only 20 women out of 100 members in the US Senate and only one African-American. At the same time, only six states — Arizona, New Hampshire, New Mexico, Oklahoma, South Carolina and Washington — had women governors and none of those states is in the top ten by population. All vice-presidents have been white males.

It is an advantage to be married. There has been only one bachelor president — James Buchanan, elected in 1857. Until 1992, it was said that scandal involving marital infidelity could rule out a possible candidate. Senator Edward Kennedy's chances of the presidency were ended by the Chappaquiddick affair, in which a young female acquaintance drowned in his car after a late-night party. Senator Gary Hart pulled out of the 1988 nomination race after the press revealed photographs of him with a scantily-clad model named Donna Rice on a yacht called *Monkey Business*. But Bill Clinton managed to secure the Democratic Party's nomination in 1992 despite allegations surrounding Gennifer Flowers, which surfaced early in the campaign. In 1980 Ronald Reagan proved that divorce was not an insuperable problem — Nancy Reagan was his second wife. The Republican presidential nominee in 2008, John McCain, had divorced his first wife in 1980 and married his current wife Cindy.

Ability to raise large sums of money

The ability to raise money is crucial to a successful bid for the presidency. Campaigns are so expensive that very few candidates can afford to finance their own campaigns. Only billionaire candidates such as Ross Perot (1992) and Steve Forbes (1996 and 2000) have been able to finance their campaigns from their own pockets. Candidates need to

raise large sums of money even before the primaries and caucuses begin, which means raising money in the year before the election itself. According to the Open Secrets website (www.opensecrets.org), President Obama raised $125.2 million in 2011 and Mitt Romney raised $56.1 million. In the first 3 months of 2012, Obama raised a further $66.4 million and Romney a further $30.2 million.

Effective organisation

During the candidate selection process, the major parties cannot endorse specific candidates. A candidate is running to *become* the Republican or Democratic presidential candidate, so candidates cannot use the party's organisational structure, either nationally or in each state. They must therefore create their own organisation. This is time consuming, expensive and demanding. But candidates who fail to put together an effective organisation will stumble badly during the campaign. It is not coincidental that candidates such as Michael Dukakis (1988) and Bob Dole (1996), who had significant weaknesses in their campaign organisations, went on to lose the general election. Indeed, an effective organisation is a key ingredient in winning the party's presidential nomination. One of the major reasons why Hillary Clinton lost to Barack Obama in the race for the Democratic presidential nomination in 2008 was his superior organisation. The most important factors behind Romney's impressive victory in the Florida Primary on 31 January 2012 were his superior fundraising and organisation in this large state compared with his main rivals Newt Gingrich and Rick Santorum.

Oratorical skills and being telegenic

In the media age, the abilities to speak well and look good on television are crucial. It would be interesting to see whether candidates such as Abraham Lincoln — lampooned for his long, gangling physique — or wheelchair-bound Franklin Roosevelt could have made it to the White House in the television age. 'I'm no good at television,' Democratic candidate Walter Mondale complained in 1984. Republican Senator Phil Gramm went even further in 1996, declaring: 'I'm too ugly to be president.'

But Mondale's 1984 opponent, President Reagan, watching a recording of himself on television, joked: 'Am I really that good?' Reagan had been a Hollywood actor before going into politics. Bill Clinton's oratorical skills and his telegenic looks were advantages that contributed significantly to his victories in 1992 and 1996. These two factors were well displayed by Barack Obama in 2008.

Sound and relevant policies

There is a danger that presidential elections are portrayed as all style and no substance. Style is important, but voters will soon detect a candidate whose campaign turns out to be a 'policy-free zone'. A candidate must have policies that are both practical and relevant. Sometimes candidates will start by majoring on one significant issue. For Democrat candidate Bill Clinton (1992) it was 'the economy, stupid!' For John McCain (2000) it was campaign finance reform. For Howard Dean (2004) it was the war in Iraq.

The invisible primary

Unlike many democracies, in which the political parties choose candidates themselves, in the US the candidates are chosen by ordinary voters. Although presidential elections are held in every fourth year, the manoeuvring in preparation for the elections begins months, if not years, beforehand. Because these events take place before the official first stage — the primaries — and because there is very little to see, this stage is often referred to as the **invisible primary**.

Key concept

> **Invisible primary.** The period between candidates declaring an intention to run for the presidency and the first contests of the primary season. The invisible primary is said to be critically important for a candidate to gain name recognition and money, and to put together the necessary organisation. There is often a high correlation between who wins the invisible primary and who actually wins the presidential nomination, though not in 2007–08.

The invisible primary is played out mainly in the media. A candidate will hope to be 'mentioned' as a possible serious presidential candidate in such newspapers as the *Washington Post* and the *New York Times,* or there might be a positive article in *Time* magazine. There might be offers of an in-depth interview on such serious political television programmes as *Face the Nation* (CBS), *News Hour* (PBS) or one of CNN's political talk shows, such as *State of the Union with John King,* or *The Situation Room with Wolf Blitzer.*

Then there are the candidates' formal announcements of their entering the presidential race. The first major Republican candidate to announce his candidacy for the 2012 presidential race was former House Speaker Newt Gingrich of Georgia, who made his announcement on 11 May 2011 — 237 days before the Iowa caucuses. Fellow Republican, Congressman Ron Paul of Texas, followed with his announcement two days later. By the end of July 2011, there were already 11 declared Republican candidates. President Obama had announced his intention to run for re-election on 4 April 2011. It was certainly unusual for the incumbent president to make his announcement before a single challenger had emerged from the opposing party.

Mitt Romney — Barack Obama's opponent in the 2012 race for the presidency

Support for a candidate at this stage is demonstrated principally by opinion polls. Some of these polls, reported regularly by the press, may be based on a certain state while others are regional. From time to time, some polling organisations may conduct

a nationwide poll. They may run head-to-head match-ups to see how candidates of one party might fare against fancied contenders from the other party. During 2011, polling organisations published frequent head-to-head match-ups between President Obama and possible Republican candidates such as Mitt Romney, Newt Gingrich and Rick Perry.

Formal events

Not all the 'invisible' primary is invisible. Some relatively formal events do occur. Between 5 May 2011 and the end of that calendar year, there were 16 televised debates between the would-be Republican candidates. It was in the tenth of these debates, on 9 November 2011 at the Oakland University of Rochester, Michigan, that Governor Rick Perry of Texas had his much-publicised memory loss when he could not recall the three federal executive departments he would close down if elected president. Governor Perry began his answer: 'Commerce, Education and the...uh, um, what's the third one there, let's see.' After almost a minute of trying to recall the third — which was later revealed as the Department of Energy — Perry ended his halting response with the word 'Oops!' to much audience amusement. Just over two months later, Perry ended his presidential bid having finished sixth in the New Hampshire primary with less than 1% of the vote.

Some states stage special events during this pre-election year. For example, in Iowa, there is the traditional Republican Iowa Straw Poll held in August of the year before the election. Otherwise known as the Ames Straw Poll after the town in central Iowa where it is held, this has become a traditional event in the invisible primary calendar since 1979. The event is essentially a fundraising dinner at which any would-be Republican presidential candidate is given an opportunity to make a speech. Its significance is doubtful as the winner of the non-binding poll rarely turns out to be the eventual Republican presidential nominee. The poll is not held in those election cycles where an incumbent Republican president is seeking renomination and re-election. Of the six times it has been held — 1979, 1987, 1995, 1999, 2007 and 2011 — on only one occasion did the straw poll winner go on to become the Republican Party's presidential candidate. That was in 1995 when Bob Dole tied as winner in the straw poll with Texas Senator Phil Gramm. In 2011, the straw poll was won by Representative Michele Bachmann of Minnesota with just over 28% of the vote. Mitt Romney, the eventual nominee, finished seventh.

For the Democrats, the traditional annual Jefferson–Jackson Day dinner provides a similar opportunity for speech making by their presidential candidates. Iowa holds its dinner in November so as to just precede its caucuses in January. It was a particularly impressive speech at that dinner in Iowa in November 2007 which helped propel the Obama campaign to victory.

Then there are visits to certain key states, especially Iowa and New Hampshire, which traditionally hold the first presidential caucuses and primary, respectively. By the time the Republican Iowa caucuses were held on 3 January 2012, the eight presidential candidates had made a total of 771 visits to the state with the eventual winner of the caucuses, Rick Santorum, topping the number of visits with 266. In contrast, Mitt Romney had made only 28 visits to Iowa.

Some candidates publish a book. Barack Obama published *Dreams of My Father* and *The Audacity of Hope* to coincide with the launch of his 2008 presidential bid. In 2010, Mitt Romney published a book entitled *No Apology: The Case for American Greatness* ahead of his presidential bid in 2012.

Fundraising

The invisible primary is also the period when money raising has to occur in earnest to accumulate a large enough 'war chest' to be taken seriously. In 1999, Elizabeth Dole ended her presidential bid during the invisible primary season, claiming that she simply could not raise enough money to be regarded as a viable candidate, while Al Gore's successful raising of huge amounts of money during 1999 deterred would-be challengers for the 2000 Democratic nomination, such as Dick Gephardt and Bob Kerrey. In 2003, Howard Dean's strong fund raising helped to propel him to the front-runner position in the Democrats' invisible primary. Table 2.4 shows the amounts of money raised by the leading Republican candidates during the invisible primary prior to the 2012 primaries and caucuses. The eventual nominee, Mitt Romney, significantly outraised his Republican rivals during this period, raising more than Ron Paul and Rick Perry — his most lucrative challengers — combined. But Perry's near $20 million haul in 2011 was insufficient to sustain his already faltering campaign. However, former Pennsylvania senator Rick Santorum's modest fund raising during this period gave no clue to his eventual success in the Republican primaries and caucuses the following year.

Front-runners

Over many election cycles, the conventional wisdom has been that it was important to end the invisible primary as the front-runner according to the opinion polls. Whichever candidate was leading in the polls just before the primaries and caucuses began was usually confirmed as the nominee. But this was not the case in the Democrat race in 2004, in which the early front-runner, Howard Dean of Vermont, crashed in the primaries. And it certainly was not the case for either party in 2008. In the *USA Today*/Gallup poll conducted on 1–2 December 2007, right at the end of the invisible primary, Hillary Clinton held a 15-percentage-point lead

Table 2.4 Total contributions for Republican presidential candidates during the invisible primary, 2011

Candidate	Total contributions: 1 April–31 December 2011 ($ millions)
Mitt Romney	56.1
Ron Paul	25.9
Rick Perry	19.8
Herman Cain	16.8
Newt Gingrich	12.7
Michele Bachmann	9.2
Jon Huntsman	5.9
Tim Pawlenty	4.6
Rick Santorum	1.2

Source: www.opensecrets.org/pres12/weekly.php

over Barack Obama. The same poll reported a 10-percentage-point lead for Rudy Giuliani over John McCain in the Republican race. Indeed, McCain was in third place, having been overtaken by Mike Huckabee. Yet it was Obama and McCain who went on to win their respective party nominations. However, in the 2012 cycle, Mitt Romney fitted the more conventional pattern of the early front-runner being confirmed as the eventual nominee.

Primaries and caucuses

Here we enter the second stage of the process for electing the president — the primaries and caucuses. A **primary** is an election to choose a party's candidate for an elective office, in this case the presidency. A few states hold **caucuses** instead. A caucus is a meeting for the selection of a party's candidate for an elective office. States that hold caucuses are usually geographically large but thinly populated, such as Iowa, North Dakota and Nevada. In 2012, 12 states held Republican caucuses. In a caucus, would-be voters must attend a meeting rather than go to a polling station. Turnout is generally lower in caucuses than in primaries and those who do turn out are disproportionately more ideological than primary voters. Hence, caucuses tend to favour more ideological candidates. In 2012, Republican presidential candidate Ron Paul, who was on the libertarian wing of his party, had some of his strongest showings in caucus states. For example, he won 36% in the caucuses in Maine and 28% in North Dakota.

Key concepts

➤ **Presidential primary.** A state-based election to choose a party's candidate for the presidency. A presidential primary shows support for a candidate among ordinary voters and chooses delegates committed to vote for that candidate at the National Party Convention.

➤ **Presidential caucuses.** A state-based series of meetings for the selection of a party's candidate for the presidency. Held in a few geographically large but thinly populated states, caucuses attract unrepresentative and very low turnouts. They fulfil the same functions as presidential primaries.

Primaries have two specific functions: to show the popularity of presidential candidates; and to choose delegates to go to the National Party Conventions. They are run under state law, which means that a great number of variations exist. The main rules of thumb are outlined below.

Timing of primaries

States must decide when to hold their primary or caucuses. The national parties usually lay down the earliest and latest possible dates — often mid-January to the beginning of June — but within that period each state can decide its own date. In readiness for the 2012 primaries and caucuses, the Republican National Committee (RNC) rules for the selection of delegates stated that only Iowa, New Hampshire, Nevada and South Carolina could hold their delegate selection contests in February 2012. All other states were to keep to a window between 6 March and 12 June. Thus when New Hampshire, South Carolina and Florida scheduled their primaries in January, and Arizona and Michigan scheduled their contests in February, the RNC stripped these states of half of their national convention delegates.

Some states, such as New Hampshire, schedule their contest on a day when no other primaries are being held, thereby hoping to give their state primary a prominence that it would not otherwise have. Other states deliberately arrange their primaries to coincide with other, often neighbouring, states, thereby creating a regional primary. In 2012, the first Tuesday in March, when ten states arranged their Republican primaries together, was dubbed **Super Tuesday**. The first Super Tuesday was held back in 1988 as an attempt by a block of southern states to increase their importance in the candidate selection process. Until 2004, Super Tuesday was in early March, but in 2008 Super Tuesday was the earliest and biggest ever with 22 Democrat and 21 Republican contests being held on 5 February.

Key term

➤ **Super Tuesday.** A Tuesday in early February when a number of states coincide their presidential primaries in order to try to gain influence for their region in the selection of major party presidential candidates.

An increasing number of states like to schedule their primary early in election year, believing that the earlier primaries have more influence over candidate selection. This recent move to early scheduling is called **front loading**. The number of states holding their primaries or caucuses before the end of March increased from just 11 in 1980 to 42 in 2008, and those 42 states included the eight largest states — California, Texas, New York, Florida, Illinois, Pennsylvania, Ohio and Michigan. California, for example, has moved from early June (1980) to early February (2008); New York moved from mid-April to early February. By 5 February 2008, 55% of the delegates to the Democratic and Republican conventions had already been chosen. In 2012, however, the rule changes put in place by the RNC meant that only 30 states had held their Republican primaries and caucuses by the end of March with big states such as Texas (3 April), New York and Pennsylvania (both 24 April) and California (5 June) still to come.

Key term

➤ **Front loading.** The phenomenon by which an increasing number of states schedule their presidential primaries or caucuses earlier in the cycle, in an attempt to increase the importance of their state in choosing major party presidential candidates.

Types of primaries

There are a number of different ways of classifying primaries by type. Let us consider two. First, primaries can be divided into **closed primaries** and **open primaries**. It is important to understand that any registered voter can vote in a primary. But in some states, when you register, you are asked to declare your party affiliation — whether you consider yourself to be a Democrat or a Republican. In a 'closed primary', only registered Democrats can vote in the Democrat primary and only registered Republicans can vote in the Republican primary. In an 'open primary', any registered voter can vote in either primary. You decide on the day of the primary. In some states, even those who describe themselves as 'independents' are allowed to participate.

Key concepts

➤ **Closed primary.** A primary election in which only registered Democrats can vote in the Democratic primary and only registered Republicans can vote in the Republican primary.

➤ **Open primary.** A primary election in which any registered voter can vote in the primary of either party.

Open primaries (see Table 2.5) allow what is called 'cross-over voting', which means that Democrat voters can opt to participate in the Republican primary and vice versa. This became an important issue in the Democratic primaries in 2008 when, in open primary states, significant numbers of independents and Republicans opted to vote in the Democratic primary and voted for Senator Barack Obama. In the 2012 Wisconsin Republican open primary, 11% of voters said they were Democrats. Whilst Romney won the primary overall with 44% of the vote to 37% for Santorum, amongst Democrats Santorum beat Romney by 20 percentage points. This suggests one of two things: either these were conservative Democrats who genuinely preferred Santorum's policies to those of either President Obama or Mitt Romney; or they were mischievous Democrats deliberately casting a vote for someone they perceived as an 'easier' opponent for the President in November.

Table 2.5 States holding open Republican primaries in 2012

Alabama
Arkansas
Illinois
Indiana
Mississippi
Montana
South Carolina
Tennessee
Texas
Vermont
Virginia
Wisconsin

There are also 'modified primaries' (see Table 2.6). These are like closed primaries, in that only registered party voters can vote, but they also allow those who have registered as independents to vote in either party's primary. So, for example, in the New Jersey primary in 2012, registered Republican voters could vote only in the Republican primary, registered Democrats could vote only in the Democratic primary, but independents could vote in either party's primary.

Primaries can also be classified according to how delegates to the National Party Conventions are won. In most primaries, candidates are awarded delegates in proportion to the votes they get. These are known as 'proportional primaries' (see Table 2.7). Most states set a threshold — a minimum percentage of votes that a candidate must receive to get any of that state's delegates, usually 15% of the vote. All Democrat and most Republican primaries are proportional primaries; but some Republican primaries are 'winner-takes-all primaries', in which whoever gets the most votes wins all that state's delegates (see Table 2.8). But in 2012, the Republican National Committee introduced a new rule which forbad any state from staging a Republican winner-takes-all primary before 1 April. As a result the number of winner-takes-all contests fell from 17 in 2008 to just 6 in 2012. This meant that it took Mitt Romney much longer to accumulate the required number of delegates to secure the nomination than it had taken John McCain in 2008. It was 29 May before Romney wrapped up the Republican nomination in 2012 compared with 5 February for McCain 4 years earlier.

Table 2.6 States holding modified Republican primaries in 2012

Georgia
Massachusetts
Nebraska
New Hampshire
New Jersey
North Carolina
Ohio
Rhode Island
Utah
West Virginia

Table 2.7 A proportional primary: the New Hampshire Republican primary, 2012

Candidate	Votes	Percentage	Delegates
Mitt Romney	97,591	39.3	7
Ron Paul	56,872	22.9	3
Jon Huntsman	41,964	16.9	2
Rick Santorum	23,432	9.4	0
Newt Gingrich	23,421	9.4	0
Rick Perry	1,764	0.7	0

Table 2.8 A winner-takes-all primary: the Arizona Republican primary, 2012

Candidate	Votes	Percentage	Delegates
Mitt Romney	238,516	46.9	29
Rick Santorum	137,128	27.0	0
Newt Gingrich	81,384	16.0	0
Ron Paul	43,794	8.6	0
Rick Perry	2,014	0.4	0

Early primaries and caucuses

Iowa

For many decades now, the early primaries and caucuses have come to be regarded as crucial. Iowa traditionally holds the first caucus. But because caucuses usually attract low turnout — the 2012 Republican caucuses in Wyoming attracted just 2,108 voters —

this is usually not regarded as being as important as the first primary. However, the 2008 Iowa caucuses proved to be very important in both the Republican and Democratic races. The Republican caucuses in Iowa were won by Mike Huckabee with 34% of the vote, easily beating Mitt Romney (25%), John McCain (13%) and Fred Thompson (13%). Less than 3 months before Iowa, in mid-October, Huckabee was polling just 8% in national polls and was in fifth place amongst the Republican candidates. Huckabee went on to win primaries in Alabama, Arkansas, Georgia and Tennessee as well as caucuses in Louisiana and Kansas and the state convention vote in West Virginia.

The Iowa result in 2008 was even more stunning in the Democratic race with the front-runner, former first lady and heir apparent Hillary Clinton finishing third (with 29%) behind John Edwards (30%) and Barack Obama (38%). This proved to be the first major stumble in the Clinton campaign, which ended with her being beaten to the nomination by Barack Obama in one of the most startling upsets in presidential nominating history.

New Hampshire

For many years it was said that a candidate could not win the presidential nomination — or even the White House — without first winning the New Hampshire primary. However, this has been proved wrong in some recent elections. None of the last three presidents — Bill Clinton (1992), George W. Bush (2000) or Barack Obama (2008) — won his party's New Hampshire primary. But the amount of time the candidates spend in the state and the level of media attention combine to make the New Hampshire primary a critical contest to win.

In five of the last eight election cycles, New Hampshire primary voters have delivered a rebuff to the front-runner of the challenging party (see Table 2.9). In the same eight elections, the New Hampshire primary confirmed the front-runner of the incumbent party on every occasion bar one — that being 2008 when front-runner Rudy Giuliani lost to John McCain (see Table 2.10). But Giuliani had announced he was not contesting the New Hampshire primary and was sitting out the race until the Florida primary just over 3 weeks later, a strategy which proved to be an utter disaster.

What is really important at this early stage is matching expectations. Take 1992, for example. The numerical winners of the Democratic and Republican New Hampshire primaries were, respectively, Senator Paul Tsongas and President George Bush. But the moral victors were Bill Clinton and Pat Buchanan. Beset by serious allegations of womanising, drug taking and draft dodging in the Vietnam War, Clinton was not expected to do well. So when he came a respectable second with 25% of the vote, Clinton was able to claim that he was 'the comeback kid'. Although Pat Buchanan finished second in the Republican primary, the fact that he managed to gain 37% of the vote against an incumbent president was an impressive performance, and far better than had been expected.

Victory in Iowa or New Hampshire, or simply exceeding expectations as Barack Obama did in Iowa in 2008, brings three big bonuses: media coverage, money and a boost in the opinion polls. Following his Iowa victory in 2008, Barack Obama enjoyed pages of favourable stories in such weeklies as *Time* and *Newsweek*. He was the cover story of *Newsweek* on 14 January. Following his New Hampshire win, John McCain made it

Table 2.9 Performance of the challenging party in the New Hampshire primary, 1984–2012

Year	Challenging party	Front-runner	New Hampshire primary winner
1984	Democrat	Walter Mondale	Gary Hart
1988	Democrat	Michael Dukakis	Michael Dukakis
1992	Democrat	Bill Clinton	Paul Tsongas
1996	Republican	Bob Dole	Pat Buchanan
2000	Republican	George W. Bush	John McCain
2004	Democrat	Howard Dean	John Kerry
2008	Democrat	Hillary Clinton	Hillary Clinton
2012	Republican	Mitt Romney	Mitt Romney

Table 2.10 Performance of the incumbent party in the New Hampshire primary, 1984–2012

Year	Incumbent party	Front-runner	New Hampshire primary winner
1984	Republican	Ronald Reagan	Ronald Reagan
1988	Republican	George H. W. Bush	George H. W. Bush
1992	Republican	George H. W. Bush	George H. W. Bush
1996	Democrat	Bill Clinton	Bill Clinton
2000	Democrat	Al Gore	Al Gore
2004	Republican	George W. Bush	George W. Bush
2008	Republican	Rudy Giuliani	John McCain
2012	Democrat	Barack Obama	Barack Obama

on to the front cover of *Time* on 4 February and the front cover of *Newsweek* the following week. In February 2008, Barack Obama was able to raise over $50 million, at that time an all-time record for 1 month's fundraising, following his impressive showings in that year's early contests. Obama also saw his poll numbers shoot up in national polling. Whereas in December 2007, the *USA Today/*Gallup poll showed him trailing Hillary Clinton by 15 percentage points, the 4–6 January 2008 poll conducted immediately after his Iowa victory showed him level with Clinton. By the end of February, Obama had a 51–39% lead.

Likewise, failing to live up to expectations can be devastating. The day after coming in third with just 15% in the Republican Florida primary in 2008, Rudy Giuliani withdrew from the race. Giuliani had staked everything on winning the Florida race and was humiliated when McCain beat him by almost 20 percentage points.

Incumbent presidents and the primaries

When an incumbent president is running for re-election as Barack Obama did in 2012, the primaries for the president's party go on with little or no coverage at all. Some states don't even bother with a primary under such circumstances, and so for example in 2012

Table 2.11 Incumbent presidents' share of primary votes : 1976–2012

President	Party	Year	Percentage of primary vote	Result of election
Ronald Reagan	Republican	1984	99	Won
George W. Bush	Republican	2004	98	Won
Barack Obama	Democratic	2012	92	Won
Bill Clinton	Democratic	1996	89	Won
George H. W. Bush	Republican	1992	72	Lost
Gerald Ford	Republican	1976	53	Lost
Jimmy Carter	Democratic	1980	51	Lost

Source: *Rhodes Cook Letter,* Vol. 13, No. 3, June 2012, p. 3

Virginia, South Carolina, Florida and New York were amongst the states that dispensed with a Democratic presidential primary. Incumbent presidents are usually renominated by their parties without any serious opposition. This was the case for Ronald Reagan in 1984, Bill Clinton in 1996, George W. Bush in 2004 and Barack Obama in 2012. That said, President Obama was somewhat embarrassed during the 2012 Democratic primaries to receive less than 90% of the primary vote in 14 states, failing even to reach 60% in West Virginia (59%), Arkansas (58%), Kentucky (58%) and Oklahoma (57%). In West Virginia, the President's opponent, Keith Judd, won more than 40% of the vote despite the fact that he was at the time serving a lengthy prison sentence for extortion. Nonetheless, as Table 2.11 shows, President Obama's showing of 92% of the total Democratic primary vote was certainly in line with other incumbent presidents who went on to win in November. Indeed, it was a better performance than President Clinton's in 1996.

But in the elections of 1976, 1980 and 1992, the incumbent president faced significant opposition from within his own party and therefore the primaries and caucuses were hard fought, even in the president's party. In 1976, Republican president Gerald Ford faced a strong challenge from the former governor of California Ronald Reagan. Four years later, President Jimmy Carter faced an equally stiff challenge from Senator Edward Kennedy in the Democratic primaries. Senator Kennedy won 12 state contests including the primaries in New York and California. And in 1992, President George H. W. Bush had to fight off a challenge from the conservative commentator Pat Buchanan in the Republican primaries. Although Buchanan did not win any of the primaries and caucuses, his 37% in the New Hampshire primary was a great embarrassment for President Bush, and Buchanan went on to win more than a quarter of the vote in a dozen states. It is not coincidental that although all these three presidents saw off their primary challengers, they all went on to lose in the general election. A strong primary challenge for the president makes him damaged goods even before he faces his real opponent in the general election. What is more, criticism made of the president from within his own party in the primaries is often recycled as damaging campaign material by his opponent later in the year. As Robin Toner wrote in the *New York Times* in February 1992 of Buchanan's criticism of President Bush in that year's Republican primaries, 'down the road, Mr Bush will confront a Democratic Party that has now been given a road map of his vulnerabilities' by Mr Buchanan. And that's exactly what happened. As a parody of President Bush's broken pledge not to raise taxes — 'Read my lips: no new taxes' — Buchanan had used the slogan, 'Read our lips: no second term.' Needless to say, this became a favourite with the campaigns of Bill Clinton and Ross Perot in the autumn of 1992. This is why, as Table 2.11 clearly shows, it is so important for an incumbent president to avoid any significant challenge in the primaries.

Voter turnout in primaries

There is no doubt that since the reforms of the nomination process in the late 1960s, participation in presidential primaries has greatly increased. Partly this has been due to the simple fact that more states hold primaries. In 1968, the last nomination cycle under the pre-reform system, just 12 million people participated in the 17 Democratic and 16 Republican presidential primaries, which represented around 11% of the voting-age population. Twenty years later in 1988, in a similar cycle with both parties having a contested nomination, 35 million people participated in the 33 Democratic and 37 Republican presidential primaries, which represented around 21% of the voting-age population. Another 20 years on, in 2008, around 58 million people participated in 37 Democratic and 39 Republican primaries, which represented around 30% of the voting-age population. But turnout in individual contests varied considerably from 53% in New Hampshire to only 17% in Louisiana.

Factors affecting turnout in primaries

Turnout does not just vary between states but also between demographic groups. Stephen Wayne (2001) found that the better-educated, the higher-income and the older members of the electorate are much more likely to vote in primaries than are younger, less educated and poorer people. In the Tennessee Republican primary in 2012, for example, nearly half of voters had a college degree, over one-quarter earned more than $100,000 per year, and three-quarters of voters were 45 or older with only 8% being under 30. There is also a widely held belief that primary voters are more ideologically extreme in their political beliefs than are general election voters, though the empirical evidence here is mixed. In the same Tennessee Republican primary, however, 41% described themselves as being 'very conservative'.

The type of primary can also affect turnout. Open primaries, which allow any registered voter to vote in either primary, are more likely to attract a higher turnout than closed primaries in which only self-identified party supporters can vote in their own primary. This is especially true when only one party has a competitive race, as was the case in 2012. Of the 11 states which held open primaries in the Republican contest in 2012, 10 saw an increase in turnout on 2008 with turnout in Wisconsin up 92% and in Mississippi up 105%. On the other hand, of the 15

states which held closed primaries in the 2012 Republican contest, only two saw an increase in turnout. In Connecticut turnout was down 61% on 2008 and in New York it was down 71%.

Turnout in primaries is dependent on two further variables. First, turnout will vary dependent upon how competitive the nomination race is. So, for example, in 2008 in the Missouri Democratic primary 825,050 people turned out to vote in the hotly contested race between Hillary Clinton and Barack Obama. Four years later, the turnout in the Missouri Democratic primary was just 72,888 as President Obama sailed to his renomination virtually unchallenged. Second, turnout will vary dependent upon whether the nomination has yet been decided or not. As a consequence, primaries scheduled early in the nomination calendar will be more likely to attract higher turnout than those coming towards the end of the cycle when the identity of the nominee is already known. In 2008, the New York Republican primary was held on 5 February — that year's Super Tuesday — when the race for the Republican nomination was still undecided and a total of 642,894 votes were cast. In 2012, the New York Republican primary was held on 24 April, by which time most of the Republican candidates had dropped out of the race, leaving Mitt Romney as the presumed nominee. Romney won 62% of the vote but the turnout was just 189,599.

Therefore, as Table 2.12 clearly shows, primary turnout both by party and by total varies hugely from one cycle to another. But this simple rule of thumb applies: the more competitive the race and the longer it lasts, the higher the turnout. The longest and most competitive nomination race was the one between Barack Obama and Hillary Clinton for the Democratic nomination in 2008, which lasted right through until the very last primaries in early June. It attracted just short of 37 million voters — far more than in any other nomination cycle. The lowest turnouts have been recorded in those contests when an incumbent president has been unchallenged for renomination: the

Table 2.12 Turnout in presidential primaries, 1976–2012

Year	Number of primaries	Primary vote: Democrats	Primary vote: Republicans	Primary vote: total
1976	27	16,052,652	10,374,125	26,426,777
1980	36	18,747,825	12,690,451	31,438,276
1984	30	18,009,192	6,575,651	24,584,843
1988	37	22,961,936	12,165,115	35,127,051
1992	39	20,239,385	12,696,547	32,935,932
1996	42	10,947,364	13,991,649	24,939,013
2000	43	14,048,951	17,157,075	31,206,026
2004	38	16,182,439	7,940,331	24,122,770
2008	41	36,848,285	20,841,211	57,689,496
2012	39	9,123,326	18,705,545	27,828,871

Source: *The Rhodes Cook Letter*, June 2012

Democrats in 1996 (Clinton) and 2012 (Obama); the Republicans in 1984 (Reagan) and 2004 (George W. Bush). When an incumbent president is challenged for the nomination — Carter (Democrat) in 1980 and George H. W. Bush (Republican) in 1992 — the turnout numbers are significantly higher. That said, the turnout in the 2012 Democratic primaries was alarmingly low and seemed to suggest a lack of enthusiasm both for the President and for his party.

The increased importance of primaries

Nowadays, presidential primaries play an important role in the process of choosing presidential candidates. They really are the only route to becoming the presidential nominee of a major party. However, that was not always the case.

In the 1950s and 1960s, most states did not hold presidential primaries. The parties preferred to control candidate selection through a series of State Party Conventions. Whereas any registered voter can vote in a primary or caucus, only certain selected party members could participate in these state conventions. Here, in the so-called 'smoke-filled rooms', decisions were made largely by the 'party bosses' — powerful state party leaders such as city mayors. It was they, and not the ordinary voters, who decided who would become the party's presidential candidate. The few primaries that were held were not decisive. In 1968, in neither party did the overall winner of the primaries get his party's presidential nomination (see Table 2.13).

This system was deemed undemocratic, elitist, non-participatory and potentially corrupt. It was reformed significantly at the instigation of the Democratic Party following the events at its 1968 National Party Convention. That convention chose Vice-President Humphrey as the party's presidential candidate despite the fact that he had not entered any primaries at all. The few votes he got were gained by voters writing in his name on the ballot paper — so-called 'write-in' votes.

Table 2.13 Presidential primary results, 1968

Candidate	Total popular vote in primaries (%)
Democratic Party	
Senator Eugene McCarthy	38.7
Senator Robert Kennedy	30.6
President Lyndon Johnson	5.1
Vice-President Hubert Humphrey*	2.2
Republican Party	
Governor Ronald Reagan	37.9
Vice-President Richard Nixon*	37.5
Governor Nelson Rockefeller	3.7

*Eventual nominees

Following Humphrey's loss to Richard Nixon in the general election that November, the Democrats established the **McGovern–Fraser Commission** to recommend reforms of the presidential nomination process. It was this commission that led to the significant increase in the number of states holding presidential primaries from 1972 onwards. Thus, the nomination process has changed dramatically over the past 40 years.

Key term

➤ **McGovern–Fraser Commission.** The commission established by the Democratic Party following the 1968 presidential election to recommend reforms to the presidential nomination process. The commission was largely responsible for the significant reforms that democratised the presidential candidate selection system, starting with the 1972 election cycle.

Strengths of the current nomination process

The current nomination system is certainly an improvement on what went before:

➤ There is an increased level of participation by ordinary voters. In 1968, the last year of the unreformed system, only 11.7 million Americans took part in the nomination process, or 11% of the voting-age population. By 1988, the figure was 35 million, or 21% of the voting-age population. And in 2008, just under 58 million Americans took part in the nomination process, or 30% of the voting-age population.

➤ There is a significant increase in the choice of candidates. In 1968, there were just five presidential candidates to choose from — three Democrats and two Republicans. In 2008, there were 15 candidates — eight Democrats and seven Republicans.

➤ The process is opened up to outsiders — politicians who do not initially have a national reputation, such as Jimmy Carter (1976), Bill Clinton (1992) and Barack Obama (2008).

➤ The power of the party bosses is done away with, thus lessening opportunities for corruption and making the process more democratic.

➤ The gruelling race through the primaries is seen by many as an appropriately demanding test for a demanding job. In 1992, Senator Paul Tsongas, who had fought back from cancer to run for the presidency, was seen to have a lighter schedule than his rivals. Although many admired Tsongas as a person and liked his policies, they saw in the primaries that he might not have the physical resilience to be president. In 2008, many suggested that Barack Obama was a stronger candidate after his gruelling primary battle with Hillary Clinton than he would have been had he won the nomination without a fight.

Weaknesses of the current nominating process

Writing in the *Washington Post* at the end of March 1996, David Broder commented on the presidential nominating process: 'Any way you look at it, this is madness.' Meanwhile, the *New York Times* editorial of 3 March described it as 'a crazy process'. Academics, too, have criticisms. Professor Robert Loevy (1995) wrote:

More voters, to be sure, take part in [presidential] primary elections than in [the old system of] caucuses and [state] conventions. But what of the *quality* of that participation? Primary voters often know little about the many candidates listed on the ballot. They may drop in at the primary election booth between a trip to the drug store and the local supermarket and give little more thought to choosing candidates than to choosing among brands of toothpaste or canned vegetables.

Widespread voter apathy and boredom

As we have already seen, although more people do participate in the nominating process than was the case 45 years ago, the turnout in the presidential primaries various enormously from one election cycle to another. In a year when an incumbent president is running for re-election and therefore only one party has a genuine nomination contest, turnout in the primaries is only around 17%. It was 17.5% in 1996 when President Clinton was running for re-election, and 17.2% in 2004 when George W. Bush was running for re-election. Even when no incumbent president was running in 2000, turnout was still only 19%. But in 2008, with no incumbent president and a highly competitive race in the Democratic Party between a woman and an African-American, turnout soared to just over 30%.

Voters are unrepresentative of the voting-age population

Low turnout would not matter too much if those who did vote were a representative cross-section of the voting-age population — but there is some evidence to suggest that they are not. As we have seen, primary voters tend to be older, better educated, wealthier and maybe more ideological than the voting-age population as a whole. As a result, certain types of candidate — especially more ideological candidates — tend to do better in the nomination process than they should do. In 2012, Ron Paul — a libertarian Republican — won at least 10% of the vote in 40 primaries and caucuses, and in five of those contests his vote exceeded 25%. In the states which held caucuses, Paul's average vote was over 21%, whereas in states which held primaries his average vote was just 12%, showing that issues of unrepresentativeness are magnified in caucus states.

Process is far too long

In 1960, Senator John Kennedy announced his candidacy for the presidency just 66 days before the first primary. In readiness for the 2004 campaign, Senator John Kerry announced his candidacy 423 days before the first primary. Even Barack Obama in 2008 announced his candidacy 332 days before the first primary. Table 2.14 shows the significant effect of the McGovern–Fraser reforms in the early 1970s in this respect. However, the process is not usually quite as long in an election cycle in which the incumbent president is seeking re-election. In 2012, for example, the eventual Republican nominee, Mitt Romney, announced his candidacy on 2 June 2011, which was just 222 days before the New Hampshire primary, over 3 months later in the cycle than Obama's announcement 4 years earlier. Furthermore, because of party rule changes introduced

Table 2.14 Number of days before the first primary that the eventual nominee of the challenging party announced candidacy, 1960–2012

Year	Challenging party	Presidential candidate	Days before first primary
1960	Democrat	John Kennedy	66
1964	Republican	Barry Goldwater	67
1968	Republican	Richard Nixon	40
1972	Democrat	George McGovern	414
1976	Democrat	Jimmy Carter	449
1980	Republican	Ronald Reagan	105
1984	Democrat	Walter Mondale	372
1988	Democrat	Michael Dukakis	293
1992	Democrat	Bill Clinton	138
1996	Republican	Bob Dole	252
2000	Republican	George W. Bush	253
2004	Democrat	John Kerry	423
2008	Democrat	Barack Obama	332
2012	Republican	Mitt Romney	222

Table 2.15 Date upon which Republican presidential candidate secured contested nomination, 1988–2012

Year	Republican candidate	Date nomination secured
1988	George H. W. Bush	26 April
1996	Bob Dole	26 March
2000	George W. Bush	16 March
2008	John McCain	5 February
2012	Mitt Romney	29 May

before the 2012 Republican primaries — rules which limited the holding of early primaries and made it more difficult for states to hold winner-takes-all primaries — Mitt Romney took much longer to wrap up the Republican nomination than had John McCain in 2008, as Table 2.15 shows.

Process is very expensive

This is something of a circular argument. Candidates need to raise a large amount of money, so they need to start their campaigns early. Campaigns are therefore much longer and much more expensive. With the onset of 'front loading', there is now little time to raise money once the primaries have started. It has to be done before they begin, so candidates start early. By the end of 2011, President Obama had already raised $125.2 million and his eventual Republican opponent, Governor Romney, had raised $56.1 million. By the end of June 2012, these figures had increased, respectively, to $300.1 million and $153.2 million (see Table 2.16).

Table 2.16 Total money raised by Obama and Romney to June 2012

Period	Raised by Obama ($ millions)	Raised by Romney ($ millions)
April–June 2011	45.4	18.3
July–September 2011	40.8	13.9
October–December 2011	39.0	23.9
January–March 2012	66.4	30.2
April–June 2012	108.5	66.9
Totals	**300.1**	**153.2**

Source: www.opensecrets.org

Process is too dominated by the media

In the pre-reform era, decisions about candidates were made by a small group of professional politicians. They were people who knew the candidates. The role for the media was small. But in today's process, the decision-makers — ordinary voters — must rely on the media for information about the candidates. Some think the media ill-suited for this role. The media become the new 'king makers', the replacements of the latter-day 'party bosses'. Loevy (1995) is critical of this. He writes:

> Our present nominating process has become a televised horse race focusing more on rival media consultants and advertising executives than on competing ideas, programmes, or even the character of the candidates...Popularity polls, slick spot ads and television coverage of the early primaries offer episodes and spectacles and the average citizen is hard pressed to distinguish significance from entertainment.

This has become increasingly the case with the introduction of the intra-party televised debates both before and during the primaries. In the 2008 election cycle, for example, there were 17 Democratic and 15 Republican debates before the Iowa caucuses plus a further 9 Democratic and 6 Republican debates once the caucuses and primaries were under way. That made for a total of 47 televised debates — even before the candidates were chosen. In the 2012 Republican nomination race, the polls during 2011 and early 2012 seemed to be driven almost exclusively by the candidates' performance in the Republican candidate debates. When Governor Rick Perry of Texas forgot his lines in a televised debate on 9 November 2011, his poll ratings quickly fell thereafter. Equally, when former House Speaker Newt Gingrich gave an extremely robust defence of his private life in a debate in January 2012, his poll numbers soared.

Primaries can all too easily develop into bitter personal battles

In the 2000 Republican primaries, a McCain television commercial accused George W. Bush of not telling the truth, likening Bush to President Clinton. 'That's about as low as you can get,' shot back an angry Governor Bush. Other campaigns that became notoriously bad-tempered were those between George Bush and Pat Buchanan in 1992, and between Jimmy Carter and Ted Kennedy in 1980. It is no coincidence that the eventual nominees

in both these contests went on to lose in the general election. Voters do not have much confidence in disunited parties. Hillary Clinton was accused of making a number of personal attacks on Barack Obama during the 2008 Democratic primaries and, though defeated in the primaries, she still insisted on having her name placed in nomination at the Democratic National Convention in August, perpetuating the impression of disunity.

Lack of 'peer review'

Back in the pre-reform era, presidential candidates were selected largely by other professional politicians. This constituted what is known as 'peer review' — the judgement of one's colleagues or equals. They had a good idea of what qualities were required to be a successful president. Nowadays, however, candidates are chosen by ordinary voters who cannot be expected to know much about presidential qualities, let alone whether this governor or that senator possesses any of them. As a result, primaries tend to test *campaigning* qualities rather than *presidential* qualities. Professors Cronin and Genovese (1998) draw attention to this state of affairs:

> What it takes to become president may not be what is needed to govern the nation. To win a presidential election takes ambition, money, luck and masterful public relations strategies. To govern a democracy requires much more. It requires the formation of a governing coalition and the ability to compromise and bargain. 'People who win primaries may become good presidents, but it ain't necessarily so,' wrote columnist David Broder.

Professor Jeane Kirkpatrick has spoken of how professional politicians are 'uniquely qualified' to choose presidential candidates because 'they know the nature of the political job'. Professor Austin Ranney bemoans the fact that the parties are now 'the prizes, not the judges' in the nomination process. In an effort to bring back some element of peer review into the selection process, the Democrats introduced so-called 'super delegates' at their 1984 convention. They have had a presence at the Democratic convention ever

---

Strengths and weaknesses of primaries   DEBATE

Strengths
- increased participation
- increased choice of candidates
- process opened up to outsiders
- power of party bosses abolished
- a gruelling race for a gruelling job

Weaknesses
- can lead to widespread voter apathy
- voters are unrepresentative
- process is too long
- process is too expensive
- process is too dominated by media, especially television
- can develop into bitter personal battles
- lack of 'peer review'

since. Their role went unnoticed for 20 years, but in 2008 they played a significant role in the nomination of Barack Obama. Neither Obama nor his chief rival, Hillary Clinton, gained the required absolute majority of delegate votes through the primaries and caucuses. Obama was therefore dependent on the votes of super delegates — Democrat members of Congress, governors and Democratic National Committee members — to put him over the 2,210 delegate total required to win the nomination.

How to improve the nomination process further

No one is suggesting that the reforms introduced in the early 1970s have been completely useless, or that there should be a return to the era before the reforms were adopted, with party bosses in smoke-filled rooms, but there are a number of suggested reforms which some think would further improve the nomination process. The reforms are mostly concerned with the timing of primaries and attempts to increase the role of professional politicians without losing the democratic elements of the current system. Possible reforms include a move to regional primaries in which states in one region — the South, the Midwest and so on — would all vote on the same day. Another suggestion is to give greater weight to the votes of elected politicians — members of Congress, state governors and the like — at the party conventions when they come to choose the presidential nominee.

Are primaries really that important?

One final thought on presidential primaries. Are they really important? Do they really choose the presidential candidates of the major parties, or do they merely confirm the front-runners who emerged during the 'invisible primary'? Between 1960 and 2012 there were 14 presidential elections and therefore 28 major party presidential candidates chosen. On 22 of those 28 occasions, the candidate who was finally chosen was the same as the candidate who was the front-runner before a single vote was cast in any primary or caucus. In the Republican Party during this period, 13 of the 14 front-runners were confirmed as presidential candidates, 2008 being the one exception when John McCain was chosen rather than the pre-primary front-runner Rudy Giuliani. But in the Democratic Party, in 1968, 1972, 1988, 2004 and 2008 the primaries did play a significant role and chose a candidate who was not the front-runner before the start of the formal nominating process.

So although the overall statistic suggests that primaries are not that important, two of the last three election cycles — 2004 and 2008 — have suggested the contrary. For in those two elections, three of the four eventual nominees — John Kerry (Democrat, 2004), Barack Obama (Democrat, 2008) and John McCain (Republican, 2008) — were not the pre-primary front-runners. And the only front-runner who was confirmed in the primaries — Republican George W. Bush in 2004 — was the incumbent president. Certainly no one who studies the 2008 presidential nomination races would conclude that the primaries were not important. Indeed, the Democrats' choice of Obama over Clinton must go down as the biggest upset in presidential nomination politics for at least 40 years.

Choosing the vice-presidential candidates

In the past three decades, a new third stage in the election process has opened up — that of choosing the vice-presidential candidates. Until 1980, the vice-presidential candidate or 'running-mate' was always chosen and announced during the National Party Convention, the next major stage of the election cycle. Indeed, until 1956 the convention delegates actually chose the running-mate. But for 20 years — from 1960 through to and including 1980 — the presidential candidate himself made the selection and merely announced it during the convention, traditionally on the third day of the proceedings, just before delivering his own acceptance speech.

But then in 1984, the Democratic presidential candidate Walter Mondale broke with tradition and announced his selection of New York congresswoman Geraldine Ferraro as his running-mate 4 days before the Democratic convention gathered in San Francisco. From then on, each subsequent Democratic presidential nominee followed suit, announcing his vice-presidential candidate ahead of the party's convention. Indeed, in 2004, presidential candidate John Kerry announced his selection of John Edwards almost 3 weeks before that year's Democratic convention. It was not until 1996 that the Republicans jumped on the pre-convention announcement bandwagon when presidential candidate Bob Dole announced his choice of Jack Kemp, the former New York congressman and Bush housing secretary, as his running-mate the day before the Republican convention convened in San Diego. Since then, both party nominees have announced their vice-presidential candidates ahead of their convention. In 2012, Romney's announcement that he had chosen Congressman Paul Ryan of Wisconsin to be his running-mate came 16 days before their convention gathered in Tampa, Florida.

Strategies for choosing vice-presidential candidates

'Balanced ticket'

When choosing the vice-presidential candidate, it is often said that a presidential candidate looks for a **balanced ticket**. 'Balance' might be looked for in terms of geographic region, political experience, age and ideology, maybe even gender, race and religion. The best recent example of a balanced ticket was probably in 2008 when Barack Obama chose as his vice-presidential running-mate Senator Joe Biden of Delaware. Biden at 65 was a balance to Obama's youthful 47. Biden had served in the Senate for almost 36 years compared with Obama's less than 4 years. Biden also brought significant foreign policy expertise, having served as chairman of the Senate Foreign Relations Committee. Needless to say, there was also a balance of race.

Key term

> **Balanced ticket.** A tactic used by a presidential candidate in selecting the vice-presidential candidate in an attempt to increase voter appeal for their 'ticket'.

'Potential in government'

But the balanced ticket strategy is not always the one used in making the choice of running-mate. The presidential candidate may think more long term and choose his running-mate not for what they might bring to the campaign but what they might bring to the White House. In other words the focus will be on governing rather than campaigning. This was clearly the strategy adopted by Governor George W. Bush in 2000 in choosing Dick Cheney. Bush had no Washington experience at all and was generally thought to lack gravitas. His choice of Cheney as his running-mate was made with an eye to what he would need should he win the election, someone to help him run not only the White House but the whole executive branch of the federal government. Cheney had served as both White House chief of staff to President Ford and secretary of defense to Bush's father. Between these two tours of duty in the executive branch, Cheney had been a member of Congress, rising to become the Republican whip in the House of Representatives — the number-two spot in the House Republican leadership team. Cheney also brought that much valued quality of gravitas to the Republican ticket. It was probably this strategy of choosing for governing rather than campaigning that motivated Mitt Romney to choose Paul Ryan in 2012.

'Party unity'

A third possible strategy in vice-presidential selection is to promote party unity, but this is rarely adopted. One way of reuniting the party after the primaries is for the eventual nominee to choose one of his former rivals as his running-mate. This was the strategy adopted by Ronald Reagan in choosing George H. W. Bush in 1980. Bush had been Reagan's principal rival in the Republican primaries and by choosing him as the number two on the ticket Reagan reunited the party after a somewhat bitter personal battle. The trouble is, however, that former party rivals have often said such harsh things

Table 2.17 Timing of the announcement of the vice-presidential candidate before/during the National Party Convention: 1980–2012

Year	Republican	Timing of announcement	Democrat	Timing of announcement
1980	George H. W. Bush	Convention: Day 3	[Walter Mondale]	[Incumbent]
1984	George H. W. Bush	[Incumbent]	**Geraldine Ferraro**	4 days before
1988	Dan Quayle	Convention: Day 2	**Lloyd Bentsen**	5 days before
1992	[Dan Quayle]	[Incumbent]	**Al Gore**	4 days before
1996	**Jack Kemp**	1 day before	[Al Gore]	[Incumbent]
2000	**Dick Cheney**	6 days before	**Joe Lieberman**	6 days before
2004	[Dick Cheney]	[Incumbent]	**John Edwards**	20 days before
2008	**Sarah Palin**	3 days before	**Joe Biden**	2 days before
2012	**Paul Ryan**	16 days before	[Joe Biden]	[Incumbent]

Candidates in **bold** named *before* the National Party Convention.

about each other during the primaries that it would be somewhat implausible to think they could suddenly become partners on the ticket. Had Barack Obama adopted this strategy in 2008 he would have chosen Hillary Clinton as his running-mate, and had Mitt Romney used it in 2012 he would have chosen either Rick Santorum or Newt Gingrich.

National Party Conventions

We now move to the fourth stage of the presidential election process — the holding of the National Party Conventions. The Democrats and Republicans — and some third parties — usually hold a **National Party Convention** during August or early September of election year which usually lasts for 3 or 4 days. It is traditional for the challenging party to hold its convention first. In 2012, the Republicans met in Tampa, Florida, from 27 to 30 August, while the Democrats met in Charlotte, North Carolina, from 4 to 6 September. The venue is decided at least a year in advance by each party's National Committee. Conventions are attended by delegates, most of them chosen in the primaries and caucuses. The US — and the world's — media also turn up. Each day of a convention will have a theme and a prime-time speaker. For the first time in 2012, both conventions actually ran for only 3, rather than the usual 4, days. Some interpreted this as a sign of their declining importance.

> **Key concept**
> ➤ **National Party Convention.** The meeting held once every 4 years by each of the major — and some minor — parties to select their presidential and vice-presidential candidates and write a party platform.

Formal functions

The National Party Conventions were traditionally said to perform three formal functions.

Choosing the party's presidential candidate

In theory, the conventions choose the party's presidential candidate in a roll-call vote, in which each state's delegates announce which candidate they wish to vote for. In the pre-reform days, delegates came to the convention and made up their minds in the convention hall, but these days, the vast majority of delegates arrive at the convention as 'committed delegates' — committed, that is, to vote for a particular candidate in the first ballot if that candidate is still in the race. As the number of committed delegates is known beforehand — because it is decided in each state primary or caucus — the result of the convention ballot to choose the presidential candidate is, these days, a foregone conclusion.

To win the presidential nomination, a candidate must receive an absolute majority of the delegate votes. In 2012, there were 2,286 Republican delegates so Mitt Romney required 1,144 votes to win his presidential nomination.

It would be more accurate to say that the convention confirms — rather than chooses — the party's presidential candidate. Not since the Republican convention of 1976 has the

Table 2.18 National Party Conventions, 1980–2012: venues and candidates

Year	Republican Party		Democratic Party	
	Venue	Candidate	Venue	Candidate
1980	Detroit	Ronald Reagan	New York	Jimmy Carter
1984	Dallas	Ronald Reagan	San Francisco	Walter Mondale
1988	New Orleans	George H. W. Bush	Atlanta	Michael Dukakis
1992	Houston	George H. W. Bush	New York	Bill Clinton
1996	San Diego	Bob Dole	Chicago	Bill Clinton
2000	Philadelphia	George W. Bush	Los Angeles	Al Gore
2004	New York	George W. Bush	Boston	John Kerry
2008	Minneapolis	John McCain	Denver	Barack Obama
2012	Tampa	Mitt Romney	Charlotte	Barack Obama

choice of the presidential candidate really been in any doubt at the opening of either party's convention. In that year, President Gerald Ford defeated the former Governor of California, Ronald Reagan, by 1,187 votes to 1,070 votes. Had 60 delegates switched from Ford to Reagan, Reagan would have won.

If no candidate gains an absolute majority on the first ballot, balloting continues until one candidate does. During these ballots, delegates become free agents, no longer committed to vote for a certain candidate. Furthermore, new candidates could enter at this stage. In the 15 elections between 1896 and 1952 there were eight occasions when either one or both parties required more than one ballot to choose their presidential candidate. In the next 15 elections — between 1956 and 2012 — there were no such occasions. Hardly surprising, as this function is now performed by the primaries, not the conventions, thus diminishing the importance of modern-day conventions.

Choosing the party's vice-presidential candidate

As we have already seen, the convention's role in choosing the vice-presidential candidate has also been lost in the last three decades. The convention is no longer even the forum for the announcement of the running-mate — the last convention at which a running-mate was announced was the Republican convention in 1988. So here is a second significant function which the modern-day convention has lost.

Deciding the party platform

The **party platform** is a document containing policies that the candidate intends to pursue if elected president (see Box 2.1). It is put together by the Platform Committee under the direction of the party's National Committee. The Platform Committee holds hearings around the country during the first 6 months of the election year. In 2008, the Democrats held more than 1,600 'listening sessions' in communities across all 50 states, in which nearly 30,000 people from all walks of life participated. The Republicans invited visitors to their website to 'share your thoughts, participate in polls, and communicate

directly with the policy-makers who will be shaping the party's agenda'. The National Committee then agrees to the draft platform, which is presented to delegates at the National Party Convention. There may be debates at the convention on various parts of the platform — known as 'planks'. More recently, however, parties have sought to avoid heated debates on policy issues at their conventions. The media often portray such debates as evidence of a divided party.

Key term

➤ **Party platform.** A statement of a party's policies for an upcoming presidential election that is used during the campaign to win support from voters. It contains the policies that the party's candidate intends to pursue if elected president.

Much of what is in party platforms is little more than support for motherhood, the American Dream and apple pie (see Box 2.1). But there are significant differences on certain policies. For example, the 2012 Republican platform stated on the issue of abortion and the right to life:

> We assert the sanctity of human life and affirm that the unborn child has a fundamental right to life which cannot be infringed.

The Democratic platform, on the other hand, asserted that:

> The Democratic Party strongly and unequivocally supports *Roe v. Wade* and a woman's right to make decisions regarding her pregnancy including a safe and legal abortion, regardless of ability to pay. We oppose any and all efforts to weaken or undermine that right.

Box 2.1 Party platforms

'Republicans believe in the Great American Dream enabling everyone to have a chance to own, invest, build and prosper. "The American Dream" is not a stale slogan. It is the lived reality that expresses the aspirations of all our people.'

Republican Party platform, 2012

'We believe in restoring the basic values that made our country great and restoring for everyone who works hard and plays by the rules the opportunity to find a job that pays the bills and most of all give your children the kind of education that allows them to dream even bigger and go even further than you ever imagined.'

Democratic Party platform, 2012

Informal functions

Given that all three of the formal functions of the National Party Conventions are now questionable, it might appear that there is little point in holding them. The importance of the conventions is in their informal, or hidden, functions.

Promoting party unity

This may be the most important function of all. The primaries can turn into bitter personal battles, and it is vital that internal party wounds are healed before the general election campaign begins. Divided parties are rarely winning parties. The convention gives a golden opportunity to heal the wounds.

At the 2008 Democratic convention, it was important that the party portrayed a united front following the bitter personal rivalry during the primaries between Barack Obama and Hillary Clinton. By the time the primaries ended in early June, Hillary Clinton — and her husband, the former president — felt aggrieved that she had not triumphed in a nomination race that was widely thought to be hers for the taking. Both had seemed to suggest that Obama did not have the experience or leadership qualities to be president. But at the convention, both Clintons endorsed Barack Obama wholeheartedly in their respective speeches. Speaking on the second night of the convention, Hillary Clinton declared herself to be 'a proud supporter of Barack Obama' and went on to state: 'Barack Obama is my candidate, and he must be our president.' Picking up his wife's theme the following night in his speech, former President Bill Clinton declared to rapturous applause from the delegates: 'Last night, Hillary told us in no uncertain terms that she is going to do everything she can to elect Barack Obama. That makes two of us!'

There are, however, examples of conventions at which party unity was not rebuilt: the 1992 Republican convention, where President George H. W. Bush remained at loggerheads with his primary election rival, Pat Buchanan; and the 1980 Democrat convention, where President Carter and Senator Edward Kennedy continued their unfriendly rivalry. It is no coincidence that Bush and Carter were both defeated later in the year. In 2008, Republican Congressman Ron Paul, who had won some significant support in the Republican primaries and caucuses, refused to endorse John McCain at the Republican convention and held a rival event across town.

Enthusing the party faithful

In the general election campaign there is a lot of hard work to do. It is vital that the party faithful in all the 50 states feel enthusiastic and committed as they head home to fight for their party and candidate during the nine-week campaign. There will be meetings to organise, phone calls to make, literature to distribute and voters to transport to and from the polls, and they will be at the forefront of the organisation. The convention provides an ideal opportunity to enthuse the party faithful through speeches as well as through appearances by the party's past champions and heroes. In 2012, an inspirational speech at the Democratic convention by former president Bill Clinton brought the delegates to their feet and clearly enthused the party faithful to return to their states and work for President Obama's re-election.

Enthusing the ordinary voters

It is equally important to enthuse the ordinary voters. As they are not present in the convention hall, this must be done through television. There is one golden opportunity to gain the attention of the ordinary voters during the convention and that is when the

newly adopted presidential candidate delivers his **acceptance speech** — traditionally on the convention's final night (see Box 2.2).

 Key term

➤ **Acceptance speech.** The nationally televised speech delivered by a party's presidential candidate in prime time on the final night of the National Party Convention.

Most voters will have paid little, if any, attention to the primaries. Now that the candidates have been selected and the policies finalised, voters may well tune in and take their first serious look at the party, its candidate and its policies. First impressions can be important, especially if the candidate is running for national office for the first time — as Governor Bush was doing in 2000. Indeed, Bush was the first politician to win the presidential nomination of his party at the first attempt since Senator Barry Goldwater in 1964. This meant that Bush had to introduce himself more thoroughly to the US voters in his convention speech.

Box 2.2 Extracts from President Obama's acceptance speech, 2012

➤ 'The choice you face is between two different paths for America, a choice between two fundamentally different visions for the future.'

➤ 'I won't pretend the path I'm offering is quick or easy. I never have.'

➤ 'You didn't elect me to tell you the things you wanted to hear. You elected me to tell you the truth.'

➤ 'The path we offer may be harder but it leads to a better place.'

➤ 'A new tower rises above the New York skyline; al Qaeda is on the path to defeat; and Osama bin Laden is dead.'

Opinion polls register the immediate effect of the conventions, with instant polls showing what, if any, increase the candidate has enjoyed as a result of the speech. The increase in a candidate's poll rating as compared with the last pre-convention poll is referred to as 'bounce'. In the elections between 1972 and 2008, the average 'bounce'

Mitt Romney and running-mate Paul Ryan in the 2012 presidential race

Table 2.19 Post-convention 'bounce', 1972–2012

Year	Challenging party candidate	Bounce	White House party candidate	Bounce
1972	George McGovern (D)	0	Richard Nixon (R)	+7
1976	Jimmy Carter (D)	+9	Gerald Ford (R)	+5
1980	Ronald Reagan (R)	+8	Jimmy Carter (D)	+10
1984	Walter Mondale (D)	+9	Ronald Reagan (R)	+4
1988	Michael Dukakis (D)	+7	George H. W. Bush (R)	+6
1992	Bill Clinton (D)	+16	George H. W. Bush (R)	+5
1996	Bob Dole (R)	+3	Bill Clinton (D)	+5
2000	George W. Bush (R)	+8	Al Gore (D)	+8
2004	John Kerry (D)	−1	George W. Bush (R)	+2
2008	Barack Obama (D)	+4	John McCain (R)	+6
2012	Mitt Romney (R)	−1	Barack Obama (D)	+3

Source: www.gallup.com

for the candidate of the challenging party was just over 6 percentage points, and for the White House party candidate just under 6 points. As Table 2.19 shows, both Mitt Romney and Barack Obama scored below-average bounce after their respective conventions in 2012. Indeed, Romney became the first Republican candidate to score a negative bounce since this particular poll calculation began back in the 1960s. This reflected the generally lack-lustre nature both of the Republican convention as a whole and of Romney's acceptance speech in particular. This table also shows some evidence that post-convention bounce may be declining and some analysts put this down to the increasingly partisan nature of modern-day politics in America. Whereas in previous decades voters were more open to being impressed by either party's convention, in today's highly partisan climate a clear majority of voters hold such polarised views that they are unlikely to change their voting intentions as the result of a party's convention or a candidate's speech.

The importance of post-convention 'bounce' can be exaggerated. In an analysis of the impact of political conventions since 1960, Professor Larry Sabato of the University of Virginia concluded that post-convention polls signal the eventual outcome of the election only about half the time. 'You could flip a coin and be about as predictive,' says Sabato. 'It's really surprising how quickly convention memories fade.'

The importance of modern-day conventions

A *Washington Post–ABC News* poll published towards the end of August 2008 asked the following question: 'As you may know, the Democrat and Republican parties will be holding their national conventions in the next few weeks. How important will these conventions be in helping you decide how to vote for president in November?' A mere 29% of respondents said the conventions would be 'important' while 71% said they would be 'less important'. Only 12% described the conventions as 'extremely important'. So as far as the voters go, modern-day conventions are seemingly of little importance.

Unsurprisingly, many political commentators agree. They suggest that, in comparison to the conventions of years ago, modern-day conventions are of little importance. The parties seek to deliver scripted, sanitised conventions, devoid of much political content. No longer are the conventions addressed by an endless line of politicians. Modern-day conventions feature choreographed videos along with stars of stage and screen as well as ordinary citizens who have a captivating story to tell. The party conventions of 2012 featured an ageing film star in Clint Eastwood, an Iraq war veteran and a worker from General Motors. Even the traditional 'roll call' — once one of the highlights of the convention — has been shuffled away from prime time lest its predictability encourage viewers to reach for their remote controls.

Television coverage of the conventions has declined significantly in recent years. In 1968, the three terrestrial television companies — ABC, CBS and NBC — put out 46 hours of coverage of that year's Republican convention. Forty-four years later, in 2012, the same three companies managed just 9 hours of coverage of the Republican convention — 1 hour on each evening on each channel. The only comprehensive television coverage was to be found on the cable news channels — CNN, MSNBC, Fox News, PBS and C-SPAN. This decline in convention coverage by the three terrestrial television stations is a result not only of the hugely increased choice that Americans now have with regard to TV channels, but also of the decline in the importance of the conventions themselves. When asked in 2012 if it was possible to recapture Americans' interest in the conventions, NBC's Brian Williams suggested that one could always try including some Olympic events — 'floor vault is a personal favourite,' deadpanned the news anchorman, 'or badminton, but it takes up a lot of floor space.' But on the other side of the coin, in 2008 more people watched the convention speeches by Barack Obama, John McCain and Sarah Palin than watched the Olympics opening ceremony in Beijing, the finale of *American Idol* or the Academy Awards.

But it would be wrong to write off the National Party Conventions as useless: they do still perform important functions. Not only are they a time for celebrating a glorious past but they can also be important in identifying the rising stars of the future. In 2004, a little-known state senator from Illinois wowed the Democratic convention with his impressive keynote address. His name was Barack Obama, and just 4 years later he returned to the convention as its presidential nominee.

National Party Conventions can still be of importance because millions of Americans who have shunned the campaign the whole year will often tune in for the key moments of the conventions. 'That's what makes the convention critically important,' stated Professor Cal Jillson in an interview with *National Journal* in August 2012. He went on: 'Even though the junkies have been riveted for a year, a good half of the public is just about to start paying attention.' As election scholar Stephen Wayne (2001) put it, the conventions 'may have become less newsworthy, but they are still important'.

Are National Party Conventions still important?

DEBATE

Yes

➤ the only time the national parties meet together
➤ opportunity to promote party unity
➤ opportunity to enthuse party members and activists
➤ introduce new vice-presidential candidate
➤ presidential nominee's acceptance speech is key moment in campaign
➤ can lead to significant post-convention 'bounce' in polls
➤ many voters don't tune into the campaign until the conventions start
➤ a significant number of voters make their decision during the conventions

No

➤ presidential candidate now decided during the primaries
➤ no second ballot at either convention since 1952
➤ vice-presidential candidate now announced before the convention convenes
➤ party platform agreed by the platform committee before the convention
➤ television coverage much reduced
➤ both 2012 conventions reduced to 3 days

The general election campaign

Now we come to the fifth of the seven stages in the process for electing the president. The previous four have all been concerned with candidate selection and confirmation. The contest up to this point has been an intra-party contest. Now it becomes an inter-party contest as the presidential nominees of the two major parties and their respective running-mates slug it out during the nine-week campaign between the beginning of September and first week of November. There are two major issues here — campaign finance and the role of television in the campaign.

Campaign finance

The Federal Election Campaign Act of 1974, a direct result of the Watergate scandal which brought down President Nixon, made a number of significant changes (see Box 2.3), hoping to reduce candidates' reliance on a few, very wealthy donors — known as 'fat cats' — and equalise the amount of money spent by both the major parties.

The objectives of these reforms were praiseworthy and they were partly successful. But the law was found to have too many loopholes and was weakened by both the Supreme Court and Congress. In 1976, in *Buckley v. Valeo*, the Supreme Court ruled that limitations on what individuals or political action committees (PACs) could spend either supporting or opposing a candidate infringed

Former president Richard Nixon, who resigned after the Watergate scandal

1st Amendment rights and were therefore unconstitutional. In 1979, Congress further weakened the law by allowing parties to raise money for such aspects as voter registration and get-out-the-vote drives as well as 'party-building' activities. This so-called 'soft money' would soon be regarded by most observers as out of control, leading to the need for further reform.

Further reform eventually came in 2002, mainly through the endeavours of two senators, Republican John McCain and Democrat Russell Feingold. This was the Bipartisan Campaign Reform Act, commonly called the McCain–Feingold law (see Box 2.4). The 2004 election saw the appearance of so-called 527 groups, named after the section of the US tax code under which they operate. 527s such as America Coming Together and Swift Boat Veterans for Truth raised and spent millions of dollars, most of it donated by a few super-rich and largely unknown people.

In the 2008 election, Barack Obama raised huge amounts of money through the internet from small donors. The huge success of his electronic fundraising may well ensure that this becomes a model for future presidential campaigns. Obama also became the first major party presidential candidate to forgo the federal matching funds — worth $84 million in 2008 — during the general election campaign. McCain took the federal money, but in doing so had to limit himself to that as a cap for his general election spending. With Obama raising huge amounts of money during the final weeks of the campaign — he raised $150 million in September alone — McCain was at a significant disadvantage, and it showed. Significantly in 2012, neither Obama nor Romney took federal matching funds, indeed neither did any of Romney's main rivals in the Republican primaries. Except for the $18.2 million each party got from these funds towards its national convention, the era of matching funds seemed to be over.

Box 2.3 Federal Election Campaign Act (1974)

The Federal Election Campaign Act:

➤ limited individual contributions to a candidate to $1,000

➤ limited corporate contributions to a candidate to $5,000

➤ forbad donations from foreign donors

➤ limited candidates' expenditure to $10 million in the primaries and a further $20 million in the general election: these figures were index-linked for inflation, rising to $45.6 million and $91.2 million respectively by 2012

➤ provided 'matching funds' from federal taxpayers on a dollar-for-dollar basis for contributions up to $250

➤ established the Federal Election Commission (FEC) to enforce and regulate the new system

Box 2.4 Bipartisan Campaign Reform Act (2002)

➤ National party committees banned from raising or spending 'soft money'.

➤ Labour unions and corporations forbidden from funding issue advertisements directly.

➤ The use of union and corporate money to broadcast advertisements that mention a federal candidate within 60 days of a general election or 30 days of a primary prohibited.

➤ Fundraising on federal property forbidden.

➤ Increased individual limits on contributions to individual candidates or candidate committees to $2,300 (2007–08), to be increased for inflation in each odd-numbered year.

➤ Banned contributions from foreign nationals.

➤ 'Stand By Your Ad' provision, resulting in all campaign ads including a verbal endorsement by the candidate with the words: 'I'm [candidate's name] and I approve this message.'

Super PACs

The more recent significant development in campaign finance followed the landmark Supreme Court decision in *Citizens United v. Federal Election Commission* (2010) which granted to corporate and labour organisations the same rights of political free speech as individuals, thereby granting to such groups the right of unlimited independent political expenditure. This decision — plus another by the United States Court of Appeal, *Speechnow.org v. Federal Election Commission* (2010) — led to the setting up of independent expenditure-only committees, commonly known as **Super PACs**. These Super PACs played a significant role in the fundraising and spending in the 2012 presidential election. Their role received mixed reviews. Supporters see Super PACs as a positive consequence of deregulation that provides an important outlet for political speech, advocating independent calls for the election or defeat of specified candidates. Opponents, however, contend that they are yet another outlet for unlimited money in electoral politics that, while legally independent, are merely functional extensions of one or more campaigns.

Key concept

➤ **Super PACs.** Fundraising committees which are permitted to receive unlimited contributions and make unlimited expenditures aimed at either electing or defeating candidates in federal elections. Otherwise known as independent expenditure-only committees (IEOCs), they are forbidden from making any direct contributions to federal candidates or parties.

Three Super PACs dominated the scene during the 2012 presidential election. Super PAC Restore Our Future spent $142.6 million during the election cycle, of which $88.5 million was spent advocating the defeat of President Obama and $14 million the election of Governor Romney. This was followed by American Crossroads, another conservative

Super PAC, which spent $124.1 million, of which $103.4 million was spent advocating the defeat of the President and $6.7 million advocating Romney's election. Third in line was a liberal Super PAC, Priorities USA, which spent their entire budget of $77.7 million advocating Romney's defeat. By Election Day, 1,117 Super PACs had spent $710 million during the presidential election cycle, of which 48% was spent by the three largest Super PACs. This raises two further points of potential concern. That three Super PACs could spend as much as the over 1,100 remaining groups showed a worrying inequality of resources. That of the combined expenditure of these three groups ($344.4 million), $269.6 million (or 78%) was spent in negative campaigning showed a worrying trend towards negativity.

The role of television

Television can be divided into two groups: old television, meaning the terrestrial channels — ABC, CBS, NBC and PBS; and new television, meaning the cable channels, such as CNN and MSNBC. Television carries a variety of programmes that contribute to the presidential election.

News, interview and talk show programmes

➤ **News coverage**. This is where most Americans gain their knowledge of the campaign, be it from the 24-hour-a-day style programme of CNN or ABC's *World News Tonight*. These programmes constitute mainly news reporting of the day's events with a small amount of analysis and comment.

➤ **Political comment programmes.** These include the Sunday morning talk shows on the terrestrial channels, such as *Meet the Press*, as well as *The News Hour* each weekday evening on PBS. These programmes have in-depth interviews by respected interviewers and attract a more politically aware audience.

➤ **Chat shows.** The most notable show used to be CNN's *Larry King Live*. The interviews on this programme tended to be less searching and were aimed at a less politically aware audience. After the interview there was a phone-in that gave a chance for viewers to put their questions to the night's guest. The programme ran for 25 years but was replaced in 2011 by *Piers Morgan Tonight*. In 2000, both Gore and Bush appeared on *The Oprah Winfrey Show* with the black celebrity talk show host. In 2008, Oprah Winfrey made a specific endorsement of Barack Obama, even appearing at some Obama rallies alongside the candidate. In October 2000, George W. Bush appeared in a 13-minute segment of *The Late Show with David Letterman* — longer than the total time he appeared on the evening news of all three networks (ABC, NBC and CBS) during the whole month. In 2008, the satirical show *Saturday Night Live* featured a wickedly funny impersonation of Republican vice-presidential candidate Sarah Palin by comedian Tina Fey.

Political commercials

The use candidates can make of the free media is limited. They need to buy time on commercial television to air their political commercials, or 'spots' as they are often called. Political commercials started on television in 1952 when Republican candidate Dwight Eisenhower put out a 30-second biographical spot titled *The Man from Abilene*. There was also a series of policy-based spots called *Eisenhower Answers America*, in which Eisenhower gave short answers to questions put by ordinary Americans.

To the biographical and policy commercials, the 1960s added the negative commercial. In 1964, the campaign of President Johnson came up with what became known as the *Daisy Girl* commercial, in which the image of a little girl counting and pulling out the petals of a daisy suddenly turns into a nuclear countdown and explosion. The spot, aired only once, did not even mention Johnson's political opponent, Senator Barry Goldwater. But viewers made the connection unprompted. This poses an interesting question about political advertising: whether it actually changes people's minds, or merely confirms what they already know about a particular candidate. Goldwater was already known to advocate what some saw as a rather trigger-happy foreign policy. The *Daisy Girl* commercial merely reinforced many voters' fears about a Goldwater presidency.

Negative commercials can backfire too. In 1988, a spot about crime featured the story of Willie Horton, a criminal who had been let out of a jail in Massachusetts — the state

---

Box 2.5　Television commercials from the 2012 election

Barack Obama: *Always*

Barack Obama: Those ads taking my words about small business out of context. They're flat out wrong. Of course Americans build their own businesses. Every day, hard-working people sacrifice to meet a pay roll, create jobs and make our economy run. And what I said was that we need to stand behind them, as America always has, by investing in education and training, roads and bridges, research and technology. I'm Barack Obama, and I approve this message, because I believe we're all in this together.

Mitt Romney: *Give me a break*

Announcer: As the economy gets worse, Barack Obama calls on Bill Clinton to help his failing campaign.

Bill Clinton: [Video of Clinton speaking to camera in an Obama ad] It's about which candidate is more likely to return us to full employment.

Announcer: He's a good soldier, helping his party's president. But what did Bill Clinton say about Barack Obama in 2008?

Bill Clinton: [Video showing footage of Clinton speaking at a rally in 2008 during the New Hampshire primary] Give me a break! This whole thing is the biggest fairy tale I've ever seen.

Announcer: Twenty-three million Americans struggling for work; the middle class falling further behind.

Bill Clinton: Give me a break!

Mitt Romney: I'm Mitt Romney and I approve this message.

Source: www.livingroomcandidate.org/commercials/2012

of which Bush's opponent, Michael Dukakis, was governor — and had then committed rape and murder. When it later transpired that Horton was black, the Bush campaign was accused of playing on fears about black people and crime.

Perhaps a safer bet is to use humour in negative commercials, attempting to poke fun at political opponents. In 1992, President Bush's campaign created a spot featuring two politicians — both with their faces blanked out to conceal their identity — making opposing speeches on such issues as free trade, drugs and the Persian Gulf War. As, one at a time, the faces of the politicians were revealed, the voice-over said: 'One of these politicians is Bill Clinton. Unfortunately, so is the other!' And then there is always the sugary, positive commercial, the most memorable of which has to be Ronald Reagan's 1984 commercial, *Prouder, Stronger, Better*, but more usually known by its opening line, 'It's morning again in America!'

Another potential pitfall of television commercials is that the words a candidate uses in one election can be replayed by an opponent 4 years later to draw attention to the fact that promises might have been broken. Some of General Eisenhower's answers from the 1952 *Eisenhower Answers America* spots were reused in 1956 by the Democrats under the title of *What's That Again, General?* In 1992, President Bush found his 1988 'Read my lips — no new taxes' promise replayed by the Clinton campaign.

The 2012 campaign brought us the usual variety of commercials — positive and negative, biographical and policy orientated, comments from ordinary Americans, scenic shots of 'America the Beautiful' as well as less scenic shots of closed factories and homeless people. As usual, few minds were probably changed by them but they did doubtless reinforce voters' views of Obama and Romney — either for better or for worse.

Activity

Go to the Living Room Candidate website at **www.livingroomcandidate.org** and then click on an election year to watch the TV ads mentioned in this chapter. They're all there, and many more. You can also watch a selection from the 2012 election. You might try to select what you think are the most and least effective ads of a particular campaign.

Presidential debates

Televised **presidential debates** between the major party candidates have now become a traditional part of the campaign. Debates have varied in number and format since they were first used, but a pattern has now developed: three 90-minute debates between the two major parties' presidential candidates and one 90-minute debate between their vice-presidential candidates, occurring usually between late September and mid-October.

Key term

➤ **Presidential debates.** Debates held between the two major party presidential candidates (usually three in number) that occur during September and October of the presidential election year. There is also traditionally one debate between the two vice-presidential candidates.

As can be seen in Table 2.20, the first debates were held in 1960, but it was another 16 years before televised debates were held again. Over the years, different debate formats have evolved. Initially, the candidates, standing behind podiums some distance from each other, were asked questions by one moderator. This developed into a panel of up to three members of the press who asked questions. A non-participatory audience was introduced in 1976.

Then, in 1992, what has become known as the 'Town Hall' style of debate was tried for the second of the three debates. The candidates did not stand behind podiums but were seated on bar stools, facing an audience of undecided voters who put questions directly to the

Table 2.20 Number of general election televised debates: 1960–2012

Year	Presidential debates	Vice-presidential debates
1960	4	0
1964	0	0
1968	0	0
1972	0	0
1976	3	1
1980	2*	0
1984	2	1
1988	2	1
1992	3	1
1996	2	1
2000	3	1
2004	3	1
2008	3	1
2012	3	1

* Only Ronald Reagan and third-party candidate John Anderson participated in the first debate. The second debate was between President Jimmy Carter and Ronald Reagan.

Source: www.presidency.uscb/edu/debates.php

candidates. A moderator was there merely to keep order. This format has been used for one of the three debates in each election cycle since 1992. The 2000 debates saw another new format — the roundtable discussion in which the candidates talked *with* each other rather than at each other or an audience. In 2012, the three presidential debates sampled all these three styles: the first had the candidates at two separate podiums; the second was a Town Hall style debate; at the third, the candidates sat round a table with the moderator. The vice-presidential debate between Joe Biden and Paul Ryan used the roundtable format.

The only time a third-party candidate was allowed to participate was in 1992, when independent candidate Ross Perot took part in the three presidential debates and his

running-mate, James Stockdale, joined the vice-presidential debate. In 1980, President Carter refused to show up at a debate to which third-party candidate John Anderson had been invited, so there was one debate between the two challengers — John Anderson and Republican candidate Ronald Reagan. Carter showed up only for the debate to which just Reagan and he had been invited.

Carter v. Reagan, 1980

For all their hype, the debates have only rarely provided moments of vintage political theatre or been significant in shaping the outcome of the race. Three exceptions stand out. The first was in the debate held on 28 October 1980, in Cleveland, Ohio, between President Jimmy Carter and his Republican challenger, Ronald Reagan. At the end of their 90-minute debate, each candidate was given 3 minutes to make a closing statement. President Carter went first and made remarks that were well meaning but eminently forgettable. Then Governor Reagan closed:

> Next Tuesday all of you will go to the polls, will stand there in the polling place and make a decision. I think when you make that decision, it might be well if you ask yourself, are you better off than you were 4 years ago? Is it easier for you to buy things in the stores than it was 4 years ago? Is America as respected throughout the world as it was? Do you feel that our security is as safe, that we're as strong as we were 4 years ago?

Reagan had cleverly posed a series of questions which he knew the majority of voters would answer in the negative. And with Election Day less than a week away, he managed to shape the way voters would make up their minds in these vital last days of the campaign. Support for President Carter fell away badly following the debate and on Election Day he won only six states, plus the District of Columbia, for a total of just 49 Electoral College votes.

Ronald Reagan, US president 1981–89

Reagan v. Mondale, 1984

Ronald Reagan also featured in the second memorable debate moment. Four years later, almost to the day — 21 October 1984 — President Reagan was taking part in the second and final debate of the campaign with his challenger, former Vice-President Walter Mondale. By this time Reagan was already 73, and age was becoming an issue in the campaign. Henry Trewhitt, diplomatic correspondent for the *Baltimore Sun*, one of the four panellists asking the questions that evening in Kansas City, Missouri, posed the following question:

> Mr President, I want to raise an issue that I think has been lurking out there for 2 or 3 weeks and cast it specifically in national security terms. You already are the oldest President in history. And some of your staff say you were tired after your most recent

encounter with Mr Mondale. I recall yet that President Kennedy had to go for days on end with very little sleep during the Cuban missile crisis. Is there any doubt in your mind that you would be able to function in such circumstances?

Reagan shot back his jokey response as quick as a flash:

Not at all, Mr Trewhitt, and I want you to know that also I will not make age an issue of this campaign. I am not going to exploit, for political purposes, my opponent's youth and inexperience.

The audience erupted in laughter and applause. That was the end of the age issue! Reagan went on to a 49-state victory in the election.

Obama v. Romney, 2012

The third example when a presidential debate had a significant effect on the course of the campaign was the first debate between President Obama and Governor Romney in 2012. Up to this point in the campaign, the President had a comfortable and seemingly enduring lead in the polls and with neither the selection of Paul Ryan as his running-mate nor his acceptance speech at the Republican convention having boosted Romney's poll numbers, the race looked to be settling down to a predictable and comfortable win for the President. But then came the first debate. Romney was animated, coherent and quite aggressive. He seemed to be genuinely enjoying the moment and, dare one say, looked 'presidential'. The President looked thoroughly disengaged, bored and flat. He let many of Romney's claims go unchallenged and looked as if he was enduring rather than enjoying the occasion. Indeed, Joe Klein writing in his *Time* magazine column stated that this was 'one of the most inept performances by a president' in a televised debate.

The polls after the debate were of one mind: Romney was the overwhelming winner. The Gallup Poll found that of those who watched the debate, 72% thought that Romney had won with only 20% making Obama the winner (see Table 2.21). This 52-percentage-point margin was the largest in TV debate history. What was perhaps even more remarkable was that even a majority of those viewers who identified

Table 2.21 Viewers' verdict on the first presidential debate, 2012: responses to the question 'Regardless of which candidate you happen to support, who do you think did the better job in last night's debate?'

	Romney (%)	Obama (%)	Both/Neither/No opinion (%)
All debate watchers	72	20	9
Republicans	97	2	1
Independents	70	19	11
Democrats	49	39	12

Source: Gallup

themselves as Democrats thought that Romney had won the debate — by 10 percentage points. But more than that, the debate changed the shape of the race and Romney, who had failed to gain any bounce at all from his convention, now found his poll numbers rising at the expense of the President. Within a week of the debate Romney was leading in both the Gallup seven-day tracking poll and the poll-of-polls published by the Real Clear Politics website. This was the first time Romney had led in both.

But most debates are not 'game-changing' events. We have been able to find only three examples from the 30 presidential debates broadcast thus far. Indeed, in two of the three examples given above of debates that were regarded as game-changers, the particular moment lasted no more than a minute or two. The remainder of the debate is entirely forgotten. It is therefore true to say that the vast majority of the nearly 60 hours of presidential and vice-presidential debates broadcast between 1960 and 2012 passed into political obscurity within minutes of the debate's conclusion. The election of 2012 showed that the presidential debate can play a significant part in a campaign, but that is still more the exception than the rule.

Debate rules of thumb

Four rules of thumb are worth noting about presidential debates, three of which were illustrated in the debates of 2012.

> **Style is often more important than substance.** What you say is not as important as how you say it and how you look. In the second Bush–Clinton debate in 1992, the camera caught Bush at one moment looking at his watch. He appeared eager to end his discomfort. In the first Gore–Bush debate in 2000, Gore appeared overly made-up. He interrupted Bush frequently and, while Bush was answering, made audible sighs and rolled his eyes. Within days, Gore was being ridiculed on *Saturday Night Live* as a 'smarty pants'. Just after the start of the second — Town Hall style — debate, Gore strode across the stage to stand right next to Bush while the latter was still speaking. Bush merely gave him a quizzical glance. And in the first debate in 2012, we have seen that President Obama was widely criticised for the passive style which he adopted throughout. Again, it wasn't so much what the President did or did not say as his manner and style that lost him that debate.

> **Verbal gaffes can be costly.** When, in 1976, President Ford mistakenly claimed that Poland was not under the control of the Soviet Union, it was an expensive error. When, in 1980, President Carter tried to personalise an answer by mentioning how he and his 10-year-old daughter Amy had talked about nuclear weapons, the cartoon artists had a field day at Carter's expense. In 2000, Gore was caught out in the first debate making some exaggerated claims to which the Bush campaign immediately drew attention after the debate. There were no obvious or serious gaffes by the candidates during the 2012 debate, although the following remark by Mitt Romney during the second debate when talking about his attempts to appoint women to top jobs when he was governor of Massachusetts caused a few chuckles at the

governor's expense: 'I went to a number of women's groups and said, "Can you help us find folks," and they brought us whole binders full of women.'

➤ **Good sound bites are helpful.** Many voters do not watch the full debate but they do see the sound bite the television networks clip out for their breakfast shows the next morning. In 1996 when debating Senator Dole, President Clinton was asked whether he thought 73-year-old Bob Dole was too old to be president. His answer provided a perfect sound bite: 'I don't think Senator Dole is too old to be president. It's the age of his ideas that I question.' In the final debate in 2008, John McCain got a good sound bite at Barack Obama's expense when Obama kept on trying to link McCain to the unpopular President George W. Bush. 'Senator, I am *not* President Bush,' commented John McCain. 'If you wanted to run against President Bush you should have run 4 years ago.' In the final debate in 2012, President Obama accused Governor Romney of favouring 'the foreign policy of the 1980s, the social policy of the 1950s, and the economic policy of the 1920s'.

➤ **Debates are potentially more difficult for incumbents than for challengers.** Incumbents have a record to defend and they have words spoken 4 years earlier that can be thrown back at them this time around. In 1980, challenger Ronald Reagan had jauntily dismissed President Carter's attacks with a nod of the head, a smile and the words: 'There you go again.' Four years later Reagan unwisely tried the same phrase on challenger Walter Mondale, who was ready for it:

Now, Mr President, you said, 'There you go again.' Remember the last time you said that? You said it when President Carter said that you were going to cut Medicare. And what did you do right after the election? You went out and tried to cut $20 billion out of Medicare.

The supposed-to-be-silent audience burst into applause and Reagan looked distinctly uncomfortable.

But not only do incumbents have a record to defend, they also nearly always go into the debates as the perceived front-runner, hence expectations on them are higher. We saw that this was a problem for President Obama in 2012. Also, the debate format itself is a great leveller. That the challenger appears on the same platform as the president of the United States and has equal air time brings the president down to the level of an ordinary politician. Furthermore, presidents often go into the debates somewhat rusty in their debate technique. Between June 2011 and February 2012, Governor Romney participated in 19 debates with his fellow Republican presidential candidates. In contrast, the last time President Obama had appeared in a televised debate was October 2008.

All the evidence suggests that, as with televised commercials, debates often do more to confirm what the voters already feel about the candidates than to change many voters' minds. They might also help to convert passive supporters — those who will not turn out and vote on Election Day — into active voters.

Viewing figures

Viewing figures for the debates vary significantly from one election cycle to another. The all-time high point for presidential debate viewership is still the 1980 debate between President Carter and his Republican challenger Ronald Reagan, which logged nearly 81 million viewers. The presidential debates of 1984 and 1992 averaged around 66 million viewers, while the debates in 1996 and 2000 were watched by an average of only 40 million viewers. However, the last three elections have seen a significant increase in viewer numbers with an average of 53.4 million in 2004, 57.4 million in 2008 and 64.0 million in 2012. What was extraordinary in 2008, however, was the over 69 million who watched the vice-presidential debate between Joe Biden and Sarah Palin. It even beat the estimated 67 million who watched the vice-presidential debate between Dan Quayle and Lloyd Bentsen back in 1988. Do American viewers watch debates in the expectation of seeing a presumed weak or controversial candidate implode? In contrast, fewer than 29 million people watched the debate between Dick Cheney and Joe Lieberman in 2000.

Election Day: voting behaviour in presidential elections

Finally, after almost 18 months from the first candidacy announcement, through the invisible primary, the Iowa caucuses, the New Hampshire primary, Super Tuesday, the securing of the nomination, the choosing of running-mates, the national conventions and a 9-week campaign, Election Day arrives — the Tuesday after the first Monday in November when eligible voters may go to the polls to choose between the candidates.

Voter turnout has been a topic of some debate in recent elections. After peaking at a high of 67% of the voting-age population in the 1960 election, voter turnout dropped in each of the next five presidential elections to 54.7% in 1980. After some small increases, turnout fell to just 51.4% in 1996. But the next three elections all registered increases in turnout (see Table 2.22), reaching 62.3% by 2008. But there was a significant drop in 2012 to 58.2%.

The result of a presidential election is decided principally in the swing states. A large number of states will almost always vote for the Democratic candidate — Massachusetts, New York, California and Illinois, for example. Other states are nowadays solidly Republican — Texas, Georgia, Kansas and South Carolina, for example. But there are

Table 2.22 Percentage of eligible electorate who voted: 2000–2012

Year	Percentage of eligible electorate who voted
2000	54.2
2004	60.4
2008	62.3
2012	58.2

Table 2.23 Number of visits made by Obama and Romney to swing states: May to Election Day, 2012

State	Number of visits made by President Obama	Number of visits made by Governor Romney
Colorado	11	10
Florida	14	17
Iowa	9	6
Nevada	10	6
New Hampshire	6	12
North Carolina	2	4
Ohio	16	19
Virginia	14	15
Wisconsin	6	2

Source: www.nationaljournal.com/hotline

a number of swing states, such as Ohio, Florida and Virginia, which will vote for the Democratic candidate in one election and then the Republican in another. Ohio has now voted for the winner in the last 13 presidential elections, stretching all the way back to 1964. Indeed, it is the swing states where the campaign is fought out, as is shown by Table 2.23. Obama and Romney made a total of 35 visits to Ohio between May and Election Day, 31 to Florida and 29 to Virginia.

For those Americans who *do* vote in a presidential election, what are the most important factors that help to determine how they vote? There are nine possible factors.

Party affiliation

Despite all that is said about the weakness of US political parties, party affiliation seems to be an important determinant of voting behaviour. In 12 out of the 16 presidential elections between 1952 and 2012, the party that managed to gain the highest level of support from its own identifiers was the party that won the election. In 2004, 89% of Democrats voted for Kerry, but 93% of Republicans voted for Bush. However, in both 2008 and 2012, while Obama won respectively 89% and 92% of the Democratic vote, McCain and Romney won respectively 90% and 93% of the Republican vote. What was significant in both elections was that far more Democrats turned out to vote than Republicans, thereby wiping out the Republicans' minor advantage.

Elections are often said to be decided by so-called 'independent voters'. In seven of the nine elections from 1980 through to 2012, the candidate who won the majority of the independent votes won the election. But 2012 was one of those two exceptions with Romney beating Obama amongst independent voters 50% to 45%. A poll conducted by the *Washington Post* and the Kaiser Family Foundation in July 2012 found that the one thing that independent voters were looking for from the two major parties was cooperation and compromise between them. When independent voters were asked, 'What's more important — parties sticking to their positions or cooperating across party lines, even if this means

compromising?' only 24% of independents wanted the parties to stick to their positions whilst 70% wanted them to cooperate and compromise across party lines. When the same question was asked of self-identified Democrats and Republicans, the figures of those who wanted their party to compromise across party lines fell to 54% and 43% respectively.

Gender

In nine out of the ten elections between 1964 and 2000, women were significantly more supportive of the Democrat candidate than men. This is what we call the **'gender gap'**, meaning that men and women vote in a distinctly different fashion. In 2000, Bush gained the votes of 53% of men but only 43% of women. Gore, on the other hand, gained the votes of only 42% of men but 54% of women. The gap was even wider in 1996, when men split equally between Clinton and Dole but women favoured Clinton by 16 percentage points. But in 2004 the gender gap narrowed slightly. Bush enjoyed an 11-percentage-point advantage among men while Kerry held only a 3-percentage-point advantage among women. But the gender gap was back in 2008, and in 2012 Obama gained an 11-percentage-point advantage among women whilst Romney had a 7-point advantage amongst men.

Key concept

> **Gender gap.** The gap between the support given to a candidate by women and the support given to the same candidate by men. In US elections, women have traditionally supported Democratic candidates more than men, while the reverse has been true of Republican candidates.

The reason for the gender gap is often thought to be connected with policy differences between the two parties. In five major policy areas — abortion, defence, law and order, gun control and women's rights — the Democrats tend to take positions that are more favoured by women. Democrats are pro-choice on abortion, tend to favour lower levels of spending on defence, oppose capital punishment and support gun control. It was the Democrats who pushed — albeit unsuccessfully — for an Equal Rights Amendment to the Constitution protecting the civil rights of women. In 2012, Romney further struggled with women voters after two Republican Senate candidates made injudicious remarks about rape; neither was his inelegant phrase about having been brought 'binders full of women' when making appointments as governor of Massachusetts exactly helpful. For many women, therefore, the Republican Party simply failed to pass the credibility test in 2012.

Race

The most significant minority racial groups in the American electorate are African-Americans and Hispanics. In the nine elections between 1980 and 2012, African-Americans never gave less than 83% support to the Democrats. President Clinton was said to have a particular affinity with African-Americans during his presidency, and they were his most loyal group of supporters, especially during the difficult period of his impeachment and trial. With Barack Obama as the first African-American presidential candidate for a major party in 2008, the share of black people voting Democrat rose from 88% in 2004 to 95% in 2008. Black turnout was also up, accounting for 13% of the electorate in both 2008 and 2012 compared with 11% in 2004.

Hispanics are a growing group. According to the 2000 census, they formed 12% of the population, but by the 2010 census this figure had increased to over 16%. Furthermore, because they are a young group and a significant proportion are not yet of voting age, their full political importance is yet to show. The states where Hispanics make up more than 25% of the population include California, Nevada, Arizona, Texas and New Mexico. Hispanics are a disparate group — from Mexico, Puerto Rico and Cuba, as well as other Central American countries. Bush's Republican campaign in 2000 made a significant pitch for the Hispanic vote. Bush himself speaks fluent Spanish. His brother, Jeb Bush, the former governor of Florida, is married to a Hispanic. The Republican vote among Hispanics increased significantly from 20% in 1996 to 31% in 2000 and to 43% in 2004. But in 2008, the figure was 31% and down to 27% in 2012, with Obama holding a 44-percentage-point lead amongst Hispanic voters in 2012. As Hispanics become a larger cohort within the voting-age population in future decades, they will become an increasingly important racial group for the two parties to attract.

Religion

There are certain important trends in voting according to religion. First, Protestant voters tend to vote Republican, giving a majority of their votes to every Republican candidate from Ronald Reagan in 1980 to Mitt Romney in 2012. Second, Catholic voters have tended to vote Democrat, giving a majority of their votes to Clinton in both 1992 and 1996, and to Gore in 2000. However, the Democrats' 'pro-choice' stance on abortion can cause problems for Catholic voters, whose church is unmistakably 'pro-life'. In 2004 Bush won 52% of the Catholic vote against a Democrat who was a Catholic, though the majority of Catholic voters returned to the Democratic Party in both 2008 and 2012, Obama having a 2-percentage-point lead among this group of voters in 2012. Third, Jewish voters vote solidly for Democrats. They gave 78% support to Clinton in both of his elections and 79% to Gore in 2000. One might have expected a rather higher percentage in 2000, given that Joe Lieberman, Gore's running mate, was Jewish (the first Jew to appear on a major party's national ticket). The 69% vote by Jewish voters for Obama in 2012, however, was their lowest vote for a Democratic candidate since 1984, reflecting their unease about Obama's first-term policy positions towards Israel.

Table 2.24 shows the continuing correlation between frequency of attendance at religious services and voting for Republican candidates. Those 2012 voters who attended a religious service more than once a week cast 63% of their votes for Mitt Romney, whilst amongst those who stated they never attended such services, only 34% voted for

Table 2.24 Frequency of attendance at religious services and candidate support, 2012

Attend religious services	Proportion of electorate (%)	Voted for Obama (%)	Voted for Romney (%)
More than once a week	14	36	63
Once a week	28	41	58
A few times a month	13	55	44
A few times a year	27	56	42
Never	17	62	34

Source: www.foxnews.com/politics/elections/2012-exit-poll

Romney. Despite his Mormon faith, Romney gained the votes of 78% of white evangelical Christians, a higher percentage than John McCain had won in 2008.

Age

Table 2.25 shows that in 2012 there was a close correlation between age and voting. The younger the voters, the more likely they were to vote Democratic; the older they were, the more likely they were to vote Republican. President Obama received his strongest support from 18–29-year-olds; Governor Romney's strongest support came from those aged 65 and over. As with gender and race, this is linked to the policies espoused by the parties: the Democrats being more attractive to younger voters. Governor Romney even complained after the election that the President's Affordable Care Act provision, which allowed those up to 26 years old to stay on their parent's health insurance, was a 'gift' to young voters.

Wealth

The gender gap may have widened in recent elections but the wealth gap has narrowed. It is not nearly as big as it was back in the New Deal period; not even as large as when President George H. W. Bush was elected in 1988. Then, the Republicans carried the highest income group by 25 percentage points — and the Democrats carried the lowest income group by the same margin.

In 2012, Obama did win those earning under $35,000 by 28 percentage points, but Table 2.25 shows that the disparity between the two candidates in other wealth groups was much less, with Romney's support increasing as personal income increased. As a rule, Obama had won the Wal-Mart/beer vote and Romney had won the Starbucks/wine vote.

Geographic region

There are two important trends when it comes to voting in relation to geographic region. First, the Northeast has become the new heartland of the Democratic Party. Gone, as we shall see in Chapter 3, are the days of the Democrats' 'solid South'. Now it is the 'solid Northeast'. In the seven elections from 1984 through to 2008, the Northeast gave the Democratic Party candidate his largest percentage of the vote. In 2012, the Democrats won every north-eastern state. But the bad news for the Democrats is that the Northeast is the one region that has a declining proportion of the nation's population.

Table 2.25 Who voted for whom, 2012

Category	Proportion of electorate (%)	Voted for Obama (%)	Voted for Romney (%)
All	100	51	48
Party and ideology:			
Democrats	38	92	7
Republicans	32	6	93
Independents	29	45	50
Liberal	25	86	11
Moderate	41	56	41
Conservative	35	17	82
Gender:			
Men	47	52	49
Women	53	55	44
Race:			
White	72	39	59
African-American	13	93	6
Hispanic	10	71	27
Asian	3	73	26
White men	34	35	62
White women	38	42	56
Black men	5	87	11
Black women	8	96	3
Hispanic men	5	65	33
Hispanic women	6	76	23
Religion:			
All Protestant	53	42	57
White Protestant	39	30	69
White evangelicals	26	21	78
Catholic	25	50	48
Jewish	2	69	30
Mormon	2	21	78
Attend religious services:			
Weekly	42	39	59
Occasionally	40	55	43
Never	17	62	34
Age:			
18–29	19	60	37
30–44	27	52	45
45–64	38	47	51
65+	16	44	56
Family income:			
Under $30,000	20	63	35
$30,000–49,999	21	57	42
$50,000–99,999	31	46	52
$100,000–199,999	21	44	54
$200,000–249,999	3	47	52
Over $250,000	4	42	55
Population area:			
City over 500,000	11	69	29
City 50,000–499,999	21	58	40
Suburbs	47	48	50
Small town	8	42	56
Rural	14	37	61

Second, the South has moved from being 'solid' for Democrats to being very supportive of Republicans. This was shown most clearly when in 1996 the South was the only region in which the Democratic ticket of Clinton and Gore — both southerners — failed to beat the Republican ticket of Dole and Kemp, neither of whom was from the South. In 2000, the Republicans won every state in the South, including Gore's home state of Tennessee, and they did the same again in 2004. In 2008, Barack Obama managed to flip three southern states — Virginia, North Carolina and Florida — into the Democratic column. In 2012, the Republicans won back North Carolina, leaving Obama with just two southern states.

Population area

There is a high degree of correlation between voting and population area, in that the more densely populated areas tend to vote Democratic, while the more sparsely populated areas tend to vote Republican. The battleground of an election is therefore often in the suburbs. The Democrats have won at least 60% of the vote in cities over 500,000 in each of the last eight elections, with the exception of 1992 when independent candidate Ross Perot kept the Democratic vote down to 58% in big cities. But in ten of the last 11 presidential elections, the party that won the suburbs won the election. The one exception was 2012 when Romney beat Obama in the suburbs by 50% to 48%.

Policies

Policies can be an important determinant of voting. Which policies they are tends to vary from one election cycle to another. The state of the economy can be critical and 2012 was no exception as Table 2.26 shows, with 59% of voters naming the economy as the most important issue. Given the state of the economy in November 2012 it is surprising that Romney gained only a 4-percentage-point advantage amongst these voters. The President had clearly succeeded in persuading enough voters both that recovery was under way and also that the economic difficulties which he had faced in his first term were so severe that he could not be blamed for failing to turn things around in 4 years. The data in this table also show that the Republicans reaped a meagre harvest for all their carping about Obama's healthcare reforms. Only 18% of voters said it was important and of those voters, three-quarters gave their vote to the President.

Table 2.26 Policy issues and candidate support, 2012

Which issues mattered most	Proportion of electorate (%)	Voted for Obama (%)	Voted for Romney (%)
The economy	59	47	51
Healthcare	18	75	24
Federal budget deficit	15	32	66
Foreign policy	5	56	33

Why Obama won in 2012

There were six main reasons why Barack Obama won the 2012 presidential election.

The incumbency factor

Since 1796, 31 presidents have run for re-election. Twenty-two of them have won and only nine have lost. Trying to defeat an incumbent president — especially one with a united party behind him — is well-nigh impossible. Presidents Ford (1976), Carter (1980) and George H. W. Bush (1992) were all defeated having already faced significant opposition in the primaries earlier in the year. In 2012, President Obama was nominated virtually unopposed. Any Republican candidate would therefore have had a difficult time defeating him. The American voters' default position tends to be to re-elect presidents to a second term as they did with Bill Clinton (1996), George W. Bush (2004) and now Barack Obama.

Obama's early and effective attacks on Romney

This leads to a second reason — Obama's brilliant use of his early advantage whilst Governor Romney was still fighting in the Republican primaries. Remember, Romney did not wrap up the Republican nomination until the end of May. Before Romney could introduce himself to the nation as the presumptive Republican nominee, the Obama campaign had already introduced the former Chief Executive Officer of Bain Capital, according to Beth Reinhard in a *National Journal* article, as a 'tax-dodging, job-outsourcing villain who would shred the safety net holding up the elderly and the poor'. This was done mostly in a blizzard of negative TV ads aired in swing states. 'I think they were very smart in defining him early. The ads paid off,' commented Republican strategist Rick Tyler. 'I don't think he ever recovered.' So in the third week of July, whilst Romney was off on his less than successful European tour, the Obama campaign were spending $1.2 million on negative ads which played 1,947 times on Ohio TV stations alone. 'Mitt Romney's not the solution. He's the problem,' intoned the announcer at the end of each ad. In response the Romney campaign did nothing. They had little money to do anything with. As a result, an election that should have been a referendum on Barack Obama's economic stewardship turned into one on Mitt Romney's character.

He ran the better campaign

This leads to a third reason for Obama's victory — that he ran by far the better campaign in terms of voter registration, organisation, use of money and get-out-the-vote operation. As Democratic strategist Joe Trippi commented: 'The Obama campaign knew [that because of the economy] they weren't supposed to get re-elected, so they figured out who they needed to register to vote and turn out to change that.' By the spring of 2012, Obama had more field offices open than all his potential Republican rivals combined. This was critical in swing states. By the summer, whilst Romney had 52 offices open across Florida, Obama had 106; Romney had 40 offices open in Ohio, but the President

had 131. On Election Day, the African-American share of the vote in Ohio jumped from 11% in 2008 to 15%. In Ohio, 96% of African-American voters voted for the President. In Florida, the Hispanic share of the vote jumped from 14% in 2008 to 17%; some 60% of Hispanics in Florida voted for Obama.

Romney — the man and his gaffes

A fourth reason for Obama's victory was Mitt Romney himself. Mitt Romney is no Bill Clinton or even George W. Bush: he lacks the common touch to get alongside and talk with ordinary Americans. Despite swapping his business suits in 2008 for jeans in 2012, in the words of one journalist covering the Romney campaign, 'In factories and fast-food restaurants, Romney was an awkward presence, uneasy at making small-talk with voters.' In the UK in 2012, Prime Minister David Cameron was accused of running a government which was an 'omni-shambles'. In the USA, meanwhile, the Republicans were running a 'Romney-shambles'.

Then there were the verbal gaffes (see Box 2.6), the most damaging of which was the 47% remark secretly filmed during a Romney fund-raiser. Furthermore, Romney had moved so far to the right to win the Republican primaries that he found it very hard to convincingly move back to the political centre before Election Day. So much of what he said during the closing weeks of the campaign directly contradicted what he had said in the primaries and at the Republican convention. Obama enjoyed poking fun at this flip-flopping, suggesting to cheering crowds that his opponent was suffering from 'Romnesia'. Was Romney the 'severely conservative governor' he had boasted of being earlier in the campaign, or was he 'moderate Mitt'? Voters were confused, not being able to discern which Mitt Romney would turn up in the Oval Office were he to win. Thus, despite his resurgence following the first TV debate, 'it was too late to overcome an image of incompetence, aloofness and lack of definition' (Michael Hirsh, *National Journal*).

Box 2.6 Some Romney gaffes

'I like to fire people.'

'[My wife] Ann drives a couple of Cadillacs.'

'I fought against long odds in a deep blue state, but I was a severely conservative governor.'

'The answer [for illegal immigrants] is self-deportation.'

'I'm outraged by the attacks on American diplomatic missions in Libya and Egypt and by the death of an American consulate worker in Benghazi. It's disgraceful that the Obama administration's first response was not to condemn attacks on our diplomatic missions, but to sympathise with those who waged the attacks.'

'There are 47% who are with Obama, who are dependent on government, who believe they are victims, and who believe the government has a responsibility to care for them.'

'I went to a number of women's groups and said, "Can you help us find folks," and they brought us whole binders full of women.'

The Clinton and Bush effects

President Obama received a helping hand from two slightly surprising sources — his two immediate predecessors. Back in 2008, Barack Obama and Bill Clinton seemed to be at odds with one another over Obama's defeat of Hillary Clinton for that year's Democratic presidential nomination. Bill Clinton made frequent and angry outbursts against Mr Obama, at one time seeming to dismiss his campaign as 'the biggest fairy tale I've ever seen'. Indeed, the Romney campaign was using that clip of an angry Bill Clinton in one of its TV ads in 2012 (see Box 2.5). What a difference 4 years makes, for in President Obama's re-election campaign, it was Bill Clinton who perhaps made a more eloquent and persuasive argument for re-electing the President than even the President himself. He appeared in numerous Obama TV ads endorsing the President, and his speech at the Democratic convention was a real barnstormer.

But even more surprisingly, Barack Obama received some help from his immediate predecessor George W. Bush. When exit pollsters asked voters, 'who is more to blame for the current economic problems: Barack Obama or George W. Bush?' a staggering 53% said Bush whilst only 38% said Obama. Presidents can normally get away with blaming current problems on their predecessors for maybe a year or two, but after 4 years the voters would normally consider blaming one's predecessor as unconvincing buck-passing. Not in 2012. And of those 53% who blamed Bush, a staggering 85% voted for Obama and just 12% for Romney, whereas amongst the 38% who blamed Obama, Romney received 94% of their votes. Clearly had the 'blame' factor been reversed and the majority blamed Obama, it would have been Governor Romney in the winner's enclosure on Election Night.

The October Surprise

The term 'October Surprise' has been used in American politics for some 40 years. Its first manifestation was during the closing stages of the 1972 presidential election between President Nixon and his Democratic challenger George McGovern. On 26 October — just 12 days before Election Day — Nixon's national security adviser Henry Kissinger announced that 'we believe that peace is at hand' in Vietnam. This completely pulled the rug from under McGovern's anti-war campaign and he went on to lose in 49 states. An October surprise is an unexpected development or event so late in the campaign that the side it disadvantages does not have time to adequately respond to it before Election Day.

The difference between the 2012 October Surprise and those in previous election cycles (see Box 2.7) was that this one was a natural rather than a political phenomenon, namely Hurricane Sandy which wreaked havoc in the mid-Atlantic and the Northeast and especially in the states of New York and New Jersey just days before the election. The arrival of Hurricane Sandy stopped Romney's post-debate momentum in its tracks and took him out of the news headlines for three critical days. With Romney relegated to being photographed loading emergency supplies onto lorries heading for the worst-affected areas, the President was pictured taking charge of the response in the Situation Room

Box 2.7 Previous 'October surprises'

1972: White House announcement of 'peace is at hand' in Vietnam. Advantage: President Nixon; disadvantage: George McGovern.

1980: President Carter's announcement of possible imminent release of 52 American hostages held in Iran for almost 1 year but the news quickly turned out to be inaccurate. Advantage: Ronald Reagan; disadvantage: President Carter.

1992: Indictment of former Secretary of Defense Caspar Weinberger, a close colleague of George Bush during the Reagan administration, on matters relating to the Iran-Contra affair. Advantage: Bill Clinton; disadvantage: President Bush.

2000: Press disclosure that George W. Bush had paid a $150 fine for a drink-driving incident in 1976. Advantage: Al Gore; disadvantage: George W. Bush.

at the White House. It was also the majority opinion that the President played his roles of comforter- and commander-in-chief to great effect. When the Republican governor of New Jersey, Chris Christie — one of Obama's sharpest critics — publicly described the President's actions as 'outstanding', the media began to talk of a possible Sandy Effect on the final days of the race. Exit pollsters found that of the 64% of voters who said the President's handling of the crisis was a factor in their decision, 62% voted for Obama and just 36% for Romney. It is also worth pointing out that New York and New Jersey were two of only five states in which Obama increased his share of the vote compared with 2008.

The Electoral College

However, the president is not elected by the popular vote but through the Electoral College. This is the final stage of the process. In the vast majority of elections the candidate who wins the popular vote also wins in the Electoral College. But in 2000, though Al Gore won the popular vote, George W. Bush won in the Electoral College (see Table 2.27); hence he rather than Gore became president. But more of that anon. First of all we need to understand how the Electoral College system works.

How it works

In the **Electoral College**, each state is awarded a certain number of Electoral College votes. This number is equal to that state's representation in Congress — the number of senators (2 for every state) plus the number of representatives. Thus in 2012, California had 55 (2 + 53) while Wyoming had just 3 (2 + 1). There are 538 Electoral College votes. To win the presidency, a candidate must win an absolute majority, which is 270.

Key term

> **Electoral College.** The institution established by the Founding Fathers to elect the president indirectly. The Electoral College never meets. Instead, the presidential Electors who make up the Electoral College meet in their state capitals to cast ballots for president and vice-president.

The popular votes for each candidate are counted in each state. In all but two states whichever candidate wins the most popular votes receives all the Electoral College votes of that state — the so-called 'winner-takes-all' rule. This 'rule', however, is not in the Constitution. It is purely a convention that developed during the 19th century in most states. The exceptions are Maine and Nebraska.

The Electoral College never meets together. Its members — called Electors — meet in their respective state capitals on the Monday after the second Wednesday in December. They then send their results to the vice-president of the United States in Washington DC. The vice-president formally counts the Electoral College votes and announces the result to a joint session of Congress in early January. Thus, on 6 January 2001, Vice-President Al Gore had the dubious privilege of announcing his own defeat at the hands of Governor George W. Bush of Texas by 271 Electoral College votes to 266.

What if no candidate wins an absolute majority of Electoral College votes? This could happen either if a 269–269 split occurred between two candidates, or if more than two candidates won Electoral College votes. The former situation almost occurred in 2000. The latter situation might have occurred in 1968 when third-party candidate George Wallace won five states with 45 Electoral College votes.

Under such circumstances, the president would be elected by the House of Representatives from the three presidential candidates with the most Electoral College votes. Each state would have one vote. The winner would require an absolute majority — 26 of the 50 votes. Balloting would continue until one candidate emerged as the winner. Meanwhile the vice-president would be elected by the Senate from the *two* vice-presidential candidates with the most Electoral College votes. Each senator would have a vote. The winner would require an absolute majority — 51 of the 100 votes. Again, balloting would continue until this occurred. Only twice has the Electoral College failed to come up with a winner and the election been thrown to Congress — in 1800 and 1824.

Strengths of the Electoral College

It is not difficult to come up with criticisms of the Electoral College, but the Founding Fathers invented the system because of some presumed strengths, two of which are still of some relevance today.

It preserves the voice of the small-population states

The small-population states, as in 1787, still worry that, were the Electoral College to be abolished, the votes of their inhabitants would become almost worthless, swept aside by the size of such states as California, Texas, New York and Florida. If this was a concern in 1787, it should be even more of a concern now. In the first presidential election, held in 1788, of the 13 states that took part, the smallest had 3 Electoral College votes while the largest — Virginia — had 12: that is, four times as many. But in 2012, California had 55 Electoral College votes — more than 18 times as many as states such as Wyoming and Alaska with just 3.

It tends to promote a two-horse race

This is important in an election for the president, who is both chief executive and head of state — a symbol of national unity. In such a two-horse race, the winner will therefore tend to receive more than 50% of the popular vote, a definite aid to uniting the nation. In 26 of the 38 elections held between 1864 and 2012 — that is, over two-thirds — the winner gained more than 50% of the popular vote. But three of the 12 elections in which this did not occur were 1992, 1996 and 2000.

Weaknesses of the Electoral College

An institution devised over 200 years ago still nominally elects the president of the United States. Many critics see it as beset with problems and potential malfunctions. Here are five criticisms made of the Electoral College.

Small states are over-represented

By 2012, California had 55 Electoral College votes representing its 37 million inhabitants. Wyoming had 3 representing its half-a-million inhabitants. Thus California receives one Electoral College vote for every 675,000 people. Wyoming receives one Electoral College vote for every 185,000 people. Put another way, if California were to receive Electoral College votes on the same basis as Wyoming, it would have not 55 Electoral College votes but 200.

Winner-takes-all system distorts the result

In 1996, Bill Clinton won only 49% of the popular vote, yet he won just over 70% of the Electoral College votes (see Table 2.27). In the 11 elections between 1972 and 2012, the Electoral College could be said to have seriously distorted the result on eight occasions. Although this distortion did not occur in the 2000 and 2004 elections, the phenomenon returned in both 2008 and 2012. In 2012, Obama's 51% of the popular vote was translated into 61.7% of the Electoral College vote.

It is also possible for the candidate who wins the popular vote to lose the Electoral College vote. This is what occurred in 2000. Al Gore won 48.4% of the popular vote to George W. Bush's 48%. But in the Electoral College, Bush came out the winner by 271 votes to 266. This was the third occasion in the nation's history that this had occurred, the other two occasions being 1876 and 1888 (see Table 2.28). It almost occurred in both 1960 and 1968: in 1960, Nixon was only 0.3% behind Kennedy in the popular vote yet lost in the Electoral College by 303 to 219; in 1968, Humphrey was only 0.5% behind Nixon in the popular vote yet lost in the Electoral College by 301 to 191.

Unfair to national third parties

In 1980, Congressman John Anderson, running as an independent, won 6.6% of the popular vote. In 1992, another independent candidate, Ross Perot, won 18.9% of the popular vote. In 1996, as the Reform Party candidate, Perot won 8.5% of the popular vote. In 2000, Green Party candidate Ralph Nader won over 3 million votes (2.9%). None of these candidates won a single Electoral College vote. Take Perot in 1992: in only one state — Mississippi — did he fail to gain at least 10% of the popular vote, yet in only one state — Maine — did he succeed in getting over 30% of the popular vote. Regional

Table 2.27 Distortion of victory by Electoral College votes, 1972–2012

Year	Winner	Party	Popular vote (%)	EC vote (%)	% distortion
1972	Richard Nixon	Republican	60.7	96.6	35.9
1976	Jimmy Carter	Democrat	50.1	55.2	5.1
1980	Ronald Reagan	Republican	50.7	90.9	40.2
1984	Ronald Reagan	Republican	58.8	97.5	38.7
1988	George H. W. Bush	Republican	53.4	79.2	25.8
1992	Bill Clinton	Democrat	43.0	68.8	25.8
1996	Bill Clinton	Democrat	49.2	70.4	21.2
2000	George W. Bush	Republican	47.9	50.4	2.5
2004	George W. Bush	Republican	51.0	53.1	2.1
2008	Barack Obama	Democrat	52.7	67.8	15.1
2012	Barack Obama	Democrat	51.0	61.7	10.7

Table 2.28 Elections in which the popular vote winner lost in the Electoral College

Year	Candidates	Popular vote (%)	Electoral College votes
1876	Samuel Tilden (D) Rutherford Hayes (R)	51.0 47.9	184 185
1888	Grover Cleveland (D) Benjamin Harrison (R)	48.6 47.8	168 233
2000	Al Gore (D) George W. Bush (R)	48.4 47.9	266 271

third-party candidates fare better. In 1968, American Independent Party candidate George Wallace won 13.5% of the popular vote — considerably less than Perot's 1992 figure — yet, because his support was concentrated in the Deep South, he managed to win five states with 45 Electoral College votes.

'Rogue' Electors

Many states have state laws requiring Electors to cast their ballots for the state-wide popular vote winner, but others do not, leaving open the possibility that so-called 'rogue' or 'faithless' Electors will cast their ballots some other way. Seven of the 13 presidential elections since 1960 have seen this occur (see Table 2.29). In 2000, a Washington DC Elector refused to cast her Electoral College vote for Al Gore in protest at the city's lack of congressional representation. She left her ballot blank. Even more oddly in 2004, a Minnesota Elector voted for John Edwards for president (though spelling his name incorrectly as 'John Ewards') but none of the ten Minnesota Electors admitted voting for Edwards for president instead of John Kerry. All ten Electors then voted for John Edwards for vice-president. This was the first time that an Elector had — knowingly or unknowingly — voted for the same candidate for both offices. When the Electoral College voted on Monday 15 December 2008, there were no rogue votes at all with Barack Obama receiving 365 electoral votes and 173 for John McCain.

Table 2.29 Rogue Electors since 1960

Year	State	Number of Electors	Elector should have voted for	Elector voted for
1960	Alabama	8	John Kennedy	Harry Byrd
	Mississippi	6	John Kennedy	Harry Byrd
	Oklahoma	1	Richard Nixon	Harry Byrd
1968	North Carolina	1	Richard Nixon	George Wallace
1972	Virginia	1	Richard Nixon	John Hospers
1976	Washington	1	Gerald Ford	Ronald Reagan
1988	West Virginia	1	Michael Dukakis	Lloyd Bentsen
2000	Washington DC	1	Al Gore	[Abstained]
2004	Minnesota	1	John Kerry	John Edwards

President and vice-president of different parties

At the beginning of the Republic, when political parties in the way they are understood today did not truly exist, it did not matter if the president and vice-president were of different parties, as a result of the system used in the case of Electoral College deadlock. In 2000, however, it was certainly possible that the House of Representatives could have chosen Republican George W. Bush as president and the Senate could have chosen Democrat Joseph Lieberman as vice-president.

Strengths and weaknesses of the Electoral College

Strengths
➢ preserves the voice of the small-population states
➢ usually promotes a two-horse race, therefore winner is likely to receive more than 50% of the popular vote

Weaknesses
➢ small-populated states are over-represented
➢ winner-takes-all system can distort the result
➢ possible for a candidate to lose the popular vote but win in the Electoral College
➢ unfair to national third parties
➢ 'rogue' or 'faithless' Electors
➢ potential problems regarding system to be used if Electoral College is deadlocked

Possible reforms

Because it is so easy to see weaknesses within the Electoral College system, numerous reforms have been suggested. Some, requiring only changes in state or federal law, are relatively minor. Any major reform is likely to require a constitutional amendment, and because these amendments need to be passed by two-thirds majorities in both houses of Congress as well as by three-quarters of the state legislatures, such reforms are unlikely to come about.

Congressional district system

The most widely advocated reform would be for the other 48 states to adopt the system used in Maine in Nebraska which involves awarding one Electoral College vote to a candidate for each congressional district (the constituencies used to elect members of the House of Representatives) that they win and two electoral votes to the candidate who is the state-wide winner. In 2008, Nebraska did split its five Electoral College votes. Although John McCain won the state, Barack Obama won the presidential vote in the 2nd congressional district, thus winning one Electoral College vote, while McCain won the other four — one each for winning the other districts, and two for winning the state-wide vote.

But, as Table 2.30 shows, this reform would lead to the results being only marginally different. Indeed, in 2000 the Maine system would have produced a *less* proportionate result, with Gore losing in the Electoral College by 38 votes rather than by four. Neither would it have helped Ross Perot in either 1992 or 1996. In 2004 it would have exaggerated Bush's winning margin significantly.

A proportional system

Another possible reform would be to allocate Electoral College votes in each state proportional to the popular vote in that state. There would then be a more equable allocation of Electoral College votes. Such a system would be much fairer to national third parties too, but then it would also encourage more voters to vote for such parties, thereby making it more likely that no candidate would gain an absolute majority of Electoral College votes and throwing the election into Congress.

Direct election

Some opinion polls have recently shown that Americans would support a move to a directly elected president — what is called the Direct Election Plan. 'Most Americans don't think the Electoral College is as fair as a direct election would be,' states Robert Richie, director of the Center for Voting and Democracy, which is headed by

Table 2.30 Winner-takes-all and Maine systems compared, 1992–2008

Year	Candidates	Winner-takes-all system	Maine system
1992	Bill Clinton (D) George Bush (R) Ross Perot (I)	370 168 0	322 216 0
1996	Bill Clinton (D) Bob Dole (R) Ross Perot (Reform)	379 159 0	345 193 0
2000	George W. Bush (R) Al Gore (D)	271 267	288 250
2004	George W. Bush (R) John Kerry (D)	286 252	317 221
2008	Barrack Obama (D) John McCain (R)	365 173	301 237

former third-party presidential candidate John Anderson. In a Gallup poll conducted the weekend after the 2000 election, 61% favoured a direct election for president compared with only 35% for keeping the Electoral College. However, opinion polls don't themselves change anything. Only a constitutional amendment could bring about this particular reform. With the small-population states wedded to the current system, the requirement of a two-thirds majority in both houses of Congress, and equal representation of large- and small-population states in the Senate, success is unlikely.

Congressional elections

Thus far we have studied in detail the race for the US presidency. But there are other elections in the United States of which we need to be aware. Both houses of the US Congress — the House of Representatives and the Senate — are now directly elected. It was not always the case. Until the passage of the 17th Amendment in 1913, the Senate was indirectly elected — senators were appointed by the state legislatures. But from 1914, there have been direct elections to the Senate, as well as to the House of Representatives. Congressional elections are held every 2 years and on alternate occasions these elections coincide with the presidential election. So, for example, in 2008, there was both a presidential election and congressional elections, and as these are held on the same day it is quite difficult to distinguish why people vote the way they do in one election as opposed the other.

Key questions answered in this section

➤ How often are elections for the House and Senate held?

➤ What trends are discernible in congressional elections?

➤ What is the coattails effect?

➤ What is split-ticket voting?

➤ What is incumbency and why is it so strong?

➤ Why are there so few competitive seats in the House?

➤ What factors determine voting behaviour in congressional elections?

➤ What trends are discernible in mid-term elections?

Timing of congressional elections

Congressional elections occur every 2 years. Members of the House of Representatives serve 2-year terms while senators serve 6-year terms, but one-third of senators are up for re-election every 2 years. Thus, in every cycle of congressional elections, the whole of the House of Representatives and one-third of the Senate are up for re-election. These elections, like those for the president, are held on the Tuesday after the first

Monday in November. In years divisible by 4 (e.g. 2008, 20012), congressional elections coincide with the presidential election. Elections in the years between presidential elections (e.g. 2010, 2014) are therefore called **mid-term elections**, as they fall midway through the president's 4-year term of office.

Key concepts

➤ **Congressional elections.** Elections held every 2 years for the whole of the House of Representatives and one-third of the Senate.

➤ **Mid-term elections.** The elections for the whole of the House of Representatives and one-third of the Senate that occur midway through the president's 4-year term of office.

Constitutional requirements

The Constitution lays down certain requirements regarding age, citizenship and residency for those wishing to be elected to the House and the Senate. These are set out in Table 2.31. In terms of residency, many large states have passed a state law requiring representatives to be resident in the **congressional district** that they represent. This is known as the **locality rule**.

Table 2.31 Constitutional requirements for representatives and senators

Category	Representative	Senator
Age	At least 25 years old	At least 30 years old
Citizenship	US citizen for at least 7 years	US citizen for at least 9 years
Residency	Resident of state they represent	Resident of state they represent

Key terms

➤ **Congressional district.** A geographic division of a state from which a member of the House of Representatives is elected. Congressional districts within a state are denoted by numbers; thus a House member represents, for example, the 32nd district of California or the 10th district of New York.

➤ **Locality rule.** A state law that requires members of the House of Representatives to be resident not just within the state but also within the congressional district they represent.

The nomination process

The first task for someone wishing to gain a seat in Congress is to secure the nomination of one of the two major parties. Third-party candidates very rarely win seats in Congress. Securing the nomination might mean running in a congressional primary.

These differ from presidential primaries in that the winner of the congressional primary automatically becomes that party's candidate in the general election. Congressional primaries are held in the months prior to the November election, usually between May and September.

Sometimes even an incumbent senator or representative might be challenged for the nomination in the upcoming election and therefore will have to contest a primary. For incumbent senators, defeat in a primary is highly unusual. In the elections between 1982 and 2012, only eight incumbent senators were defeated in primaries and one of those was a senator who had been appointed to fill the vacancy of a retired senator and another was a senator who had switched parties. Two others — Democrat Joe Lieberman of Connecticut in 2006 and Republican Lisa Murkowski of Alaska in 2010 — managed to get re-elected despite their defeat in the primary, Lieberman as an independent and Murkowski as a write-in candidate. In 2010, Republican senator Bob Bennett of Utah was denied a place on the Republican primary ballot by his State Party Convention. The only recent senator to be defeated in a primary was Republican Richard Lugar of Indiana in 2012.

During the same 30-year period, 62 incumbent House members were defeated in primaries, including 19 in 1992 and 13 in 2012. But considering that every 2 years around 400 House members seek re-election, an average of only five or six primary defeats per election cycle is not high. In 2012, of the 13 House incumbents who lost in the primaries, eight were defeated by fellow incumbents in primaries in which two incumbents were running. This often happens in those election cycles which come immediately after the 10-yearly census and the resulting reapportionment of congressional districts in many states. Of the five who lost to challengers in 2012, two were running in districts which had been substantially redrawn to their disadvantage whilst another had been embroiled in controversy for some time. Republican John Sullivan of Oklahoma suffered the only genuine upset of the 2012 House primaries.

Trends in congressional elections

Because congressional elections coincide in every alternate cycle with the presidential election — people may be voting at the same time for president, senator, representative — it is difficult to separate voting intentions in these elections from the votes that people cast for the presidency. As a consequence, most analysis of congressional elections comes from the mid-term elections, in which voters are not casting a presidential ballot. Four trends are discernible when it comes to voting in congressional elections.

Coattails effect

It is sometimes possible to discern a **coattails effect**, which occurs when a strong candidate for a party at the top of the ticket — for president, or in mid-term elections for state governor — can help other party candidates get elected at the same time. The picture is of these other candidates riding into office clutching the coattails of the

Table 2.32 Shift in House and Senate seats at presidential elections: 1960–2012

Year	President	Party	House shift	Senate shift
1960	Kennedy	D	−22	−2
1964	Johnson	D	+37	+1
1968	Nixon	R	+5	+6
1972	Nixon	R	+12	−2
1976	Carter	D	+1	0
1980	Reagan	R	+33	+12
1984	Reagan	R	+14	−2
1988	Bush (41)	R	−2	0
1992	Clinton	D	−9	0
1996	Clinton	D	+3	−2
2000	Bush (43)	R	−1	−4
2004	Bush (43)	R	+3	+4
2008	Obama	D	+21	+8
2012	Obama	D	+8	+2

presidential or gubernatorial candidate. Few modern-day presidents have enjoyed much in the way of a coattails effect. The only clear example, as shown in Table 2.32, was Ronald Reagan for the Republican Party in 1980. In that November the Republicans gained 33 seats in the House and a staggering 12 seats in the Senate, when no fewer than nine incumbent Democrat senators were defeated.

In some recent elections, there has been a reverse coattails effect. In 1992, for example, Democrat Bill Clinton won the presidency, but in the same election Democrats lost nine seats in the House and made no gains in the Senate. Again in 2000, the Republicans lost seats in both houses, including four in the Senate, despite George W. Bush's win in the presidential race. In 2008, the Democrats gained seats in both the House and the Senate (see Table 2.32), but there was little evidence of a true coattails effect, with many Democrat members of Congress running ahead of Barack Obama in the popular vote in their state or district. In 2012, Obama's Democrats made modest gains in both houses but more despite than because of the President.

Key term

> **Coattails effect.** The effect of a strong candidate for a party at the top of the ticket helping other candidates of the same party to get elected at the same time.

The question of whether the president has strong coattails is an important one, as Gary Jacobson (2009) points out in his study of congressional elections. Sheer numbers

matter. Presidents can usually get more done in Congress the more seats their party holds in the House and the Senate. It is also the case that members of Congress who have been elected with the president's help are more likely to support the president than those who believe they have been elected despite the president. As Jacobson comments:

> Members of Congress who believe that they were elected with the help of the president are more likely to cooperate with him, if not from simple gratitude, then from a sense of shared fate. They will prosper politically as the administration prospers. Those convinced that they are elected on their own, or despite the top of the ticket, have less reason to cooperate.

Finally, a partisan sweep in both the presidential and congressional races sends a message to all politicians in Washington. Even members from the opposition party who survived will be wary of falling foul of a popular president.

Split-ticket voting

There is evidence of **split-ticket voting**, which occurs when someone votes for the candidates of different political parties for different offices at the same election. People might vote for a Republican president but a Democrat member of Congress. At the mid-term election, they might vote for a Democrat governor but a Republican member of Congress. Because elections in the United States are more candidate- and issue-orientated than simply party-orientated, ticket splitting does not seem odd to American voters. There is some evidence that voters think in terms of divided government — a president of one party but Congress controlled by the other party. In 1996, the Republicans, having virtually admitted that their presidential candidate Bob Dole would lose, appealed to voters in the last days of the campaign to re-elect a Republican-controlled Congress. They did just that.

Ticket splitting will often result in a state supporting a presidential candidate from one party but, at the same election, a senatorial candidate from the other party. In 2012 this occurred in six states — five going for Republican Mitt Romney in the presidential race but electing a Democrat senator, whilst Nevada voted for President Obama but re-elected Republican senator Dean Heller. In West Virginia, only 35% of voters supported Obama in the presidential race whilst 61% voted to re-elect Democratic senator Joe Manchin. Clearly there were a lot of ticket-splitters in West Virginia in 2012.

Key term

➤ **Split-ticket voting.** The practice of voting for candidates of two or more parties for different offices at the same election. The opposite — voting for candidates of the same party for different offices at the same election — is called straight-ticket voting.

Table 2.33 House members: retired, defeated, re-elected, 1992–2012

Year	Retired	Sought re-election	Defeated in primary	Defeated in general election	Total re-elected	% re-elected who sought re-election
1992	67	368	19	24	325	88.3
1994	48	387	4	34	349	90.2
1996	50	383	2	21	360	94.0
1998	33	401	1	6	394	98.3
2000	32	403	3	6	394	97.8
2002	38	397	8	8	381	96.0
2004	29	404	2	7	395	97.8
2006	28	405	2	22	381	94.1
2008	32	402	4	19	379	94.3
2010	37	396	4	54	338	85.4
2012	40	390	13	27	350	89.7

Table 2.34 Senators: retired, defeated, re-elected, 1992–2012

Year	Retired	Sought re-election	Defeated in primary	Defeated in general election	Total re-elected	% re-elected who sought re-election
1992	7	28	1	4	23	82.1
1994	9	26	0	2	24	92.3
1996	13	21	1	1	19	90.5
1998	5	29	0	3	26	89.6
2000	5	29	0	5	24	82.8
2002	5	28	1	3	24	85.7
2004	8	26	0	1	25	96.1
2006	4	29	1*	6	23	79.3
2008	5	30	0	4	26	86.7
2010	12	25	3†	2	21	84.0
2012	10	23	1	1	21	91.3

* In 2006, Senator Joe Lieberman (D — Connecticut) was defeated in the Democratic primary but was then re-elected as an independent Democrat.
† In 2010, Senator Lisa Murkowski (R — Alaska) was defeated in the Republican primary but was then re-elected as a write-in candidate.

Strong(ish) support for incumbents

There is also evidence of quite strong support for incumbents, with some high re-election rates during the past two decades, especially in the House. The early 1990s showed a temporary blip in this trend with the rise — but almost as quick fall — of the term limits

movement and a 'throw the bums out' mentality among many voters. Even at this time, although Congress as an institution and members of Congress in general were held in low esteem, voters often thought that their senator or representative was doing a good job and deserved to be re-elected. It was as if the voters' slogan was: 'Throw the bums out — but my member of Congress isn't a bum!'

After higher than average turnover rates in the early 1990s, the four elections held between 1998 and 2004 saw re-election rates in the House of over 95%. But the trend reversed again between 2006 and 2012 with 145 incumbents defeated in those four elections compared with just 41 in the previous four. Those 145 members correspond to exactly one-third of the House membership. But re-election rates continue to be high in the Senate with only ten incumbents defeated in the three election cycles between 2008 and 2012.

Fewer competitive races in House elections

Between 1992 and 2004, there was a significant trend towards fewer genuinely competitive seats in elections for the House of Representatives. A competitive seat is one that was won by the incumbent by less than 10 percentage points. Table 2.35 shows that in 1992 there were 111 races decided by less than 10 percentage points, but this figure had fallen to just 31 by 2004. This means that following the 2004 congressional elections, the vast majority of House members — 404 out of 435 — were

Table 2.35 Number of close races in House elections: 1992–2012

Year	Number of House close races
1992	111
1994	87
1996	80
198	43
2000	42
2004	31
2006	58
2008	60
2010	108
2012	65

in what would be called safe seats. They had little to fear in terms of electoral defeat. However, the next three election cycles — 2006, 2008 and 2010 — saw an increase in the number of competitive House elections, but the figure had fallen to just 65 in 2012. This means that in the 2014 mid-term elections some 370 House members could be fairly certain of being re-elected without a significant contest.

The most significant cause of the downward trend in competitive seats was thought to have been the drawing of congressional district boundaries in many states to create safe seats. The decline of competitive districts in House elections has been a contributory factor to higher levels of partisanship in the House in recent years. With the vast majority of members now representing rock-solid Democrat or Republican districts, there is very little incentive to bipartisanship. Indeed, quite the opposite — there is every incentive to please only one's own party. House members in safe seats have more to fear from an intra-party challenge in a primary than from an inter-party challenge in the general election.

Voting behaviour in congressional elections

There is much debate over voting behaviour in congressional elections. The difficulty comes in differentiating voting behaviour in congressional elections that coincide with presidential elections from voting behaviour in those that do not. Data on voting behaviour in presidential election years tend to focus on how voters cast their *presidential* ballot, not their congressional ones. When it comes to mid-term elections, there is evidence of voting being both 'national' and 'local'. In 1994 and 2002, the Republicans in particular attempted — with some success on both occasions — to 'nationalise' the mid-term elections. In 1994 they achieved this through their ten-point policy document called the *Contract with America*, a policy programme to which nearly all House Republican candidates signed up. It became the nationwide focus of the 1994 campaign.

Local issues

That having been said, voters in congressional elections tend to cast their ballots upon local issues and the record of the incumbent. Farm subsidies decide votes in Kansas and Iowa, but not in New Jersey. The regulation of the logging industry decides votes in Oregon and New Hampshire, but not in Texas. Policies to stop illegal cross-border immigration decide votes in Texas and New Mexico, but not in Kansas. Levels of money being committed to interdict coastal drug smuggling decide votes in Florida, but not in Colorado.

Record of incumbent members

Voters consider carefully the record of incumbent members of Congress — especially their attendance at roll-call votes in the House or Senate and how they cast those votes. The senior senator from Kentucky, Republican Mitch McConnell, first won his seat back in 1984 by defeating two-term Democrat Walter Huddleston. McConnell, a 42-year-old county judge at the time, little known state-wide, defeated Senator Huddleston on the issue of his frequent absences from votes in the Senate and his failure to look after the state's interests. 'I can't think of a single thing that Huddleston has done for Kentucky, and no one else can either,' ran McConnell's slogan. He aired a series of state-wide television commercials which showed a pack of bloodhounds trying, in vain, to track down the senator around Washington. 'Has anyone around here seen Senator Huddleston?' the commercials asked repeatedly. The senator had missed almost a quarter of all the roll-call votes in the Senate that year.

In 1992, Senator Alan Dixon (D — Illinois) was defeated mainly for just one vote he cast during 1991 — to confirm Clarence Thomas as an associate justice of the Supreme Court. And two Maryland House members, Wayne Gilchrest (R) and Albert Wynn (D), were defeated in their respective congressional primaries in 2008 partly because of controversial votes they cast on the 2002 vote to authorise President George W. Bush to use troops in Iraq.

In 2008, Republican Senator Elizabeth Dole was defeated in North Carolina on the issues of being ineffective, failing to look after the interests of North Carolinians, and being too supportive of an unpopular president — George W. Bush. The Democratic Senatorial Campaign Committee ran a series of TV ads in support of their candidate, Kay Hagen, criticising Dole for her apparent failings. One ad featured a couple of elderly, casually-dressed men, sitting in rocking chairs on a house porch discussing Senator Dole. It is an extremely clever ad, as it obliquely appears to raise the issue of Dole's age — she was 72 at the time — whilst mocking her as ineffective and too supportive of President Bush (see Box 2.8).

In the 2012 congressional races, Democrat John Barrow found himself in a very tight re-election race in Georgia's 12th Congressional District. Redistricting had not been kind to him, making the district much more Republican leaning than before. Barrow was also the last remaining white Democratic congressman in the Deep South. He needed to reach out to conservative Republicans as well as to the significant African-American community and traditional Democrat voters. His TV ad, *Nobody*, first aired on 15 October, just 3 weeks before Election Day, did the job brilliantly (see Box 2.9). In the

Box 2.8 TV ad against Senator Elizabeth Dole, 2008 — *Rocking Chairs*

'I'm telling you Liddy Dole is 93.'

'93?'

'Yep, she ranks 93rd in effectiveness.'

'After 40 years in Washington?'

'After 40 years in Washington, Dole is 93rd in effectiveness, right near the bottom.'

'I've read she's 92.'

'Didn't I just tell you she's 93?'

'No, 92% of the time she votes with Bush.'

'What's happened to the Liddy Dole I knew?'

'She's just not a go-getter like you and me.'

Box 2.9 TV ad by Congressman John Barrow of Georgia, 2012 — *Nobody*

[Talking to camera sitting on a chair in his home with a rifle propped up to his right.]

I'm John Barrow and long before I was born my grandfather used *this* little Smith and Wesson here [pulls handgun from back pocket] to help stop a lynching. And for as long as I can remember my father had *this* rifle [reaches to hold rifle] real handy just to keep us safe. That's why I support the 2nd Amendment and that's why I'm proud to be endorsed by the NRA. I approve this message because these are my guns now, and ain't nobody goin' to take 'em away.

ad, Barrow appealed to African-Americans by relating the story of how his grandfather had used a handgun to stop a lynching, whilst appealing to conservative Republicans with his NRA endorsement and support for the 2nd Amendment. Barrow was re-elected with 54% of the vote and a 7-percentage-point margin over his Republican challenger, a much wider margin than had been expected.

Mid-term congressional elections

As we have already observed, the congressional elections which come 2 years after the presidential election — in 2010 and 2014, for example — are called mid-term elections, coming as they do midway through the president's 4-year term of office. These mid-term elections for the whole of the House and one-third of the Senate display certain characteristics of their own.

President's party tends to lose

There is evidence that the president's party usually loses seats in both houses in mid-term elections. In the mid-term elections between 1962 and 2010, the president's party has lost an average of 23 House seats and between two and three Senate seats. As Table 2.36 shows, 2002 is the only year in the last 50 years in which the president's party gained seats in both houses in the mid-term elections. The reasons are twofold. If a president has had a coattails effect in the presidential election 2 years before, it is likely that his party's House candidates, now devoid of his presence on the ticket, will do less well. The years 1966 and 1982 are examples of this phenomenon. Furthermore,

Table 2.36 Losses by president's party in mid-term congressional elections, 1962–2010

Year	Party holding presidency	Gains/losses for president's party in:	
		House	Senate
1962	D	−4	+3
1966	D	−47	−4
1970	R	−12	+2
1974	R	−48	−5
1978	D	−15	−5
1982	R	−26	+1
1986	R	−5	−8
1990	R	−8	−1
1994	D	−52	−8
1998	D	+5	0
2002	R	+5	+2
2006	R	−30	−6
2010	D	−63	−6

voters often see the mid-term elections as a chance to express their disappointment or disapproval with the president's previous 2 years in office. In 2010, voters clearly expressed their disappointment with, among other things, President Obama's failure to deliver on his promises to turn around the American economy as well as, for some, their opposition to his healthcare reform legislation.

Congressional elections, 2010

In 2010, the Democrats lost 63 seats in the House, making this the worst mid-term performance by the president's party 2 years into a presidential term since the Republicans lost 75 House seats in 1922. Their loss of six Senate seats was not quite as bad as their 1994 losses just 2 years into President Clinton's first term. In the House they lost three standing committee chairmen with 98 years of congressional service between them as well as 52 members who had been elected in the previous two election cycles. Many of those who lost were Democratic House members in districts which had voted for Republican John McCain in 2008. Of the 39 so-called 'McCain-Democrats' who ran for re-election, 28 (72%) lost. Of the 11 who won, nine had voted 'no' on the final passage of President Obama's healthcare reform bill earlier in the year.

The Democrats' losses in the Senate were mainly in open races following the retirement of the Democratic incumbents in Illinois, Indiana, North Dakota and Pennsylvania. Two incumbent Democrats lost — Blanche Lincoln in Arkansas and Russell Feingold in Wisconsin. The Democrat losses in the Senate could have been even worse had the Republicans not chosen Tea Party-backed candidates in Colorado, Delaware and Nevada who, having run accident-prone campaigns, went on to lose to vulnerable Democrats.

Compared with their vote 2 years earlier, the Democrats saw their share of the vote plummet amongst key groups of voters: down 6 points amongst white voters, down 7 points amongst men, down 8 points amongst women, down 9 points amongst 18–29-year-olds, down 10 points amongst Catholics, and down a staggering 14 points amongst self-identified independent voters. The latter told exit pollsters that having voted for Obama in 2008 as the 'agent of change', he had so far governed as the president of 'more of the same' — more big government spending, more congressional earmarks on legislation, more liberal policies, too much time on healthcare reform and far too little on boosting a stagnant economy and creating jobs. It almost seemed that winning the vote of independents was now the key to winning national elections. As Bob Benenson wrote in *CQ Weekly* ('Pendulum pushed well to the right', 8 November 2010):

> The prominence of this frustrated and relatively non-ideological amalgamation of voters in tipping national elections will require both parties to navigate a minefield of difficult strategic and tactical decisions over the next couple of years.

Propositions, referendums and recall elections

Finally, in this chapter on elections and voting, we consider some forms of direct democracy used by some states but not by the federal government. By direct democracy we mean a system of government in which political decisions are made directly by the people rather than by their elected representatives. Some states practise a more direct form of democracy through the use of propositions, referendums and recall elections. We shall consider each in turn, but it is important to remember that we are talking here about *state* governments, not the federal government. The federal government uses none of these forms of direct democracy.

Key questions answered in this section
➤ What are propositions, referendums and recall elections?
➤ What are the pros and cons of direct democracy?

Propositions

A **proposition**, more commonly in the USA referred to as an 'initiative', is a process that enables citizens to bypass their state legislature by placing proposed laws, and in some states, constitutional amendments, on the ballot. The first state to adopt this form of direct democracy was South Dakota in 1898. Since then, 23 other states have included the proposition or initiative process in their constitutions, the most recent being Mississippi in 1992. That makes a total of 24 states with a proposition process.

Key concept
➤ **Proposition.** A mechanism, commonly known as an initiative, by which citizens of a state can place proposed laws — and in some states, constitutional amendments — on the state ballot.

There are two types of proposition: direct and indirect. In the direct process, proposals that qualify go directly on the ballot. In the indirect process, they are submitted to the state legislature, which must decide what further action should follow. Rules regarding this indirect process vary from state to state. In some states, the proposition question goes on the ballot even if the state legislature rejects it, submits a different proposal or takes no action at all. But in other states, the legislature can submit a competing proposal on the ballot along with the original proposal.

When it comes to the rules regarding getting a proposition on to the state ballot paper, no two states are exactly the same. However, there are a few general rules of thumb and the process in most states includes the following steps by which the proposed proposition must be:
➤ Filed with a designated state official.
➤ Reviewed for conformance with state legal requirements.

- Given a formal title and brief summary for inclusion on the ballot paper.
- Circulated to gain the required number of signatures from registered voters, usually a percentage of the votes cast for a statewide office (e.g. US senator, state governor) in a preceding general election.
- Submitted to state officials for verification of signatures.

The number of signatures required to place a proposition on a state ballot varies from state to state. In Alaska, 10% of the total votes cast in the last general election is required. In California it is just 5% of the votes cast for governor in the last election if the proposition is for a new state law, but 10% if the proposition seeks to amend the state constitution. If enough valid signatures are obtained, the question then goes on the ballot or, in states with the indirect process, is sent to the state legislature. Once a proposition is on the state ballot, the general requirement for passage is a majority vote. In the decade running from 2000 to 2010, voters approved 45% of all initiatives proposed.

Recent examples of propositions

In 2008, there was much publicity given to the vote on California's Proposition 8 to ban same-sex marriage. The vote was 52–48% in favour of the ban. At the same time, California voters approved a measure (52–48) to spend billions of dollars on a high-speed rail system from Los Angeles to San Francisco and also approved (63–37) a measure to give farm animals more space in their enclosures. They also defeated a measure (48–52) which would have required under-18s to inform their parents before seeking an abortion, but approved a measure supported by the then governor, Arnold Schwarzenegger, to take away from state legislators the task of redrawing state legislative districts and give it to an independent, bipartisan commission.

In 2010, there were 42 initiatives on the ballot: 18 (43%) were approved and 24 were rejected. This was the lowest number of initiatives in a mid-term election since 1986. The headline results were:

- **Medical use of marijuana:** rejected in all four states that had it on the ballot — California, Arizona, Oregon and South Dakota.
- **Secret ballots for labour (trade) union elections:** approved in Arizona, South Carolina and Utah.
- **Banning affirmative action programmes:** Arizona voters approved Proposition 107, which prohibited the state from discriminating for or against individuals on the basis of race or ethnicity, effectively banning any form of affirmative action.
- **Greenhouse gases:** California voters rejected Proposition 23, which would have suspended a state law requiring reductions in greenhouse gas emissions.

In 2012 there were again 42 initiatives on the ballot. Voters approved 17 (40%) and defeated the remaining 25. The headlines in this election cycle included:

- **Same-sex marriage:** Maryland, Maine and Washington State all approved same-sex marriage initiatives.

➤ **Use of marijuana:** Colorado and Washington State made legal history by approving measures to legalise and control the recreational use of marijuana, but voters in Oregon rejected a similar measure. Massachusetts voters approved the medical use of marijuana whilst voters in Arkansas rejected it.

Advantages of propositions

There are four often-stated advantages of the proposition. First, it provides a way of enacting reforms on controversial matters that state legislatures are often unwilling or unable to act upon — campaign finance reform, the medical use of marijuana, term limits for state legislators, for example. Second, the existence of the proposition process can increase the responsiveness of state legislatures and increase state legislators' performance and accountability. Third, having propositions on the ballot — especially controversial ones — can help to increase voter turnout. This was certainly the case with the same-sex marriage ban proposition on the Ohio ballot in 2004, which attracted large numbers of conservative Republican voters who also voted for President George W. Bush on the same ballot, thus tipping the state into the Republican column in that election. Fourth, propositions may increase citizen interest in state issues and encourage other forms of participation in the political process — membership of pressure groups, for example.

Disadvantages of propositions

There are, however, some perceived disadvantages. Propositions lack flexibility. Once a measure is drafted, approved and put on the state ballot, it cannot be amended until after it has been adopted, and in some states the legislature is severely limited in its power to amend laws passed by proposition. So whereas legislation passed through the normal legislative process can be amended during the process in order to attract wider support or forestall a potential weakness in its wording and effect, propositions are, in comparison, set in stone from the start. The proposition process, therefore, lacks the benefits of the legislative process — debate, compromise, hearings, public input and amendment. Proposition elections are also vulnerable to manipulation by special interests — high-spending campaigns and media advertising blitzes featuring somewhat simplistic and misleading argument can carry the day.

Pros and cons of propositions   DEBATE

Pros
➤ provide a way of enacting reforms on controversial issues
➤ increase responsiveness and accountability
➤ help increase voter turnout
➤ increase citizen interest in state policy issues

Cons
➤ lack the flexibility of the legislative process
➤ vulnerable to manipulation by interest groups

Referendums

A referendum is an electoral device, available in all 50 states, by which voters can effectively veto a bill passed by the state legislature. Referendums are in many ways similar to propositions, but the major difference is that rather than citizens taking the initiative, referendums follow from something the state legislators themselves have already done. In some states, the state legislature is required to refer certain measures to the voters for their approval in a referendum. For instance, a number of states require that changes to the state constitution must be approved in a statewide referendum. In other states, changes in state tax must be approved in this way. In 2012, there were 115 referendums put on the ballot by state legislatures.

But 24 states go further than this and have a provision called a popular referendum. In states such as Alaska, Colorado and New Mexico which have the popular referendum, if the state legislature passes a law that voters do not approve of, they may gather signatures to demand a referendum on the law. Generally, there is a 90-day period after the law is passed during which the petitioning must take place. Once enough signatures have been gathered and verified, the new law appears on the ballot for a popular vote. While the referendum is pending, the law does not take effect. If voters approve the law in the referendum, it takes effect as scheduled. If voters reject the law, it is null and void — a kind of popular veto.

Recall elections

A recall election is a procedure which enables voters in a state to remove an elected official from office before their term has expired. Recall elections can be seen as a direct form of impeachment. Impeachment is a legal process whereby politicians can remove one of their own from office. The recall election is a political process whereby ordinary voters can remove a politician from office. Nineteen states currently permit the recall of elected officials by this process, though as Box 2.10 shows only eight have ever used it.

Recall of state governors

There have been three recall elections of state governors. In 1921, the voters of North Dakota removed Governor Lynn Frazier by recall election. In 2003, the Democrat governor of California, Gray Davis, was defeated in a recall election by the Republican candidate Arnold Schwarzenegger, who then went on to serve as governor of the state until January 2011. But the most recent and high-profile example was the recall of the Republican governor of Wisconsin, Scott Walker, in June 2012, in which Governor Walker beat his Democrat opponent, Milwaukee mayor Tom Barrett, by 53% to 46%. This recall election was triggered by opposition to Governor Walker's implementation of changes to state employee pension schemes and the limiting of the collective bargaining rights of trade unions within the state.

Box 2.10	States with recall procedures for state officials

Alaska	Kansas	New Jersey
Arizona (1)	Louisiana	North Dakota (1)
California (9)	Michigan (4)	Oregon (3)
Colorado	Minnesota	Rhode Island
Georgia	Montana	Washington (1)
Idaho (2)	Nevada	Wisconsin (18)
Illinois		

Figures in brackets indicate number of recall elections
held for state governors or legislators.

Source: www.ncsl.org

Recall of state legislators

But it is not only state governors who can be the subject of recall elections in these 19 states but state legislators as well. Between 1913 and 2012, there were 36 recall elections of state legislators. Recall elections having been used only sporadically between 1913 and the 1980s — there were only 12 such elections involving state legislators in 70 years — there were then six during the 1990s, two successful and four unsuccessful. Only four recall elections were held between 1996 and 2010, two successful and two unsuccessful. But there were then 11 recall elections involving state legislators in 2011, and a further four in 2012. Of those 15, five of the individuals were recalled and the other ten survived.

The recall election is clearly a device which increases democratic accountability, for it makes elected officials directly accountable not only at election time but potentially at any time during their term of office. But some critics see the recall election as demeaning of the democratic process by allowing voters to indulge in what one might term 'buyer's regret' — changing one's mind after short-term dissatisfaction. Certainly, were the recall election to be used with any degree of frequency, it could easily destabilise the governing process by increasing instability and uncertainty. Many believe that, short of an elected official committing some crime or impeachable offence, voters should have to live with the consequences of the votes they have cast and not be able to change their minds in mid-term. The exit poll conducted at the time of the gubernatorial recall election in Wisconsin showed that 60% of voters thought that the recall mechanism should be used only in case of misconduct by an elected official and another 10% said that recall elections were never appropriate. Of the 60% who thought that recall elections should occur only in cases of misconduct, as opposed to policy disagreements, those voters supported Governor Walker by 37 percentage points — 68% to 31%. Of the 10% who thought that recall elections should never be used, Walker won by 81 percentage points — 90% to 9%.

UK/US comparison

Elections and voting

(i) Election of US president and UK prime minister

There are nine basic characteristics of the election of the US president:

➤ The selection of candidates takes place immediately prior to a general election.

➤ The selection of candidates is conducted through party primaries and caucuses in which any registered voter may participate. It is lengthy, time consuming and expensive.

➤ Party officials usually play only a limited role in candidate selection.

➤ The general election campaign is centred largely on the media and includes TV advertising and TV debates between the major-party candidates.

➤ The general election campaign is again lengthy and costly and is largely a candidate-centred campaign.

➤ Turnout in US presidential elections is generally between 50 and 60%.

➤ The president is elected by the Electoral College rather than by the popular vote.

➤ There is a $2\frac{1}{2}$-month transition period following the election before a new president takes over.

➤ Should a vacancy occur between elections, the vice-president automatically completes the president's unfinished term of office. There is no new election.

There are ten basic characteristics of the election of the UK prime minister:

➤ The prime minister is elected not in a direct election as prime minister but as party leader.

➤ Party leadership elections are held at almost any time except immediately prior to a general election.

➤ The selection of leadership candidates is controlled by the party hierarchy, mostly by the party's MPs at Westminster.

➤ Party members have some role to play in the election of party leaders but ordinary voters cannot participate.

➤ A party leader becomes prime minister when his party becomes the largest single party in the House of Commons.

➤ Party leaders play an increasingly important role in the general election campaign but this is still largely a party-centred campaign.

➤ The media play an increasing role in UK general elections but there is no TV advertising.

➤ The general election campaign is much shorter and less expensive than in the USA.

➤ A newly elected prime minister takes office immediately.

➤ A change of prime minister may occur between general elections if the majority party in the House of Commons changes its leader. Also an unscheduled election may be precipitated should the government fall in a vote of no confidence.

(ii) US congressional and UK parliamentary elections

There are six basic characteristics of US congressional elections:

➢ They are fixed-term elections.

➢ Both houses of Congress are subject to election.

➢ Candidates may be chosen in party primaries in which any registered voter may participate.

➢ Mid-term elections usually result in a loss of seats in both houses for the president's party.

➢ Re-election rates for incumbents are very high, especially in the House, and only a relatively small number of House seats are truly competitive.

➢ Congressional elections may result in 'divided government' with the president's party being in the minority in both houses.

There are six basic characteristics of UK parliamentary elections:

➢ Traditionally, they were not fixed-term elections and could occur at any time up to 5 years after the previous election. There were, for example, two elections in 1974. But now they are fixed at every 5 years in years divisible by five: 2015, 2020, etc.

➢ Currently only the House of Commons is elected but the coalition government published proposals in 2012 for a mostly elected second chamber.

➢ Candidates are chosen only by party members, not ordinary voters.

➢ By-elections often result in a loss of seats for the prime minister's party.

➢ Incumbency rates are lower than in the US House of Representatives with more truly competitive seats.

➢ The prime minister is the leader of the party which has the most seats in the House of Commons after the general election.

(iii) Voting behaviour in US and the UK general elections

One can compare voting behaviour in US and UK general elections by considering the role played by the following factors in each:

➢ policies

➢ party leaders

➢ the campaign

➢ the economy

➢ the record of the previous administration

➢ turnout

One can also compare voting behaviour in each system as to how people vote according to:

➢ gender

➢ race

➢ economic status

➢ region

➢ party identification

➢ social class

Exam focus

Short-answer questions

1 Why is the invisible primary thought to be so important?
2 Do the National Party Conventions still fulfil any useful functions?
3 How important are the TV debates during the presidential general election campaign?
4 Which groups of voters tend to support the Democratic Party, and why?
5 Why are US presidential election campaigns so long?
6 What effect does the Electoral College have on the presidential race and its outcome?
7 What opportunities exist in the USA for direct democracy?
8 Analyse the significance of mid-term elections.
9 Assess the extent to which incumbents have an advantage over challengers in congressional elections.

Essay questions

1 Does public participation in the presidential nomination process advance or hinder democracy?
2 Does television enhance democracy or merely trivialise the issues in presidential elections?
3 What are the major concerns regarding campaign finance in presidential elections?
4 Should the Electoral College be reformed, abolished or left as it is?
5 Money, policies or personality: which is most important in winning the presidency today?
6 How do Americans decide how to vote in presidential elections?
7 To what extent are mid-term elections merely a referendum on the performance of the president?

Further reading

Ashbee, E., 'Primaries and caucuses evaluated', *Politics Review*, Vol. 18, No. 2, November 2008.

Bennett, A. J., *US Government and Politics: Annual Update 2013*, Philip Allan Updates, 2013 (gives a detailed survey of the 2012 presidential election).

Bennett, A. J., *The Race for the White House from Reagan to Clinton: Reforming Old Systems, Building New Coalitions*, Palgrave, 2013.

Bennett, A. J., *The Battle for the White House, Bush to Obama: Nominations and Elections in an Era of Partisanship*, Palgrave, 2013.

Chapter 3

Political parties

Political parties are an essential element of any democracy. So it may come as something of a surprise to find that political parties do not play as important a role in US politics as might at first be expected. A number of the traditional functions played by parties — organisation, fundraising, communication, policy formulation — are not the sole prerogative of parties in the US political system. To some extent, these functions have been usurped by pressure groups, political action committees, candidate-centred organisations and the media. The size of the USA also makes the national political parties weaker than is the case in a small nation-state such as the United Kingdom, and we must not forget that the US parties are very much state-based organisations.

The USA is nonetheless said to have a two-party system, and, because it has a first-past-the-post electoral system, this might not come as too much of a surprise. In terms of the institutions of government, the Democrats and the Republicans dominate the scene to an extraordinary degree. Third parties seem to have only a minor role to play in US politics. Thus, we have something of a paradox to explain: a political system in which the two major political parties are both relatively unimportant and yet dominate the political scene.

Key questions answered in this chapter

➤ What is the link between the major parties and ideology?

➤ What is the organisational structure of the major parties?

➤ Does the USA have a two-party system?

➤ What role is played by third parties?

➤ Are the US parties in a period of decline or renewal?

➤ What is the Tea Party movement and how important is it?

Links to follow up

The first place to go for information on political parties is **www.politics1.com**, which has comprehensive information on both the two major parties and on a host of third and minor parties. Click on 'Political Parties' on their website. The two major parties each have a website: **www.democrats.org** and **www.rnc.org**

To follow up information on ballot access for third and minor parties, go to **www.ballot-access.org**

Major parties and ideology

The names of the two major parties immediately suggest that they are not ideologically exclusive parties, for 'democracy' and 'republicanism' are two all-embracing ideologies, if ideologies they are. An ideology is a collectively held set of ideas and beliefs. Some ideologies, such as fascism and socialism, are narrow in their compass, but this is not so with the two being considered here. Indeed, Barack Obama, who is a Democrat (i.e. a member of the Democratic Party), is also a republican, in that he believes in the principles of republican government. Likewise, George W. Bush, who is a Republican (i.e. a member of the Republican Party), is also a democrat, in that he believes in the principles of democratic government.

Because the parties' names do not necessarily suggest an ideological colour, we find that commentators, and even politicians themselves, attach ideological labels ahead of the party names. Thus, there are 'conservative Democrats' and 'liberal Democrats'; 'conservative Republicans' and 'moderate Republicans'. George W. Bush ran his 2000 election campaign calling himself a **compassionate conservative**. In the USA ideology and region are often linked. The South tends to be more conservative; the Northeast and the west coast tend to be more liberal or libertarian. Thus, for both parties to be viable in all regions of the country, they need to take on the ideological colours of the region. Southern Democrats such as Senator Mark Pryor of Arkansas are more conservative than New England Democrats such as Senator Patrick Leahy of Vermont. Similarly, New England Republicans such as Senator Susan Collins of Maine are more liberal than southern Republicans such as Senator Richard Burr of North Carolina.

 Key concept

> **Compassionate conservative.** A term popularised by George W. Bush during his 2000 presidential election campaign to denote a strand of conservative Republican philosophy which took a more compassionate view on such issues as welfare, education, immigration and poverty.

Ideological differences

That said, it is still possible to discern some clear ideological differences between the two major parties. This can be done most easily by looking at the stands the parties tend to adopt on certain high-profile political issues. Table 3.1 shows the parties' stands

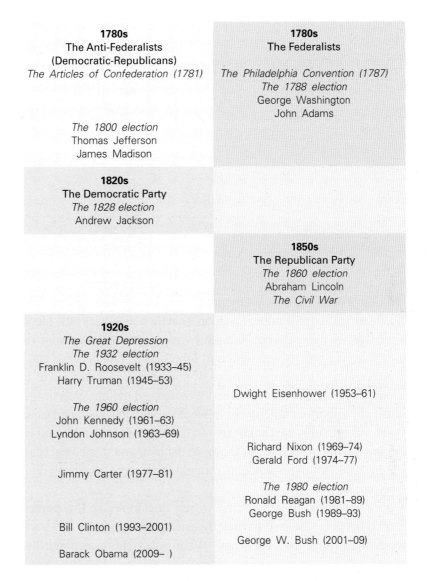

Figure 3.1 The development of America's two major parties

on ten key policy issues. All these issues will be debated in any modern-day, national political campaign. We are not, of course, suggesting that *all* Democrats oppose the death penalty or *all* Republicans support prayer in schools, but we can say that, in general, *most* Democrats tend to oppose the death penalty and *most* Republicans tend to support school prayer. This can be seen in the positions taken by presidential candidates as well as in the voting patterns on these issues in Congress.

It is possible to suggest that the ideological pattern of Democrats — support for abortion and gay rights, opposition to prayer in public schools — is one that could be described as '**liberal**'. Equally, one could suggest that the ideological pattern of Republicans — support for cutting taxes and the death penalty and opposing abortion

Table 3.1 Differences between Democrat and Republican positions on ten key policy areas

Key issue	Democrat position	Republican position
Increased spending on social welfare programmes	Support	Oppose
A 'get tough' attitude to criminals and crime	Oppose	Support
Death penalty	Oppose	Support
Gun control	Support	Oppose
A woman's right to an abortion	Support	Oppose
Increased defence spending	Oppose	Support
Rights for gays and lesbians	Support	Oppose
'The federal government should do less'	Oppose	Support
Prayer in public (i.e. state) schools	Oppose	Support
Stricter controls on immigration	Oppose	Support

rights — is one that could be described as '**conservative**'. Such ideological leanings can be clearly seen in the way Americans vote for the two major parties (see Table 3.2).

It used to be the conventional wisdom that there was very little ideological difference between the two major parties, that they were in the famous phrase of Professor Denis Brogan 'like two bottles with different labels, both empty', or if you prefer Professor Clinton Rossiter: 'They are creatures of compromise, coalitions of interest in which principle is muted and often silenced.' When asked the question in 1972: 'Do you think there are any important differences in what the Republicans and Democrats stand for?' 44% said 'no' and only 46% said 'yes'. As Table 3.3 shows, the trend has been towards Americans seeing the parties as far more distinct, and this has accelerated since 2000 so that by 2008 78% of respondents thought there were important differences between the two parties.

A similar change is discernible when one looks at the perceived ideological difference between the two parties by asking the question: 'Do you think one party is more conservative than the other?' When asked this question in 1992, 57% said the Republican Party was the more conservative and just 12% the Democratic Party, but 31% said there was no difference between them in terms of conservative ideology. By 2008, the percentage naming the Republican Party as the more conservative had increased to 67% whilst those saying there was no difference had declined to 17% (see Table 3.4).

Key concepts
> **Liberal.** A view that seeks to change the political, economic and social status quo in favour of the well-being, rights and liberties of the individual, and especially those who are generally disadvantaged by society.
> **Conservative.** A view that seeks to defend the political, economic and social status quo and therefore tends to oppose changes in the institutions and structures of society.

Table 3.2 Ideological voting in the 2012 election

Position		% of all voters	Voted for Obama (%)	Voted for Romney (%)
Liberal		25	86	11
Conservative		35	17	82
White Evangelical	Yes	26	21	78
	No	74	60	37

Table 3.3 Answers to the question: 'Do you think there are any important differences in what the Republicans and Democrats stand for?', 1972–2008 (percentages)

	1972	1976	1980	1984	1988	1992	1996	2000	2004	2008
No difference	44	42	34	30	35	35	35	33	20	21
Yes, different	46	47	58	63	60	60	64	64	76	78

Source: www.electionstudies.org/nesguide

Table 3.4 Answers to the question: 'Is one party more conservative than the other?', 1972–2008 (selected years, percentages)

	1972	1976	1984	1988	1992	2004	2008
Yes, Republicans	57	54	53	57	57	68	67
Yes, Democrats	15	17	15	12	12	17	16
No: both the same	33	28	32	31	31	15	17

Source: www.electionstudies.org/nesguide

Ideological debates

Democratic Party

Both major parties have experienced internal ideological debates during the past two decades. Within the Democratic Party this has been between what might be described as old-fashioned, liberal Democrats and New Democrats. Many within the party saw the defeats in the 1968 and 1972 presidential elections, and again in the 1984 and 1988 presidential elections, as a repudiation of old-style Democrat ideology. The candidates in those four elections were all old-style liberals from the North — Hubert Humphrey of Minnesota (1968), George McGovern of South Dakota (1972), Walter Mondale also of Minnesota (1984) and Michael Dukakis of Massachusetts (1988). The Democrats' only victory during this period was with a southerner — Jimmy Carter of Georgia in 1976.

Out of the ashes of these defeats was born the Democratic Leadership Council (DLC). The DLC sought to reposition the Democratic Party further to the centre of US politics. It was their candidate, Governor Bill Clinton of Arkansas, who finally broke the succession of defeats and became the first Democrat since Franklin Roosevelt to serve two full terms as president. But to what extent did Bill Clinton's attempt to reshape the

Democratic Party during the 1990s outlive his presidency? There is some evidence to suggest that the answer to this is 'not a great deal'. The first piece of evidence was that when Al Gore ran for the Democrats in 2000 he did not put himself forward as the 'let us continue' candidate, as Lyndon Johnson did in 1964. Quite the opposite. Gore seemed to distance himself from President Clinton, maybe for reasons more of personal ethics than of policy shifts. Even the fact that Gore failed in his bid to win the presidency seemed to suggest that the country in general, and maybe even Democrats in particular, did not want to see a continuation of the Clinton agenda.

Following Gore's defeat in 2000, the party turned not to a Clinton-style New Democrat in 2004 but to Massachusetts Senator John Kerry, someone who was much more clearly identified with old-style Democrats of same-state senator Ted Kennedy and former governor Michael Dukakis — the latter defeated by Bush in 1988. This was followed by the 2008 nomination of Senator Barack Obama. In winning the nomination that year, Obama ran successfully against the combined campaigning of Bill and Hillary Clinton. Just 8 years after leaving the White House, the former first couple seemed to have lost their hold over the Democratic Party. The party opted instead for a candidate who in 2007 was, according to *National Journal*, the most liberal member of the US Senate. In winning the presidency in 2008, Barack Obama was therefore the first liberal Democrat to do so since John Kennedy in 1960. That said, by 2012 the Clintons were clearly held in high esteem and that might suggest that Bill Clinton's ability to shape the future of the party may still become a reality.

Republican Party

The Republican Party has for decades been engaged in an ideological debate within the party. In the 1960s this was seen in the fight between conservatives led by Senator Barry Goldwater of Arizona — the party's defeated 1964 presidential candidate — and the moderate Governor Nelson Rockefeller of New York. Indeed, the term 'Rockefeller Republican' was used by those on the conservative wing of the party as one of scorn. The battle between these two ideological wings was evident in almost every presidential election cycle. In 1976, the moderates had the upper hand, as Gerald Ford won a close nomination contest against Governor Ronald Reagan of California. But following Ford's defeat in that election, Reagan returned triumphant in 1980, winning re-election by a landslide in 1984.

The 'succession' of Reagan's vice-president, George H. W. Bush, in the 1988 election was seen as putting the moderates back in charge. The first President Bush represented the 'eastern establishment' wing of the party and gave key jobs to those of a similar ideological perspective, such as Secretary of State James Baker. The second President Bush sought initially to blur these ideological issues within the Republican Party with his 'compassionate conservative' label. 'Compassionate' had overtones of 'Rockefeller Republicanism', while 'conservative' spoke of 'Reagan Republicanism'. But the ideological battle was still there. In domestic policy it was seen in the inclusion in Bush's first cabinet of people as diverse as conservative John Ashcroft (Attorney General) and moderate Christine Todd Whitman (Administrator of the Environmental Protection Agency). In foreign policy it was seen, at least to begin with, in the inclusion of conservative Donald Rumsfeld (Secretary of Defense) and moderate Colin Powell (Secretary of State).

But as the George W. Bush presidency unfolded, most observers thought Bush looked more conservative than compassionate. Ashcroft and Whitman did not last long. Powell clearly lost out to the foreign policy hawks — Defense Secretary Rumsfeld (until he resigned in late 2006) and Vice-President Cheney. Bush appointed conservative judges John Roberts and Samuel Alito to the Supreme Court. And when it came for Republicans to choose a successor to George W. Bush in the 2008 Republican primaries, the front-running candidates — Rudy Giuliani, the former Mayor of New York, and Mitt Romney, the former Governor of Massachusetts — clearly looked nothing like Bush at all from an ideological perspective. Even the eventual nominee, Senator John McCain of Arizona, was a party maverick and frequent Bush critic. The candidate who looked most like Bush, the former Arkansas governor Mike Huckabee, came a respectable second in the nomination race, but was unable to build any significant support outside the southern, white evangelical Christian wing of the party. Just as Clinton's ideological stance was rejected by his party once he left office, so was that of George W. Bush by the Republican Party. And as we shall see later in this chapter, the Tea Party movement would also have a significant effect on the party's ideological standpoint.

The polarisation of American politics

The break-up of the solid South

In 1960, 100 years after the start of the Civil War, **the solid South** was still intact: whether you were black, white, liberal or conservative, you voted for the Democrats. Southerners would sometimes describe themselves as 'yellow dog Democrats', meaning that, even if the Democrats put up a yellow dog as an election candidate, they would still vote Democrat. As a result of the 1960 election, of the 106 members of the House of Representatives from the South, 99 were Democrats. All 22 southern senators and all 11 southern state governors were Democrats. That was the extent of the solid South. In the presidential election of that year, the Democrat candidate John Kennedy won eight of the 11 southern states. There was little to suggest that the solid South was about to disintegrate, but in the ten subsequent presidential elections (1964–2000), the Democrats won a majority of the South on only one occasion — in 1976, with southerner Jimmy Carter. By 1992 and 1996, they could not even win the South with a presidential ticket made up of two southerners — Bill Clinton of Arkansas and Al Gore of Tennessee.

 Key concept

> **The solid South.** A term used to refer to the Democratic Party's solid political and electoral control of the South during the century between the Civil War and the 1960s.

Indeed, the 1990s brought the final seismic shift. In 1994, the Republicans shot to majority status in the House and Senate and among state governors in the South. They now controlled 64 House seats to the Democrats' 61, 13 Senate seats to the Democrats' nine, and six state governorships to the Democrats' five (see Table 3.5). The Democrats largely lost their southern conservative wing, which shifted to their more natural political home — the Republican Party. States like Texas, Georgia and Alabama which had been solidly Democrat for decades were becoming increasingly dominated by Republican politicians.

The break-up of the solid South led to the two major parties becoming more ideologically distinct. A significant group of conservative voters had crossed from the Democratic Party and joined the Republicans. The result was to make the Republican Party more conservative and the Democratic Party more homogeneous as a left-of-centre party. Remember that it was not just voters who moved — some politicians moved too. Such noted conservative luminaries of the Republican Party as the late Strom Thurmond of South Carolina and former Texas senator Phil Gramm were once Democrats but switched to the Republican Party, believing that they would find more of an ideological home there. So, as Table 3.5 shows so clearly, the Democrats' hold in the South finally collapsed in the mid-1990s, though in 2006 and 2008 they managed to stage a small but seemingly temporary recovery. Democrat losses in the South continued in both 2010 and 2012, by which time the Democrats controlled not a single governor's mansion in the South, and held only six Senate seats and just 40 of 138 House seats. In just 50 years, the political landscape of the South had been almost completely reversed.

The '50-50 nation' and 'red v. blue'

By the time we reached the 21st century, commentators were talking of an increasingly polarised electorate and this was popularised in two phrases: America as a '50-50 nation' and the 'red states v. blue states'. Both these phrases were essentially born out of the results of the 2000 presidential and congressional elections.

In the 2000 presidential election, both major-party candidates ended up with around 49% of the popular vote. The Electoral College divided 271–267. In the House of Representatives it was 221–212 with two independents, while the Senate split exactly 50–50. In 2004, things swung a fraction in the Republicans' favour: 51–48% in the popular vote; 286–252 in the Electoral College; 232–202 in the House; 55–45 in the Senate. In the presidential election, only three states changed hands from 2000 — New Mexico, New Hampshire and Iowa. New Mexico — which in 2000 was a solitary island of Blue in the Red Sea — switched to the Republicans. New Hampshire — which in 2000 was a solitary piece of Red in the Blue Northeast — switched to the Democrats. And the Republicans

Table 3.5 The break-up of the solid South, 1960–2012

Year	House: Democrats–Republicans	Senate: Democrats–Republicans	Governors: Democrats–Republicans
1960	99–7	22–0	11–0
1962	95–11	21–1	11–0
1964	89–17	21–1	11–0
1966	83–23	19–3	9–2
1968	80–26	18–4	9–2
1970	79–27	16–5	9–2
1972	77–31	14–7	8–3
1974	81–27	15–6	8–3
1976	80–28	16–5	9–2
1978	78–30	15–6	8–3
1980	69–39	11–10	6–5
1982	82–34	11–11	9–2
1984	80–36	12–10	8–3
1986	78–38	16–6	6–5
1988	77–39	15–7	6–5
1990	77–39	15–7	8–3
1992	77–48	13–9	8–3
1994	61–64	9–13	5–6
1996	54–71	7–15	5–6
1998	54–71	8–14	4–7
2000	53–71	9–13	5–6
2002	55–76	9–13	4–7
2004	49–82	4–18	4–7
2006	54–77	5–17	5–6
2008	59–72	7–15	4–7
2010	38–94	6–16	2–9
2012	40–98	6–16	0–11

enticed Iowa away from the Democrats' Great Lakes peninsula. In other words, after 2004 the electoral map looked even more tribal than did the one 4 years earlier.

And so America was portrayed as two rival societies: Red America versus Blue America. Red America, it was claimed, was rather more male than female. It was overwhelmingly white, though in certain areas it was increasingly Hispanic. It was overwhelmingly Protestant (and specifically, evangelical) but has been joined of late by practising Catholics. It was wealthy, rural or suburban, and unmistakably conservative. In Red America, the majority of voters think that the federal government does too many

things which would be better left to private businesses and individuals, and they tend to think that federal income taxes should be cut, even if that means cuts in federally funded services.

By contrast, Blue America, it was claimed, was more female than male. It was still a rainbow coalition of white, black, Asian and Hispanic. Churchgoing was not that important in Blue America. It was less wealthy, predominantly urban and unmistakably liberal. In Blue America, the majority of voters think that the federal government should do more to solve problems, and they tend to think that federal income taxes should be increased — certainly on the more wealthy — in order to protect federally funded services.

Shades of purple?

The trouble with the red v. blue debate is that it is somewhat simplistic. It makes things appear to be more polarised than they are. Even in the presidential race, while there are some states that vote consistently for one party's candidate — Massachusetts, New York and California for the Democrats, Wyoming and Oklahoma for the Republicans — in 2008, nine states that had voted for Republican George W. Bush in 2004 voted for Democrat Barack Obama, including Indiana, which Bush had won by 21 percentage points just 4 years earlier, though it switched back to the Republican column in 2012.

When we then start to look at congressional and state elections, the picture becomes even more complex. The red v. blue map of America would tell us, for example, that West Virginia is a Red state. But both its United States senators are Democrats. Its three-member state delegation in the House of Representatives includes Democrat Nick Rahall. It has a Democrat governor and the Democrats control both houses of the state legislature. On the other hand, Maine we are told is a Blue state. Yet neither of its United States senators are Democrats. Even Massachusetts, New York and California, which we have just described as being pretty blue, have all had Republican governors within the past two decades. Massachusetts managed four consecutive Republican governors between 1991 and 2006 — William Weld, Paul Cellucci, Jane Swift and Mitt Romney. So in most states, it is not so much Red and Blue as differing shades of purple.

Why the red–blue divide?

American politics back in the 1950s, 1960s and 1970s was said to be all about bipartisanship. There were liberal Democrats and conservative Democrats; there were conservative Republicans and moderate Republicans. The two major parties were non-ideological and both encompassed a huge philosophical range. But today, Washington politics seems to be all about **partisanship**. The two major parties are much more ideologically distinct and homogeneous. As we shall see in Chapter 5, when it comes to voting in Congress, the two parties tend to behave more like parties in a parliamentary system such as Britain. Indeed, when a moderate Republican senator, Olympia Snowe of Maine, announced her retirement in 2012 she said that one of the reasons she was leaving was the chamber's 'dysfunction and political polarisation'. And in an opinion piece in the *Washington Post*, she added:

Congress is becoming more like a parliamentary system where everyone simply votes with their party and those in charge employ every possible tactic to block the other side. But that is not what America is all about and it's not what the Founders intended. In fact, the Senate's requirement of a supermajority to pass significant legislation encourages its members to work in a bipartisan fashion.

Key concept

➤ **Partisanship.** A term used to denote a state of affairs in which members of one party regularly group together in opposition to the members of another party. Partisanship is therefore typified by high levels of party discipline, frequent occurrences of party-line voting, and little if any cooperation and compromise between politicians of different parties.

But the old 'coalition' parties seem to be disappearing. Why? There are four factors worthy of serious consideration — all of which occurred either during or since the 1980s.

➤ The first thing that happened was the presidency of Ronald Reagan (1981–89). Reagan wooed conservatives away from the Democratic Party while making it more uncomfortable for moderates to remain in the Republican Party.

➤ The second thing that happened was the end of the Cold War. From 1941 to the end of the 1980s, the two major parties looked ideologically similar because they both accepted the foreign policy consensus — the need for unity in the face of the threat from the Soviet Union. The collapse of the Soviet Union ended the need for that consensus.

➤ The third factor was the rise of what one might call the partisan presidency. Presidents such as Eisenhower, Ford, Carter and the first George Bush tended to govern from the political centre, as unifying figures. They were presidents of whom many Americans approved, but who few 'loved' or 'hated'. Then came the presidency of Bill Clinton (1993–2001). The Clinton years were something of a paradox. For although Clinton ran as a 'New Democrat' and sometimes adopted Republican policies and themes ('the era of big government is over'), his presidency proved highly divisive. Clinton, the first baby-boomer president, reopened the divisive issues of the 1960s — sex, the role of women and the nature of authority and morality. Clinton was followed by George W. Bush (2001–09).

Like Clinton, Bush proved to be a divisive president. In 2000, Bush had run for office as 'a uniter, not a divider'. But the circumstances of his election — the disputed count in Florida — immediately made him a divisive character. The events of 9/11 suddenly transformed him into the Uniter-in-Chief, and in the months immediately after the attacks on New York and Washington, Bush enjoyed bipartisan support both in Congress and in the country. But the military operation in Iraq quickly ended all that, and Bush's largely unpopular war once again divided the country. The Obama presidency has continued this partisan tone, seen in the reaction to 'Obamacare' and the rhetoric of some of Obama's critics.

> And while all this was going on, a fourth factor — technology — came into play. Direct mail, talk radio, cable television, mobile phones, e-mail and the internet all enabled ideological soul mates not only to communicate with each other more effectively, but also to evangelise. These New Media are quickly replacing the Old Media — newspapers, journals (such as *Time* magazine), network television (ABC, CBS, NBC) — as the shaper of public opinion. What this means is that while Americans used to read, hear and see a spectrum of comment, now they tune in or log on to the channel or the website that merely reinforces their existing views or prejudices. Thus partisanship is increased and the political debate becomes less civil.

Organisational structure of the two major parties

As we saw in Chapter 1, the USA has a decentralised form of government based on the principle of federalism. If government is decentralised, political parties are likely to be decentralised too. This can best be seen by asking the questions: 'Who is the leader of the Democratic Party?' and 'Who is the leader of the Republican Party?' The former question might elicit the answer of 'President Obama', but that is questionable. As Chapter 6 explains, the president may be able to exercise very little leadership in Congress, even among those members of his own party. President Obama was, after all, elected as *president* in a national election, not as party leader in an internal party election. Contrast that with the position of the British prime minister.

National committees

The only manifestation of party structure at the national level is the national committees — the Democratic National Committee (DNC) and the Republican National Committee (RNC). Both have offices in Washington DC. Each has a chair elected by fellow committee members. As of January 2013, the DNC chair was Debbie Wasserman Schultz, who is a member of the House of Representatives from Florida; the RNC chair was Reince Priebus of Wisconsin, yet few ordinary voters will have heard of them. The DNC and RNC organise the parties' respective National Conventions (see Chapter 2) — the most public manifestation of the parties. However, it is difficult to think of conventions made up of between 2,000 and 4,000 people, meeting for only 4 days every 4 years, being responsible for very much.

Conventional wisdom has therefore been that the national committees of both parties are fairly weak affairs and that we would be better to think of American political parties as decentralised, state-based parties. However, a very public disagreement between the national and state parties occurred during the 2008 presidential nomination process. The national committees of both major parties had agreed the rules for the holding of state-based presidential primaries and caucuses. Both had laid down explicit rules concerning the dates between which states could schedule their nominating contests. The DNC's Rules and Bylaws Committee had stated that only

Iowa, New Hampshire, Nevada and South Carolina could hold primaries or caucuses before 5 February 2008. But the state parties of Michigan and Florida scheduled their contests, respectively, on 15 and 29 January. In response, the DNC voted in August 2007 to strip both state parties of their National Convention delegates. A later compromise allowed the Michigan and Florida delegates to attend the convention but with only half a vote each.

The Republicans faced a similar problem and in October 2007 the then chairman of the RNC, Mike Duncan, imposed a 50% cut in the number of delegates allocated to New Hampshire, South Carolina, Florida, Michigan and Wyoming for breaching national party rules regarding the scheduling of primaries and caucuses. 'It's very important that our party upholds and enforces the rules that we unanimously voted into place at the Republican National Convention in 2004,' said Duncan. His decision was endorsed by the full RNC on 8 November by 121 votes to 9. The Republicans faced a similar national–state party spat during the 2012 primaries when five states ignored national rules about delegate selection and as a result had their delegate allocation cut by half.

Congressional committees

Each party has a series of committees in both houses of Congress overseeing policy and campaigning (see Box 3.1). The chair of the Democratic Senatorial Campaign Committee, Senator Patty Murray of Washington, was given much of the credit for the Democrats' successful 2012 Senate campaign, which resulted in the party winning two seats, boosting its number of Senate seats from 51 to 53 (plus 2 independents) and this in a cycle when they were defending 23 of the 33 seats and expected to suffer significant losses.

State-level organisation

Everything else to do with political parties in America is at the state level, where there is a bewildering variety of organisation, laws and customs, and considerable power is vested in the state governors and mayors of big cities. Indeed, it is worth remembering that the so-called *National* Party Conventions are merely the coming together of the delegates from the *state* parties, chosen in *state-run* primaries. There are State Party Committees (headed by the State Party chair) and State Party Conventions. Below that exist party committees at county, city and ward levels. Although big-city 'machine' politics still exists in some regions, the picture of the cigar-chomping, fedora-hatted political 'boss' is now somewhat outdated. Mayor Richard Daley, often thought of as the last of the big-city party bosses, died in 1976.

Increasingly, the state and local parties are dominated by two new kinds of party activist. First, there are the 'issue activists' — people committed to a particular political issue, such as civil rights or women's rights — and, second, there are what might be called 'candidate activists' — people who have come into politics through working on the campaign of a particular candidate.

Box 3.1 Congressional party committees

➤ Senate Democratic Policy Committee (Chair: Sen. Chuck Schumer, New York)

➤ Senate Republican Policy Committee (Chair: Sen. John Barrasso, Wyoming)

➤ House Democratic Steering and Policy Committee (Chair: Rep. Nancy Pelosi, California)

➤ House Republican Steering Committee (Chair: Rep. John Boehner, Ohio)

➤ House Republican Policy Committee (Chair: Rep. James Lankford, Oklahoma)

➤ Democratic Senatorial Campaign Committee (Chair: Sen. Michael Bennet, Colorado)

➤ National Republican Senatorial Campaign Committee (Chair: Sen. Jerry Moran, Kansas)

➤ Democratic Congressional Campaign Committee (Chair: Rep. Steve Israel, New York)

➤ National Republican Congressional Committee (Chair: Rep. Greg Walden, Oregon)

The two-party system

A **two-party system** might be defined as one in which two major parties regularly win at least 80% of the popular vote in general elections, regularly win at least 90% of the seats in the legislature and alternately control the executive branch of government. If these criteria are used in the USA, then US politics is clearly a two-party system.

Key concept

➤ **Two-party system.** A party system in which two major parties regularly win the vast majority of votes in general elections, regularly capture nearly all of the seats in the legislature and alternately control the executive branch of government.

As Table 3.6 shows, in the 12 presidential elections between 1968 and 2012, the Democrats and Republicans accounted for more than 80% of the popular vote on every occasion. Indeed, in eight of these 11 elections, their combined vote exceeded 95%. This is the case in terms of Electoral College votes too. In only one of these 12 elections — 1968 — did the Democrats and Republicans fail to win all the Electoral College votes — rogue Electors apart.

When it comes to seats in Congress, the picture is clearly that of a two-party system. Following the 2012 elections, only two members of the Senate, Bernie Sanders of Vermont and Angus King of Maine, were not sitting as either Democrats or Republicans. Sanders is the longest-serving independent member of Congress, having been elected to the House of Representatives in 1990 and then to the Senate in 2006. But although elected as an independent, he is opposed by only a Republican candidate at each election. The Democrats, with whom he invariably votes, allow him a free run. King is a former independent governor of Maine and has announced he will caucus with the Democrats.

Even in terms of state government, the picture is the same. In January 2013, 49 of the 50 state governors were either Democrats or Republicans, the only exception being Lincoln Chafee of Rhode Island, but even he is a former Republican senator. Every president since 1853 has been either a Democrat or a Republican. That is 41 straight presidential elections won by the two major parties over a 160-year period.

The reasons for the US two-party system

➤ The first-past-the-post electoral system makes life difficult for national third parties. As we shall see in greater detail later on in this chapter, third-party support is usually widespread but shallow. They pick up a fraction of the vote in almost every state but under a winner-takes-all system they receive no reward at all. A national third-party candidate on the ticket merely lowers the percentage of the vote needed by the major-party candidate to win the election.

Table 3.6 Combined Democrat and Republican vote in presidential elections, 1968–2012

Year	Combined Democrat and Republican vote (%)
1968	86
1972	98
1976	98
1980	92
1984	99
1988	99
1992	81
1996	91
2000	97
2004	99
2008	99
2012	99

➤ When the two major parties encompass such a wide ideological spectrum — from Congresswoman Barbara Lee and Senator Barbara Boxer, both of California, on the Democrats' left, to Congressman Ben Quayle of Arizona and Senator Tom Coburn of Oklahoma on the Republicans' right — there is not much room left for any other parties to attract substantial support. The two major parties are ideologically all-embracing.

➤ The phenomenon of primary elections helps to make the major parties more responsive to the electorate, minimising the need for protest voting. Protest votes often go to third parties.

Other theories

Some analysts challenge the simple assumption that the USA has a two-party system and come up with other theses. Some argue that the two major parties have become so ideologically indistinct that it is meaningless to talk of a two-party system. Democrats in the 1990s were stealing such Republican issues as welfare reform and deficit reduction. A *Democrat* president — Bill Clinton — was declaring that 'the era of big government is over'. The current decade has seen a *Republican* president adding a new executive department to Washington's bureaucratic labyrinth. This is US parties as Tweedledum and Tweedledee — the two identical characters from *Alice through the Looking Glass* who spend their time arguing about their apparent differences.

Does the US have a two-party system?

Yes

➤ All presidents since 1853 have been either a Democrat or a Republican.

➤ Democrats and Republicans combined regularly win over 95% of the vote in presidential elections and win all the votes in the Electoral College.

➤ In January 2013, all 435 members of the House of Representatives were either Democrats or Republicans.

➤ In January 2013, 98 of the 100 senators were either Democrats or Republicans and both of the 'independents' caucus with the Democrats.

➤ Congress is therefore completely dominated by the two major parties, which control all the leadership positions, including committee chairmanships.

➤ In January 2013, 49 of the 50 state governors were either Democrats or Republicans and the one 'independent' was a former Republican senator.

➤ In January 2013, 49 of the 50 state legislatures were controlled by either Democrats or Republicans and the one that was not (Nebraska) was non-partisan.

No

➤ The USA has a 50-party system as the individual state parties are organisationally autonomous and ideologically varied.

➤ Some states are virtually one-party states where one party wins virtually every election — federal, state or local.

➤ The USA has a no-party system as candidates are often more important than parties, split-ticket voting is quite common and divided government is a frequent phenomenon.

➤ Third parties played a significant role in the presidential elections of 1992, 1996 and 2000.

➤ Many modern-day Americans are more likely to join a group such as the Tea Party movement, the Occupy movement or a pressure group than a political party.

Writing in the *Washington Post* in 1997, political commentator Mark Shields stated: 'As of today, the country has two Republican parties, separated by the issue of abortion.' But this verdict seems at variance with observations earlier in this chapter.

A more convincing argument is to suggest that the USA has not a two-party system, but a 50-party system. The term 'two-party system' seems to convey the idea of two disciplined, centralised national parties with national leaders and national policy programmes. Although this description might be more appropriate now than it was two decades ago, parties in the USA are still essentially decentralised, state-based parties with no national 'leader' in the accepted sense and no national policy programme — except maybe for 4 months of every fourth year when these state-based parties must unite in a presidential campaign. The idea of a 50-party system reminds us that the Texas Republican Party is a very different creature from the Massachusetts Republican Party; that the California Democratic Party is a very different animal from the Georgia Democratic Party. This is the natural consequence of federalism and a country in which every election — even the presidential one — is a state-based election run largely under state laws by state officials. We have only to remember the events in Florida following the 2000 presidential election to see that even the presidential election is nothing like a national election in the accepted sense.

Furthermore, even if the USA were thought to have a two-party system, the fact that political power is so often divided makes this less obvious. For a two-party system is one in which the two major parties tend to *alternate* control of the levers of power, whereas in the USA, the two parties so often have their hands on the levers of power *at the same time* — one party controlling the White House and the other controlling one or both houses of Congress. As someone commented in the aftermath of the 2012 elections, 'The US is — for the moment at least — a two-party system with no-party rule.'

Third parties

Despite the domination of US politics by the Democrats and Republicans, third parties do exist. There are different types: national, regional and state-based; permanent and temporary; issues-based and ideological. The best-known third parties are national: the Reform Party, the Libertarian Party and the Green Party; these three had candidates on the ballot in all 50 states in the 2000 presidential election. Regional third parties are those such as Strom Thurmond's States Rights Party (founded 1948) and George Wallace's American Independent Party (founded 1968). The Green Party and the Libertarian Party are examples of permanent third parties, while the Reform Party and the American Independent Party are examples of temporary third parties. The Green Party and the Prohibition Party are both examples of issue-based third parties, while the Socialist Party and the Libertarian Party are examples of ideological third parties.

Impact of third parties

What the USA does not have are national, permanent third parties that regularly win a sizeable proportion of the votes in general elections. There are reasons for this. The status of third parties in US politics is something of a paradox: they are both unimportant and important. Their unimportance is shown in Table 3.7 — their combined popular vote in 2012 was less than 2%. But their potential importance is shown in the fact that in five of the nine presidential elections between 1968 and 2000, a third party played a significant role (see Table 3.8). On three of those occasions — in 1968, 1992 and 2000 — it could be argued that a third party decided the outcome.

In the 2000 presidential election, Nader's 2.7% for the Green Party almost certainly cost Al Gore the presidency. In Florida, where Bush won by just 537 votes, Nader polled nearly 100,000 votes. In New Hampshire, where Bush won by just 7,000 votes, Nader had over 22,000 votes. And exit poll data suggested that at least half of those Nader voters would have been Gore voters — and the other half would probably not have voted at all had Nader not been on the ballot.

Table 3.7 Third-party support in the 2012 presidential election

Candidate	Party	Popular votes	Popular vote (%)
Gary Johnson	Libertarian	1,218,570	0.98
Jill Stein	Green	434,725	0.35
Virgil Goode	Constitution	118,551	0.09
Roseanne Barr	Peace and Freedom	56,349	0.04
Rocky Anderson	Justice	38,889	0.03
Tom Hoefling	America's	33,509	0.03
Others	[Various]	118,314	0.10

Table 3.8 Effect of third parties in recent presidential elections

Year	Candidate	Party	Vote (%)	Effect
1968	George Wallace	American Independent Party	13.5	Split Democrat vote, leading to Republican victory
1980	John Anderson	National Unity Party	7.0	Took votes mainly from Democrats
1992	Ross Perot	–	19.0	Took votes mainly from Republicans, leading to Democrat victory
1996	Ross Perot	Reform Party	9.0	Took votes mainly from Republicans
2000	Ralph Nader	Green Party	2.7	Took votes almost exclusively from Democrats, leading to Republican victory

In the 2012 elections, third-party candidates were little more than bit-part players. True, independent candidate Angus King won the open Senate seat in Maine, but elsewhere the influence of third parties was pretty negligible. In the Maryland Senate race, independent candidate Rob Sobhani — an author and self-proclaimed energy expert — won 17% of the vote. In the Montana Senate race, Libertarian Party candidate Dan Cox won 6.5% when the margin between the two major party candidates was less than 4 percentage points. And in the Nevada Senate race, the Independent American Party candidate David Vanderbeek got just under 5% of the vote with only just over 1 percentage point separating the Democrat and Republican candidates.

Ralph Nader, Green Party candidate who probably contributed to Al Gore's defeat in 2000

Third-party difficulties

Third parties face eight difficulties in their attempts to win votes in elections.

Electoral system

The electoral system is a first-past-the-post, winner-takes-all system. All elections — whether for president, Congress or state or local office — use this system, which makes life difficult for national third parties. Regional third parties can do well. In 1968 George Wallace won 45 Electoral College votes with 13% of the vote, but his votes were concentrated in a small number of southern states. In 1992, Ross Perot won no Electoral College votes with 19% of the vote. Perot's votes, by contrast, were spread throughout the entire USA.

Matching funds

Third parties are disadvantaged by the way they qualify for 'matching funds' in presidential elections. Major-party candidates qualify by raising at least $5,000 in contributions of $250 or less in at least 20 states — not a difficult requirement. But third-party candidates qualify only by winning at least 5% of the popular vote in the previous election. There are two problems with this. First, very few third parties achieve this. In the last 50 years, only three third-party candidates — Wallace (1968), Anderson (1980) and Perot (1992 and 1996) — have managed it. Second, as many third parties are temporary parties, they often contest only one election as, for example, John Anderson did. This rule accounts for the oddity that Perot did not qualify for 'matching funds' in 1992 when he was attracting almost one-fifth of the votes, but Reform Party candidate Patrick Buchanan did qualify in 2000 when he was attracting less than one-hundredth of the votes.

Ballot access laws

Third parties are disadvantaged by the states' ballot access laws. Laws in each state regulate how third-party candidates can qualify to get their name on the ballot. Some, such as those in Tennessee, are straightforward. Tennessee requires just 25 signatures on a petition. Little wonder that there were seven third-party and independent candidates on the ballot for the Senate seat in Tennessee in 2012 (see Table 3.9). Other states, such as New York and California, are much more demanding. In New York, a third-party candidate must gain a certain number

Table 3.9 Candidates for the US Senate seat in Tennessee, 2012

Candidate	Votes
Bob Corker (Republican)	1,504,081
Mark Clayton (Democratic)	704,708
Martin Pleasant (Green)	38,412
Shaun Crowell (Libertarian)	20,913
Kermit Steck (Constitution)	18,589
James Higdon (Ind)	8,077
Michael Long (Ind)	8,062
Troy Scoggin (Ind)	7,151
David Gatchell (Ind)	6,513

of signatures in every county in the state. In California, the number of signatures required is equal to 1% of the electorate in the state. In 1980, John Anderson estimated he had to gather around 1.2 million signatures nationwide to get on the ballot in all 50 states. He had to spend around $3 million doing just that.

Lack of resources

Third parties' lack of resources is, to some extent, exacerbated by the two previous points. It is hard for third parties to qualify for 'matching funds'. They must spend much of their hard-earned cash on ballot access petitions rather than on real campaigning. People are understandably reluctant to give money to parties that they know are going to lose: this creates something of a 'catch 22' situation.

Lack of media coverage

Third parties suffer from a lack of media coverage. News programmes do not think them sufficiently newsworthy. The parties can rarely afford the cost of making — let alone of airing — television commercials. Their candidates are usually barred from appearing in both state and national televised debates. In 2000, only Bush and Gore appeared in the three presidential debates. Nader was excluded.

Lack of suitable candidates

The sixth problem for third parties is that they tend to suffer from a lack of well-known and well-qualified candidates. Consider the difficulties experienced by John Anderson (1980) and Ross Perot (1992 and 1996) in trying to attract suitable running-mates. Anderson had to settle for a former Governor of Wisconsin, Patrick Lucey. In 1992, Perot, despite talk of such big names as Colin Powell, had to settle for Admiral James Stockdale. In 1996, it was the equally odd Orson Swindle. Lucey, Stockdale and Swindle might pass as a likely name for a Washington law firm, but in terms of elective politics they were no-hopers.

Allegations of extremism

The two major parties often have little difficulty in portraying third-party candidates as ideological extremists. Many of them are. If they weren't, they would be running under the umbrella of either the Democrats or Republicans. Republicans smeared pro-segregationist George Wallace with the slogan: 'If you liked Hitler, you'll love Wallace.' Candidates from the Constitution Party, the Libertarian Party or the Socialist Party are not difficult to paint as ideologues. Americans have a deep-seated fear of political extremism, especially that of the left. The 'red scares' after both world wars and the McCarthy witch-hunts of the 1950s are examples of this.

Co-optation

What if a third party, against all the odds, does well in pre-election opinion polls and even wins a significant number of votes on Election Day? Wallace did in 1968, as did Perot in 1992. This success brings with it a final problem for a third party: the adoption of its key policies by one or both of the major parties. It happened to Wallace when Republican President Richard Nixon launched his 'southern strategy' to woo Wallace voters in the run-up to the 1972 election. It happened to Perot when both Democrat President Bill Clinton and the congressional Republicans adopted policies to deal with

Do third parties play any significant role in US politics? DEBATE

Yes

- Ross Perot won 19% of the popular vote in the 1992 presidential election and contributed to President Bush's defeat. His Reform Party also won 9% of the vote in 1996.
- The Green Party's 2.7% of the vote in 2000, whilst numerically small, meant that Al Gore probably lost the election as a result of that party's support in certain states.
- George Wallace's American Independent Party won 13.5% of the vote and 46 Electoral College votes in 1968.
- Both Wallace and Perot, though losing the election, had a significant impact on the policy debate both during and after their respective elections: Wallace regarding issues of race and ethnicity; Perot regarding the economic and the federal budget deficit.
- Some states (e.g. Alaska, Maine, New York) have quite vibrant third parties which can play a significant role in state and local races.

No

- The two major parties dominate presidential elections.
- The two major parties dominate Congress.
- The two major parties dominate state politics.
- The Democrats and Republicans, upon seeing a threat from a third party, tend to co-opt its policies, thereby curtailing the third party's electoral popularity.

Perot's flagship policy — the federal budget deficit. By 2000 the federal budget was in surplus and the Reform Party's vote had fallen from 19% in 1992 to 0.4% in 2000. Political scientists call this 'co-optation'.

It is, however, important to ask: what are the aims of third parties? For in the cases of Wallace and Perot, one could argue that it was not to win the presidency, but to have a significant effect on the policy debate. In this, Wallace and Perot scored a significant victory. Nader's ability to affect the outcome of the 2000 election is another case in point. It would therefore be inaccurate to write off all third-party candidates as 'failures'. Although third parties often fail in electoral terms — they get few votes — they may, as in 2000, affect the outcome of the election both in certain states and possibly nationally, as well as the policy agendas of one or both of the two major parties.

Theories of party decline

It was David Broder who popularised the idea that US political parties were in serious decline. In 1972, he published a book with the ominous title *The Party's Over: The Failure of Politics in America*. The first three words of that title caught on as being shorthand for the demise of America's two major political parties. Earlier, Denis Brogan remarked that America's two major parties were 'like two bottles with different labels, both empty'. Then came Ruth Scott's volume *Parties in Crisis* (1979), followed 5 years later by Martin Wattenberg's *The Decline of American Political Parties*.

Broder's title has often been taken out of context, however. What he wrote was:

It is called *The Party's Over* not in prophecy but in alarm. I am not predicting the demise of the Republicans or the Democrats. Party loyalties have been seriously eroded, the Democrat and Republican organisations weakened by years of neglect. But our parties are not yet dead...Whatever the fate of our political parties, for America the party *is* over.

There are four factors to consider regarding theories of **party decline**.

 Key concept
> **Party decline.** The theory, popular in the last three decades of the 20th century, that political parties were in decline in terms of membership, functions and importance — both in elections and in Congress.

Candidate selection

The parties have lost control over presidential candidate selection (see Chapter 2). Whereas until the late 1960s, presidential candidates were largely selected by 'party bosses' in 'smoke-filled rooms', now they are chosen largely by ordinary voters in presidential primaries. This is a significant loss of clout for the parties.

Communication with voters

Parties have lost their traditional function as the communicator between politicians and the voters, and vice versa. Politicians who wished to communicate with the voters would do so through a party rally. The same party-organised function gave the voters a chance to communicate with politicians, either through a formal question-and-answer session, or by heckling. Today, politicians communicate their message largely through television, while voters 'speak back' to the politicians through opinion polls. The role of the party is cut out.

Candidate- and issue-centred voting

Campaigns in the television era have become less party-centred and more candidate- or issue-centred. Voters tend to cast their ballots, not for a party, but because they feel strongly attracted either to a candidate or to an issue that he or she is espousing.

One effect of such candidate- or issue-centred voting was **split-ticket voting**. Split-ticket voting refers to voting for candidates of different parties for different offices at the same election. One might, at the same election, vote for a Republican president but a Democrat congressman, for example. Table 3.10 shows that split-ticket voting reached something of a peak in the 1970s and 1980s but has declined

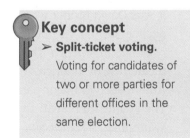 **Key concept**
> **Split-ticket voting.** Voting for candidates of two or more parties for different offices in the same election.

Table 3.10 Split-ticket voting in presidential elections: 1972–2008 (percentages)

	1972	1976	1980	1984	1988	1992	1996	2000	2004	2008
Dem Pres/ Rep Cong	5	9	8	6	7	10	13	10	7	9
Rep Pres/ Dem Cong	25	16	20	20	18	12	4	9	10	10
Total	**30**	**25**	**28**	**26**	**25**	**22**	**17**	**19**	**17**	**19**

Table 3.11 Voters by party identification, 1972–2012 (percentages)

	1972	1976	1980	1984	1988	1992	1996	2000	2004	2008	2012
Democrat	41	40	41	37	35	36	37	32	35	39	38
Independent	34	37	34	34	36	38	35	34	32	29	29
Republican	23	23	23	27	28	25	27	33	33	32	32

somewhat in elections since 1992. Another effect of candidate- and issue-centred voting was the rise of 'independent' voters — those who do not identify with either of the two major parties (see Table 3.11). The rise in both split-ticket voting and the number of independent voters especially between 1972 and 1992 fuelled theories of party decline.

Emergence of 'movements'

The emergence of the Tea Party and Occupy 'movements' during the first decade or so of this century show the extent to which many Americans are more prone to join a 'movement' than a traditional party. Each of these movements has sought to exert political influence on the Republican and Democratic parties respectively. Americans therefore seek to influence the parties more from without than from within. The extent to which the Tea Party movement has managed to get its preferred candidates chosen in certain congressional races over the wishes of the Republican Party leadership is, some would suggest, yet another manifestation of the decline of political parties.

Theories of party renewal

Theories of party decline were popular in the 1970s and 1980s. More recently, however, many commentators have been arguing that US political parties are undergoing renewal. How can these theories of **party renewal** be supported?

Key concept

➢ **Party renewal.** The theory which suggests that parties, far from being in decline, are increasingly important in elections, in fundraising and in Congress.

Theories of party decline were exaggerated

It is probably the case that the theories of party decline were exaggerated. Parties might be less important than they used to be, but they still play a significant role in US politics. Both parties could echo the words of Mark Twain: 'The report of my death was an exaggeration.' The death of the Republican Party was reported following the Watergate affair and Nixon's resignation; its candidate was back in the White House in just over 6 years. The death of the Democratic Party was reported following the leftward shift of the party in the 1960s, 1970s and 1980s, but the party was resurrected by the New Democrat model of the Clinton–Gore ticket in 1992. And when all is said and done, the two major parties controlled the White House, Congress and the vast majority of state governorships throughout the entire 20th century. As that century closed, only two seats in Congress and only two state governorships were not controlled by the two major parties.

Increased party involvement in presidential nominations

The parties have fought back and regained some control over the presidential nomination process. In the mid-1980s, the Democratic Party introduced 'super delegates' — elected office holders who are given *ex officio* seats at the Democratic National Convention as uncommitted delegates. By 2000, these super delegates accounted for almost 20% of the delegate votes at the Democratic National Convention. In the same year, it was possible to see how the choice of the Republican Party 'establishment', Governor George W. Bush, triumphed over the preferred choice of a significant number of rank-and-file Republican voters, Senator John McCain. The fact that Governor Bush enjoyed the almost unanimous support of the Republican Party hierarchy still counted for a lot, even in a system dominated by presidential primaries. Much the same could be said of the choice by the Democrats of John Kerry over Howard Dean in 2004. And in 2008, the role of the super delegates in the Democratic Party was highly significant in awarding the presidential nomination to Barack Obama rather than Hillary Clinton.

The national parties have also issued regulations in each recent presidential election regarding the timing of primaries and caucuses and the selection of delegates by the state parties. Admittedly these rules have not always been adhered to, but where state parties have transgressed, the national party has handed out a sanction in the form of reducing the size of that state party's National Convention delegation. The Republican National Committee also laid down new rules for the 2012 presidential primaries concerning the holding of winner-takes-all primaries, which had a significant effect on the nomination race.

Nationalisation of campaigns

Party renewal has been seen in moves towards the nationalising of electoral campaigns. This was especially true of the Republican Party in the mid-term elections of 1994 and 2002. In 1994, the Republicans campaigned around a ten-point policy programme called ***Contract with America***. The brainchild of Congressman Newt Gingrich, this national policy document was supported by nearly all Republican House candidates in that election. It promised that, under a Republican-controlled Congress, votes would be held within the first 100 days of such a Congress on ten policy issues of interest to conservative voters, such as a constitutional amendment providing for a balanced budget and congressional term limits. Then, in 2002, the Republicans launched another successful nationalised mid-term election, resulting in the White House gaining seats in both houses of Congress in a mid-term election for the first time since 1934. The Democrats followed suit in the 2006 mid-term elections with their 'Six for 06' agenda, which accompanied their retaking control of both houses of Congress after 12 years in the minority. Four years later, the Republicans published their 'Pledge to America' in advance of the 2010 mid-term elections, which listed the policies they would bring to the floor in the 112th Congress (2011–12) if they won control of either or both houses.

Key term

➤ **Contract with America.** The Republican Party policy document that was behind the party's campaign to win control of the House of Representatives in the 1994 mid-term elections. The brain-child of Republican congressman Newt Gingrich, it laid out ten policies that Republicans promised to bring to a vote on the House floor during the first 100 days of the new Congress, if they won the election — which they did. The policies included a balanced budget constitutional amendment, anti-crime legislation, welfare reform and congressional term limits.

Increased partisanship in Congress

A final pointer to party renewal came with increased levels of partisanship in Congress. If parties were declining in importance, a decline in partisanship could be anticipated. After all, if parties no longer matter, why should their members continually disagree? But in 1995, recorded votes in the Senate showed the highest levels of partisanship

---

Party decline versus party renewal

Party decline
➤ parties' loss of control over presidential candidate selection
➤ parties have been bypassed by federal matching funds in presidential elections
➤ parties have lost their traditional function as communicator between politicians and voters and vice versa
➤ campaigns have become more candidate centred and television orientated and less party orientated
➤ rise in split-ticket voting (though this has started to decline)
➤ rise in 'movement' politics (e.g. Tea Party, Occupy)

Party renewal
➤ party decline theories often exaggerated weakness of parties
➤ revitalisation of parties (e.g. New Democrats, super delegates)
➤ modernisation of national party structures
➤ imposition of national rules regarding presidential primaries and delegate selection
➤ nationalisation of mid-term election campaigns (e.g. 'Pledge to America' — Republicans, 2010)

since 1922, and in the House of Representatives the highest levels of partisanship since 1910. Partisanship reached a crescendo during the impeachment and trial of President Clinton in 1998 and early 1999. The votes in the House of Representatives on the Articles of Impeachment were largely along party lines. Increased levels of partisanship have also been seen clearly in both the reaction to the Supreme Court's ruling in *Bush v. Gore* (2000) and a prolonged stand-off between presidents — both Clinton and George W. Bush — and the Senate on their nominations to the federal courts. Partisanship is a significant pointer to party renewal.

The Tea Party movement

Origins and 'organisation'

The Tea Party movement has been one of the most extraordinary, unusual and confusing phenomena to hit American politics in decades. For a start, it is not a political party, but then neither is it like most pressure groups. It is a 'movement'. Even the name is odd. The movement takes its name from the so-called Boston Tea Party of 1773, a protest by American colonials against what they viewed as unfair taxation imposed on them by the British government — taxation without representation. In protest against the tax on tea, some angry Bostonians tipped more than 300 chests of tea from three vessels into Boston harbour on 29 November 1773.

The modern Tea Party movement took its name both to ally itself with the anti-big government sentiments of the original tea partiers, and because the word 'tea' serves as an acronym for their rallying cry: 'Taxed Enough Already'. The movement came into existence as a grassroots — bottom-up, rather than top-down — organisation following the legislation Congress passed in reaction to the economic downturn, the

---

Box 3.2 **Tea types: a brief guide to Tea Party groups**

Tea Party Nation: this group held the first ever Tea Party convention in February 2010 but another scheduled for 2011 was first postponed and then cancelled (www.teapartynation.com).

Tea Party Patriots: the movement's largest membership organisation (www.teapartypatriots.org).

Tea Party Express: a political action committee which has sponsored bus tours, drawing thousands to local rallies and building local membership, as well as spending money on behalf of conservative candidates (www.teapartyexpress.org).

National Tea Party Federation: a discussion forum for Tea Party organisers; coordinates responses to attacks on the Tea Party movement (www.thenationalteapartyfederation.com).

Americans for Prosperity: trains activists in many states; organises rallies; spends money to air TV ads (http://americansforprosperity.org).

FreedomWorks: advises members where to find local rallies and events; hosts activists for training seminars in Washington (www.freedomworks.org).

Source: adapted from *National Journal*, 11 September 2010, p. 17

banking collapse and the meltdown on Wall Street. Specifically, the Tea Party movement opposed the passage of such legislation as the Emergency Economic Stabilisation Act of 2008 (commonly known as the bank bailout scheme) and the American Recovery and Reinvestment Act of 2009 (commonly known as Obama's economic stimulus package).

Just as there are numerous types of tea, so there are different types of Tea Party. This is what is so confusing about the whole Tea Party thing: it is not an organisation, it is more of a non-organisation — highly decentralised and almost leaderless. It has no offices, no headquarters. It is based in activists' homes, on their laptops, I-phones and Blackberries. As Jonathan Raunch remarked in a recent *National Journal* article ('Group Think', 11 September 2010):

> Strange though it may seem, this is a coordinated network, not a hierarchy. There is no chain of command. No group or person is subordinate to any other. The tea parties are jealously independent and suspicious of any efforts at central control.

Tea partiers believe that it is centralisation, leadership and top-down organisation which is at the root of the problems in Washington DC and in the national political parties. They want to avoid being tainted by the same diseases. Think of them as a kind of political form of *Wikipedia* — their units are self-funded and their members mostly work for free. Hardly surprising, therefore, that Washington insiders, the press, politicians and lobbyists, all of whom work on a 'who's-in-charge' basis, find the Tea Party movement thoroughly confusing. As Box 3.2 shows, the Tea Party movement is something like a confederacy — a loose collection of independent bodies that don't always agree amongst themselves. Because of its right-wing ideology, it is often asked what effect, if any, the movement might have on Republican Party politics.

Beliefs and core values

What do its supporters believe in? In essence, the Tea Party creed can be stated as:
- strict adherence to the Constitution and to the original intentions of the Framers
- limited government
- reducing the size and scope of the federal government
- reducing US government spending and taxation
- reducing the national debt and the federal budget deficit

Terms which one would associate with Tea Party supporters are: conservatism, populism, libertarianism and fiscal responsibility. The *Contract from America* — deliberately meant as a follow-on from the Republican Party's 1994 *Contract with America* — listed such items as simplification of the tax system, repeal of President Obama's healthcare legislation and a constitutional amendment requiring a balanced budget. Before the 2010 mid-term elections, the Republicans published their *Pledge to America* as an obvious bid for Tea Party support.

First and foremost, Tea Party supporters want a smaller, more modest, more limited federal government. Asked in a 2010 poll, 'How much has President Obama expanded the role of government in addressing economic problems?' 89% of Tea Party folk answered

'too much'. Amongst ordinary Americans, the figure was 37%. Asked, 'Which is more important: creating jobs through government spending or lowering the federal budget deficit?' 76% of Tea Party supporters said the latter. Amongst ordinary Americans, the figure was just 42%. Asked, 'Which do you prefer: smaller government with fewer services or bigger government with more services?' 92% of Tea Party supporters said the former. Amongst ordinary Americans, the figure was 50%.

Tea partiers protesting against US government spending and taxation

The Tea Party and Congress

The Tea Party Caucus in the House of Representatives came into existence in July 2010 as a group of 28 Republican House members, a quarter of whom came from Texas. By March 2011 the Caucus had 61 members, all Republicans, with the chair of the group being Michele Bachmann of Minnesota, who was about to become a candidate in the Republican presidential primaries for 2012. Thirty-six of these 61 Caucus members represented congressional districts in the South. Meanwhile the Tea Party Senate Caucus numbered four — Jim DeMint of South Carolina, Mike Lee of Utah, Rand Paul of Kentucky and Jerry Moran of Kansas, again all Republicans. Those 61 House Tea Party Caucus members were quite a mixed bunch. They did include 10 of the 14 most conservative Republicans, as measured by the *National Journal*'s 2012 vote ratings. These included Jeff Miller of Florida, Duncan Hunter of California and Pete Sessions of Texas. But the Caucus also included some centrist Republicans such as David McKinley of West Virginia, who had the nineteenth most liberal voting record amongst House Republicans in 2011. It also included some House Republicans who held libertarian-leaning views, such as Roscoe Bartlett of Maryland and Denny Rehberg of Montana, both of whom would lose their seats in 2012. But some prominent Tea Party supporting members of Congress declined to join the Caucus, such as Ron Paul of Texas in the House and Marco Rubio of Florida in the Senate.

There is no doubt that during the 112th Congress (2011–12) the Republican delegation in the House of Representatives was on occasion pushed significantly to the right by the Tea Party Caucus, especially when the debates and votes concerned the role of the federal government, or fights over federal spending. It was largely as a result of pressure from the Tea Party that House Speaker John Boehner pushed for deep cuts in the final months of the 2011 budget debate, bringing the federal government to the brink of shutdown. The

Tea Party Caucus also pressured the Republican leadership into resisting all attempts to include tax increases as part of any deal over raising the federal debt ceiling. Indeed on this matter, Tea Party members of Congress were probably out of step with Tea Party supporters in the country, who polls showed wanted an agreement with the President to raise the debt ceiling so as not to risk damaging an already fragile economy.

The Tea Party and elections

2010 elections

Having burst onto the political scene in 2009, the first elections in which the Tea Party was influential were the mid-terms in November 2010. Its role seemed to be to try to nominate and elect Republican candidates who were truly conservative rather than more moderate Republicans disparagingly referred to as 'RINOs' – **R**epublicans **I**n **N**ame **O**nly. Their initial success was in the congressional primaries of that year, in which Tea Party supporters managed to deny Senator Lisa Murkowski of Alaska the Republican nomination in favour of Joe Miller, a Tea Party activist. In states with open races, the Tea Party was successful in getting its favoured candidates onto the November ballot in Delaware, Nevada and Colorado. But all these four Tea Party candidates lost in the general election in November. Murkowski eventually managed to get re-elected as a write-in candidate. As a result, the Republicans ended up with 47 seats in the Senate — up from the 41 they had before the mid-terms, but four short of the 51 they needed to win back party control from the Democrats. Republican congressman Spencer Bachus of Alabama went so far as to suggest that it was the Tea Party movement that 'cost us control of the Senate'.

But the Tea Party did have its victories. In Utah, Senator Bob Bennett was denied a fourth term at the nomination stage when he failed even to make it onto the primary ballot. Utah Republicans thought Bennett not sufficiently conservative in his Senate voting record. The eventual Republican nominee Mike Lee was another Tea Party member and he went on to hold the seat easily for the party in November. Another Tea Party favourite, Marco Rubio, held on to the Republican Senate seat in Florida. Rubio had won the party nomination over the early front-runner, the state's popular Republican governor Charlie Crist, a noted moderate. And in Kentucky, Tea Party supporter Rand Paul — son of perennial presidential candidate Ron Paul — held on to the seat vacated by the retirement of Jim Bunning.

2012 elections

It seems a strange irony that, in the first presidential election held after the formation of the Tea Party movement, the Republican Party should nominate Mitt Romney as its presidential candidate. Clearly the large field of Republican candidates included a number who were much closer to the Tea Party than the former governor of Massachusetts. The chair of the Tea Party Caucus in the House of Representatives, Michele Bachmann, shot to prominence by winning the Ames Straw Poll in Iowa in August 2011. But when the

same state held its caucuses on 3 January 2012, Ms Bachmann finished sixth with less than 5% of the vote. She pulled out of the presidential race 2 days later. Others who went on to inherit the Tea Party mantle — businessman Herman Cain, former Pennsylvania senator Rick Santorum, and former House Speaker Newt Gingrich — all, sooner or later, fell by the wayside as Romney emerged as the party's 2012 presidential nominee.

In the 2012 Senate races, the Tea Party scored some more primary upsets. Their most famous scalp was that of the six-term veteran from Indiana, Richard Lugar, who lost his primary bid to run for a seventh term. Lugar was defeated by Tea Party-backed Richard Mourdock by a stunning 60% to 39% margin. Then in the open race in Texas, another Tea Party supporter, Ted Cruz, defeated the state's Lieutenant Governor and clear front-runner David Dewhurst in the run-off primary by 57% to 43%. Another Tea Party favourite, Todd Akin, won the Republican nomination to take on Senator Claire McCaskill in Missouri. Although Cruz went on to an impressive win in Texas, both Mourdock and Akin threw away races that were considered Republican shoo-ins with ill-judged remarks about rape. There will be those in the Republican hierarchy who will be ruing the fact that the Tea Party has cost their party at least five Senate seats in the last two election cycles — those in Delaware, Nevada and Colorado in 2010 and Indiana and Missouri in 2012.

Activity

Using the websites mentioned in Box 3.2 and any other sources you have available, find out more about the activities, aims and achievements of the various branches of the Tea Party movement. You could put together a short piece or a debate setting out the strengths and weaknesses, as you see them, of the Tea Party movement. Try to assess whether or not you think the movement will still be active and as important in 10 years' time and give reasons for your conclusion.

UK/US comparison

Political parties

There are seven basic characteristics of political parties in the USA:

➤ Party organisation is largely decentralised with limited power vested in the national party leadership and organisation.

➤ Party platforms are relatively unimportant documents and are not seen as a list of specific commitments.

➤ The term 'party leaders' refers to the leadership in Congress, though during the period of a presidential election campaign, the presidential candidates may be thought of as party leaders.

➤ The major parties have become more ideologically cohesive in recent years, though both parties still encompass quite a range of ideological positions.

➤ Levels of party discipline in Congress, though much higher than in previous decades, are still lower than in the UK House of Commons.

➤ Parties operate within a two-party system, though this needs to be seen alongside the state and regional variations that exist in both parties.

➤ Third parties play a very limited role.

There are six basic characteristics of political parties in the UK:

➤ Party organisation is largely centralised, though following devolution and the introduction of some directly elected mayors, regional and local parties are now more autonomous than used to be the case.

➤ Party manifestos are relatively important documents and are seen as a list of specific commitments — a contract between the party and the voters as to what the party would do if elected to government.

➤ The term 'party leaders' refers to the national leaders of the parties, who are elected through a system involving both the party hierarchy and party members.

➤ The major parties are less ideologically distinct than was the case in the 1970s and 1980s.

➤ Levels of party discipline in the House of Commons, though lower than in previous decades, are still relatively high.

➤ Parties operate within a system in which two parties are dominant, but third parties play a significant role.

Exam focus

Short-answer questions

1 Is it true to say that Republicans are conservative and Democrats are liberals?
2 What was the Solid South and why did it disappear?
3 What does it mean and to what extent is it true to say that the USA can be divided into red states and blue states?
4 How influential is the left within the Democratic Party?
5 Explain the factors that limit the electoral impact of minor parties.

Essay questions

1 Does the USA still have a two-party system?
2 'The ideological differences between the Democratic and Republican parties are far greater than the differences within them.' Discuss.
3 Why do third parties in the USA always fail?
4 'Moderate conservatism is a declining force in the Republican Party.' Discuss.
5 'The theory of "party decline" is increasingly out of date.' Discuss.

Further reading

Ashbee, E., 'The Tea Party: mid-term bickering?', *Politics Review,* Vol. 21, No. 1, September 2011.

Bennett, A. J., *US Government & Politics: Annual Survey 2011*, Chapter 8, Philip Allan Updates, 2011.

Knight, J., 'The Republicans: where do they go from here?', *Politics Review,* Vol. 20, No. 1, September 2010.

Knight, J., 'The Democrats: what next?', *Politics Review,* Vol. 21, No. 4, April 2012.

Maisel, L. S., *American Political Parties and Elections: A Very Short Introduction*, Oxford University Press, 2007.

Chapter 4

Pressure groups

Pressure groups are regarded as having important implications for a modern democracy. Through them, citizens can participate in the political process between elections. They can also use their membership of them to pressurise all three branches of the federal government — the legislature (Congress), the executive (the president and the bureaucracy) and the judiciary (headed by the Supreme Court). In a country like the United States, with a participatory tradition and an open form of government, pressure groups seem to take on added importance. They benefit from numerous 'access points' within the political system. They also benefit from a weak and fragmented party system and from election campaigns that are often issue based rather than merely party based.

Key questions answered in this chapter

- ➤ What is the theoretical basis of pressure group activity?
- ➤ What types of pressure group exist in the USA?
- ➤ What are their traditional functions?
- ➤ Why do people join a pressure group?
- ➤ What methods do pressure groups use?
- ➤ What impact do they have?
- ➤ How effectively are pressure groups regulated?
- ➤ What are their merits and demerits?
- ➤ Which factors lead to pressure group success?

Links to follow up

The best website to start your study of pressure groups is **www.politics1.com/issues.htm**. Here you will see a wealth of pressure group sites listed by topic, including abortion, affirmative action, environment, 1st Amendment and free speech, guns, social security and seniors, and women. What is especially useful on this site is that both sides of an issue are clearly represented so, for example, you have both pro-choice and pro-life groups listed under abortion and pro- and anti-gun groups listed under guns.

If you want to follow up the money side of pressure groups, then visit **www.opensecrets.org** and click on the 'Influence and Lobbying' button on the home page.

You can also visit the website of a leading Washington lobbyist firm such as Ogilvy Government Relations at **www.ogilvygr.com** and click on their 'What We Do' button.

Pluralism

The Founding Fathers, meeting in Philadelphia in the summer of 1787, did not talk about pressure groups. They weren't contacted by powerful firms from K Street — the street in Washington DC around which today's lobbying firms congregate. But they did talk a lot about 'factions' in the society they were trying to organise and govern. And 'factions' to the likes of James Madison would probably have been an anathema. What Madison called 'the causes of faction' were, to him, a threat to a stable and secure democracy. But they were also 'sown in the nature of man'. Madison worried that groups would be more likely to oppress than liberate and therefore he believed the aim of all right-thinking people should be how to 'cure the mischiefs of faction'.

The theoretical basis of pressure group activity is to be found in what political theorists call **pluralism**. Pluralism has been written about and debated by a host of eminent political philosophers through the years. In *The Governmental Process*, published in 1951, David Truman claimed that politics could be understood only by studying the way different groups interacted with one another. In the 1960s, it was Robert Dahl's study of local politics in New Haven, Connecticut, that became the classic study of pluralism in the USA. His famous book, *Who Governs?*, was written as an answer to another classic of political science, C. Wright Mills' *The Power Elite* (1956). Mills had argued that the United States was ruled by a small governing elite — wealthy and powerful individuals — and that, as a consequence, ordinary Americans had little real control over how they were governed or who governed them. Dahl, on the other hand, claimed that US society was based not on **elitism** but on pluralism. In three critical areas — political party nominations, urban redevelopment and public education — Dahl claimed that widely differing groups of ordinary Americans were both active and influential. Dahl's theory was that democracy was not so much a theory about '50% plus one' as a 'process in which there is a high probability that an active and legitimate group in the population can make itself heard effectively at some crucial stage in the process of making decisions'. Hence, to Dahl, democracy was all about compromise — compromise between competing groups.

 Key concepts

➤ **Pluralism.** A theory which suggests that political power in a society does not rest simply with the electorate or with the governing elite, but is distributed amongst a number of groups representing widely different interests within society.

➤ **Elitism.** A theory which suggests that political power in a society rests with a small group who gain power through wealth, family status or intellectual superiority.

Types of pressure group

Pressure groups are quite different from political parties. Whereas political parties seek to win control of government, pressure groups seek to influence those who have control of government.

Key term

➢ **Pressure group.** An organised interest group in which members hold similar beliefs and actively pursue ways to influence government. Unlike political parties, which seek to win control of government, pressure groups are principally interested in influencing those who determine policy.

Pressure groups vary considerably in size, wealth and influence. Pressure groups in the United States operate at all levels of government — federal, state and local — and seek to bring their influence to bear on all three branches of government. As a result there are numerous typologies of pressure groups. First of all, one can divide pressure groups into two broad categories: institutional groups and membership groups (see Table 4.1).

Institutional pressure groups

Institutional pressure groups seek to represent other organisations and groups. In this first category, therefore, come business and trade groups such as the American Business Conference, the National Association of Manufacturers and the National Automobile Dealers Association. Of great importance are the US Chamber of Commerce, which represents thousands of different businesses across the nation, and the labour unions, most of which represent a particular trade, such as the United Auto Workers or the Teamsters representing truck drivers. The American Federation of Labor–Congress of Industrial Organizations (AFL–CIO) is the US equivalent of the British Trades Union Congress. Not only industry has such groups: there are institutional groups representing the interests of America's agriculture, such as the American Farm Bureau Federation, the National Farmers' Union and Associated Milk Producers Incorporated.

Table 4.1 Categorisation of pressure groups into institutional and membership groups

Institutional groups	Membership groups
Business/trade groups	Single-issue groups
Labour unions and agricultural groups	Ideological groups
Professional groups	Group rights groups
Intergovernmental groups	Public interest groups Think-tanks

Institutional groups include professional pressure groups, such as the American Medical Association, the National Education Association and the American Bar Association. Then there are intergovernmental pressure groups — those that lobby one level of government on behalf of another, such as the National Governors' Conference.

Membership pressure groups

Membership pressure groups seek to represent individual Americans rather than organisations and groups. Americans like to join groups, but they are selective. They are more likely than, for example, their European counterparts to join social, charitable, civic, political and religious groups, although they are less likely to join trade unions. On the whole, however, Americans join, subscribe, write, phone, petition, protest and march more than the citizens of most nation-states.

The membership groups they join may be single-issue groups, such as the National Rifle Association (NRA), Mothers Against Drunk Driving (MADD), or the National Abortion and Reproductive Rights Action League. Equally, they might join an ideological group, such as the American Conservative Union, People for the American Way, or the American Civil Liberties Union (ACLU).

Alternatively, they might join a group that represents individuals with a common gender, ethnic, religious or social characteristic, such as the National Organization for Women (NOW), the National Association for the Advancement of Colored People (NAACP), the Christian Coalition of America, or the American Association of Retired Persons (AARP). They might, on the other hand, join a public interest group: for instance, Common Cause, Friends of the Earth, or the Sierra Club.

Think-tanks are a particularly important type of public interest group and they are especially numerous in the United States. Think-tanks conduct research, write reports, write articles for publication in leading broadsheet newspapers, publish journals and books, organise conferences and give evidence to congressional committees. Most have a particular ideological slant. On the liberal side come the Institute for Policy Studies and the Brookings Institution. On the conservative side are the Heritage Foundation and the American Enterprise Institute.

Functions of pressure groups

Pressure groups perform five basic functions, although not all pressure groups perform all these functions.

Representation

Pressure groups may perform a representative function. They are a means whereby US citizens can have their views represented and their grievances articulated. They are an important link between the public and the politician, the governed and the government. They provide a channel of easy access through which ordinary citizens can voice their opinions. For many Americans, pressure groups will be the most important way in which their strongest-held views are represented. One's senator or representative, for example, will have many calls upon their representative role — a great variety of constituents, their political party and the administration being three of the most important. But through a pressure group, the woman, the African-American, the gun owner, the business person, the environmentalist, the Christian, the farmer or the retired person can have their views represented in all three branches of government at the federal, state and local levels.

Citizen participation

Pressure groups increase the opportunities for ordinary citizens to participate in the decision-making process between elections. In the USA, political participation is seen as a virtue. True, elections occur more frequently in the USA than they do in the UK. But when all is said and done, Election Day is merely 1 day in a year — or with a primary, maybe 2 days in a year. Many Americans seek far greater, more frequent participation in the democratic process. Pressure groups also offer an opportunity to participate in a specific policy area — pro-guns, anti-abortion, pro-environment or anti-war, or whatever policy or issue this particular citizen feels deeply about.

Public education

Pressure groups attempt to educate public opinion, warning people of the possible dangers if issues are not addressed, as well as the likely effects of decisions made by the government. As Jeffrey Berry and Clyde Wilcox (2007) comment:

> With their advocacy efforts, publications and publicity campaigns, pressure groups can make people better aware of both policy problems and proposed solutions.

Agenda building

Pressure groups may perform the function of agenda building. In so doing they attempt to influence the agendas of political parties, legislators and bureaucrats to give priority to their members' interests. They may attempt to bring together different parts of US society — for example, business groups, religious groups, state governments and professional organisations — to work together to achieve a common interest. An example given by Berry and Wilcox is of the manufacturers and distributors of CDs, video cassettes and computer software working together to get governments to pay attention to the problem of piracy of such goods. As a result of such coordinated agenda building, China promised to close down factories that were illegally duplicating American goods.

Programme monitoring

Pressure groups may scrutinise and hold government to account in the implementation of policies, to try to ensure that promises are fulfilled, policies delivered and regulations enforced. After the passage of the Bipartisan Campaign Reform Act in 2002 — commonly known as the McCain–Feingold Act — the Campaign Finance Institute commissioned a

> ## Box 4.1 League of Women Voters: Take Action
>
> **WELCOME TO THE LEAGUE'S ACTION CENTER**
>
> Here you will find all the tools, tips and information you need to advocate for the League's priority issues. To receive our free action alerts on urgent issues join our Grassroots Lobby Corps.
>
> **HOW ARE YOUR MEMBERS OF CONGRESS VOTING ON KEY GOOD GOVERNMENT ISSUES?**
>
> One of the best ways to arm yourself for taking action on key issues is to understand how your elected officials have reacted to important legislation. The League has compiled the results of recent congressional votes including nine Senate votes and six House votes on key legislation ranging from ethics reform to civil liberties, from children's healthcare to global climate change. This includes a list of each member of Congress and his or her votes on the League's priority issues.
>
> Our key votes page provides you with the opportunity to enter your zip code to find out how your Representatives and Senators have voted on key legislation. Additionally, you can click on any of the key votes to understand more about the legislation, as well as a map of the country to find out how all members of Congress from one state voted.
>
> Source: www.lwv.org

set of studies by scholars on the law's impact on the funding of campaigns. As a result of such monitoring, pressure groups such as the National Rifle Association (NRA) and the American Civil Liberties Union (ACLU) will sometimes bring cases to the state and federal courts, asking the judicial branch of government to monitor the effects of legislation.

How does all this work in practice? Let us consider a few current key policy areas and the functions being performed by pressure groups associated with them.

Prescription drugs

Take the issue of prescription drug provision, especially for senior citizens. The American Association of Retired Persons (AARP) boasts some 40 million members over the age of 50. Even politicians who do not agree with the AARP's policy positions cannot ignore its political clout. The Pharmaceutical Research and Manufacturers of America, representing more than 100 American drug companies, is lobbying hard for legislation that would give the private sector — not the federal government — the management role in administering any prescription drug programme for senior citizens. Add to those two groups the United Seniors Association — a conservative grassroots group with some 1.5 million members — and the 11-million-member AFL–CIO, which claims that proposed legislation too often favours drug company profits rather than the wallets of senior citizens, and you have an extraordinary amount of lobbying going on.

In his January 2005 State of the Union Address, President George W. Bush announced a top priority reform of social security to allow for private retirement accounts. Numerous pressure groups immediately got involved in campaigns on both sides of the argument — some, like Business Roundtable, mobilised support for the President's plan while others, like the AARP, mobilised opposition. Club for Growth, a conservative economic group, ran television advertisements, trying to persuade Americans to back the plan. The AARP, on the other hand, organised forums, mailed messages to its members and ran advertisements in national newspapers warning that in their view the plan was a huge gamble. 'If we feel like gambling,' some advertisements said, 'we'll play the slots.'

The environment

Another example is the area of the environment and, specifically, clean air. There is lobbying from industrial groups such as the Alliance of Automobile Manufacturers, whose former boss Andrew Card was White House chief of staff between 2001 and 2006, and environmental groups such as the Sierra Club and Environmental Defense.

Broadband technology

The provision of broadband technology is of concern to phone companies and cable television companies as well as to the representatives of high-tech industry, such as Silicon Valley's TechNet association and the Consumer Electronics Association, and the Hollywood film and music industry — the Motion Pictures Association of America and the Recording Industry Association of America. Not only providers but also consumers have pressure groups. The Consumer Federation of America and the Center for Digital Democracy want curbs on the provider companies to prevent them acting as broadband gatekeepers and thereby hindering consumers' easy access to news and information.

Between them, such organisations fulfil the functions of pressure groups within these policy areas.

Reasons for joining a pressure group

Berry and Wilcox (2007) suggest three different classes of benefit which go some way to explaining why Americans join pressure groups. These are the benefits that the leadership of pressure groups offers to members. Some pressure groups offer benefits of more than one type. Let us consider each of these benefits in turn.

Material benefits

One reason why people join a pressure group is because they believe something worthwhile will result from the group's activities — material benefits. Ordinary Americans either directly or by implication ask themselves the questions: (1) 'If I donate money to this particular group, what will I get in return?' and (2) 'If I donate this money, what will society get in return?' Berry and Wilcox define material benefits as 'the tangible rewards that individuals or companies get in return for their donations' to a particular pressure group. Material benefits might come in the form of information. Most groups publish a regular newsletter or magazine. The Sierra Club sends out a glossy *Sierra* magazine. It is a mix of serious articles and items to catch the more peripheral supporter — photographic competitions or lists of sponsored hiking tours.

Join the National Rifle Association and you can receive any one of a number of regular publications — *American Hunter, American Rifleman, Women's Outlook* or *America's First Freedom*. They are all free to paid-up members. Not only are there these publications, but pressure groups will make wide use of the internet to pass on information to members. There are audio and video clips to play, links-related sites, advertisements for relevant publications and e-mail alerts.

Then there are what might be called service benefits which are available to members. These vary depending on the type of group. The US Conference of City Mayors, for example, offers help to individual mayors when they are visiting Washington DC to lobby government personnel. The AARP, on the other hand, offers its 40 million members a whole range of service benefits — a mail discount pharmacy, a motor club and health insurance, to name but three.

Also included in material benefits are changes in policy which the pressure group will deliver to the advantage of its members. As we shall see later, pressure groups achieve this through a variety of methods, operating through all three levels of government — federal, state and local — and focusing on all three branches of government — the legislature, the executive and the courts.

Purposive benefits

But many Americans join a pressure group not to gain any material benefit for themselves but to be part of a movement, a cause — to try and make their society, or even the world, a better place. This is the difference between joining the AARP and joining Amnesty International. In joining the former, one's primary aim will probably be to gain material benefits for oneself in old age. Nothing wrong with that. But in joining Amnesty International, one's primary aim will almost certainly be more altruistic — trying to draw attention to examples of torture, human rights violations and political imprisonment in countries with authoritarian regimes, and then to bring the pressure of public opinion on such regimes to respect the human rights and liberties of their citizens. Such pressure groups are more likely to attract members from the more highly educated and wealthy members of society. Membership will give something of a 'feel good' factor to those who join, a feeling that they are playing their — admittedly small — part in the betterment of society, either at home or abroad, or both.

Solidarity benefits

While some join pressure groups for material benefits (what's in it for them) and others for purposive benefits (what's in it for others), there is a third group of people who join a pressure group for what might be called solidarity benefits. A solidarity benefit is a social benefit that is brought about principally from interacting with like-minded people. These groups centre their activities especially around local meetings that their members will attend. In the American terminology, they will form what are called local chapters. So, for example, if as an American you are a keen bird watcher, you may well join the National Audubon Society, not so much to preserve wetlands or other bird habitats, but more to join the local chapter. In Virginia, for example, you could join one of the local chapters, the Northern Shenandoah, Richmond, Norfolk or Virginia Beach. In mid-September, you could attend the annual Eastern Shore Birding and Wildlife Festival, which includes guided hikes and boat trips off the state's Atlantic coastline.

Methods used by pressure groups

Pressure groups use four principal methods in fulfilling their functions.

Electioneering and endorsement

Since the campaign finance reforms of the 1970s, considerable changes have taken place in the role of pressure groups and political fundraising. The reforms limited the amount that any pressure group could give to a candidate in a federal election. What the reforms encouraged, therefore, was the setting up of **political action committees** (PACs) that could make such donations. A PAC is an organisation whose purpose is to raise and then give campaign funds to candidates for political office.

Key term

➤ **Political action committees.** Pressure groups that collect money from their members and then give it to candidates and political parties that support their interests.

The role of PACs from 2006

The 2006 mid-term elections were the first to be run under the McCain–Feingold law of 2002, which had made the most significant changes to federal election finance laws since those of the 1970s. The 2006 mid-terms were also hotly contested, with the opportunity for the Democrats to regain control of both houses of Congress for the first time in 12 years, a target which they achieved. These factors combined to make these elections the most expensive to date — an increase of 25% on what had been spent in 2002 — and much of this increase was by PACs. In his study of the 2006 mid-terms, Larry Sabato (2008) found that PAC spending exceeded $1 billion for the first time ever in an election cycle. And with an increased emphasis on hard-dollar fundraising, PACs have grown in number and importance since the passage of the McCain–Feingold law, with over 400 new PACs created in the first 4 years following the law's enactment.

Tables 4.2 and 4.3 show the top 12 House and Senate candidates in terms of PAC receipts during the 2012 election cycle. There were no losers in the House top 12, but Democrats Jim Matheson in Utah and John Barrow in Georgia put their PAC money to good use to fend off strong challenges in unpromising states. On the Senate side, the only top 12 loser was Scott Brown of Massachusetts, who had won a special election in 2010 to fill the vacancy caused by the death of Edward Kennedy. Brown, a Republican in the bluest of the blue states, lost to Democrat Elizabeth Warren by 8 percentage points despite his PAC money advantage.

Table 4.2 House of Representatives top 12 PAC recipients: 2012 election cycle

House member	District	Party	PAC receipts ($)	Result
Dave Camp	Michigan 4	R	3,042,354	Won 63%
Eric Cantor	Virginia 7	R	2,686,034	Won 59%
Steny Hoyer	Maryland 5	D	2,584,691	Won 62%
Fred Upton	Michigan 6	R	2,553,231	Won 54%
Kevin McCarthy	California 23	R	2,420,467	Won 74%
John Boehner	Ohio 8	R	2,304,850	Unopposed
Tom Latham	Iowa 3	R	2,029,665	Won 52%
Patrick Tiberi	Ohio 12	R	1,920,199	Won 63%
James Clyburn	South Carolina 6	D	1,793,202	Won 94%
Jim Matheson	Utah 4	D	1,760,341	Won 49%
John Barrow	Georgia 12	D	1,647,648	Won 54%
Joseph Crowley	New York 14	D	1,553,143	Won 83%

Source: www.fec.gov

Table 4.3 Senate top 12 PAC recipients: 2012 election cycle

Senator	State	Party	PAC receipts ($)	Result
Orrin Hatch	Utah	R	3,557,253	Won 65%
Scott Brown	Massachusetts	R	2,693,721	Lost 46%
Debbie Stabenow	Michigan	D	2,680,496	Won 58%
Kirsten Gillibrand	New York	D	2,416,313	Won 72%
Bill Nelson	Florida	D	2,262,097	Won 55%
Jon Tester	Montana	D	2,182,717	Won 49%
Bob Casey	Pennsylvania	D	2,115,238	Won 54%
Dean Heller	Nevada	R	2,110,277	Won 46%
Robert Menendez	New Jersey	D	2,098,866	Won 58%
Bob Corker	Tennessee	R	2,085,707	Won 65%
Ben Cardin	Maryland	D	2,028,819	Won 54%
Tom Carper	Delaware	D	2,003,925	Won 66%

Source: www.fec.gov

The biggest PAC contributor in the 2010 election cycle overall was, as usual, the National Association of Realtors — representing America's estate agents — who donated a total of just under $3.8 million to federal candidates. They also spent a further $7 million in independent expenditures on behalf of federal candidates. The biggest corporate PAC donor was the telephone, internet and digital television provider AT&T ($3.2 million) whilst the biggest labour union donor was the International Brotherhood of Electrical Workers ($2.9 million) followed by the Teamsters Union ($2.3 million).

However, what pressure groups get for this money is open to question. Research has yet to prove any clear link between PAC contributions and the way members of Congress cast their votes on the floor of the House or Senate. Members of Congress are more likely to be influenced by direct lobbying than by donations to their campaigns. By the 2011–12 election cycle, so-called 'Super PACs' had emerged and their role in the 2012 presidential election is discussed in Chapter 2.

Candidate endorsement

Pressure groups will also actively support or oppose presidential and congressional candidates on the basis of the candidates' positions on the policy areas of concern to them. In 2012, the pro-life group the National Right to Life endorsed Republican candidate Mitt Romney while the pro-choice group NARAL endorsed Barack Obama.

Every 2 years, the League of Conservation Voters (LCV) publishes its 'dirty dozen' list — the 12 candidates with what they regard as the worst record on environmental conservation. Its 'dirty dozen' list for the 2012 congressional elections included seven members of Congress, of whom six were defeated (see Table 4.4). However, the success rate and the effect of the League may be somewhat overstated, for sometimes names are not added to the list until it is fairly certain that the candidate will be defeated. For example, the name of Congressman Tim Holden of Pennsylvania was not added to the 'dirty dozen' list until just a week before he was defeated in the Democratic primary in April 2012.

Another example of pressure group electioneering and endorsing could be seen in 2008 by looking at the AARP (the American Association of Retired Persons) website. This included a voter guide in which AARP had put a series of questions not only to the two

Table 4.4 Congressional candidates on the 'dirty dozen' list, 2012

Candidate	Party	Senate/ House	Incumbent/ Challenger/Open race	State	Election outcome
George Allen	R	Senate	Open race	Virginia	Defeated
Dan Benishek	R	House	Incumbent	Michigan	Re-elected
Ann Marie Buerkle	R	House	**Incumbent**	New York	**Defeated**
Francisco Canseco	R	House	**Incumbent**	Texas	**Defeated**
Tim Holden	D	House	**Incumbent**	Pennsylvania	**Defeated**
Dan Lungren	R	House	**Incumbent**	California	**Defeated**
Josh Mandel	R	Senate	Challenger	Ohio	Defeated
Linda McMahon	R	Senate	Open race	Connecticut	Defeated
Dennis Rehberg	R	House	**Incumbent**	Montana	**Defeated**
Joe Walsh	R	House	**Incumbent**	Illinois	**Defeated**
Heather Wilson	R	Senate	Open race	New Mexico	Defeated

Defeated incumbents in **bold**.
Source: www.lcv.org

leading contenders in the presidential election but to the candidates in the 435 House races and 35 Senate races. In North Carolina's 8th District, Republican incumbent Robin Hayes was in a close race with his Democrat challenger Larry Kissel. Two years earlier, Hayes had defeated Kissel by fewer than 500 votes out of over 120,000 — 50.2% to 49.8%. The AARP put ten questions to the two candidates, all relating to issues of particular interest to seniors. On all ten questions, Kissel's response was identical to the AARP position. For example, Kissel opposed diverting Social Security payroll taxes to individual retirement accounts (IRAs). So does the AARP. Kissel supported providing an automatic payroll deduction for employee IRAs. So does the AARP. Kissel supported increasing consumer choice and control for people needing long-term care. So does the AARP. On none of these ten questions did Congressman Hayes's position receive the endorsement of the AARP. The Republican incumbent lost to his Democrat challenger — 45% to 55%.

Another Republican House member facing a tough re-election bid in 2008 was Vern Buchanan in Florida's 13th District. Buchanan was also facing a rematch with his 2006 Democratic opponent, whom he had beaten by a mere 0.2% of the vote. But Buchanan's Florida constituency, based around the gulf coast city of Sarasota, has a significant number of retirees. Buchanan's position agreed with the AARP on eight out of the ten questions posed. The only trouble was that his Democrat opponent, Christine Jennings, had a perfect 10/10 score. But Buchanan clearly recognised that even if he had to be out of step with other Republican House candidates, it was more important to be in step, as much as possible, with the interests of his elderly constituents. The Republican incumbent won 55–37%.

Lobbying

Perhaps the most effective method of **lobbying** is the provision of accurate, detailed, up-to-date information to those who need it. Legislators and bureaucrats are busy people who have many demands made upon their limited time and resources. Legislators, in particular, must appear knowledgeable about and take positions on a bewildering number of policy issues. Pressure groups are often the only source of information.

Key concept

➤ **Lobbying.** An attempt to exert influence on the policy-making, legislative or judicial process by individuals or organised groups.

In order to facilitate this method of operation, pressure groups maintain offices in Washington DC, state capitals and other major cities. This allows them to be on hand to lobby members of federal, state and local government. The presence of lobbyists in Washington DC itself is almost overwhelming and is often referred to as the 'K Street corridor', named after the street in the capital where the offices of many lobbyists are located (see Table 4.5). Some of the most notable lobbying firms in Washington

Table 4.5 Examples of 'K Street corridor' lobbyists

Lobbyist	Washington DC address
American Legion	1608 K Street, NW
American Public Transportation Association	1666 K Street, NW
General Aviation Manufacturers Association	1400 K Street, NW
Institute for Mental Health Initiatives	2175 K Street, NW
Leadership Conference on Civil and Human Rights	1629 K Street, NW
Leather Industries of America	3050 K Street, NW
Media Access Project	1625 K Street, NW
Mehlman Capitol Strategies	1750 K Street, NW

are built around former presidential aides and cabinet officers whose visibility and experience helps to attract clients, especially those who need to lobby the executive branch of government. There is, for example, the Duberstein Group, started by Kenneth Duberstein, a former White House chief of staff to President Reagan, with headquarters just five blocks west of the White House at 2100 Pennsylvania Avenue. John Ashcroft, George W. Bush's former Attorney General, has opened a lobbying firm called the Ashcroft Group.

Pressure groups also provide legislators with voting cues. Liberal Democrats look to such groups as the AFL–CIO, the NAACP and Americans for Democratic Action (ADA) to provide reassurance that they are taking the right stand on a particular issue. Conservative Republicans find the American Conservative Union (ACU), Americans for Constitutional Action (ACA) and the US Chamber of Commerce equally helpful. Pressure groups such as ADA, the AFL–CIO and the ACU publish regular ratings of legislators, showing how often — or how rarely — a particular legislator has supported the policy positions in line with the views of that particular group.

When the AFL–CIO published its Senate Scorecard for the first session of the 112th Congress (2011), it ranked each senator on how they had voted on what the AFL–CIO regarded as 19 key votes during that year. These included votes on the American Jobs Act and the Balanced Budget Amendment. At the approval end of the scale, five senators — all Democrats — had 100% ratings, having voted in agreement with the AFL–CIO position on all 19 votes. These included Tom Harkin of Iowa and Jeff Merkley of Oregon. The lowest rating for a senator was just 7% for Republican Dean Heller of Nevada.

Publicity

Pressure groups frequently launch public relations campaigns in order to educate the people at large. Such publicity takes a number of different forms. It might involve television advertising — often known as 'issue advertising'. The role that insurance companies played in killing off President Clinton's healthcare reforms in 1993–94 was certainly decisive. More recently, the AARP mounted a television campaign against

President George W. Bush's proposal to reform Social Security to create private retirement accounts. Television advertisements showed a demolition crew responding to a complaint of a clogged kitchen drain by knocking down the house. The ad tried to persuade viewers that the President's plan was something of an over-reaction to the more minor problems associated with the funding of Social Security. The AFL–CIO has also launched numerous negative publicity campaigns aimed at Republican legislators opposed to increases in the federal minimum wage.

When the Food and Drug Administration announced plans to ban saccharin due to possible links with cancer, the Calorie Control Council — which has close links with the Coca-Cola Company — ran an advertisement campaign denouncing the proposal.

Public policy journals — whose circulation includes almost all members of Congress, senior staff at the White House and executive departments and agencies — are also used for the placement of advertisements. The 30 August 2008 edition of *National Journal* — a low-circulation but high-reputation Washington weekly — carried advertisements from the American Hospital Association, the Independent Community Bankers of America, the Nuclear Energy Institute, the Renewable Fuels Association, the American Academy of Family Physicians, and Consumers United for Energy Solutions. The latter's advertisement included a bipartisan list of 130 members of Congress who were supporting renewable and alternative energy programmes, thereby, in the words of the advertisement, 'putting progress ahead of politics'.

Roadside hoardings, bumper stickers and badges are among other methods used for pressure group publicity. Pressure groups send some publicity directly to law-makers in the form of informative or promotional DVDs. A campaign to encourage Congress to tighten laws on the production of veal meat bombarded members with a video entitled *Murder on the Menu*.

Organising grassroots activities

Grassroots activities by members are often thought to be the most effective of pressure groups' methods, especially when these activities are aimed directly at legislators or policy-makers. Such grassroots activities may include the organisation of a postal 'blitz' on Congress, the White House or a government department. However, knowing that members of Congress pay little attention to the arrival of sack loads of identical letters or postcards, pressure groups encourage their members to frame their own communications. There are even firms that exist to orchestrate mail, e-mail and telephone blitzes.

Marches and demonstrations are sometimes aimed at state and federal court houses, where other forms of lobbying are inappropriate. Whenever the United States Supreme Court delivers a judgement on a controversial issue such as abortion, school prayers, capital punishment, gun control or minority rights, the pavement outside the Supreme Court building in Washington DC is filled with people from pressure groups representing the opposing sides of the argument.

Some groups may go further and resort to violence and disorder. The bombing of the federal government building in Oklahoma City in 1995 was linked to militia groups on the extreme right of US politics. Some of the more extreme anti-abortion groups have set fire to and bombed abortion clinics, intimidating staff who work in them and women who visit them, and even shooting doctors who carry out abortions. In 1999, there were violent demonstrations by anti-globalisation protesters in Seattle, Washington, during the World Trade Organization's ministerial conference being held in the city.

The wrecked federal government building in Oklahoma City bombed by right-wing militants on 19 April 1995

The impact of pressure groups on issues

Pressure groups are big business. The total federal lobbying revenue in 2010 amounted to just short of $3.5 billion. And that sum includes only that income which must be disclosed under federal law. On top of that, clients spent at least hundreds of millions of dollars more on grassroots lobbying, public relations, consulting, strategic advice and many other forms of lobbying that make up the Washington lobbying sector. It is hardly surprising, therefore, that pressure groups have had a significant impact in a number of policy areas.

Environmental protection

Towards the end of the 19th century, when both industrialisation and 'westward expansion' were well under way, the matter of environmental conservation became important. This is when the Sierra Club was formed. It was followed in the early 20th century by the Wilderness Society and the National Wildlife Federation. Such groups have been behind the push towards stricter laws for environmental protection.

Women's rights

Groups such as the League of Women Voters and the National Organization for Women pushed — unsuccessfully — for the passage of an Equal Rights Amendment to the Constitution during the 1970s and 1980s. They have remained very active in US politics, campaigning on such issues as equal pay and job opportunities for women. In addition, they have been involved in the debate over attempting to root out sexual harassment in the workplace, with some high-profile cases in the US military.

Women's groups have also been deeply involved in moves to try to increase the number of women being elected to Congress. The pressure group EMILY's List — an

acronym for '**E**arly **M**oney **I**s **L**ike **Y**east' — supports female candidates early in the election process so that they will be able to demonstrate their ability to raise money later on in the electoral cycle and win seats.

Abortion rights

Both the 'pro-choice' and 'pro-life' lobbies have been active in US politics during the past three to four decades. Since the 1973 *Roe v. Wade* decision by the Supreme Court, pro-choice pressure groups have fought to preserve the constitutional right of women to have an abortion, whereas pro-life groups have fought to have it both narrowed and overturned. Most recently, they have been involved in the debate over the practice of so-called 'partial birth abortions'. When Congress initially tried to ban such types of abortion, President Clinton vetoed the bills, once in 1996 and again in 1997. And in 2000, the Supreme Court refused to allow states to ban this type of abortion. But once George W. Bush had signed a partial birth abortion ban into law, the Supreme Court, in 2007, upheld the ban. In pursuing their respective agendas, both sides in the debate have lobbied the Senate over presidential judicial appointments, most clearly seen in the fights over the nominations to the Supreme Court of Robert Bork in 1987 and Clarence Thomas in 1991, but also in the confirmation of John Roberts in 2005 and Samuel Alito in 2006.

Gun control

The National Rifle Association (NRA) is arguably one of the most powerful pressure groups in US politics, with a membership of some 3 million. It was formed in 1871 as a group dedicated to teaching Americans how to use guns. Since the 1960s, however, it has been influential in stopping what it sees as encroachment on citizens' rights to own and use legal firearms. It seeks to uphold the strictest interpretation of the 2nd Amendment right to 'keep and bear arms'. It also works to oppose tougher gun

Roadside hoarding advertising the National Rifle Association

control laws put forward at any level of government. The NRA opposed the Brady Bill and the assault weapons ban, as well as laws requiring background checks on those purchasing guns and the mandatory sale of trigger locks with handguns. It played a significant role in the Supreme Court case of *District of Columbia v. Heller* in 2008 and became involved in the national debate on gun control following the killing of 20 children and 6 teachers by a 20-year old gunman at Sandy Hook Elementary School in Newtown, Connecticut, in December 2012. The debate below shows some comments made by members of Congress about the influence of the NRA in the immediate aftermath of the cinema shootings in Aurora, Colorado, in July 2012. (You can see an example of an election TV ad featuring an NRA endorsement in Box 2.9 in Chapter 2.)

> ## 'How much influence does the National Rifle Association have on the gun control debate in Congress?'
>
> **DEBATE**
>
> ### Democrat members of Congress:
> - 'The NRA has been effective in ensuring that there has been relatively little gun control debate in recent years.'
> - 'They "own" Congress.'
> - 'Thanks to the NRA, you can't even discuss the issue in a rational way, let alone pass commonsense gun control measures like restricting the number of bullets in a clip.'
> - 'The NRA "owns" the Republican Party.'
> - 'Right now, a very large number of members are afraid to upset the NRA.'
>
> ### Republican members of Congress:
> - 'Few if any interest groups are in the same league as the NRA. They are well funded, they have a committed and active grassroots network, and members of Congress both fear and respect them as a political force.'
> - 'The NRA has influence because the majority of Americans agree with their principles.'
> - 'The NRA is the best single-issue lobby group in politics, bar none.'
> - 'Their membership is vast and deep and protecting our constitutional rights is an important advocacy.'

Source: 'Congressional insiders poll', *National Journal*, 28 July 2012, pp. 10–11

Economic inequality

The collapse in the banking and finance sectors which began in America during the latter years of the presidency of George W. Bush gave rise to the international Occupy movement to pressure governments to address the specific issue of economic inequality. The first protest to receive the full focus of the media was the occupation of Zuccotti Park in New York City on 17 September 2011 by the Occupy Wall Street movement. Within a month, similar protests had sprung up within each of the 50 states as well as a well-publicised protest in Washington DC. The movement became known initially through its slogan — 'We are the 99%' — a reference to the concentration of wealth among the top 1% of income earners. The movement was initially seen as something of a democratic awakening, not only in the United States but worldwide. There is no doubt that in the early weeks of the protests, the Occupy movement drove a good deal of the substance of public and political debate. The Obama administration, the Democratic Party leadership and the American labour union movement initially all showed some interest in and sympathy for the core beliefs and objectives of the movement. Some saw it in America as the left's answer to the Tea Party movement.

But a year on, and the movement had all but disappeared, certainly from the streets of American cities, if not from the political debates of would-be sympathisers within the government and left-leaning political parties. The movement's critics pointed out some obvious flaws and weaknesses. First, unlike the Tea Party movement, Occupy never tapped into the political system. Whilst Tea Partiers were encouraged to participate in choosing like-minded candidates and vote in elections, the main tactic of the Occupy movement

seemed to be purely sedentary. Occupiers seemed to be under the mistaken belief that by just sitting in public places, doing nothing, week after week, they would prompt some kind of action from others. Second, once the movement took on a more violent, confrontational approach, the civic authorities closed down the encampments, citing fears about public health and public safety. Third, their 'leadership' was even more disparate and unfocused than that of the Tea Party movement. The movement was also skewed much more towards the young — the very group who are notoriously bad at taking their protests from the street to the ballot box. The Democratic Party could look at the Occupiers and feel fairly confident that it had little to fear from them in any upcoming election.

The impact of pressure groups on government

Impact on Congress

Pressure groups seek to influence the way House and Senate members vote. They do this by a number of methods. First, they make direct contact with members of Congress as well as senior members of their staff. Visit the website of almost any pressure group and you will find directions as to how to contact your members of Congress with regular updates on the current state of relevant legislation going through Congress.

Second, they make contact with the relevant congressional committees — especially those who chair or are ranking minority members on those committees. As we shall see in Chapter 5, Congress does most of its work in committees — specifically the standing committees. So it is no surprise that most of the work of legislative lobbyists is directed at committees. Standing committees have significant power to amend legislation which they consider during the legislative process. This provides pressure groups with one of their most valuable access points into the legislative process. One lobbyist commented: 'You have to start at the bottom. You have to start at the subcommittee level. If you wait until the bill gets to the floor [of the House or the Senate], your efforts will very seldom work.' Because the membership of congressional committees is relatively small — about 16 in the Senate, and 40 in the House of Representatives — and also fairly constant, lobbyists find it easy to build a close working relationship with the members of the particular policy-specific committees in which they are interested. Indeed, it soon becomes two-way traffic: not only do lobbyists contact members of Congress to lobby for their policy position, but members of Congress contact lobbyists as a source of information and support. Committee staff are another target of pressure group activity. Staff members are often more accessible than their bosses. Berry and Wilcox (2007) quote a lobbyist for a large manufacturer as saying: 'If you have a [committee] staff member on your side, it might be a lot better than talking to the member of Congress.'

Third, pressure groups attempt to organise constituents to write to, telephone, e-mail or visit their member of Congress to express either support for or opposition to a certain policy. This is most likely to occur just before a high-profile committee hearing, floor debate or final passage vote.

Fourth, as we saw earlier, pressure groups publicise the voting records of House and Senate members, sometimes offering their own rankings, and at election time they endorse supportive and oppose non-supportive incumbents by fundraising and media advertising.

Impact on the executive

Pressure groups seek to maintain strong ties with relevant executive departments, agencies and regulatory commissions. This is especially the case when it comes to the regulatory work of the federal government — regulations, for example, regarding health and safety at work, business, the transport and communications industries, and the environment.

Problems can emerge when regulatory bodies are thought to have too cosy a relationship with the particular group that they are meant to be regulating. Are they acting as 'watchdogs' or 'lapdogs'?

Edward Ashbee and Nigel Ashford (1999) identify another close link, between 'producer groups' — such as companies, labour unions or small business federations — and relevant government departments and agencies seeking protection, funding, subsidies or price guarantee mechanisms.

Some pressure groups will find themselves courted by the White House for their support. In 2005, President George W. Bush's political director in the White House, Karl Rove, had frequent contacts with Christian Right groups in what turned out to be an unsuccessful effort to reassure them that the President's nominee for the Supreme Court, Harriet Miers, was a like-minded conservative who could be trusted to act in their interests on the Court. Rove had hoped that these groups would then lobby members of the Senate to confirm Ms Miers to the Court. In the event, they lobbied to have her defeated. Instead, Ms Miers withdrew.

Impact on the judiciary

Pressure groups take a lively interest in the nominations the president makes to the federal courts, especially those to the US Supreme Court. As we shall see, nominations to the courts are for life and the Supreme Court has very significant power, for example, to interpret the Constitution and declare acts of Congress unconstitutional, thereby affecting the everyday life of ordinary Americans. The American Bar Association evaluates the professional qualifications of nominees and their evaluation can play a significant role in the confirmation process conducted by the Senate.

Pressure groups can hope to influence the courts by offering *amicus curiae* (friends of the court) briefings. Through these, pressure groups have an opportunity to present their views to the court in writing before oral arguments are heard. Pressure groups have used this method to great effect in recent decades, in such areas as the civil rights of racial minorities, abortion and 1st Amendment rights. One of the most active pressure groups in the courts is the American Civil Liberties Union (see Box 4.2).

In 2005, the American Civil Liberties Union was at the Supreme Court in the case of *McCreary v. ACLU*, in which the Court ruled that a display of the Ten Commandments

in a Kentucky courthouse was unconstitutional. A much lower-profile pressure group, Parents Involved in Community Schools (PICS), brought a landmark case to the Supreme Court in 2007, *PICS v. Seattle School District*, in which the Court declared it unconstitutional to assign students to public (i.e. state-run) schools solely for the purpose of achieving racial balance. And in 2008, the National Rifle Association played a significant role in the landmark case of *District of Columbia v. Heller*, in which the Supreme Court declared Washington DC's ban on handguns to be unconstitutional.

Access points

One of the reasons why pressure groups are so important and influential in the USA is the number of access points that the US system of government provides. By 'access points' we mean points in the governmental and political system at which pressure groups can gain access to the decision-making process. Access points are provided at all three levels of government — federal, state and local — and in all three branches — the legislature, the executive and the judiciary. They are also provided in the electoral process at all three levels of government. Access by pressure groups is enhanced in the USA because of the openness of the political system and by the fact that high levels of democratic participation are encouraged.

In this chapter, we have seen pressure groups gaining access to the electoral process through campaigning, electioneering, fundraising and endorsing. And, of course, there are primaries as well as general elections, elections for both houses of Congress as well as the president, and then state and local elections — for state governors, state legislators, city mayors, even judges in some states. Add to that the state propositions and initiatives which we looked at in Chapter 2. They give yet another opportunity for pressure groups to gain access to the political system.

We have seen pressure groups as gaining access in Congress. Unlike the UK Parliament, which is dominated by the twin powers of the executive and highly disciplined political parties, the US Congress is open to all kinds of pressure — both on the floor of each chamber and in the committee rooms. The congressional committee system provides literally hundreds of access points to pressure groups to provide information, appear as witnesses, make written submissions, amend legislation, and scrutinise the actions of the executive branch. Pressure groups not only have committees to lobby but sub-committees too. They not only have members of Congress to lobby, but their staff as well — and the committee staff. And the same is true in the state legislatures in the 50 state capitals across the nation.

Then there is access to the executive branch of government — not just to the White House, but to all the various departments, agencies and regulatory commissions which make up the federal bureaucracy. Add to that the access which pressure groups can gain to the executive branches of the 50 state governments — in Albany, New York, or in Sacramento, California.

Finally, pressure groups have access to the judicial branch within the federal and state governments. By the filing of *amicus curiae* briefs, pressure groups have had a very significant influence on some landmark decisions in the federal and state courts.

Regulation of pressure groups

In a nation where 1st Amendment rights are the very breath of politics, it is difficult to regulate anything that fundamentally concerns freedom of speech and expression. The 1st Amendment states that: 'Congress shall make no law...abridging the freedom of speech, or of the press; or the right of the people to peaceably assemble, and to petition the government for a redress of grievances.' For over 100 years, pressure groups have sheltered under the protection of this amendment and have successfully pleaded its guarantees in court.

Earlier attempts at lobbying reform

It was not until the passage of the Federal Regulation of Lobbying Act in 1946 that Congress started to regulate significantly the activities of pressure groups. This Act required lobbyists to register with the clerk of the House of Representatives and the secretary of the Senate if they raised money 'to be used principally to aid the passage

or defeat of any legislation by the Congress of the United States', but its provisions went largely ignored. Thirty years later the Lobby Disclosure Bill failed to make it on to the statute book — because of powerful lobbying from pressure groups.

It was largely as a consequence of the Watergate affair and the subsequent passage of campaign finance reform legislation that the regulation of pressure groups came about. The campaign finance reform of the 1970s gave rise to the huge growth of PACs. There was public disquiet over buying influence in Congress as a consequence of a congressional scandal known as 'Abscam' — the attempts of influential Arab interests to bribe leading members of Congress.

In the 1990s, Congress passed further regulatory legislation by expanding the definition of what qualified as a pressure group and thereby making more groups register. Congress also passed significant restrictions on lobbyists by banning gifts to members of Congress, including the 'wining and dining' of members and the paying of honoraria — writing or speaking fees paid by pressure groups to members of Congress.

Honest Leadership and Open Government Act (2007)

When the Democrats took control of both houses of Congress in January 2007 for the first time in 12 years, they moved quickly on the subject of lobbying reform. Within 9 months, President Bush was signing the Honest Leadership and Open Government Act (2007) into law. The legislation had received bipartisan support, passing the House of Representatives by 411 votes to 8, and the Senate by 83 votes to 14.

Some of the major provisions of this legislation are shown in Box 4.3. Although President Bush signed the bill into law, he noted that this was merely a first step towards significant lobbying reform and that Congress had not helped itself by passing legislation which placed different standards on the members of the two houses.

In an article in *National Journal* ('Good times, bad times', 22 March 2008), Peter Stone and Bara Vaida commented that as a result of the 2007 lobbying reform:

> Gone are the days when lobbyists could buy meals and gifts for lawmakers and their staffers and could finance entertainment, corporate jets and junkets. Lobbyists and their firms must now file three times the number of reports with Congress than in years past. Even more ominous, the new law exposes lobbyists and their employers to potential prison time and hefty fines if they fail to follow the regulations.

So as a result, pressure groups have had to stop sponsoring trips for members of Congress and their staff. The Sierra Club, for example, can no longer take members of Congress to see the National Wildlife Refuge in Alaska, or visit national parks, which had been an important way for the organisation to demonstrate the impact of environmental regulations. Meetings and meals between lobbyists and either members of Congress or their staff are now taking place in their offices or in one of the House or Senate cafés. There is even some evidence of some law-makers paying for lobbyists' meals — a strange reversal of roles. 'I've been bought dinner by a couple of senators

Box 4.3 Honest Leadership and Open Government Act 2007: some major provisions

Closing the revolving door

➤ Prohibits senators from gaining undue lobbying access by increasing the 'cooling off' period for senators from 1 to 2 years before they can lobby Congress.

➤ Prohibits cabinet officers or other very senior executive branch personnel from lobbying the department or agency in which they worked for 2 years after they leave their position.

➤ Prohibits senior Senate staff and Senate officers from lobbying contacts with the entire Senate for 1 year, instead of just their former employing office.

➤ Prohibits senior House staff from lobbying their former office or committee for 1 year after they leave House employment.

Prohibiting gifts by lobbyists

➤ Prohibits lobbyists from providing gifts or travel to members of Congress with knowledge that the gift or travel is in violation of House or Senate rules.

➤ Prohibits senators or their staff from accepting gifts from registered lobbyists.

➤ Requires entertainment and sports tickets offered by registered lobbyists to be valued at market rates.

Full public disclosure of lobbying activity

➤ Requires lobbyist disclosure filings to be filed quarterly rather than half-yearly as before.

➤ Increases civil penalty for knowing or wilful violations of the Lobby Disclosure Act from $50,000 to $200,000 and imposes a criminal penalty of up to 5 years for knowing and corrupt failure to comply with the Act.

➤ Requires the Government Accountability Office to audit annually lobbyist compliance with disclosure rules.

Congressional pension liability

➤ Denies congressional retirement benefits to members of Congress who are convicted of bribery, perjury, conspiracy or other related crimes in the course of carrying out their official duties as a member of Congress.

Prohibiting use of private aircraft

➤ Requires that candidates, other than those running for a seat in the House, pay the fair market value of air fares when using non-commercial jets to travel. (This affects Senate, presidential and vice-presidential candidates.)

➤ Prohibits candidates for the House from using non-commercial aircraft.

and congressmen,' claimed Wayne Berman, managing director of Ogilvy Government Relations, a Washington-based lobbying firm. 'I think the 2007 ethics reforms have had a significant impact.'

Another possibly unintended consequence of the Honest Leadership and Open Government Act was a sudden rush for the exit doors on Capitol Hill among congressional staff, eager to beat the new rules which came into effect on 1 January 2008. Eighteen senior staffers left Capitol Hill in the last 6 weeks of 2007. Four senators — Trent Lott

of Mississippi, Orrin Hatch of Utah, Debbie Stabenow of Michigan, and Maria Cantwell of Washington — all lost their chiefs of staff to Washington lobbying firms during that period.

It was also noticeable that lobbyists became a target for both presidential campaigns in 2008. Barack Obama refused all campaign donations from registered lobbyists. In a speech in February after having just won the Wisconsin primary, Obama declared: 'Washington has become a place where good ideas go to die because lobbyists crush them with their money and influence.' And in a speech on the Senate floor, John McCain commented: 'Only by breaking the iron triangle of big money, special-interest lobbyists, and the legislation they buy can sovereignty be restored to the American people.' McCain's campaign website pointed out that he had battled the 'revolving door by which lawmakers and other influential public officials leave their posts and become lobbyists for the special interests they have aided'.

Arguments for pressure groups

The arguments in favour of pressure groups tend to follow the functions they may usefully perform, as discussed above. First, they provide legislators and bureaucrats with useful information and act as a sounding board for legislators at the policy formulation stage in the legislative process. Second, they bring some kind of order to the policy debate, aggregating views and channelling the wishes of the clients and members whom they seek to represent. Third, they broaden the opportunities for participation in a democracy. Fourth, pressure groups can increase levels of accountability both for Congress and for the executive branch. Fifth, they increase opportunities for representation between elections, as well as offering opportunities for minority views to be represented that would be lost in the big tent of political parties. Sixth, they enhance the two fundamental rights of freedom of speech and freedom of association.

The US political process is one that is conducive to pressure group activity. There are many access points in the democratic process where pressure groups can have their say. This is especially the case in Congress, where the decentralisation of power, the autonomy of committees, and the lack of strict party discipline when it comes to voting, all make Congress an institution that is far more open to persuasion by pressure groups than most national legislatures. The number of access points is merely increased by the federal division of powers, which allows many important decisions to be made in the host of state and local governments across the USA.

Arguments against pressure groups

But pressure groups can come in for something of a bad press. Do they enhance democracy? Are they a 'good thing' or merely a 'necessary evil'? Several arguments are made against the activities of pressure groups.

The revolving-door syndrome

Many pressure groups work through hired lobbyists employed by lobbying firms — many based in Washington DC — whose full-time job is to lobby government. There is nothing inherently wrong with that. A criticism that can be made, however, is that a high proportion of these professional lobbyists are former members of Congress or former congressional staff members. This is what is known as the **revolving-door syndrome**: people walk out of the political door, so to speak, perhaps having just been defeated in an election, but immediately re-enter the political world as a Washington lobbyist. Federal law forbids former public officials from taking up a job as a lobbyist within a year of leaving public office, but after that year has elapsed, the traffic through the revolving door from public official to professional lobbyist is quite heavy.

Key term

> **Revolving-door syndrome.** The practice by which former members of Congress (or the executive branch) take up well-paid jobs with Washington-based lobbying firms and then use their expertise and contacts to lobby the institution of which they were once a member.

Critics argue that this constitutes an abuse of public service. People exploit their knowledge of and contacts within Congress or the executive branch of government in order to further the interests of their pressure group clients and in so doing make large sums of money for themselves. It is alleged that serving politicians may favour particular group interests because they are hoping for a job representing that interest, should they lose their public office.

The 2010 mid-term elections saw an unusually large number of law-makers leave Capitol Hill either through voluntary retirement or electoral defeat, a total of 119 in all. According to the website Open Secrets (**www.opensecrets.org**) and the Center for Responsive Politics, of the 81 who had found new employment, 31% had joined lobbying firms and a further 22% had become lobbying clients. Former Democrat senator Chris Dodd of Connecticut, for example, now works for the Motion Picture Association of America.

According to Craig Holman, a government affairs lobbyist for Public Citizen, the revolving-door syndrome has two fundamental problem areas: 'first, you have to wonder what lawmakers are giving in exchange for their potentially lucrative employment, and second, once they leave office, are they exploiting their relationships in office for profitable gain?'

The iron-triangle syndrome

The **iron triangle** is a term used to describe a strong relationship that many commentators of US politics see existing between pressure groups and the relevant congressional committees on the one hand and the relevant government department or agency on the other. This cosy relationship — the term 'cosy triangle' is sometimes used — guarantees policy outcomes to the benefit of all three parties involved. One example

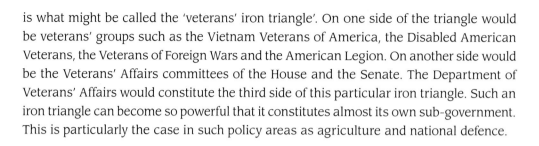

is what might be called the 'veterans' iron triangle'. On one side of the triangle would be veterans' groups such as the Vietnam Veterans of America, the Disabled American Veterans, the Veterans of Foreign Wars and the American Legion. On another side would be the Veterans' Affairs committees of the House and the Senate. The Department of Veterans' Affairs would constitute the third side of this particular iron triangle. Such an iron triangle can become so powerful that it constitutes almost its own sub-government. This is particularly the case in such policy areas as agriculture and national defence.

Key term

➤ **Iron triangle.** A term used to describe a strong relationship between pressure groups, the relevant congressional committees and the relevant government department or agency in an attempt to guarantee the policy outcomes to the benefit of all three parties involved.

The iron triangle is linked with the revolving-door syndrome. A Pentagon general might, after the lawful waiting period, end up as a lobbyist for a missile manufacturer. Similarly, a former staff member from the Senate Armed Services Committee might get a job lobbying for a defence contractor.

The existence of these iron triangles raises the question of whether pressure group activities are compatible with a pluralist society. A pluralist society is one in which political resources such as money, expertise and access to both government and the mass media are spread widely and are in the hands of many diverse individuals and groups. Many see pressure groups as fostering an elitist view of society in which the aforementioned political resources are in the hands, not of the many, but of the few.

Inequality of groups

Defenders of pressure groups would have us believe that at the very least pressure groups operate within a series of 'competing elites'. They see US politics as a system in which pressure groups, along with political parties, bureaucrats, business people, trade unions, the media, educators, lawyers and so on, compete for influence over those who make policy. They would argue that, because each group represents the interests of its own clients, this is entirely compatible with a democratic society. Such an argument is associated with those on the right of the political spectrum.

Those on the left criticise pressure groups because they see this 'competition' as being one that is often unequal. As early as the 1950s, President Eisenhower warned against what he saw as the power of the 'military-industrial complex'. At around the same time, the noted American political philosopher C. Wright Mills continued this theme in his 1956 book *The Power Elite*.

There are a number of policy areas in which pressure groups representing the opposing sides of the argument are clearly unequal, for example the area of the environment. Many would argue that the resources of big business often outweigh the resources of the environmental protectionists. In the policy area of gun control, a battle between the

National Rifle Association on the one hand and Handgun Control Inc. on the other is clearly unequal. In the debate over health issues and tobacco smoking, the resources of one side have traditionally outweighed the resources of the other. The tobacco industry spent $67.4 million on lobbying in 1998.

Special interests v. the public interest

A criticism levelled at pressure groups is that they tend to put the interests of a small group before the interests of society as a whole. The pressure groups that represent various ethnic groups within American society are a good example; the National Association for the Advancement of Colored People (NAACP), the American Jewish Congress, the Indian American Center for Public Awareness, the Organization of Chinese Americans and the National Association for Hispanic Health, to name but a few. Critics see this as pressure groups adding to a splintering, or 'atomisation', of US society.

Pressure groups tend to accentuate 'me' rather than 'we'. They spend too much time fighting for their special interest and little time working for the wider public interest. Provided their client group is satisfied, they rarely consider the implications for society as a whole. They can also lead to group stereotyping, by making it appear as if all blacks, or all Jews, or all Latinos — or women, or teachers, or airline pilots, or whoever — think the same way and want the same policy outcomes. Some would argue that part of the reason for the criticism heaped upon Supreme Court nominee Clarence Thomas in 1991 was that he was a *conservative* black who did not fit the group-think of liberal politics as espoused by the NAACP and most other black pressure groups.

Buying political influence

The late Senator Edward Kennedy once famously remarked that America has 'the finest Congress that money can buy'. You have to 'pay to play'. According to the Center for Responsive Politics, the year 1999 saw $1.45 billion spent on lobbying activities; and the lobbying business is growing at a staggering 7.3% a year. In the 2002 mid-term elections, PACs donated a total of just short of $215 million to House candidates and just over $60 million to Senate candidates. That is well over a quarter-of-a-billion dollars spent in just one mid-term election cycle.

What do lobbyists get for their money? The short answer for the critics of pressure groups is 'a disproportionate level of influence'. In her account of the 104th Congress, Elizabeth Drew (1996) claims that lobbyists acting on behalf of business corporations wrote legislation for members of Congress. She quotes a *Washington Post* story that a lobbyist for the energy and petrochemical industries wrote the first draft of a bill during that Congress and that lobbyists working for a group called Project Relief were given a Capitol Hill office to use as a 'war room' during an energy debate showdown. Meanwhile, the *New York Times* was reporting a story that a bill to weaken the Clean Water Act was written by a taskforce of lobbyists representing groups such as the

Chemical Manufacturers Association and International Paper. House Speaker Newt Gingrich, asked about the role that pressure groups played in Congress, was quoted in the *Wall Street Journal* as saying: 'As long as it's out in the open, I have no problem.' Not everyone would agree.

Using direct action

A final criticism levelled at pressure groups is their use of **direct action**, which is deemed by others to be inappropriate. This criticism is raised whenever pressure groups use what most consider unacceptable levels of violence to pursue their political agenda. In recent years it has been associated with pro and anti-abortion groups, environmentalists, anti-capitalist groups and groups of the extreme right pursuing their anti-government agenda. Violence — even shootings, bombings and murders — conducted around abortion clinics by 'pro-life' groups hit the headlines in the 1990s. Anti-capitalist demonstrations that disrupted a meeting of the World Trade Organization in Seattle, Washington, in 1999, followed by demonstrations outside the World Bank in Washington DC in 2000, brought similar condemnation, as did the bombing of the federal government building in Oklahoma City in 1995. When the Occupy movement turned violent in some American cities, support quickly evaporated amongst the ordinary citizenry.

Key concept

➤ **Direct action.** A form of pressure group activity that most often favours the use of non-violent or violent physical protest over the more traditional forms of lobbying such as e-mailing and petitions.

Pros and cons of pressure groups

Pros

➤ provide legislators and bureaucrats with useful information
➤ act as a sounding board during policy formulation
➤ provide order, priorities and aggregation to political debate
➤ broaden opportunities for participation both during and between elections
➤ can increase levels of accountability on legislators and elected executive branch members
➤ increase opportunities for representing minority interests
➤ enhance freedom of speech and freedom of association — two basic democratic rights

Cons

➤ revolving-door syndrome
➤ iron triangle relationships
➤ inequality between groups leading to unfair representation of some views
➤ concentration on 'special interest' at the expense of the 'public interest'
➤ over-influence of money
➤ some methods used by some groups

| Box 4.4 | *Fortune* magazine's top 10 most influential interest groups in Washington DC |

1 National Rifle Association (NRA)

2 American Association of Retired People (AARP)

3 National Federation of Independent Business

4 American Israel Foreign Affairs Committee

5 Association of Trial Lawyers of America

6 American Federation of Labor–Congress of Industrial Organization (AFL–CIO)

7 Chamber of Commerce of the United States of America

8 National Beer Wholesalers of America

9 National Association of Realtors

10 National Association of Manufacturers

Factors leading to pressure group success

Every so often *Fortune* magazine publishes its 'Power 25 Survey' — a list of the top 25 most influential interest groups in Washington DC. Box 4.4 shows the top 10 in its latest list. Also on the list of the top 25 were the American Medical Association (12th), the Motion Picture Association of America (16th) and the National Right to Life Committee (18th). There are a number of factors which will tend to lead to pressure group success.

Effective organisation and leadership

Of course, some groups are easier to organise and lead than others. Andrew Heywood (2011) rightly suggests, for example, that producers are easier to organise than consumers; teachers are easier to organise than students. The National Rifle Association exhibits effective organisation and leadership whilst the Occupy movement did not.

Wealth

Effective organisation and leadership is linked to a second factor, that of wealth. President Franklin D. Roosevelt once famously remarked that 'you can't do nothing if you ain't got nothing to do nothing with!' A pressure group with little or no money is unlikely to be able to successfully achieve its goals. Corporate and trade groups are often the richest. Money brings the ability to be able to do more lobbying, engage in more campaigning, and have more attractive literature and websites. Table 4.6 shows some of the financial big hitters in the past two-and-a-half decades.

Large membership

Wealth links with a third factor in pressure group success — the size of the group's membership. The larger the group, the more successful it is likely to be. The larger the group's membership, the easier it is for that group to claim that it represents a large — and therefore potentially influential — segment of society. And the larger the membership, the

Table 4.6 Top 10 pressure group donors: 1989–2012

Rank	Organisation	Total donations: 1989–2012	Political tilt
1	ActBlue	$66,869,298	Democratic Party
2	American Federation of State, County and Municipal Employees	$60,633,873	Democratic Party
3	AT&T Inc.	$49,162,460	Between both parties
4	National Association of Realtors	$44,024,138	Between both parties
5	National Education Association	$42,066,188	Democratic Party
6	Service Employees International Union	$39,714,097	Democratic Party
7	Goldman Sachs	$39,330,264	Between both parties
8	American Association for Justice	$36,432,428	Democratic Party
9	International Brotherhood of Electrical Workers	$35,728,225	Democratic Party
10	American Federation of Teachers	$34,118,316	Democratic Party

Source: www.opensecrets.org

larger the bank balance: more members means more subscriptions and donations. The American Association of Retired Persons (AARP) is reputed to be the largest in the USA with some 40 million members. The NRA is well behind with around 4 million members. One begins to see how these first three factors are largely inter-related.

Linked with the factor of the size of the membership is the factor of popularity and public support. Politicians will try to gauge how electorally costly it might be to ignore a group's views. The more popular the issue, the more pressure the group can put on government.

Status and effectiveness of the opposition

The leadership, size and wealth that a pressure group needs to succeed are partly related to the leadership, size and wealth of their direct opponents. There are very few policy areas where a pressure group has no one arguing from the opposite corner. Anti-smoking groups have to contend with the powerful and wealthy tobacco industry; environmental groups have to contend with car manufacturers' groups and groups associated with oil producers. The stronger the opposition, the stronger the group needs to be in order to win the argument.

Achievability of the group's goal

A final factor is the achievability of the group's goal. A group such as Planned Parenthood that wants to keep abortion legal has a much easier task than the National Right to Life Committee which wants a complete ban on all abortions. However, achievability may change with time and perseverance. The past three decades have seen considerable changes in public views on such matters as drink driving, capital punishment and smoking in public places. Some groups persevere and succeed whilst others are overtaken by events and become redundant.

Activity

1 Go to the website of the **AFL–CIO** at **www.aflcio.org.**

   ➤ Click on 'legislation and politics'.

   ➤ Click on 'legislative voting records'.

   ➤ Using the interactive map, research specific senators, House members or state delegations to see how their votes are rated by the AFL–CIO.

   ➤ What trends do you notice? What legislation does this group regard as 'key'?

2 Now visit the website of the **American Conservative Union** (ACU) at **www.conservative.org.**

   ➤ Click on 'ACU ratings'.

   ➤ Then click on a year or a state to bring up the ACU ratings.

   ➤ Contrast the ACU ratings with the AFL–CIO ratings for particular members or delegations.

   ➤ What conclusions do you draw?

UK/US comparison

Pressure groups

There are a number of similarities between US and UK pressure groups:

➤ There are different types of pressure group.

➤ They perform similar functions concerning representation, participation, education, agenda building and programme monitoring.

➤ Citizens in both countries have different reasons and motivations for joining a pressure group.

➤ Pressure groups in both countries use different methods: electioneering, lobbying, publicity and organising grassroots activities.

➤ Pressure groups in both the USA and the UK seek to influence a variety of policy areas.

➤ They also seek to influence government at the national, state/regional and local levels.

➤ Pressure groups in both countries are subject to regulation.

➤ Arguments for and against pressure groups are put forward in both countries.

There are, however, a number of significant differences between pressure group activity in the USA and that in the UK:

➤ The rise and importance of political action committees in the USA.

➤ More access points for pressure groups in the USA.

➤ Lower levels of party discipline in Congress than in Parliament increases the potential for pressure group influence in the US legislative process.

➤ Pressure groups in the USA focus more on the judiciary than do their UK counterparts, given the power and importance of the courts in the US system of government.

Exam focus

Short-answer questions

1 What important functions do pressure groups perform?
2 Discuss the reasons why people join pressure groups.
3 Discuss the different methods which pressure groups might use to achieve their objectives.
4 Examine the main arguments for and against pressure groups.

Essay questions

1 To what extent does pressure group activity in the USA benefit the wealthy at the expense of the poor?
2 Are US pressure groups too powerful?
3 Analyse the factors that are likely to bring success to pressure groups in the USA.
4 Have pressure groups become more important than political parties in US politics?
5 Why and how do pressure groups attempt to influence Congress?
6 Do pressure groups strengthen or weaken democracy in the USA?

Further reading

Batchelor, A., 'US pressure groups: a blight on democracy?' *Politics Review,* Vol. 19, No. 2, November 2009.

Dumbrell, J., 'Pressure groups and the US Congress', *Politics Review,* Vol. 17, No. 4, April 2008.

Hefferman, R., 'Pressure groups: do promotional groups strengthen democracy?' *Politics Review,* Vol. 22, No. 1, September 2012.

Chapter 5

Congress

The three branches of the US federal government are Congress, the presidency and the Supreme Court. Congress is the legislative branch of the federal government. Its home is in the building known as the Capitol, situated in the area of Washington known as Capitol Hill. The Capitol is a graceful domed building, the backdrop and the venue for many national occasions both joyful and sad. Presidential inaugurations occur on its west steps. The inside of the rotunda has witnessed the lying-in-state of many presidents, most notably that of President Kennedy following his assassination in November 1963.

Principally, Congress is the place where America's laws are made. It is where the 535 members of Congress work, 100 of them in the Senate, 435 of them in the House of Representatives. Their work is conducted both on the floor of the two great chambers and in the numerous committee rooms and offices that are to be found in the buildings adjacent to the Capitol.

The work of Congress can appear slow. Often it seems highly unproductive. Sometimes it is characterised by apparent gridlock. However, the Founding Fathers wanted a federal government characterised by 'limited government' and by 'checks and balances'. It was not meant to resemble the British Parliament, where a government pushes through its policy programme almost at will. The casual observer, therefore, must not be too quick to criticise Congress for what might appear to be inaction. Congress has a built-in negative bias — it was intended.

The Capitol, east facade

Key questions answered in this chapter

➤ What is the structure of Congress?

➤ What is the make-up of Congress?

➤ What powers does it possess?

➤ How do the House of Representatives and the Senate compare in terms of power and prestige?

➤ What leadership exists in Congress?

➤ How important are congressional committees?

➤ How are laws made?

➤ What determines the way members of Congress vote?

➤ To what extent and why has partisanship increased in Congress?

➤ How effective is Congress's oversight of the executive branch?

➤ What is the public view of Congress?

Links to follow up

There are many possibilities for following up your study of Congress through the internet. The place to start would be the websites of the two houses of Congress — **www.house.gov** and **www.senate.gov**. These sites have information on such things as members, the leadership, committees, legislation and votes. The sites are easy to navigate and it is possible to find out about, for example, specific members of Congress, the work currently going on in committee or how members vote. There is also the Library of Congress THOMAS website — **http://thomas.loc.gov** — which provides legislative information.

You might be interested to watch the House or Senate in session and this can be done online at **www.c-span.org**. There is live coverage of the House on C-SPAN and live coverage of the Senate on C-SPAN2. C-SPAN 3 covers committee hearings as well as other programming.

Another extraordinarily good resource on Congress is **http://congress.indiana.edu/** which is sponsored by Indiana University and hosted by former Representative Lee Hamilton. One of its most innovative features is its interactive learning modules on such topics as how a member decides to vote, public criticisms of Congress, and the legislative process.

Finally, the highly respected Washington-based journal Congressional Quarterly has a free website called Roll Call at **www.rollcall.com/politics/**

The structure of Congress

Congress is bicameral: it is made up of two houses — the House of Representatives and the Senate. This arrangement for the legislative branch of government was one of the compromises devised by the Founding Fathers at the Philadelphia Convention. Some delegates to the convention had wanted the states to be equally represented in the legislature, while others had wanted representation to be proportional to population. The compromise was to have a two-chamber structure. In the lower house (the House of Representatives) the states would be represented proportionally to their population, but in the upper house (the Senate) the states would be represented equally. This kept both the states with large populations and those with small populations content.

Another compromise was made. Some delegates wanted to see the legislature directly elected by the people, while others thought the legislators should be indirectly elected. The Founding Fathers decided that the House of Representatives would be directly elected but the Senate would be indirectly elected — appointed by the state legislatures. This arrangement for the Senate continued until 1914 when, as a result of the 17th Amendment, the first direct elections for the Senate were held.

Today, the House of Representatives is made up of 435 members. Each state has a certain number of members proportional to its population. The number of representatives for each state is reapportioned after each 10-yearly census, which is held in the zero-numbered years (e.g. 2000, 2010, 2020). Some states gain House seats, while others lose them. For example, following the 2010 census, the Texas House delegation rose from 32 to 36, while New York's fell from 29 to 27 and Ohio's fell from 18 to 16. Except in states that have just one representative, each member represents a sub-division of the state known as a congressional district.

With 50 states in the Union and each state having two senators, there are today 100 members of the Senate.

Membership of Congress

The Constitution lays down certain qualifications to become a member of either the House or the Senate, but what does Congress look like in terms of gender, race, age, occupation and religion? How representative is it?

Women have been persistently under-represented in Congress. In 1992, the Democrats tried to focus on this issue and declared 1992 'the Year of the Woman'. The title might have struck some as contrived, but the effect was dramatic, virtually doubling the number of women in Congress in just one election. Gains in the last two decades have been rather more modest, as Table 5.1 shows. The majority of the women in both houses are Democrats — the party that tends to attract the female vote. Following the 2012 elections there were a record number of women in both houses at the start of the 113th Congress: 78 in the House and 20 in the Senate (see Table 5.1). But this means that women still make up only 18% of the House and 20% of the Senate, which, needless to say, is hardly representative of American society as a whole. In this sense, Congress certainly does not 'look like America'.

Of the 78 women elected to the House in 2012, 58 were Democrats and only 20 Republicans. In the Senate, of the 20 women, 16 were Democrats, just four Republicans. The 110th Congress (2007–08) was notable for the fact that with the Democrats regaining control of Congress for the first time in 12 years, a number of women members were elected to leadership positions, most notably in the House of Representatives which elected its first woman speaker, Nancy Pelosi of California. The House Rules Committee also had its first woman chair, Louise Slaughter of New York. In the Senate, both the standing committee on Environment and Public Works and the standing committee on Rules and Administration were chaired by women — respectively Barbara Boxer and Dianne Feinstein, both of California. But with the Republicans back in control of the House of Representatives, all standing committee chairmanships have reverted to male occupants whilst in the Senate, still under Democrat control in January 2013, six standing committees had women in the chair — Agriculture (Debbie Stabenow), Appropriations (Barbara Mikulski), Budget (Patty Murray), Environment (Barbara Boxer), Rules and Administration (Dianne Feinstein) and Small Business (Mary Landrieu).

Table 5.1 Women in the House and Senate, 1979–2013

Year	Women in House	Women in Senate
1979–80	16	0
1981–82	19	1
1983–84	21	2
1985–86	22	2
1987–88	23	2
1989–90	25	2
1991–92	28	2
1993–94	47	7
1995–96	48	8
1997–98	51	9
1999–2000	56	9
2001–02	59	14
2003–04	59	14
2005–06	64	14
2007–08	71	16
2009–10	75	17
2011–12	72	17
2013–14	78	20

One of the problems in trying to increase the representation of women in Congress is that women are also under-represented in the pool of recruitment from which members of Congress are commonly drawn, namely state legislatures. Following the 2012 elections, only 24% of state legislators were women, higher than in the US Congress but significantly below the figure in the population at large. In only eight states do women make up more than 30% of state legislators — Colorado at 42% having the highest proportion of women. But there are 16 states — ten of them in the South — in which women make up less than 20% of state legislators. In Louisiana in 2013, a mere 11% of state legislators were women.

Representation by race is much better in the House of Representatives than in the Senate because the federal courts have allowed states to draw congressional district boundaries to create districts that are likely to return a Representative from an ethnic minority group. These so-called 'majority-minority districts' are often geographically distorted as they attempt to group together sometimes scattered pockets of minority voters. Figure 5.1 shows North Carolina's 12th Congressional District, which links small towns scattered for 100 miles along

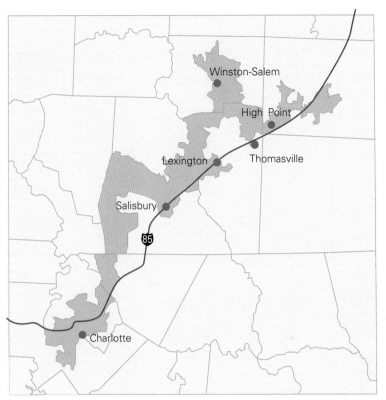

Figure 5.1 North Carolina's 12th Congressional District (shaded area)

Interstate 85. The district is currently represented by African-American Democrat Melvin Watt. The redrawing of district boundaries following the 1990 census clearly boosted African-American representation in the House, as Table 5.2 shows. By 2013, all the African-American representatives were Democrats. Between 2005 and 2008, Barack Obama of Illinois was the only African-American senator. After he had resigned following his election to the presidency, another African-American, Roland Burris, was appointed to complete the remaining 2 years of Obama's 6-year term, but he did not seek election in his own right when the term expired in 2010, leaving the Senate with no African-American members in January 2011. However, following the resignation of South Carolina Republican Jim DeMint in December 2012, Governor Nikki Haley appointed African-American congressman Tim Scott to fill the vacancy until a special election in November 2014.

Again, as with women, there is an issue about the low levels of representation of African-Americans in state legislatures — the main pool of recruitment for Congress. In 2008, in only 16 states did African-Americans make up more than 10% of the state legislature. The states with the highest percentages of African-American state legislators are Mississippi, Alabama and Georgia.

Table 5.2 African-Americans in the House and Senate, 1979–2013

Year	African-Americans in House	African-Americans in Senate
1979–80	16	0
1981–82	17	0
1983–84	21	0
1985–86	20	0
1987–88	23	0
1989–90	24	0
1991–92	25	0
1993–94	38	1
1995–96	38	1
1997–98	38	1
1999–2000	35	0
2001–02	36	0
2003–04	38	0
2005–06	41	1
2007–08	40	1
2009–10	39	1
2011–12	42	0
2013–	41	1

Table 5.3 Hispanic-Americans in the House and Senate, 1979–2013

Year	Hispanic-Americans in House	Hispanic-Americans in Senate
1979–80	6	0
1981–82	7	0
1983–84	10	0
1985–86	10	0
1987–88	10	0
1989–90	9	0
1991–92	9	0
1993–94	18	0
1995–96	18	0
1997–98	18	0
1999–2000	19	0
2001–02	18	0
2003–04	22	0
2005–06	24	2
2007–08	23	3
2009–10	23	2
2011–12	24	2
2013–	31	3

Table 5.3 shows the Hispanic-American representation in Congress over the past three decades or so. Twenty-eight of the current 31 Hispanic House members come from the nine states shown in Table 5.4 with California, Texas and Florida accounting for 20 of them. In the 113th Congress (2013–14), three states were represented in the Senate by a Hispanic-American — Florida (Republican Marco Rubio), New Jersey (Democrat Bob Menendez) and Texas (Republican Ted Cruz). These three states all have a Hispanic-American population above the 16.3% national average but Hispanics make up only 7% of the House membership and just 3% of the Senate.

One final point, which is covered later in this chapter, is the number of former members of the other house in each chamber. In 2013 there were no former senators in the House, but there were 52 ex-House members in the Senate. The reasons why House members seek election to the Senate have a lot to do with the powers of the respective houses. In 2012, 12 House members ran for the Senate — 6 Democrats and 6 Republicans. Six of them — 5 Democrats and 1 Republican — were successful (see Table 5.5).

Table 5.4 States with highest proportion of Hispanic-Americans, 2010 census

State	Percentage of Hispanic-Americans
New Mexico	46.3
California	37.6
Texas	37.6
Arizona	29.6
Nevada	26.5
Florida	22.5
Colorado	20.7
New Jersey	17.7
New York	17.6

Table 5.5 House members seeking election to the Senate, 2012

House member	Party	State	Elected/Defeated
Todd Akin	Republican	Missouri	Defeated
Tammy Baldwin	Democrat	Wisconsin	Elected
Rick Berg	Republican	North Dakota	Defeated
Shelley Berkley	Democrat	Nevada	Defeated
Joe Donnelly	Democrat	Indiana	Elected
Jeff Flake	Republican	Arizona	Elected
Martin Heinrich	Democrat	New Mexico	Elected
Mazie Hirono	Democrat	Hawaii	Elected
Connie Mack	Republican	Florida	Defeated
Chris Murphy	Democrat	Connecticut	Elected
Denny Rehberg	Republican	Montana	Defeated
Bob Turner	Republican	New York	Defeated

Powers of Congress

The powers of Congress are laid down in Article I Section 8 of the Constitution. Some of the powers are explicit: for example, Congress is given the power 'to coin money'. Other powers are vague: for example, Congress is given the power 'to provide for the common defence and general welfare of the United States'. Another way of categorising the powers of Congress is as exclusive and concurrent powers: some powers are exclusive to one house while other powers are concurrent to both houses (see Table 5.6).

Table 5.6 Powers of Congress

Nature of powers	House of Representatives	Senate
Exclusive powers	Initiate money bills Impeachment Elect president if Electoral College is deadlocked	Confirm appointments Ratify treaties Try cases of impeachment Elect vice-president if Electoral College is deadlocked
Concurrent powers	Pass legislation Override the president's veto Initiate constitutional amendments Declare war Confirm a newly appointed vice-president	

Exclusive powers of the House

The House of Representatives has three exclusive powers. First, it is given the power to initiate money bills. This is because at the beginning of the nation's history only the House was directly elected and the Founding Fathers believed that the people's directly elected representatives should have the first say in spending the people's money. Second, perhaps the House's most significant exclusive power is the power of impeachment. The House can impeach — that is, formally accuse — any member of the executive and judicial branches of the federal government. It has used this power 19 times since 1789, the most recent being federal judge Thomas Porteous in 2010. In 1998, the House impeached President Clinton. Third, if the Electoral College is deadlocked — if no candidate wins an absolute majority of Electoral College votes — then the House is charged with electing the president. The power has been used only twice — in 1800 and 1824.

Exclusive powers of the Senate

The Senate's exclusive powers are seen as more prestigious than those of the House. Two of them, in particular, give the Senate significantly more power than the House. First, the Senate alone has the power to confirm — by a simple majority — many appointments made by the president. These include all the president's appointments to the federal judiciary and a great many — though not all — of the appointments to the executive branch. As a result, whenever the president wishes to fill a vacancy in the trial, appeal or Supreme courts of the federal government, the Senate must give its consent. Similarly, an incoming president must have many of his new appointments to the executive approved by the Senate, including all the heads of the executive departments who make up the president's cabinet. Whenever a vacancy occurs, the president must seek the Senate's approval for replacement appointments. In 2013, when Secretary of State Hillary Clinton resigned, President Obama had to gain the approval of the Senate to appoint John Kerry to replace her. The Senate voted 94–3 to confirm him. An informal agreement called 'senatorial courtesy' allows a president to confer with any senator of his party from a particular state before he makes a nomination to fill a vacancy for a federal office affecting that state. This is important when it comes to appointments that the president makes to the federal trial courts.

The second significant exclusive power of the Senate is its power to ratify — by a two-thirds majority — all treaties negotiated by the president. This means that the president needs to keep the Senate fully informed throughout treaty negotiations, to avoid concluding treaties that the Senate is unlikely to ratify. In December 2010, the Senate voted by 71 votes to 26 to ratify the new Strategic Arms Reduction Treaty (START) negotiated by President Obama with his Russian counterpart Dmitry Medvedev.

Once the House has impeached someone, the Senate has the power to try that case of impeachment. This Senate trial is to determine whether the person is guilty of the offence of which they have been accused by the House. If they are found guilty by a two-thirds majority, the person is removed from office. In December 2010, Judge Thomas Porteous was found guilty by the Senate on four counts, but the Senate acquitted President Clinton in 1999.

If the Electoral College is deadlocked, the Senate must elect the vice-president.

Concurrent powers of the House and Senate

Despite the significance of the Senate's exclusive powers, it is important to remember that in many ways the two houses of Congress are co-equal, for they have five concurrent powers. First, and most importantly, the two houses are co-equal in the passage of legislation. All bills must pass through all stages in both houses; neither house can override the wishes of the other. Both must agree the same version of the bill before that bill can be sent to the president for his signature. Second, both houses must vote — by two-thirds majorities — to override the president's veto of a bill. In 2007, the Congress overrode President Bush's veto of the Water Resources Development Bill. The vote in the House was 381–40, which was 100 votes over the 281 required for a two-thirds majority. The vote in the Senate was 81–12, which was 19 votes over the 62 votes required. Third, the two houses are co-equal when it comes to initiating constitutional amendments. A constitutional amendment must be approved by a two-thirds majority in both houses before it can be sent to the states for their ratification. Fourth, both houses must concur in a declaration of war. This has occurred on only five occasions — the last one being 1941, when America declared war on Japan in the Second World War. Finally, the 25th Amendment (1967) gave to both houses the power to confirm a newly appointed vice-president. This has occurred twice — in 1973 (Gerald Ford) and 1974 (Nelson Rockefeller).

The relative importance and prestige of the House and the Senate

It is often suggested that the Senate is more powerful and prestigious than the House. We have already seen that House members often seek election to the Senate and that in 2013 there were 52 former House members in the Senate but no ex-senators in the House of Representatives. There are some significant reasons why this may be the case.

While House members represent only a congressional district, senators represent the entire state. For example, Representative Adam Schiff represents only the 28th Congressional District of California, but Senator Dianne Feinstein represents the entire state of California. She also enjoys a 6-year term in the Senate, whereas Congressman Schiff has only a 2-year term in the House. Senator Feinstein is one of only 100 in the Senate whereas Congressman Schiff is one of 435 in the House. She is likely to get more of the action. Because of the smaller size of the Senate, a senator is likely to gain a leadership position more quickly than a member of the House. Indeed Senator Feinstein was elected to chair the Senate's Rules and Administration Committee in January 2013. Congressman Schiff, meanwhile, was only 14th in the seniority rank amongst the 24 Democrats serving on the House Appropriations Committee of which he is a member. It will be a long time before he gets to a committee chairmanship in the House.

The Senate is seen as a launching pad for a presidential campaign. Presidents Harry Truman, John Kennedy, Lyndon Johnson, Richard Nixon and Barack Obama were all former members of the Senate. Six senators launched campaigns for the 2008 presidential race: Democrats Barack Obama, Hillary Clinton, Christopher Dodd and Joe Biden as well as Republicans John McCain and Sam Brownback. There were also two former senators running for the presidency in 2008: Democrat John Edwards and Republican Fred Thompson. And both parties ended up nominating an incumbent senator as their presidential candidate, which was the first time this had occurred. The Senate is also seen as a recruitment pool for vice-presidential candidates. Walter Mondale, Dan Quayle, Al Gore and Joe Biden — four of the last six vice-presidents — were either former or serving members of the Senate when elected vice-president. Indeed, the Democrats have nominated a senator or former senator as their vice-presidential candidate in every election since 1944, except for 1984 — that is, in 15 out of the last 16 elections.

Is the Senate more prestigious than the House? DEBATE

Yes, because:

- ➤ Senators represent the entire state
- ➤ Senators serve longer terms
- ➤ Senators are one of only 100
- ➤ Senators are more likely to chair a committee or sub-committee or hold some leadership position
- ➤ Senators enjoy greater name recognition state-wide and even nationwide
- ➤ the Senate is seen as a recruiting pool for presidential and vice-presidential candidates
- ➤ Senators enjoy significant exclusive powers
- ➤ House members frequently seek election to the Senate

No, because:

- ➤ both houses have equal power in the passage of legislation — Congress's key function
- ➤ both houses must approve the initiation of constitutional amendments
- ➤ members of both houses receive equal salaries

Senators enjoy significant exclusive powers — especially those concerned with the confirmation of appointments and the ratification of treaties.

However, when it comes to the passage of legislation, senators and representatives enjoy equal powers. The same goes for those other concurrent powers. Finally, it is worth noting that members of both houses receive the same salary — in January 2012, $174,000. Under a formula included in the Ethics Reform Act (1989), members of both houses can expect an annual 2.8% increase in their salaries but this was denied in 2010, 2011 and 2012.

Leadership in Congress

The main leadership posts in Congress are the Speaker of the House of Representatives, the majority and minority leaders and the standing committee chairs in both houses.

The House Speaker

The House Speaker is elected by the entire House membership at the start of each Congress: that is, every 2 years. With this method of election, it is likely that the person chosen will be the nominee of the majority party in the House at the time. The Constitution does not require the Speaker to be a serving member of the House, although all Speakers have been.

The Speaker is a potentially powerful figure in the House and has a number of specific powers:

➢ to act as the presiding officer of the House
➢ to interpret and enforce the rules of the House and decide on points of order
➢ to refer bills to standing committees
➢ to appoint select committee and conference committee chairs
➢ to appoint the majority party members of the House Rules Committee

According to the Constitution, the Speaker is next in line to the presidency after the vice-president. The passage of the 25th Amendment made this less significant, as it required the office of the vice-presidency to be filled if a vacancy should occur.

The Speaker has the power to exercise influence on the flow of legislation through the House, as well as to award committee assignments to majority party members and select House standing committee chairs. When the president and the majority of Congress are of different parties — which these days they often are — the Speaker may become a kind of 'leader of the opposition' figure, acting as spokesperson for the party not currently controlling the White House. This was the role that was played by Democrat Speaker Nancy Pelosi during the last 2 years of Republican President George W. Bush's second term and by Republican John Boehner (pronounced Bay-ner) during both the last 2 years of President Obama's first term and the opening years (at least) of his second.

Three successive speakers between 1989 and 1998 left office under unusual circumstances. Democrat Speaker Jim Wright was forced to resign in June 1989 after the House Ethics Committee announced it would charge him with 69 violations of the

House's ethics rules. His successor was another Democrat, Tom Foley. In 1994, Foley became the first Speaker to be defeated in an election since 1862 when he lost his seat in that year's mid-term elections to a Republican with no previous experience of elective office. His successor was Newt Gingrich, who himself resigned in 1998 after his party's poor showing in that year's elections. Wright and Gingrich were highly partisan figures — that was part of their problem.

In January 2007, with the Democrats in the majority in the House, the first woman Speaker was elected — Nancy Pelosi of California. She served 4 years until the Republicans regained control of the House of Representatives in January 2011, when she was succeeded by John Boehner. Republicans had criticised Speaker Pelosi for being, in their view, far too autocratic and dictatorial. But in many ways she was no different in her approach to the job than her immediate Republican predecessors Dennis Hastert and Newt Gingrich. According to a recent *National Journal* article by Major Garrett ('Being Boehner', 4 June 2011), 'Pelosi, Hastert and Gingrich all consolidated power in leadership circles.' Decisions were mostly arrived at by the Speaker plus a small coterie of the party's top leadership. They gained significant influence over who would chair the House standing committees and then largely controlled the chairmen once they were in post. Seniority — the traditional way of choosing committee chairmen — was largely ignored. The folk who ended up as committee chairs were 'Friends of Nancy'. Under these speakers, legislation tended to pass with votes drawn only from their own party caucus — Pelosi from House Democrats, Hastert and Gingrich from House Republicans. According to Garrett, 'they almost never sought bipartisan support on big-ticket bills'. Amendments to legislation tabled by the other party were routinely blocked, which caused deep animosity amongst Democrats between 1995 and 2006 and then amongst Republicans between 2007 and 2010. This way of doing business, according to Garrett, 'gave the House an "us-versus-them" edge that intensified partisan divisions and marginalised the [standing] committees'.

The model upon which Boehner has based his speakership is not that of his Republican predecessors but of Democrat Sam Rayburn of Texas, who presided over the House as Speaker from 1940 to 1961, except for two 2-year periods (1947–48 and 1953–54) when the Republicans were in the majority. Boehner, like Rayburn, has re-empowered the committees and allowed more opposition-sponsored amendments to reach the House floor. He looks for opportunities for bipartisan passage of bills. Many Democrats call the changes 'window dressing'. Some Republicans complain that the process now takes longer and the end result is less predictable, and that Boehner is too prone to back off from fights with President Obama. But in the end Speaker Boehner will be judged on results.

Majority and minority leaders

In both the House and Senate, there is a majority and minority leader. Their respective party groups in each house elect them every 2 years, at the start of each Congress. In both houses, the majority and minority leaders:

➤ act as day-to-day 'directors of operations' on the floor of their respective houses
➤ hold press briefings to talk about their party's policy agenda
➤ act as liaison between the House/Senate and the White House

The Senate majority leader plays a key role in bringing bills for debate to the Senate floor. The House majority leader plays a 'number two' role to the Speaker. The importance of these posts can be gauged by the fact that they can be used as a launching pad for a presidential candidate. Democrat Lyndon Johnson (President: 1963–69) was Senate majority leader from 1955 to 1961. Republican Bob Dole was Senate majority leader when he launched his presidential bid in 1996. Democrat Dick Gephardt had served 8 years (1995–2003) as House minority leader before launching his unsuccessful bid for the 2004 presidential nomination.

In the Senate there is also the seniority post of President Pro Tempore, which is filled by the member of the majority party with the longest continuous service in the chamber. Following the death of Hawaii's Democratic senator Daniel Inouye in December 2012, this post was filled by the senior senator from Vermont, Democrat Patrick Leahy, who was first elected to the Senate in 1974. The Constitution puts him third in line to the presidency, after the vice-president and the Speaker of the House. Other significant leadership posts are connected with the work of the congressional committees.

Congressional committees

Writing in 1885, Woodrow Wilson — 28 years later to become president — said this about Congress:

> The House sits, not for serious discussion, but to sanction the conclusions of its committees as rapidly as possible. It legislates in its committee rooms; not by the determination of majorities, but by the specially-commissioned minorities [the committees]; so that it is not far from the truth to say that Congress in session is Congress on public exhibition, while Congress in its committee rooms is Congress at work.

The most important types of congressional committee are: standing committees, the House Rules Committee, conference committees and select committees. The **committee system** of Congress is both extensive and highly important.

Key concept

➤ **Committee system.** The committee system of Congress is made up of many different types of committee, which perform legislative and investigatory functions. The most important type of committee is the standing committees which are policy specialists. The fact that it is only in the committee rooms that members of the executive branch can be directly questioned gives the committee system an added importance.

Standing committees

Standing committees exist in both houses of Congress. They are permanent, policy-specialist committees (see Table 5.7). Most standing committees are divided into sub-committees, examples of which are shown in Table 5.8. A typical Senate standing committee comprises around 18 members, while a typical House standing committee is made up of around 30–40 members. The party balance in each standing committee is in the same proportion as that which exists within the chamber as a whole. At the beginning of the 113th Congress (January 2013), the Democrats were the majority party in the Senate and the Republicans were the majority in the House. Thus, each Senate standing committee had a Democratic majority and each House standing committee had a Republican majority.

House and Senate members seek assignments on committees that are closest to the interests of their district or state. For example, Tom Harkin of Iowa and Max Baucus of Montana are both members of the Senate Agriculture Committee. Re-elected members are routinely reappointed to their former committees unless they have asked for a new assignment. Some committees — for example, Judiciary, Armed Services and Appropriations — are more prestigious than others. New members might have to wait some years to get assigned to these more sought-after committees.

Standing committees have two functions in both the House and the Senate, and a third function in the Senate only. The first common function — and the most important one — is to conduct the committee stage of bills in the legislative process. This involves holding 'hearings' on the bill at which 'witnesses' appear. These witnesses might be:

➤ other members of Congress
➤ members from the relevant executive departments or agencies, or even from the White House
➤ representatives from interest groups or professional bodies likely to be affected
➤ ordinary members of the public

Witnesses make prepared statements in front of the committee and are then subjected to questioning from committee members. The length of such hearings is determined largely by the length of the bill itself and the level of controversy that it engenders. Short, non-controversial bills attract short hearings lasting no more than a few hours. But long, controversial bills are given hearings that might last — on and off — for weeks or even months. At the conclusion of these hearings, a vote is taken by the committee on whether or not to pass the bill on to its second reading — the next stage in the legislative process.

The second common function of standing committees in both houses is to conduct investigations within the committee's policy area. Such investigations are often launched into perceived problems, as shown by examples given in Table 5.9. They attempt to answer such questions as 'Why did this happen?', 'Is current legislation proving effective?' and 'Is new legislation required?' Investigations might be held into crises or perceived policy failures. The format is much the same as for legislative hearings, with witnesses being summoned and questions asked. We shall consider this function in more detail when we study Congress's oversight function of the executive branch of government.

Table 5.7 Congressional standing committees

Senate standing committee	Chair
Agriculture, Nutrition and Forestry	Debbie Stabenow (Michigan)
Appropriations	Barbara Mikulski (Maryland)
Armed Services	Carl Levin (Michigan)
Banking, Housing and Urban Affairs	Tim Johnson (South Dakota)
Budget	Patty Murray (Washington)
Commerce, Science and Transportation	John Rockefeller (West Virginia)
Energy and Natural Resources	Ron Wyden (Oregon)
Environment and Public Works	Barbara Boxer (California)
Finance	Max Baucus (Montana)
Foreign Relations	Robert Menendez (New Jersey)
Health, Education, Labor and Pensions	Tom Harkin (Iowa)
Homeland Security and Governmental Affairs	Tom Carper (Delaware)
Judiciary	Patrick Leahy (Vermont)
Rules and Administration	Dianne Feinstein (California)
Small Business and Entrepreneurship	Mary Landrieu (Louisiana)
Veterans' Affairs	Bernie Sanders (Vermont)
House of Representatives standing committee	**Chair**
Agriculture	Frank Lucas (Oklahoma)
Appropriations	Hal Rogers (Kentucky)
Armed Services	Howard 'Buck' McKeon (California)
Budget	Paul Ryan (Wisconsin)
Education and the Workforce	John Kline (Minnesota)
Energy and Commerce	Fred Upton (Michigan)
Financial Services	Jeb Hensarling (Texas)
Foreign Affairs	Ed Royce (California)
Homeland Security	Mike McCaul (Texas)
Judiciary	Bob Goodlatte (Virginia)
Natural Resources	Doc Hastings (Washington)
Oversight and Government Reform	Darrell Issa (California)
Rules	Pete Sessions (Texas)
Science, Space and Technology	Lamar Smith (Texas)
Small Business	Sam Graves (Missouri)
Transportation and Infrastructure	Bill Shuster (Pennsylvania)
Veterans' Affairs	Jeff Miller (Florida)
Ways and Means	Dave Camp (Michigan)

Table 5.8 Examples of congressional sub-committees

Committee	Sub-committees
House Science, Space and Technology	Energy and Environment Investigations and Oversight Research and Science Education Space and Aeronautics Technology and Innovation
House Transportation and Infrastructure	Aviation Coast Guard and Maritime Transportation Economic Development, Public Buildings and Emergency Management Highways and Transit Railroads, Pipelines and Hazardous Materials Water Resources and Environment

Table 5.9 Examples of standing committee investigations during 2012

Committee	Investigation
House Homeland Security Committee	Assessing dangerous threats to our nation's borders
House Armed Services Committee	Corruption in the Afghan national security forces
Senate Judiciary Committee	The rise of Super PACs
Senate Foreign Relations Committee	Terrorist attack on the US embassy in Benghazi
Senate Commerce, Science and Transportation Committee	Impact of Hurricane Sandy on transportation systems in New York and New Jersey

Table 5.10 Senate standing committee and floor votes on various presidential nominees

Nominee	Post	President	Committee vote	Senate floor vote
Robert Bork	Supreme Court	Ronald Reagan	5–9	Rejected 42–58
John Tower	Defense Secretary	George H. W. Bush	9–11	Rejected 47–53
Clarence Thomas	Supreme Court	George H. W. Bush	7–7	Confirmed 52–48
Ruth Bader Ginsburg	Supreme Court	Bill Clinton	18–0	Confirmed 96–3
Michael Mukasey	Attorney General	George W. Bush	11–8	Confirmed 50–43
John Kerry	Secretary of State	Barack Obama	Unanimous	Confirmed 94–3

In the Senate, standing committees have a third function: to begin the confirmation process of numerous presidential appointments. The two committees that are particularly busy in this regard are the Senate's Judiciary and Foreign Relations committees. The former must hold hearings on all the federal judicial appointments made by the president; the latter holds hearings on all ambassadorial appointments. Other Senate standing committees oversee appointments made within their particular policy areas. Hearings are held at which supporters, and possibly critics, of the nominee are heard from before a vote is taken. The vote is not decisive — only recommendatory — but it is a very important clue to the likely outcome of the nomination. Because these committees are regarded as the policy specialists in their particular areas, their recommendations are rarely overturned. An overwhelming — possibly unanimous — 'yes' vote by the committee indicates that the nominee will receive easy passage on the floor of the Senate, but a close vote will indicate problems ahead. Should the majority of a committee vote 'no', the nomination is certain to be defeated, if it even gets to the Senate floor (see Table 5.10).

The standing committees of Congress have considerable power to help the parent chambers manage their huge workloads, but there are limits to their power. As congressional scholar Burdett A. Loomis (2004) points out:

> Committees are powerful but not all-powerful: they cannot legislate; they cannot require the executive to comply with their wishes; they cannot implement policies once they have been approved.

House Rules Committee

The House Rules Committee is one of the standing committees of the House of Representatives, but it performs a different function from the others. It is responsible for prioritising bills coming from the committee stage on to the House floor for their second readings. Because there is a huge queue of bills waiting for a second reading on the House floor, the Rules Committee has a vital legislative

The chamber of the House of Representatives

role to play. Its name comes from the 'rule' it gives to a bill, setting out the rules of debate by stating, for example, whether any amendments can be made to the bill at this stage. Most bills must go through the House Rules Committee if they are to reach final passage.

The Rules Committee is unusual in that its membership is much smaller and more skewed to the majority party than other standing committees. In 2013, the House Rules Committee had just 13 members — nine Republicans and only four Democrats — chaired by Pete Sessions of Texas. Chair of the House Rules Committee is considered one of the most influential posts in Congress.

Conference committees

Conference committees are required because of two important characteristics of the legislative process in Congress. First, both houses have equal power. Second, bills pass through both houses concurrently, rather than consecutively. As a consequence, there are two different versions of the same bill — a House version and a Senate version. By the

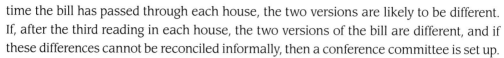

time the bill has passed through each house, the two versions are likely to be different. If, after the third reading in each house, the two versions of the bill are different, and if these differences cannot be reconciled informally, then a conference committee is set up.

All conference committees are ad hoc — set up to consider only one particular bill. The members, known as 'conferees', are drawn from both houses. Their sole function is to reconcile the differences between the House and Senate versions of the same bill. Once a conference committee has come up with an agreed version of the bill, this version must be agreed to by a vote on the floor of each house. If agreement is not forthcoming, the same conference committee may be reconvened. Another compromise will be drawn up and sent to the floors of both houses. Should that be unacceptable to one or both chambers, the bill will be sent back to the *standing* committees that first considered it.

Conference committees are important because they are likely to draw up what will become the final version of the bill. Their power is checked, however, by the ability of the House and Senate to refuse to sign up to their compromise version. But, as we shall see when we consider the legislative process in detail, conference committees are used much less frequently nowadays. The House and Senate leadership have found other ways to resolve differences in the versions of bills passed by their respective chambers.

Select committees

Select committees are sometimes known as 'special' or 'investigative' committees. Nearly all are ad hoc, set up to investigate a particular issue. But why are select committees needed when, as we have already seen, the standing committees have an investigative function? A select committee is set up when the investigation either: does not fall within the policy area of one standing committee; or is likely to be so time consuming that a standing committee would become tied up with it, thus preventing the standing committee from fulfilling its other functions.

In 2011, following the debt-ceiling crisis, a joint select committee on deficit reduction was set up. Made up of three members of each party from both chambers, the 12-member committee was meant to make a single, bipartisan proposal for deficit reduction for the next 10 years with a saving of at least $1.5 trillion, but the Democrats and Republicans on the committee failed to agree on a common plan.

Committee chairs

Those who chair standing committees are always drawn from the majority party in that house. Thus, in the 113th Congress (2013–14), all the Senate standing committees are chaired by Democrats and all the House standing committees by Republicans. The **seniority rule** states that the chair of the standing committee will be the member of the majority party with the longest continuous service on that committee. The same applies for what are called the 'ranking minority members' of each committee. Referred to by its critics as the 'senility rule', it has been modified in recent years. From the 1970s, both parties gradually introduced secret ballots for committee chairs and ranking minority members. However, it is still usually the member with the longest continuous committee service who is elected.

Key term

➤ **Seniority rule.** A rule stating that the chair of a congressional standing committee will be the member of the majority party with the longest continuous service on that committee.

Further reforms came in the 1990s, when the Republicans placed a 6-year term limit on committee and sub-committee chairs. This is the reason why in January 2013, seven of the 18 House standing committees had to select new Republican chairs. These term limits were introduced partly as a concession to the early 1990s term limit movement and partly because Republicans had for many years been critical of Democrat committee chairs who had held their posts unchallenged, in some cases, for decades. Congressman Jamie Whitten (D — Mississippi) chaired the Appropriations sub-committee on Agriculture for 43 years. Critics of committee chair term limits say that the institutional memory of the committees is lost and that power is ceded to unelected committee staff upon whom new and inexperienced chairs have to rely more heavily.

Those who chair standing committees have a number of important powers. They:
➤ control the committee's agenda
➤ decide when the committee will meet
➤ control the committee's budget
➤ influence the membership, meetings and hearings of sub-committees
➤ supervise a sizeable committee staff
➤ serve as spokesperson on the committee's policy area within Congress, to the White House and in the media
➤ make requests to the House Rules Committee (in the House) and the party leadership (in the Senate) for scheduling of legislation on the House floor
➤ report legislation to the floor of their respective chamber on behalf of the full committee

Chairing a congressional committee brings power, perks and publicity. For many, this is the pinnacle of their congressional career.

The legislative process

The legislative process in Congress is best thought of in seven stages:
1 First reading
2 Committee stage
3 Timetabling
4 Second reading

5 Third reading

6 Conference committee (*optional*)

7 Presidential action

To be successful, all bills must pass through stages 1–5 and 7. Stage 6 — the conference committee — may be avoided if both houses pass the bill in the same form or if any differences can be resolved amicably. To be successful, a bill must pass through all these stages during a Congress — that is, two years. So, for example, the 113th Congress runs from January 2013 until December 2014. Any bills not completed in one Congress must start the process again at the beginning of the next Congress.

First reading

The first reading — or introduction — is a pure formality. There is no debate and no vote. In the House, the first reading involves nothing more than placing a copy of the bill in a 'hopper' — a tray — on the clerk's desk. In the Senate, the first reading involves reading out the title of the bill on the Senate floor. Bills are then numbered, printed, circulated and sent on to the appropriate standing committee.

The most important fact to comprehend at this stage is the sheer volume of legislation that is introduced in Congress. As Table 5.11 shows, in a typical Congress, anything between 10,000 and over 14,000 bills are introduced. Of these, only around 2–4% actually make it into law. The process explains largely why this percentage is so small. The 112th Congress (2011–12) was the least productive in terms of legislation of any recent Congress, with only 238 of the 10,417 bills introduced becoming law.

Committee stage

This is the most important stage. Far more bills fail here than at any other stage. Hundreds of bills are referred to each of the standing committees in both chambers in each Congress. This is far more than they can handle. A significant number are pigeon-holed — put to one side, with no action taken on them at all, no hearings and no vote. It is those with a good deal of support — from members of Congress, the White House, the administration or interest groups, for example — that are given hearings. The hearings may be either in the full committee or in the relevant sub-committee.

There are other reasons why this stage is so important. The committee stage comes very early in the legislative process — *before* the second reading. The full House and Senate have not yet debated the bill. The standing committee members are regarded as

Table 5.11 Number of bills introduced and laws enacted, 2007–12

	110th Congress 2007–08	111th Congress 2009–10	112th Congress 2011–12
Bills introduced	14,042	10,621	10,417
Laws enacted	460 (3.3%)	383 (3.6%)	238 (2.3%)

Source: *Congressional Quarterly*

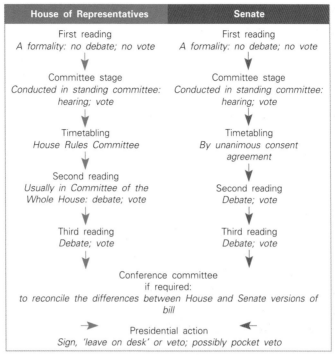

House of Representatives	Senate
First reading *A formality: no debate; no vote*	First reading *A formality: no debate; no vote*
Committee stage *Conducted in standing committee: hearing; vote*	Committee stage *Conducted in standing committee: hearing; vote*
Timetabling *House Rules Committee*	Timetabling *By unanimous consent agreement*
Second reading *Usually in Committee of the Whole House: debate; vote*	Second reading *Debate; vote*
Third reading *Debate; vote*	Third reading *Debate; vote*

Conference committee
if required:
*to reconcile the differences between House and Senate versions of
bill*

Presidential action
Sign, 'leave on desk' or veto; possibly pocket veto

Figure 5.2 The legislative process in Congress

the policy specialists in their policy area and they have the full power of amendment — anything can be added to and anything removed from the bill at this stage. Professor Vile (1999) stated that 'it is difficult to exaggerate the importance of these [standing] committees, for they are the sieve through which all legislation is poured, and what comes out, and how it comes out, is largely in their hands'.

Once the hearings have been completed, the committee holds a mark-up session — making the changes it wishes — before reporting out the bill, effectively sending it on to its next stage. The report written by the committee does four things: states the main aims of the bill; reviews the amendments made by the committee; estimates the cost of implementation; recommends future action to be taken by the full chamber.

Timetabling

By the time Congress has been in session for a few months, a huge number of bills will be waiting to come to the floor of both chambers for their second reading. While there are dozens of committee and sub-committee rooms, there is only one floor in each house. Something of a legislative traffic jam develops, with bills queuing for their turn on the House and Senate floors. Each house has its own procedure for dealing with this potential problem.

The Senate deals with it through what are called 'unanimous consent agreements'. These are, in effect, agreements between the Senate majority and minority leaders on the order in which bills will be debated on the Senate floor.

The House of Representatives deals with it through the House Rules Committee. The 'prioritising' role of the House Rules Committee makes it a kind of legislative 'gatekeeper' or 'traffic cop' — allowing some bills through but holding others back. If the Rules Committee fails to give a rule to a popular bill, House members may resort to the discharge process. A discharge petition must be signed by an absolute majority of House members — 218. Once that demanding requirement has been fulfilled, the bill is 'discharged' from the Rules Committee and comes automatically to the House floor for debate. This process was used successfully in 2001–02 on the Bipartisan Campaign Reform Act.

Second reading

This is the first opportunity for the full chambers to debate the bill. In the House, most bills are debated at the second reading in the 'Committee of the Whole House', which permits rules of debate to be in force, allowing for as many members to take part as possible. In both houses, further amendments can usually be made. Votes are taken both on amendments and on the whole bill at the end of the debate. Simple majorities are required. Votes can be either by 'voice vote' or by 'recorded vote'. In the former, members merely call out 'aye' or 'no': this is used mostly for non-controversial bills. In a recorded vote, a record of each member's vote is made. In the House this is done electronically; in the Senate by a roll-call vote with the clerk alphabetically calling the roll of the 100 senators, currently from Mr Alexander (R — Tennessee) to Mr Wyden (D — Oregon). Both procedures take 15 minutes.

In the Senate, there is the possibility of a **filibuster** taking place. Stamina is more important than relevance in conducting a filibuster. Senators have been known to read out extracts from the Constitution, the Declaration of Independence, the Bible and even the telephone directory. In 1957, Strom Thurmond conducted a filibuster against a civil rights bill that lasted for over 24 hours. On 10 December 2010, independent senator Bernie Sanders of Vermont spoke on the Senate floor against a tax deal which President Obama was trying to work out with congressional Republicans. Sanders spoke from 10.25 in the morning until just before 7 o'clock that evening, a total of just over 8½ hours.

Sometimes a group of senators will get together to conduct a filibuster. This type of filibuster was in evidence in the Senate in July 2007 when a group of Republican senators got together to filibuster the 2008 Defense Appropriations Bill, which included the demand for President Bush to withdraw American troops from Iraq. The Democrats, who controlled the Senate at the time, were happy to play along with the tactic. Senate Majority Leader Harry Reid permitted an all-night session of the Senate on the night of 17 July which coincided with an anti-war rally outside the Capitol on the same evening. The Democrats hoped that the Republican-led filibuster would give maximum coverage to the policy differences between Democrats and Republicans over the Iraq war — a policy area in which Democrats had reason to believe their policy of scaling down the war was supported by the majority of Americans.

> **Key concept**
>
> ➤ **Filibuster.** A device by which an individual senator, or group of senators, can attempt to talk a bill to death by using delaying tactics. It derives from senators' right of unlimited debate. A three-fifths vote (i.e. 60 votes) is required to end a filibuster.

A filibuster can be ended by a procedure known as 'closure' (or 'cloture'). To be successful, a closure petition must be signed by 16 senators and then voted for by at least three-fifths (60) of the entire Senate. In 1988, Senator Robert Byrd (D — West Virginia) brought a record eight closure votes to try to stop a Republican filibuster of a campaign finance reform bill. All eight failed. Until the 1970s, filibusters and cloture motions were relatively unusual events. For example, in the 91st Congress (1969–70) only 7 cloture motions were presented with 6 of those being voted on. Thirty years later in the 104th Congress (1999–2000), there were 71 cloture motions presented with votes on 58 of them. But by the 110th Congress (2007–08) a record 139 cloture motions were presented with votes on 112. The figures fell only slightly in the next two congresses. As a result of this huge increase in filibusters, Senate Majority Leader Harry Reid and Minority Leader Mitch McConnell reached a deal in January 2013 to try to limit the use of filibusters but it is unlikely to have much significant effect.

Third reading

This is the final opportunity to debate the bill. If substantial amendments were made at the second reading and/or the final vote was close, then the third reading would be likely to occur some weeks or months later and require another substantial debate. If, however, few amendments were made at the second reading and/or the final vote showed a substantial majority in favour, then the third reading would follow on almost immediately after the second reading and be very brief. At the end of the third reading, a further vote is taken.

Conference committee

Time was when if a bill was passed in different forms by the two chambers, a conference committee would be set up to reconcile the differences. Even as recently as the 103rd Congress (1993–94), around one-third of bills that needed reconciling were reconciled in conference committees. But nowadays, conference committees are frequently avoided, with any differences being resolved essentially by the majority party leadership. In the 110th Congress (2007–08), only around one in ten bills that needed reconciling were reconciled in a conference committee.

The decline in the use of conference committees began soon after the Republicans took control of both houses of Congress in 1995. In place of the formalised, bicameral conference committees, the Republicans began to use a more ad hoc, leadership-driven approach whereby one chamber was simply asked to endorse the legislation passed

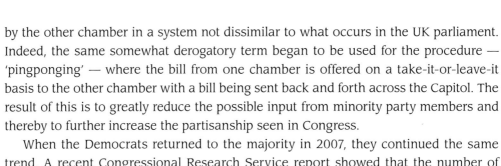

by the other chamber in a system not dissimilar to what occurs in the UK parliament. Indeed, the same somewhat derogatory term began to be used for the procedure — 'pingponging' — where the bill from one chamber is offered on a take-it-or-leave-it basis to the other chamber with a bill being sent back and forth across the Capitol. The result of this is to greatly reduce the possible input from minority party members and thereby to further increase the partisanship seen in Congress.

When the Democrats returned to the majority in 2007, they continued the same trend. A recent Congressional Research Service report showed that the number of conference committees convened declined from 62 in 1993–94, which produced 13% of the laws enacted by the 103rd Congress, to just 10 in 2007–08, yielding a mere 2% of the 110th Congress's legislative output. Many senior members of Congress decry the move away from conference committees. Democrat Kent Conrad of North Dakota, the Senate Budget Committee chair, went on record recently as stating: 'I think it is very important that conferences occur. It's a very good process. We've been getting away from that in a way that is unhealthy.' Republican senator Michael Crapo of Idaho agreed:

> When we play pingpong, rather than employ the conference process, we make mistakes. Too many bills are basically put before us as an up-or-down proposition, a *fait accompli*. That makes for a much less worthy product.

The avoidance of a conference committee was clearly seen in the passage of the $700 billion bail-out for the financial industry in 2008 as the bill bounced back and forth between the House and Senate chambers. Several House Democrats argued that even in the midst of a crisis, a conference committee would have been a better mechanism for thrashing out House and Senate disagreements: 'concerns could have been aired that in the end were not,' commented New Hampshire House Democrat Paul Hodes. Box 5.1 shows that a conference committee was not used in the process of passing President Obama's healthcare reforms in 2009–10. Again, different versions of the bill were passed back and forth between the two chambers.

Once a version of the bill has been agreed by both houses — with or without the offices of a conference committee — the bill is ready to be sent to the president.

Presidential action

The president always has three options as to what to do with a bill. At times, he has a fourth.

First, he may sign the bill into law. This he does with bills he fully supports and for which he wishes to claim some credit. An example of this would be the March 2010 signing by President Obama of the Patient Protection and Affordable Care Act. A bill-signing ceremony is arranged, usually at the White House, where a number of key House and Senate members who have supported the bill through its passage are present for a photo opportunity with the president. This is an opportunity for both credit claiming and political thank-yous. The president may also decide to sign bills out of

Box 5.1 Healthcare reform legislation: 2009–10

2009

January–July: House committees on Energy and Commerce, Education and Labor, and Oversight and Government Reform draw up proposed legislation.

July: House Speaker Nancy Pelosi unveils proposed House bill (Affordable Healthcare for America Bill) which is an amalgam of the bills drawn up by the three House committees.

9 September: President Obama addresses joint session of Congress on healthcare reform.

13 October: Senate Finance Committee reports out the Senate bill (Patient Protection and Affordable Care Bill) by a vote of 14–9.

7 November: House passes its healthcare bill by 220–215 (D: 219–39; R: 1–176).

18 November: Senate Majority Leader Harry Reid introduces Senate healthcare bill for Senate floor debate.

15 December: President meets with Senate Democrats to urge passage of healthcare bill.

21 December: Senate votes to end Republican filibuster of bill by 60–40 (D: 60–0; R: 0–40).

24 December: Senate passes its healthcare bill by 60–39 (D: 60–0; R: 0–39). But the two houses have not passed identical pieces of legislation.

2010

27 January: President uses his State of the Union address to urge final passage of healthcare bill.

21 March: House passes the Senate's bill by 219–212 (D: 219–34; R: 0–178). House immediately passes Reconciliation Bill (amendments to Senate bill) by 220–211 (D: 220–33; R: 0–178).

23 March: President holds bill signing ceremony at the White House to sign the Patient Protection and Affordable Care Act into law.

25 March: Senate passes amended version of House Reconciliation Bill by 56–43 (D: 56–3; R: 0–40). House passes the same bill by 220–207 (D: 220–32; R: 0–175).

30 March: President signs the Healthcare Reconciliation Act into law.

political expediency. In this category would come the March 2002 signing by President Bush of the Bipartisan Campaign Reform Act.

Second, the president may decide to 'leave the bill on his desk'. He does this for bills upon which he takes no position at all, or which he would like to veto but knows his veto would be overridden. These bills will become law without his signature within 10 congressional working days.

Third, the president may **veto** the bill using a regular veto. He does this to bills that he strongly opposes. Presidents use the threat of a veto as a bargaining tool with Congress. The president hopes that the threat of the veto will cause Congress to make the changes in the bill which the president has demanded. To veto the bill the president must act within 10 congressional working days of receiving it, sending it back to its house of origin with a message explaining his objections. He must veto the whole bill, not just parts of it.

> ## Key concept
>
> ➤ **Presidential veto.** A power vested in the president by Article II of the Constitution, by which he may return a bill to Congress unsigned, along with the reasons for his objection. Congress may override a presidential veto by a two-thirds vote in both houses.

Congress then has three options. It can put right the 'wrongs' identified by the president in his veto message and return the bill for his signature: this is unlikely, as they will have been well aware of his objections during the bill's passage. The second option is to attempt to override the veto. This requires a two-thirds majority in both houses — a demanding and difficult requirement that is rarely achieved. Third, they may realise that they do not have the votes to override the veto, do nothing and accept that the president has won. The last is by far the most likely option.

In 2001–05, President George W. Bush became the first president to go through an entire 4-year term without using a veto, since Martin van Buren between 1837 and 1841. Bush waited 2,006 days before issuing his first veto — well into his sixth year. In November 2007, Bush suffered his first veto override — on the Water Resources Development Bill (see Table 5.12). Bush suffered three more veto overrides in 2008, leaving him with the lowest success score on vetoes of any modern-day president at just 64% (see Table 5.13),

Table 5.12 Examples of congressional overrides of George W. Bush's vetoes

Bill	Final passage vote in:		Date of presidential veto	Veto override vote in:	
	House	**Senate**		**House**	**Senate**
Water Resources Development Bill	361–54	79–14	2 November 2007	361–54	79–14
Medicare Improvements Bill	355–59	Voice Vote	15 July 2008	383–41	70–26

Table 5.13 Regular vetoes used, overridden and percentage sustained, 1961–2012

President	Years in office	Regular vetoes used	Vetoes overridden	Percentage of vetoes sustained
John Kennedy	1961–63	12	0	100
Lyndon Johnson	1963–69	16	0	100
Richard Nixon	1969–74	26	7	73
Gerald Ford	1974–77	48	12	75
Jimmy Carter	1977–81	13	2	85
Ronald Reagan	1981–89	39	9	77
George H. W. Bush	1989–93	29	1	97
Bill Clinton	1993–2001	36	2	94
George W. Bush	2001–09	11	4	64
Barack Obama†	2009–	2	0	100

† to December 2012

and the third lowest of any president. Bush's total of just 11 regular vetoes in 8 years was the lowest for a president serving two full terms since Andrew Jackson (1829–37).

In the 224 years between 1789 and the end of Barack Obama's first term in January 2013, presidents have used the regular veto 1,497 times, and of those just 110 have been overridden by Congress. That gives the president a 93% success rate. There are two main reasons for this. First, the cards are stacked so much against Congress. The president needs only 34 supporters in the Senate to win. Second, the president will study the final passage votes of bills. If they have passed by huge majorities in both houses at the third reading or on the conference report, then he will rarely veto. If, however, the majorities have been small, he can veto with confidence, knowing that he will prevail.

The president may have a fourth option — to use a 'pocket veto'. If the bill is awaiting the president's action when the legislative session ends, the bill is lost: this is a pocket veto and cannot be overridden by Congress. A late rush of bills may arrive on the president's desk just as the legislative session ends, so this can be a significant power. President Clinton pocket-vetoed only one bill in his 8 years — the Consumer Bankruptcy Overhaul Bill in December 2000. George W. Bush used his pocket veto power in December 2007 when he killed the National Defense Authorisation Bill. Congress later passed the bill again in a slightly amended form and the President signed it into law.

For a brief period in the 1990s, President Clinton had the power of so-called 'line-item veto'. With both the regular and pocket vetoes, the president must veto the whole bill or none of it. But the line-item veto gave the president the power to veto sections, or 'items', within a bill while signing the remainder of the bill into law. This greatly enhanced the president's power over legislation. The Line Item Veto Bill was passed by the House of Representatives (232–177) and by the Senate (69–31) in March 1996 and President Clinton signed it into law on 9 April that year but it did not become operative until 1 January 1997. President Clinton used the power for the first time on 11 August 1997. But less than a year later, on 25 June 1998, the US Supreme Court, in the case of *Clinton v. New York City*, declared the law unconstitutional. President Clinton had used the power 11 times to strike 82 items from bills passed by Congress.

An assessment of the legislative process

> The cards are stacked against action by Congress. As a result, those who seek action in Congress face a far more difficult task than those whose purpose is negative. (Carr, 1974)

The beginning of this section on the legislative process showed that it is difficult to get bills passed through Congress successfully. There are eight specific reasons for this.
➢ A vast number of bills are introduced. This immediately makes the process crowded.
➢ The process itself is complicated. Professor R. V. Denenberg (1976) describes Congress as a 'bastion of negation', the process of passing laws as a 'legislative labyrinth' and the legislative process as having 'a built-in negative bias'. Box 5.1 shows how complicated the process was to enact President Obama's healthcare reform legislation in 2010. There had to be seven separate votes — four in the House and three in the Senate.

> There is the need at some stages for super-majority votes: a three-fifths majority to stop a filibuster in the Senate, as in the 21 December 2009 vote on Obama's healthcare reform (see Box 5.1); a two-thirds majority in both houses to override the president's veto.

> Power in Congress is decentralised. Much power resides with the standing committees and especially with those who chair them. Party leaders have limited powers — former Senate majority leader Bob Dole once described himself as the 'majority pleader'.

> The fact that both houses possess equal power makes the process more difficult. If, as in the UK Parliament, one house can virtually override the wishes of the other, legislation is generally more easily accomplished.

> Between 1981 and 1987, and from June 2001 to December 2002, and then from January 2011 to the time of writing, these two equal houses were controlled by different parties. In the 1980s, the Republicans controlled the Senate, but the Democrats controlled the House. In the two more recent examples, it has been the other way around.

> Even if the two houses of Congress are controlled by the same party, it may not be the president's party. He is therefore likely to find it difficult to pass the bills he wants.

> Even when party control of both the presidency and Congress does coincide, it may not count for much. Party discipline in Congress has tended to be weak. Members of Congress do not simply toe a party line.

Activity

Go to the Center on Congress website at **http://congress.indiana.edu/** then move the cursor to 'Learn About Congress' and click on 'How Does Congress Work?' On the 'How Does Congress Work?' page, under 'Interact' click on 'The Dynamic Legislative Process'. This will allow you to follow a series of films and slides which further explain how a bill becomes a law in Congress.

Voting in Congress

House and Senate members are called upon to cast a large number of votes each year (see Table 5.14). Indeed, in 2007, members of the House of Representatives voted 1,186 times, beating the previous high of 885 set in 1995. In just 4 days between 5 and 8 May 2008, members of the House of Representatives were asked to vote on the floor 66 times, including 28 times on one day — 7 May. They might be voting on budgets, amendments to bills, second or third readings, bills from conference committees, constitutional amendments or — in the Senate — on treaties or appointments made by the president. They will probably be rushing to the floor to cast their vote, having just broken off a committee hearing or a meeting with constituents or staff.

Table 5.14 Number of recorded votes in the House and Senate, 2003–12

	2003	2004	2005	2006	2007	2008	2009	2010	2011	2012
House	675	544	671	543	1186	690	991	664	949	659
Senate	459	216	366	279	442	215	397	299	235	251

Source: *Congressional Quarterly*

Box 5.2 Voting in Congress: different members' views

'As a member of the Democratic Whip team, I try to persuade others to support the party position. We need to develop better tools of persuasion. By that I mean that if members don't support the party, then they should not be given the more prestigious committee and sub-committee assignments. We ought to demand a higher level of party discipline. We are too much of an assortment of free agents.'

A Democrat House member from Colorado

'I'm in the grocery store, the baker's shop, walking down the high street, at the ball game. If constituents get fractious, you have to consider whether they have anywhere else to go — would they actually vote against you in the primary or in the general election?'

A Republican House member from New Mexico

'There are a number of inputs: the views of my staff and mail from the district, for example. There is the material coming out of the House Republican Conference, which meets every 1–2 weeks. We usually check with neighbouring Republicans, especially with Porter Goss. He represents a very similar district to the south of ours and we are both conservative Republicans. I might be influenced by [Florida Congressman] Bill Young — what you might call the Dean of the Republican state delegation in the House. There will also be those votes where I have strong personal opinions.'

Former Congressman Dan Miller (R — Florida)

'In my opinion, too many House members see themselves as "delegates", not "representatives". I believe in the Burkean view of representation and agree with the Founding Fathers that "the passions of the day should be dampened". That's why I need to exercise my own judgement. This sometimes gets me into trouble with some folks in my district. Indeed, after a recent town hall meeting, I received a letter from one irate constituent annoyed that I didn't seem to care what he thought.'

Former Congressman David Skaggs (D — Colorado)

'First, there is my own personal philosophy. I ask myself whether this bill offers a real solution to the problem. Secondly, there are the views of my district. Thirdly, there is the Democratic Party, and this particular factor has gradually diminished to the extent that party loyalty is of little or no use as a guiding principle. I'm not the most popular person with the party leadership. But the feeling is mutual.'

A Democrat House member from Ohio

'[Members like me] vote their districts before they vote their party. We practise more of a representative type of democracy.'

Former Congressman John Tanner (D — Tennessee)

'The voting card we hold in our pocket belongs to our people back home, not to the party leaders.'

Former Congressman Allen Boyd (D — Florida)

Recorded votes in the House of Representatives are nowadays taken 'by electronic device', where members have 15 minutes to cast their votes. These were introduced to cut down the time it took to read out the names of the 435 members, which is how the recorded votes used to be carried out in the House. Entering the House chamber, each member places an electronic card into a small machine affixed to the back of the bench. As the member votes by pressing one of the buttons on the machine, a matching-coloured light appears next to the name on the roll of members displayed on the front wall of the chamber above the Speaker's chair. A 'score box' on the side of the press gallery shows the tally of votes and time remaining.

What factors make members of Congress vote as they do?

There are six factors to consider. The relative importance of each factor varies from one member of Congress to another and from one vote to another.

Political party

Political party is one of a number of determinants of voting in Congress. For some members, on some issues, it may be the most important determinant. 'Party votes' sometimes occur in Congress when the issue is a contentious, ideological matter, such as civil liberties, taxation, gun control, abortion or school prayers. A 'party vote' in Congress is a vote in which the majority of one party votes against the majority of the other party. The parties have few 'sticks' or 'carrots' to encourage party voting. 'Sticks' such as the threat of de-selection do not work in a system in which voters decide on candidates in primary elections. 'Carrots' such as executive branch posts do not work in a system of 'separated institutions', in which posts in the executive and legislature do not overlap.

Despite this very low threshold for qualifying as a party vote, in most years only around 55% of votes in each chamber are party votes. In 2011, however, the House of Representatives recorded its highest ever percentage of party votes at 75.8%, indicating that in that year in three-quarters of all roll-call votes the majority of Republicans voted against the majority of Democrats. Table 5.15 gives an example of a party vote in the House of Representatives — on the passage of the American Taxpayer Relief Act in January 2013, which averted the so-called 'fiscal cliff' crisis at the time. In this vote, the majority of Democrats voted 'yes' while the majority of Republicans voted 'no' — a party vote.

So it is important to remember that party labels do not necessarily mean voting together. Conservative Democrats, like Congressman John Barrow of Georgia or Senator Mark Pryor of Arkansas, often vote with Republicans. Likewise, moderate Republicans, such as Congressman Chris Smith of New Jersey or Senator Susan Collins of Maine, often vote with Democrats. Table 5.16 shows the most conservative Democrat and liberal Republican members of each chamber during 2012. This makes clear the geographic and regional basis of political ideology in American politics. Six of the 12

Table 5.15 Final passage vote in the House of Representatives on the American Taxpayer Relief Act, 1 January 2013

	Yes	No
Total	257	167
Republicans	85	151
Democrats	172	16

Table 5.16 Most conservative Democrat and liberal Republican members of Congress, 2012

Most conservative Democrat House members	Most liberal Republican House members
Dan Boren (Oklahoma)	Chris Gibson (New York)
John Barrow (Georgia)	Tim Johnson (Illinois)
Jim Matheson (Utah)	Walter Jones (North Carolina)
Collin Peterson (Minnesota)	Robert Dold (Illinois)
Mike McIntyre (North Carolina)	Justin Amash (Michigan)
Mike Ross (Arkansas)	Steven LaTourette (Ohio)
Heath Shuler (North Carolina)	Frank LoBiondo (New Jersey)
Larry Kissell (North Carolina)	Patrick Meehan (Pennsylvania)
Henry Cuellar (Texas)	Ileana Ros-Lehtinen (Florida)
Joe Donnelly (Indiana)	Mike Fitzpatrick (Pennsylvania)
Jason Altmire (Pennsylvania)	Chris Smith (New Jersey)
Ben Chandler (Kentucky)	Michael Grimm (New York)
Most conservative Democrat senators	**Most liberal Republican senators**
Joe Manchin (West Virginia)	Scott Brown (Massachusetts)
Ben Nelson (Nebraska)	Susan Collins (Maine)
Mark Pryor (Arkansas)	Lisa Murkowski (Alaska)
Jon Tester (Montana)	Olympia Snowe (Maine)
Kay Hagan (North Carolina)	Richard Lugar (Indiana)
Mary Landrieu (Louisiana)	Dean Heller (Nevada)
Max Baucus (Montana)	John Hoeven (North Dakota)

Source: *National Journal*, 23 February 2013

most conservative House Democrats come from the South, as do three of the seven most conservative Senate Democrats. Ten of the 12 most liberal House Republicans come from the Northeast or the upper Midwest, as do four of the five most moderate Republican senators. Or look at it another way. Seventeen of the 19 most conservative Democrat members of Congress in 2012 — both in the House and the Senate — came from states which Mitt Romney won that year. Similarly, 15 of the 19 most liberal Republican members of Congress in 2012 came from states which Barack Obama won that year. The most liberal state delegations in their voting in 2012 were those from Massachusetts, Maine, Connecticut, Rhode Island and Vermont — all in the Northeast. Those delegations with the most conservative voting record were Montana, Arizona, Alabama, North Dakota and Texas. We shall have more to say about increasing partisanship in Congress later in this chapter.

Constituents

In considering the role constituents play in how members of Congress decide how to vote, we need to be aware of different models of **representation**. The model most appropriate to how most members vote in Congress is the trustee model. In this model of representation, the representative acts as the person who is vested with formal responsibility for the affairs of others. Such representation is based upon the mature and considered judgement of the legislator.

Key concept

➤ **Representation.** The term can be used in a number of different ways. Representation can be understood in terms of *how* legislators represent their constituents. In this sense there are three different models of representation — the trustee model, the delegate model and the mandate model. But the term can also be understood in terms of *who* represents the electorate. This is called the resemblance model of representation and considers how representative legislators are in terms of such factors as gender and race.

House and Senate members place a high premium on representing the interests of their constituents — and with good reasons. First, the Constitution states that they must be residents of the state they represent, so this gives them a good understanding of what 'the folks back home' are saying. Second, a number of states go further by insisting — through the 'locality rule' — that House members reside in the congressional district that they represent. Third, typical House or Senate members do not just reside in the state or district; they will have been born, raised and educated and will have worked there. Fourth, House members are especially careful about constituents' views because they have to face the electors every 2 years.

Failing to look after one's constituents can prove fatal. Two House members from Maryland — Republican Wayne Gilchrest and Democrat Albert Wynn — were both defeated in their congressional primaries in 2008 because constituents believed they were out of touch with the wishes of voters, Gilchrest for being too liberal, Wynn for being too conservative. Senator Elizabeth Dole lost her re-election bid the same year for failing to be attentive enough to the wishes of the voters of North Carolina and paying too few visits to the state. A television ad put out by her opponent, Kay Hagen, reminded North Carolina voters that Senator Dole had visited 12 states for President Bush in 2006, 'while records show Dole spent only 13 days in North Carolina'.

There are various methods by which members of Congress can find out about their constituents' views. While they are in Washington DC, members of Congress keep in touch through phone and e-mail with their offices back in the state or district. They read the local newspapers published back home — usually online. They receive visits, phone calls, letters and e-mails from constituents. The volume of written communication from constituents has increased hugely over the past

15 years or so. In 1996, members of Congress received in total 36 million letters and almost 11 million e-mails. That averaged about 90,000 communications per member of Congress. By 2004, while the number of letters received had halved to 18 million, the number of e-mails had risen to 182 million. That made an average of over 350,000 communications per member of Congress, or 1,000 per day. By 2006, the number of e-mails had risen to 313 million.

They discover what their constituents want by making regular visits back home. The frequency depends on how far 'home' is from Washington DC. Congressman Doc Hastings (R — Washington), for example, represents a district nearly 3,125 miles (5,000 kilometres) from the nation's capital. A flight from Washington DC to Seattle — the nearest large airport — takes 6–7 hours, the equivalent of flying from London to Boston. Hastings therefore makes use of the longer recess periods — for example, around Christmas, Easter, Memorial Day (May) and Independence Day (July).

Back home, House and Senate members have a variety of engagements, including:
➤ holding party and 'town hall' meetings
➤ conducting 'surgeries' with individual constituents
➤ making visits around the state/district
➤ appearing on local radio phone-in programmes
➤ interviews with representatives of the local media
➤ addressing groups such as chambers of commerce, professional groups and Round Table lunches
➤ visiting local schools, hospitals and businesses

On most issues, constituents' views are likely to be divided, with some in favour and others against. Through town hall meetings and constituency mail, the views of the discontented are more likely to be heard than those the content. One Democrat Congressman described his constituency mail as 'what folks don't like from the folks who don't like it'. It is usually not a representative cross-section of constituency opinion. Furthermore, members of Congress are meant to be more than just 'delegates' of their constituents and may need to balance other factors as well as the national good against what is perceived as being merely locally popular or electorally expedient.

It is interesting in the Senate to note how the two senators from each state vote — to what extent they have similar or different voting records. After all, because they represent exactly the same constituents, one might expect them to vote quite similarly. However, this is not always the case. In a recent analysis of voting behaviour during 2012, the *National Journal* (23 February 2013) referred to senators from the same state as falling into the categories of either 'twins' — those with very similar voting records — or 'odd couples', being those with very different voting records despite representing the same state (see Table 5.17).

The two same-state senators who voted most alike in 2012 were Democrats Jeff Merkley and Ron Wyden of Oregon. These same-state senators are almost political twins. The two same-state senators who voted most differently in 2012 were the

Table 5.17 Senate 'twins' and 'odd couples', 2012

Same state senators with the most similar voting records
Jeff Merkley and Ron Wyden (D — Oregon) Tom Coburn and James Inhofe (R — Oklahoma) Mark Warner and Jim Webb (D — Virginia)
Same state, different party senators with the most dissimilar voting records
Ron Johnson (R) and Herb Kohl (D) of Wisconsin John Thune (R) and Tim Johnson (D) of South Dakota Charles Grassley (R) and Tom Harkin (D) of Iowa

Source: *National Journal*, 23 February 2013

Wisconsin senators — Democrat Herb Kohl and Republican Ron Johnson. These really are same-state 'odd couples', a liberal Democrat and a conservative Republican representing the same constituents. It is extraordinary to realise that voters in Wisconsin elected both Kohl and Johnson despite their sharp ideological differences. Kohl retired in 2012 but has been replaced by former Representative Tammy Baldwin who ranked as the 21st most liberal House member in 2011.

The administration

The term 'the administration' refers to members of the executive branch, including the president. Much legislation voted on in Congress has been initiated by the administration.

Cabinet members — the heads of the 15 executive departments — have a keen interest in the passage of legislation affecting their policy areas. So members of the administration — from the departments and agencies as well as the White House itself — keep in contact with members of Congress through phone calls as well as meetings in an attempt to persuade them to cast their votes in certain ways. They talk with members of the relevant committees as well as with staff on Capitol Hill. Often the White House gets involved through the Office of Legislative Affairs as well as directly in the person of the president (see Chapter 6).

Senator Elizabeth Dole — her 'loyalty' to President Bush led to her re-election defeat

Any persuasion needs to be regular, reciprocal and bipartisan. It is important that members of Congress are approached not only just before an important vote comes up. It is important, too, that those from the departments and the White House are willing to do favours in return, offering a two-way street of mutual cooperation. All this needs to be done with members from both parties. For an administration to talk only with members of its own party is usually a recipe for disaster. Success tends to occur in Congress when there is a bipartisan coalition.

But supporting an unpopular president can be costly, as a number of Republican members of Congress discovered in 2008. A number of Democrat challengers in that year's congressional elections defeated incumbent Republicans by linking them to their strong support for President Bush. Republican Senator Elizabeth Dole of North Carolina lost her re-election bid against a series of Democrat television ads which continually reminded voters that '92% of the time she votes with Bush'.

Pressure groups

Pressure groups use a number of different ways to try to influence how members of Congress vote (see Chapter 4). They make direct contact with members as well as with their staff. They attempt to generate public support favourable to their position. They make visits and phone calls, provide evidence to committees, organise rallies, demonstrations and petition drives, and engage in fundraising and campaigning. Money raised is used to fund politicians who support their cause and to seek to defeat those who do not. Certain policy areas have seen significant pressure group activity in recent years, including the environment, abortion, gun control, healthcare and welfare reform.

Colleagues and staff

Because of the huge numbers of votes that members of Congress have to cast, they cannot personally know the details of all of them. They therefore rely on others to help them make a decision on a vote.

Other colleagues can be helpful. A Congressman might turn to fellow members of the same chamber and of the same party who share the same philosophy and views. Some senior members act as 'mentors' to newer members, offering advice and suggestions on votes. In the House, one could look out fellow members of the state delegation, especially those from neighbouring districts. Members of the relevant committee can be a help — especially those who chair committees or who are the ranking minority members.

Senior staff members — the chief of staff or legislative director — at the weekly staff meeting in a Capitol Hill office of a Republican House member, might be heard telling their Congressman: 'You'll want to support this', or 'This plays well in the district'. One Republican House member talked thus of the importance of his senior staff:

> You can always tell those who don't know how things work here on Capitol Hill. When they leave my office after a meeting, they thank me and then hand me copies of all their papers so that I can follow up on whatever it was we were talking about. They don't know how things work. Those who *do* know how things work thank me and then give the papers to *my staff.* I remember getting an invitation from someone in the Clinton administration and the invitation stated: 'Members only. No staff.' Who do they think it is that I talk with just before I make a decision on how to vote?

Personal beliefs

On certain votes, House or Senate members may vote according to their own personal beliefs. Issues such as abortion, capital punishment, taxation (increases or cuts), federal subsidies and defence spending are likely to bring a member's own personal philosophy to the fore. There are, for example, members of Congress who will never vote for a federal subsidy to any industry or group, while others will never vote to deny life to a fellow human being, whether through capital punishment or war.

Activity

Go to the Center on Congress website at **http://congress.indiana.edu/** then move the cursor to 'Learn About Congress' and click on 'How Does Congress Work?' On the 'How Does Congress Work?' page, under 'Interact' click on 'How a Member Decides to Vote'. This will allow you to simulate the steps towards a vote in the House of Representatives on a Flag Desecration Amendment to the US Constitution. Follow the on-screen instructions to play the simulation.

Increased partisanship in Congress

The conventional wisdom about political parties in Congress used to be that they were 'like two bottles with different labels, both empty' (D. W. Brogan). Even as recently as 1997, Mark Shields writing in the *Washington Post* famously remarked that 'as of today, the country basically has two Republican parties, separated by the issue of abortion'. But writing just a decade later Ronald Brownstein (2007) had this to say of the new era of what he termed 'hyper-partisanship' in US politics:

> The defining characteristics of this age are greater unity **within** the parties and more distinct conflicts **between** them. On almost every major issue, the distance between the two parties has widened, even as dissent within the parties has diminished.

Votes in Congress used frequently to be one group of Democrats and Republicans voting against another group of Democrats and Republicans. Looking at this more closely, votes often comprised Republicans joining with conservative Democrats on one side, with liberal Democrats and moderate Republicans on the other side. But over the past decade, conservative Democrats and moderate Republicans — the centrists of Congress — have become increasingly rare breeds. Look what happened just in the 2010 mid-term elections. Of the nine centrists in the Senate whose seats were up for re-election in 2010, four chose to retire, two were defeated in primaries, a further two were defeated in the general election, and the other — Robert Byrd of West Virginia — died before Election Day. It was much the same in the House of Representatives. Of the 60 most conservative Democrats in the House during the 111th Congress (2009–10), 37 (62%) lost in the 2010 mid-terms, and of the five most moderate House Republicans, only one was re-elected.

One of the simplest ways to understand what has happened to the parties in Congress is to take two snap shots of the US Senate: in 1982 and 2011. Back in 1982, one of the most liberal Senate Democrats was Ted Kennedy of Massachusetts. Meanwhile, the most conservative of the Senate Democrats was Ed Zorinsky of Nebraska. They rarely voted together, yet they were both Democrats. Among Republicans in the Senate in 1982, the most liberal or 'moderate' Republican was Lowell Weicker of Connecticut. In the same party was arch-conservative Strom Thurmond of South Carolina. Again, Weicker and Thurmond had little in common — except they were both Republicans. Between Weicker (the most liberal Republican) and Zorinsky (the most conservative Democrat) were 35 Democrats and 23 Republicans. In other words, 35 Democrats were more conservative than Weicker and 23 Republicans were more liberal than Zorinsky. Republican Strom Thurmond was more likely to vote with Democrat Ed Zorinsky than with fellow Republican Lowell Weicker. Likewise, Democrat Ted Kennedy was more likely to vote with Republican Lowell Weicker than with fellow Democrat Ed Zorinsky. As Figure 5.3 shows, there was a huge ideological overlap between the two parties. The differences *within* the parties were far greater than the differences *between* them.

In 2011, the most liberal Senate Democrat was Jeff Merkley of Oregon and the most conservative of the Senate Democrats was Ben Nelson of Nebraska. Among Republicans in the Senate in 2011, the most liberal Republican was Susan Collins of Maine and the most conservative of the Senate Republicans was Tom Coburn of Oklahoma. Between Collins (the most liberal Republican) and Nelson (the most conservative Democrat) there was not a single senator. In other words, all the 45 Republicans were more conservative than Ben Nelson and all 55 Democrats were more liberal than Susan Collins. As Figure 5.4 shows, there was absolutely no ideological overlap at all between the two parties. The differences *between* the parties are now greater than the differences *within*. Both parties have become more ideologically cohesive and distinct: the Democrats have become a more distinctly and cohesively liberal party; the Republicans have become a more distinctly and cohesively conservative party. It is hardly surprising that as a result of this ideological sorting of the parties in Congress there has been an increase in partisanship and polarisation.

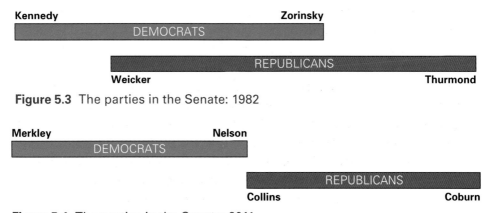

Figure 5.3 The parties in the Senate: 1982

Figure 5.4 The parties in the Senate: 2011

A factor which has led to the increased partisanship in Congress has been the disappearance of the centrist members of both parties: that is, members whose voting is more towards the political centre — conservative Democrats and liberal Republicans. It isn't just that the same people are voting in different ways, although there may be some of that, but that the people in Congress are different — more ideological, more partisan. Again, this is most clearly seen in the Senate. Over the past few election cycles, both parties in the Senate have lost prominent centrists. The Democrats have lost conservative senators such as Joe Lieberman of Connecticut and Ben Nelson of Nebraska. The Republicans have lost a number of liberal senators such as Olympia Snowe of Maine, Richard Lugar of Indiana and Lincoln Chafee of Rhode Island.

Arlen Specter of Pennsylvania, a liberal Republican, was first elected to the Senate in 1980 and was re-elected in 1986, 1992, 1998 and 2004. But in 2004, Specter almost lost the Republican primary to a much more conservative candidate, Pat Toomey. Specter's margin was only 17,000 votes out of over 1 million cast. Feeling that his centrist views now put him at odds with many Pennsylvania Republicans, Specter switched parties and became a Democrat in 2009. But Specter then lost the Democratic primary in 2010 to a much more liberal Democrat, Joe Sestak. Sestak went on to lose to Toomey in the general election. This is partisanship in microcosm — a liberal Republican who defects to the Democrats but is defeated by a much more liberal candidate in the primary, who in turn loses to a conservative Republican in November. Result — a moderate is replaced by an ideologue; a senator with a *bipartisan* voting record is replaced by a senator who will build a *partisan* voting record. The American Conservative Union, which awarded Specter a 43% rating for his voting record in the Senate, now awards his replacement Pat Toomey a 97% rating.

This is linked to another recent factor likely to increase partisanship in Congress — especially in the House — namely the rise of the Tea Party movement. Following the 2010 mid-term elections, 60 House Republicans and 4 Senate Republicans formed Tea Party caucuses in their respective houses. Take the row between President Obama and congressional Republicans over the federal debt ceiling in the summer of 2011. It was the Tea Party-endorsed House members of Congress who, in the words of Michael Hirsh in the *National Journal* ('What Just Happened?', 6 August 2011) 'hijacked a fairly routine congressional vote [to raise the debt ceiling] and threatened to send the United States into first-time default in order to fight a proxy war over their singular agenda of shrinking the federal government'.

In the House of Representatives, partisanship has also been increased by the way district boundaries are redrawn. This occurs after each 10-yearly census. In many states, it is the state legislators who are the main players in this redistricting process. What they have done in many states is to draw up districts which are safe seats for one or other party. Take California, for example. Until 2011, redistricting was controlled by the state legislators. In the 2010 mid-term elections in California, the average vote for winners of the state's 53 House seats was 66%. The politicians in the state legislature deliberately drew the boundaries so as to bring about these results. If one defines a competitive district as one in which the margin of victory is 10 percentage points or less, then only 4 of the 53 California House races were competitive in 2010. The other 49 California House members therefore had little or no incentive to talk or vote in a bipartisan fashion. All they had to do was vote in a way to please their own party supporters. Hence they voted in a highly partisan fashion. After California voters took away the redistricting power from state legislators in 2011 and gave it to an independent commission, House races in California became more competitive. In 2012 the number of competitive races in the state went up from 4 to 12.

As John Farrell wrote recently in the *National Journal* ('Divided We Stand', 25 February 2012):

> Congressional leaders now sound, and act, like their parliamentary counterparts in foreign lands — voting in rigid blocs and, in times of legislative gridlock, calling for an election to put the question to the voters. Fair enough, but the parliamentary peg does not fit into the holes of the American constitutional system. In Westminster, a new prime minister emerges from the legislative branch and takes office with a unified majority, almost guaranteed to get his or her programme enacted. But America's Founders were wary of parliamentary majorities. They designed a system to hobble a majority and force the country's varied regions, states and interests to cooperate.

Therefore as congressional scholar Thomas Mann has put it:

> There is a mismatch between our new, parliamentary-style parties and the governing system in which they have to operate. The Framers had in mind, with the Constitution's separation of powers and checks and balances, a process of negotiation. But now these negotiations don't take place. The inclination is to oppose, obstruct, discredit and nullify.

Oversight of the executive branch

Having studied Congress's power in terms of legislation, we now turn to Congress's other important function, that of oversight of the executive branch. The Constitution does not explicitly grant Congress oversight responsibility. But it does give Congress the power to make laws, and over the years oversight of the executive branch has come to be seen as an implied power of Congress. Members of Congress have to know what is going on in order to make the laws, see how the laws they have passed are working, and amend the laws. And to carry out this oversight, Congress has given itself a number of significant powers: to subpoena documents and testimony; to hold individuals in contempt if they fail to comply with Congress's demands for information; to make it illegal to lie to Congress.

We have already touched on Congress's oversight function when we were considering the work of congressional committees, for it is in the committee rooms of Congress that most of the oversight takes place. The reason for this is fundamental — the absence of

the executive branch from the chambers of Congress. Unlike in the British parliament, the executive is not present, so there is no opportunity for Question Time in Congress. It is only in the committee rooms where members of the executive branch can be questioned. And we have also seen that because the standing committees of Congress are permanent policy specialist bodies, they can wield a considerable degree of clout. The question arises, however, whether congressional oversight is effective. Does Congress act as a watchdog or a lapdog?

There is quite a bit of agreement — as well as much evidence to support the theory — that congressional oversight of the executive is only really effective when Congress is not controlled by the president's party. Exhibit A in this argument is the fact that almost all modern-day examples of the Senate's rejection of presidential nominations, whether to the executive or judicial branches, have come when the president's party has not controlled the Senate. It was a Democrat Senate in 1987 which rejected Republican president Ronald Reagan's nomination of Robert Bork to the United States Supreme Court. The same was true of the Senate's 1989 rejection of George H. W. Bush's nomination of John Tower to be secretary of defense. In reverse, it was a Republican Senate which, in 1999, rejected both Bill Clinton's nomination of Ronnie White to be a federal trial court judge and his Nuclear Test Ban Treaty.

Exhibit B would be the relationship between Congress and President George W. Bush during his 8-year term. Throughout most of the first 6 years (2001–06), Bush's Republican Party controlled both houses of Congress. There was a brief 18-month period between June 2001 and December 2002 when the Democrats controlled the Senate, but by only one vote, and much of this period coincided with the President's sky-high approval ratings following the attacks on New York and Washington on 11 September 2001. During these years, congressional oversight was light if not at times almost non-existent. Democrat Congressman Steny Hoyer of Maryland pointed out that oversight activity during this period was low even by the standards of other periods of united government. So, for example, in 1993 and 1994 when Democrats controlled Congress during Democrat Bill Clinton's first 2 years, there were 135 investigative hearings held. In contrast, in 2003 and 2004 the Republican-controlled Congress held only 37 investigative hearings.

But that all changed following the Republicans' loss of control in both houses in the 2006 mid-term elections. Indeed, some Republicans even conceded that had they done a better job of oversight when they held the majority, they might not have been so severely punished by the voters. Once the Democrats took control on Capitol Hill in January 2007, the President found himself facing some feisty committee chairs such as Patrick Leahy of Vermont, Carl Levin of Michigan and Robert Byrd of West Virginia in the Senate, while in the House Henry Waxman of California now chaired the standing committee on Oversight and Government Reform, and John Dingell of Michigan chaired the House Energy and Commerce Committee. 'We are not a potted plant, watching the administration function,' commented the House Foreign Affairs Committee chairman Tom Lantos. The

Senate Appropriations Committee chairman Robert Byrd told the secretaries of state and defense, and the chairman of the Joint Chiefs of Staff in February 2007: 'Congress is not a rubber stamp or a presidential lapdog, obedient and unquestioning. Oversight, oversight, oversight is among our most important responsibilities, and oversight, oversight, oversight has been lacking for far too long' (see Box 5.3).

It wasn't long before heads started to roll. 'In just 3 weeks, more people were forced out of their [executive branch] jobs than in the entire prior 6 years under this administration,' declared Democrat Congressman Rahm Emanuel of Illinois in 2007. Four high-profile executive branch officials had just gone, forced out by relentless and critical questioning by congressional committees — two generals and the Army Secretary over the scandal concerning veterans' healthcare at the Walter Reed Army Medical Center in Washington DC, plus the Attorney General — Alberto Gonzales — because of his role in firing eight US attorneys for what appeared to be political rather than professional reasons.

Box 5.3 'Congress's Oversight Offensive' by David Broder

Ten weeks into the new Congress, it is clear that revelation, not legislation, is going to be its real product. For the first 6 years of the Bush administration, White House personnel were allowed free rein to carry out whatever policy or political assignments they wished — or supposed that the President wanted done. A Congress under firm Republican control was somnolent when it came to oversight of the executive branch. No Republican committee chairman wanted to turn over rocks in a Republican administration.

You have to feel a twinge of sympathy now for the Bush appointees who suddenly find unsympathetic Democratic chairmen such as Henry Waxman, John Conyers, Patrick Leahy and Carl Levin investigating their cases. Even if these appointees are scrupulously careful about their actions now, who knows what subpoenaed memos and e-mails in the files will reveal about the past?

They will pay the price for the temporary breakdown in the system of checks and balances that occurred between 2001 and 2007, when the Republican Congress forgot its responsibility to hold the executive branch accountable.

It was a fundamental dereliction of duty by Congress, and it probably did more to encourage bad decisions and harmful actions by executive branch political appointees than the much-touted lobbying influence. In reality, many Republican members of Congress did not mind what was happening because they were able to get favours done in that permissive climate.

Democrats find it easier to investigate than to legislate. With their major initiatives, from a minimum-wage boost to a shutdown of the Iraq war, stymied by Republican opposition, the Democrats are understandably making 'accountability' their new goal — meaning more and more investigations. Last week, House Speaker Nancy Pelosi and Majority Leader Steny Hoyer held a news conference to celebrate the fact that the House had already conducted more than 100 oversight hearings on executive agencies. And, they promised, that was just the beginning. As Hoyer put it: 'Today is a new day in Congress. The days of see no evil, hear no evil and speak no evil are over. The United States Congress will no longer be a potted plant or a signer of blank cheques.'

Source: www.washingtonpost.com, 18 March 2007

Box 5.4 Senate Committee on Foreign Relations

PRESIDING: Senator Menendez

DATE: Wednesday, January 23, 2013

TIME: 9.00 AM

LOCATION: Senate Hart 216

SUBJECT: Benghazi: The Attacks and the Lessons Learned

WITNESS: The Honorable Hillary Rodham Clinton, Secretary of State

The congressional Democrat majority also turned its attention to the administration's foreign policy, most specifically in Iraq and Afghanistan as well as to the so-called War on Terror, the detention and trial of terrorist suspects in Guantánamo Bay, and the use by the American government of the procedure known as waterboarding in its interrogation of terrorist suspects, as well as the wider issue of the use of torture. In January 2013, the Senate Foreign Relations Committee held a widely publicised hearing on the terrorist attack in Benghazi (Libya) on 11 September 2012, at which the then Secretary of State Hillary Clinton was the star witness (see Box 5.4).

But to some, congressional oversight — especially at times of divided government — is just a polite phrase for trying to embarrass the president and his administration. Republican Senator Jim DeMint of South Carolina described Democrats' oversight of George W. Bush in 2007 as 'political posturing and demagoguing' which 'hasn't really changed anything'. According to Brian Friel in the *National Journal* ('The Watchdog Growls', 24 March 2007), just as Republicans spent much of 1998–99 trying to make President Clinton look unethical, so the Democrats spent much of 2007–08 trying to make President Bush look incompetent.

Finally, it is worth asking whether all this oversight activity by Congress ultimately produces wiser policies and more effective implementation. According to congressional scholars Norman Ornstein and Thomas Mann ('The Hill Is Alive with the Sound of Hearings', www.aei.org, 21 March 2007): 'While the constitutional arsenal of Congress is powerful, it has limited ability to quickly reverse the course set upon by a determined president.' But, they continue: 'Oversight keeps an administration on its toes; the lack of oversight, and the expectation that there will be none, leads to complacency, arrogance and maladministration.' Ironic, therefore, that the congressional Republicans might be held responsible for some of the failings of George W. Bush's Republican administration merely because they didn't criticise enough.

The public view of Congress

Despite all this activity, Congress has declined in public esteem. By October 2011, a CBS News/*New York Times* poll found that only 9% of Americans approved of the way Congress was doing its job — an all-time low and significantly lower even than the approval ratings of President Obama. A cartoon in the *Miami Herald* showed a couple sitting on a sofa watching the TV coverage of disgraced cyclist Lance Armstrong. 'Lance Armstrong is a liar, a hypocrite, a con-man, a bully, a crook and an egomaniacal sociopath!' shouts the man, to which his wife replies, 'So when do you think he'll run for Congress?' Dissatisfaction with Congress is evident amongst supporters of both parties. The ambivalence comes in voters' views of their own senators and representatives, whom they hold in much higher esteem than the institution as a whole; hence re-election rates remain high, though not as high as they were a decade or so ago.

But voters tend to regard 'Washington politicians' as a whole with great scepticism. In six of the seven presidential elections from 1976 to 2000, the winner was a former state governor, not a Washington insider, though this pattern changed in 2008 with the nomination by both parties of incumbent senators. In 2012, however, no incumbent senator ran for the presidential nomination of either party — the first time this had occurred since the election of 1944. In the minds of many, Congress is still epitomised by **gridlock** and a 'do-nothing' mentality. Significant policy concerns such as the federal budget deficit, taxation, gun control, social security and immigration reform remain largely unresolved. Many Americans' view of Congress can be summed up in the bumper sticker that reads: 'What's the opposite of progress? **Congress!**'

Key concept

➢ **Gridlock.** A term derived from traffic jams at major intersections of US cities, signifying the failure to get action on policy proposals and legislation in Congress. Gridlock is thought to be exacerbated by divided government and partisanship.

Activity

Go to the Center on Congress website at **http://congress.indiana.edu/** then move the cursor to 'Learn About Congress' and click on 'How Does Congress Work?' On the 'How Does Congress Work?' page, under 'Interact' click on 'Public Criticisms of Congress'. This will enable you to learn more about the criticisms ordinary Americans make about Congress.

UK/US comparison

The US Congress and the UK Parliament

There are eight basic characteristics of Congress:
➢ Both houses are directly elected by fixed-term elections.
➢ There is a strict separation of personnel between the legislature and the executive.
➢ Both houses have equal legislative power.
➢ The Senate is, nonetheless, regarded as more powerful and prestigious than the House and many House members seek to advance their political career by election to the Senate.

- The work of standing committees is of great importance.
- Congressional oversight of the executive branch is done almost exclusively through the committees of Congress and is thought to be performed more thoroughly when the two branches are controlled by different parties.
- Congress is almost entirely made up of members from the two major parties.
- Party is only one of a number of important factors that influence the way members of the House and the Senate vote.

There are seven basic characteristics of the UK Parliament:

- Only the House of Commons is directly elected (though proposals were published in 2012 for a substantially elected second chamber). The length of time between these elections had traditionally been governed only by a maximum period of 5 years, although the Coalition introduced the Fixed-term Parliament Act (2011).
- Members of the executive are also members of the legislature, most of them in the House of Commons.
- The House of Commons has greater power over legislation.
- The House of Commons is regarded as more powerful than the House of Lords, and members move from the Commons to the Lords only on retirement.
- Parliamentary oversight of the executive is done both in the chambers and in committees and is often hampered by the executive's control of parliamentary procedure, their guaranteed majority in the Commons and high levels of party discipline.
- Parliament contains many members from third parties and, in the House of Lords, of no party allegiance at all.
- Party is usually the most important factor that influences the way members of the House of Commons vote and is relatively important for some members of the House of Lords.

Exam focus

Short-answer questions

1 To what extent are the two chambers of Congress equal in power and influence?
2 How important are the exclusive powers held by the House and the Senate?
3 How significant is the role of political parties in Congress?
4 What is the role of committee chairmen in Congress, and why have they been the subject of criticism?
5 How does Congress attempt to exercise oversight over the executive branch?

Essay questions

1 Is Congress truly representative of America?
2 Why is the Senate regarded as more prestigious than the House of Representatives?

3 To what extent does Congress remain a powerful body?
4 Examine the claim that it is in the committee rooms that the real work of Congress is done.
5 Why is it easier to defeat legislation in Congress than to pass it?
6 How effective is Congress's oversight of the executive branch?
7 How do members of Congress decide how to vote?

Further reading

Ashbee, E., 'Congress: An obstacle to effective government?', *Politics Review*, Vol. 22, No. 2, November 2012.

Batchelor, A., 'Why are US congressional committees so important?', *Politics Review*, Vol. 18, No. 4, April 2009.

Bennett, A. J., 'Congress: watchdog or lapdog?', *Politics Review*, Vol. 19, No. 3, February 2010.

Dumbrell, J., 'Pressure groups and the US Congress', *Politics Review*, Vol. 17, No. 4, April 2008.

Mann, T. E. and Ornstein, N. J., *It's Even Worse than It Looks: How the American Constitutional System Collided with the New Politics of Extremism*, Basic Books, 2012.

Moxon, K., 'US healthcare reform', *Politics Review*, Vol. 20, No. 2, November 2010.

Chapter 6

The presidency

> I, Barack Hussein Obama, do solemnly swear that I will faithfully execute the Office
> of President of the United States, and will to the best of my ability, preserve, protect
> and defend the Constitution of the United States. So help me God.

With these words, Barack Obama became the 44th president of the United States at (just after) 12 noon eastern standard time on Tuesday 20 January 2009. Unfortunately, between them, Chief Justice John Roberts, who was administering the oath, and the President-elect (as he still was), fluffed their lines in front of a crowd of over one million. So the following day, at 7.35 p.m., the Chief Justice dropped by the White House to meet up with the President (as he now was) to do it again! And this time there was no crowd, no family, no television cameras — and no fluffing of lines. Was it necessary to do it again? Probably not. But the White House commented that the oath was repeated 'out of an abundance of caution'.

Caution is not a word many people associated with Mr Obama's predecessor, George W. Bush. But the office of the US president is often misunderstood by casual observers for two reasons. First, they tend to see the president as a one-man band when in fact he is part — though admittedly an important part — of an orchestra. Hence, this chapter is entitled 'The presidency' rather than 'The president', drawing to our attention the organisation rather than simply the person. Second, they tend to think of the president as 'the most powerful man in the world'. True, the president does have a considerable amount of power, more in foreign policy than in domestic policy.

Barack Obama becomes the 44th
president of the United States of America

Whereas in foreign policy the president can use his formidable commander-in-chief powers, when it comes to domestic policy, he is far more limited — hedged around with numerous checks and balances, especially from Congress. President Johnson was once heard to remark: 'The only power I've got is nuclear, and I'm not allowed to use that.'

The US presidency is therefore something of a paradox: power and weakness. The president has to be both commander-in-chief and 'bargainer-in-chief'. He has considerable formal powers, but there are formidable limits on his use of those powers. To run the federal bureaucracy, mould public opinion and get on with Congress, the president needs to be an effective administrator, communicator, persuader, facilitator and leader.

Key questions answered in this chapter

- ➢ What kind of presidency did the Founding Fathers envisage?
- ➢ What are the formal powers of the president?
- ➢ How has the office of the vice-president been transformed in recent decades?
- ➢ What problems does the president face in dealing with the federal bureaucracy?
- ➢ How is the cabinet appointed, what happens at cabinet meetings and how important is the cabinet?
- ➢ What role is played by the Executive Office of the President?
- ➢ How can the president get his way with Congress?
- ➢ What are the characteristics of the 'partisan presidency'?
- ➢ Who controls American foreign policy — the president or Congress?
- ➢ What is 'presidential power' and what limits exist upon it?

Links to follow up

The place to start in studying the presidency online is the White House website at: **www.whitehouse.gov**. It is easy to navigate and has a good archive of material.

One of the best academic websites on the US presidency is the American Presidency Project based at the University of California at Santa Barbara. The web address is **www.presidency.ucsb.edu**. You will find detailed information on matters ranging from the State of the Union Address to presidential vetoes.

Another useful resource specifically for information on the federal bureaucracy is **www.usa.gov**. Individual departments and agencies all have their own websites, and if it is statistics you are after then try **www.fedstats.gov**.

The creation of the presidency

The Founding Fathers created a president who would be both head of state and head of the government. This is important to remember. The US president is not just another politician; he — and perhaps one day, she — is the personification of the nation. 'I am

both king and prime minister,' remarked President Theodore Roosevelt. The arrival of the president at a formal, public function is greeted by a military band playing 'Hail to the Chief'. The White House may not have the grandeur of Buckingham Palace, but it is certainly a good deal more imposing than 10 Downing Street.

Second, the Founding Fathers created a singular executive. 'The executive power shall be vested in a president of the United States of America' are the opening words of Article II of the Constitution. It is important to remember this when considering the president's cabinet, for it is not — and cannot be — a decision-making body. President Truman had on his Oval Office desk a sign that read simply: 'The buck stops here.'

Third, they created an indirectly elected president. The president was to be chosen by the Electors — the great and the good — in an Electoral College. As Chapter 2 explains, this system has been adapted into a direct election, although the mechanism of the Electoral College still survives.

Finally, they created a limited — a checked — president. The Founding Fathers feared tyranny, and especially they feared tyranny by the executive branch. As a result, they hedged the president with a host of checks and balances (see Chapter 1). Thomas Cronin and Michael Genovese (1998) have written:

> The men who invented the presidency did not wish to create a ruler. Instead they hoped to create conditions where leadership might from time to time flourish. A ruler commands; a leader influences. A ruler wields power; a leader persuades.

Students of the US presidency need to understand that the office is often a limited and, for its main occupant, a frustrating one.

Table 6.1 American presidents since 1961

President	Party	Years in office
John Kennedy	Democrat	1961–63
Lyndon Johnson	Democrat	1963–69
Richard Nixon	Republican	1969–74
Gerald Ford	Republican	1974–77
Jimmy Carter	Democrat	1977–81
Ronald Reagan	Republican	1981–89
George H. W. Bush	Republican	1989–93
Bill Clinton	Democrat	1993–2001
George W. Bush	Republican	2001–09
Barack Obama	Democrat	2009–

The powers of the president

The powers of the president are his tasks, functions or duties. They are laid out in Article II of the Constitution. Essentially, they have been the same for every president — from George Washington to Barack Obama, and all the 42 presidents in between.

Propose legislation

Article II of the Constitution states: '[The president] shall from time to time give to the Congress information of the State of the Union, and recommend to their consideration such measures as he shall judge necessary and expedient.' This gives the president the power to propose legislation to Congress which he may do through the annual State of the Union Address. But the president can propose legislation at any time by, for example, calling a press conference or making an announcement at a public event. President Obama used his 2010 State of the Union Address to promote help for small businesses, infrastructure building projects, financial reform, a new National Export Initiative and financial aid for higher education students, as well as his flagship healthcare reform legislation.

Box 6.1 The President's schedule: 25–26 July 2012

(all times Eastern Daylight Time)

Thursday 25th

11.00 a.m.	President and Vice-President receive the Presidential Daily Briefing
11.30 a.m.	President meets with Veterans' Affairs Secretary Eric Shinseki
12.30 p.m.	President meets Vice-President for lunch
2.10 p.m.	President holds a cabinet meeting
4.45 p.m.	President and Vice-President meet with Secretary of Defense Leon Panetta

Friday 26th

9.40 a.m.	President and Vice-President receive the Presidential Daily Briefing
10.15 a.m.	President signs the United States–Israel Enhanced Security Act
11.00 a.m.	President and Vice-President meet with US Ambassador to Afghanistan Ryan Crocker
11.30 a.m.	President and Vice-President meet with Secretary of State Hillary Clinton
1.10 p.m.	President attends a campaign event, Washington DC
4.45 p.m.	President departs White House en route to McLean, Virginia
5.25 p.m.	President attends a campaign event
7.35 p.m.	President delivers remarks at a campaign event
8.35 p.m.	President arrives at White House

Source: www.whitehouse.gov

Submit the annual budget

The budget is really just another piece of legislation, but it is potentially the most important. The Office of Management and Budget (OMB) draws up the annual federal budget for the president. The OMB is part of the president's own bureaucracy, which is known as the Executive Office of the President (EXOP). The president then submits the budget to Congress. This is followed by a lengthy bargaining process between the president and Congress — especially lengthy if the presidency and Congress are controlled by different political parties.

Sign legislation

Once bills have been passed through a lengthy and complicated legislative process in Congress (see Chapter 5), they land on the president's desk. He has a number of options, but the most likely is that of signing the bill into law. He will do this to bills for which he wishes to take some credit. Elaborate bill-signing ceremonies are often held, attended by House and Senate members who have been particularly supportive, relevant members of the administration, as well as interested parties who will be affected by the new legislation. At the bill-signing ceremony at the White House for the Patient Protection and Affordable Care Act in March 2010, President Obama invited not only the Democratic Party leadership in Congress but also the widow of the late senator Edward Kennedy, who had made healthcare reform one of his life's ambitions. Also present was 11-year-old Marcelas Owens of Seattle who became an advocate for reform after his mother died without health insurance.

Veto legislation

As well as signing bills into law, the president has the option of vetoing them. The regular veto is a much-used presidential weapon. Even the threat of it can be an important bargaining tool. Altogether, from George Washington to George W. Bush, presidents have used just under 1,500 regular vetoes. Congress may attempt to override the president's veto, but is rarely successful. George W. Bush's 63.6% success rate with vetoes (see Table 6.2) is the third lowest of any president. The president may have the power of pocket veto at his disposal, too, but this can be used only at the end of a congressional session. Pocket vetoes cannot be overridden by Congress. President George H. W. Bush used 15 pocket vetoes, while both Bill Clinton and George W. Bush used just one each. During his first term President Obama used two regular vetoes. The House of Representatives failed in its attempts to override each of them, the first by 143 to 245 and the second by 185 to 235.

Act as chief executive

The opening 15 words of Article II of the Constitution grant the president all executive power. Thus, the president is chief executive — in charge of running the executive branch of the federal government. This, as explained later in this chapter, is a huge job and much of the day-to-day running is delegated to those who run the federal

Table 6.2 Presidential vetoes: 1961–2012

President	Years	Total vetoes	Regular vetoes	Pocket vetoes	Vetoes overridden	Success rate %
John Kennedy	1961–63	21	12	9	0	100
Lyndon Johnson	1963–69	30	16	14	0	100
Richard Nixon	1969–74	43	26	17	7	73.1
Gerald Ford	1974–77	66	48	18	12	75.0
Jimmy Carter	1977–81	31	13	18	2	84.6
Ronald Reagan	1981–89	78	39	39	9	76.9
George H. W. Bush	1989–93	44	29	15	1	97.7
Bill Clinton	1993–2001	37	36	1	2	94.6
George W. Bush	2001–09	12	11	1	4	63.6
Barack Obama†	2009–	2	2	0	0	100

† to 31 December 2012

government's principal departments and agencies. Modern presidents have needed their own bureaucracy — EXOP — to help them to coordinate the work of the federal government.

Nominate executive branch officials

The president has the power to nominate hundreds of officials to the executive branch of government. An incoming president — such as Barack Obama in 2009 — has a host of such posts to fill. The most important of these are the heads of the 15 executive departments such as the Treasury, State and Agriculture. In addition, there are lower-level officials in all these departments, as well as ambassadors, agency heads and members of regulatory commissions. The Senate must confirm all these appointments by a simple majority vote. Appointments continue to be made throughout the president's term of office.

Nominate all federal judges

Nomination of judges involves the president in making hundreds of appointments. He must fill vacancies not only on the federal Supreme Court, but also on the federal trial (district) and appeal (circuit) courts. All judicial appointments are for life and therefore assume a special importance. They must be confirmed by a simple majority vote in the Senate.

Act as commander-in-chief

This power was particularly important for presidents in office from the 1940s to the 1980s. Whether it was Franklin Roosevelt fighting the Second World War, Harry Truman in Berlin and Korea, Kennedy in Cuba, or Lyndon Johnson and Richard Nixon in Vietnam, presidents were seen as playing a highly significant role as commander-in-chief. Then came the demise of the Soviet Union and the break-up of the communist bloc in eastern Europe during the presidencies of Reagan and George H. W. Bush. It was the same

Bush who successfully fought the Persian Gulf War in 1991. The post-Cold War era saw a diminution of the president's commander-in-chief role. The decade from 1991 to 2001 brought no significant foreign policy engagement by a US president, nothing on the scale of Korea, Vietnam or the Gulf War. The events of 11 September 2001 changed all that, however, and George W. Bush found himself thrust into the role of a wartime president.

In this area, Congress's checks are more questionable. The Constitution gives Congress the power to declare war, but that power has not been used since 1941. The president now asks Congress to 'authorise' his use of troops. Congress passed the Gulf of Tonkin Resolution in 1964, giving President Johnson the power 'to take all necessary measures' in Vietnam. Congress passed authorising resolutions in 1991 and 2002 before US troops were used in Kuwait and Iraq respectively. Congress also has the 'power of the purse' with which to check presidential war making, but this has not always proved effective.

Negotiate treaties

The president's seal of office shows an eagle clutching a bundle of arrows in one claw, symbolising the commander-in-chief role, and an olive branch in the other to symbolise his peace-making role. Modern-day presidents have used this power to negotiate such treaties as the Strategic Arms Reduction Treaty (Ronald Reagan), the Chemical Weapons Ban (George H. W. Bush) and a nuclear arms treaty with Russia (Barack Obama).

The president's seal of office

The president's power is checked by the Senate, which must ratify treaties by a two-thirds majority. Table 6.3 shows that during the 20th century the Senate rejected seven treaties. The first and last were significant in that they were major treaties. In 1999, President Clinton failed even to gain a simple majority for the Comprehensive Test Ban Treaty, let alone the two-thirds majority required.

Pardon

Presidents possess the power of pardon and, as can be seen from Table 6.4, use the power with varying degrees of frequency. In 1974, President Ford pardoned his predecessor, Richard Nixon, over all Watergate-related matters. President Clinton caused a storm on his final day in office in January 2001 when he pardoned 140 people including fugitive Mark Rich, whose former wife had made large monetary donations to Clinton's election campaigns and had given expensive personal gifts to the President and first lady. In contrast with Clinton's 140 pardons in one day, George W. Bush pardoned only 189 people in 8 years and Barack Obama pardoned only 22 people in his first term.

Head of State

Not only do presidents perform all these formal constitutional functions, but they must also perform the role of head of state. This is most clearly seen at times of national tragedy when the president takes on the role of comforter-in-chief, sometimes of

Table 6.3 Senate rejection of treaties during the 20th century

Date	President	Treaty	Senate vote
19 March 1920	Woodrow Wilson (D)	Versailles	49–35
18 January 1927	Calvin Coolidge (R)	Commercial rights	50–34
14 March 1934	Franklin Roosevelt (D)	St Lawrence Seaway	46–42
29 January 1935	Franklin Roosevelt (D)	World Court	52–36
26 March 1960	Dwight Eisenhower (R)	Law of Sea Convention	49–30
8 March 1983	Ronald Reagan (R)	Montreal Protocol	50–42
13 October 1999	Bill Clinton (D)	Comprehensive Test Ban	48–51

Table 6.4 Presidential pardons by administration: 1969–2012

President	Party	Dates	Years	Pardons
Richard Nixon	Rep	1969–74	$5\frac{1}{2}$	926
Gerald Ford	Rep	1974–77	$2\frac{1}{2}$	409
Jimmy Carter	Dem	1977–81	4	566
Ronald Reagan	Rep	1981–89	8	406
George H. W. Bush	Rep	1989–93	4	77
Bill Clinton	Dem	1993–2001	8	456
George W. Bush	Rep	2001–09	8	189
Barack Obama†	Dem	2009–	4	22

† to 31 December 2012

mourner-in-chief. President George W. Bush played this role in the weeks following the attacks on the United States on 11 September 2001. It was the President who addressed the nation that night from the Oval Office and did so again at the prayer service in the Washington National Cathedral three days later, seeking to bind the nation's wounds and lift its fallen spirits. More recently we saw President Obama play this role following the devastation caused by Hurricane Sandy in October 2012, as well as in the aftermath of the killing of 20 children and 6 adults at Sandy Hook Elementary School in Newtown, Connecticut, in December of the same year.

The vice-president

Selection, election and appointment

As we explained in Chapter 2, the selection of vice-presidential candidates is now made by the party's presidential candidate before the opening of the party's national convention. The presidential and vice-presidential candidates then run together, on what is called a 'joint ticket'. On Election Day, people vote for the ticket of, for example, Obama–Biden or Romney–Ryan. In other words, the people elect the vice-president along with the president.

Table 6.5 US vice-presidents since 1969

Vice-president	Party	Years in office
Spiro Agnew	Republican	1969–73
Gerald Ford*	Republican	1973–74
Nelson Rockefeller*	Republican	1974–77
Walter Mondale	Democrat	1977–81
George H. W. Bush	Republican	1981–89
Dan Quayle	Republican	1989–93
Al Gore	Democrat	1993–2001
Dick Cheney	Republican	2001–09
Joe Biden	Democrat	2009–

*Appointed

When choosing the vice-presidential candidate, it is often said that a presidential candidate looks for a **balanced ticket**. 'Balance' might be looked for in terms of geographic region, political experience, age and ideology, maybe even gender, race and religion. In 2008, Barack Obama adopted something of a balanced ticket strategy in choosing his vice-presidential running-mate, Senator Joe Biden of Delaware. Biden at 65 was a balance to Obama's youthful 47. Biden had served in the Senate for almost 36 years compared with Obama's less than 4 years. Biden also brought significant foreign policy expertise having served as chairman of the Senate Foreign Relations Committee. There was also, of course, a balance in terms of race.

Key term

➤ **Balanced ticket.** A tactic used by a presidential candidate in selecting the vice-presidential candidate in an attempt to increase voter appeal for their 'ticket'.

Since 1967 and the passage of the 25th Amendment, there are circumstances under which the vice-president may be appointed rather than elected. Should the vice-presidency become vacant, the president has the power to appoint a new vice-president, who must be confirmed by a simple majority vote of both houses of Congress. This has occurred twice. In 1973, Vice-President Spiro Agnew resigned, having pleaded 'no contest' to a charge of income tax evasion. President Nixon then appointed Congressman Gerald Ford as vice-president. Ford was duly confirmed by votes of 92–3 and 387–55 by the Senate and House of Representatives respectively. Less than a year later, Nixon resigned from the presidency over the Watergate affair. Vice-President Ford therefore became president. He then appointed the former governor of New York, Nelson Rockefeller, as the new vice-president. Rockefeller was confirmed by congressional votes of 90–7 and 287–128.

Powers of the vice-president

The Constitution originally gave four powers to the vice-president.

➤ He is the presiding officer of the Senate, but this is a function that the vice-president rarely performs. The Senate deputes usually junior members of its chamber to chair debates.

➤ The vice-president is granted the power to break a tied vote in the Senate. Indeed, it is only to perform this function that a vice-president will usually attend the chamber. Dick Cheney cast a tie-breaking vote in April 2001 to protect President Bush's $1.6 trillion tax cut. In the 28 years between 1981 and January 2009, vice-presidents were called upon to break tied votes on 19 occasions — eight by Dick Cheney (2001–09), seven by George H. W. Bush (1981–89) and four by Al Gore (1993–2001). Dan Quayle (1989–93) never used this power and neither did Joe Biden during his first term as vice-president (2009–13).

➤ The vice-president is given the task of counting and then announcing the result of the Electoral College votes. Thus in January 2001, outgoing Vice-President Gore had to announce his own defeat in the previous November's election, and in January 2013 Vice-President Biden announced his own successful re-election along with that of President Obama.

➤ The first three powers are either of little importance or occur rarely — or both. It is the final power that gives the office of vice-president its potential importance. The vice-president becomes president upon the death, resignation or removal of the president from office. This has occurred on nine occasions: four times following the assassination of the president; four times following the natural death of the president; and once following the resignation of the president (President Nixon in August 1974). The insignificant powers of the office, coupled with this potential importance, led the first vice-president, John Adams, to remark of the post: 'In this I am nothing; but I may be everything.'

More recently, the vice-president has acquired a fifth power: to become acting president if the president is declared, or declares himself, disabled. This is another provision of the 25th Amendment, passed in 1967. The power has been used three times: on 13 July 1985, when President Reagan was hospitalised briefly; on 29 June 2002 and 21 July 2007, when President George W. Bush required sedation in order to undergo a colonoscopy. On these two occasions, Cheney was acting president for just over 2 hours.

The increasing importance of the vice-presidency

The list of those who have held the office of vice-president falls into three distinct groups. Initially, the vice-president was seen as the 'president in waiting'. During much of the first two decades of the nation's history, the vice-president was the person who came second in the balloting of the Electoral College. Thus, the office was held by such prominent politicians as John Adams (1789–97) and Thomas Jefferson (1797–1801). The 12th Amendment (1804), however, changed all that. From then on, the vice-president was

elected on a joint ticket with the presidential candidate. For the next century and a half, the vice-presidency was either filled by people who were nonentities or not filled at all. A list of vice-presidents between 1805 and the mid-20th century looks like an extract from 'who *wasn't* who' with names such as Hannibal Hamlin (1861–65) and Schuyler Colfax (1869–73). Since then the vice-presidency has grown in importance for several reasons.

➤ As the role of the federal government and the president's responsibilities grew, presidents began to see the vice-presidency as a source of help in running the executive branch of government. Beginning with the Eisenhower–Nixon administration (1953–61), vice-presidents were given more high-profile tasks and became in some cases significant presidential advisers. Since Nixon's time as vice-president, all vice-presidents have been ex officio members of the cabinet. Walter Mondale (1977–81) was the first vice-president to be shown the presidential daily briefing (PDB) — the intelligence briefing given to the president at the start of each day. Mondale was also the first vice-president to be given an office in the West Wing — the building that houses the Oval Office. All his successors have seen the PDB and had the same office.

➤ This has had the effect of attracting more significant people to seek the office, which is now always occupied. Over the past 50 years, therefore, the list of vice-presidents has been a distinguished one, including such famous names as Lyndon Johnson, Hubert Humphrey and Al Gore. Of the 11 vice-presidents who held office between 1953 and 2008, four went on to become president, while a further three were selected as their party's presidential candidate.

➤ Modern-day vice-presidents have taken on new roles. Many have played a key role in legislative liaison with Congress. This is the role that Dick Cheney — himself a former member of the House of Representatives — played for President George W. Bush, and is the role that Joe Biden has played in the Obama administration.

➤ The vice-president often becomes the party worker, electioneer and fund-raiser. Cheney played this role in the run-up to the 2002 mid-term elections, as did Biden during both the 2010 and 2012 election cycles.

➤ The vice-president may become a major spokesperson for the administration. This has certainly been the case with the three most recent vice-presidents. Al Gore became a regular face at the podium on environmental issues as well as over government efficiency drives. Dick Cheney spoke out a good deal on foreign policy issues, as has Joe Biden.

➤ Finally, in an era of Washington-outsider presidents — governors Carter, Reagan, Clinton and George W. Bush — vice-presidents have often played the Washington-insider role, guiding the president around the potential pitfalls of Washington politics. These four presidents were ably served in this regard by their respective insider vice-presidents: Walter Mondale, George H. W. Bush, Al Gore and Dick Cheney. Obama might also be added to this list of Washington-outsiders, having served less than four years in the Senate when he was elected president in 2008. And, as we shall see, he has been ably assisted by consummate Washington-insider Joe Biden, especially in terms of liaison with Congress where Biden served for over three decades.

Joe Biden as vice-president

When Joe Biden became vice-president in January 2009, he brought with him the same wealth of Washington experience that a number of his predecessors — Dick Cheney, Al Gore and George H. W. Bush — had brought. And like these three predecessors, he would serve a president who entered office having little or no experience of how Washington worked. Biden's 36 years' service on Capitol Hill — all served in the Senate — was longer than that of any vice-president. With this background, Biden quickly became the point-man for the Obama administration in Congress. 'I'm a Senate guy,' Biden told *New York Times* reporter Matt Bai in a June 2009 interview. 'It's been my whole life.' According to Bai, 'part of Biden's White House portfolio is to act as

Joe Biden — Vice-President to Barack Obama

unofficial ambassador to the Senate, carrying information back and forth between his old colleagues and his new boss'. Biden's role was critical for the President on such big-ticket issues as the economic stimulus package, the middle-class taskforce, tax relief and the Unemployment Reauthorisation Act as well as the negotiations to end the debt ceiling crisis in 2011. Biden's role as White House–Congress mediator was on show again in December 2012 when it was he and Senate Minority Leader Mitch McConnell who put together the final deal to avoid the so-called 'fiscal cliff'. Obama also put Vice-President Biden in charge of drawing up proposals on gun control measures following the Connecticut school shooting in December 2012.

Another of Biden's strengths has been his ability to play devil's advocate in policy discussions and to ask the difficult questions. Every president needs someone to play that role and it helps when it is played by someone with the 'regular Joe' good humour which Biden exudes. His former Senate colleague John Kerry put it this way:

> The Vice-President is asking great questions and he understands these issues very, very deeply. He knows the issues and the personalities very well.

It is because of this role that some who work with Biden have described him as being rather like 'a skunk at a picnic'. Biden does have his weaknesses, not least his proneness to verbal gaffes, but even these are mostly laughed off both by Biden and by his colleagues. As another former Senate colleague, Lindsey Graham, put it: 'If there

were no gaffes, there would be no Joe!' The White House line is clear — that Biden is far more of a help than a hindrance. In a recent *National Journal* column, Michael Hirsh (1 January 2013) described Biden as 'maybe the most influential vice-president ever', for in terms of the sheer number of issues Biden has influenced in a short time, he is bidding to surpass even Dick Cheney to win that accolade. Comments Hirsh:

> In modern times, the vice-presidency has grown in stature from being for the most part a funeral-attending, snooze-inducing post, barren of almost all constitutional duties to something [under Biden] of almost a conjoined twin to the presidency, organically linked and indivisible from the Oval Office.

And unlike his immediate predecessor Dick Cheney, Joe Biden may yet set his sights on the Oval Office when President Obama completes his second term in 2016. Biden would be 73 at the time of the next presidential election, making him a year older than John McCain when he ran for the presidency in 2008. Having voted in his home town of Wilmington, Delaware, on 6 November 2012, he was asked by a member of the media if this was the last time he would be voting for himself, to which the Vice-President teasingly replied, 'No, I don't think so.'

The federal bureaucracy

But the executive branch of government is more than just the White House. There is a vast federal bureaucracy, which those who work in the White House are trying to coordinate. Some of that federal bureaucracy is based in downtown Washington, but there are significant parts spread throughout all 50 states.

The federal bureaucracy grew significantly during the 20th century as the size and scope of the federal government itself expanded. This expansion was brought about by a number of important developments in US society, such as industrialisation, immigration, westward expansion, the New Deal and the development of modern means of communication such as road, rail and air, as well as the telephone, radio and the new electronic media. Furthermore, the USA's development into a world power from the 1950s — and into the world's sole superpower by the end of the century — added to the responsibilities laid at the door of the federal government. Such a rapid and significant expansion brought problems to presidents from Franklin Roosevelt onwards which would have been almost — if not entirely — unknown to their predecessors. Even in the last two decades, two new executive departments have been created, reflecting the growing importance of the policy areas for which they have oversight — Veterans' Affairs and Homeland Security. The federal bureaucracy has now grown to a size quite unimaginable at the beginning of the 20th century.

The **federal bureaucracy** can be defined as the administrative system of the national government that carries out policy. The term is synonymous with 'the executive branch of government' or 'the administration'. To some, 'bureaucracy' is also synonymous with excessive red tape, delay, over-manning, inefficiency and waste, as well as an over-commitment to routine, hierarchy and 'process', and a resistance to change.

Key concept

➤ **Federal bureaucracy.** The unelected, administrative part of the executive branch of the federal government, made up of departments, agencies and commissions that carry out policy on a day-to-day basis. The word 'bureaucracy' also has overtones of 'red tape', systems dedicated to routine, resistance to change and inefficiency.

By 2010, the federal bureaucracy had just under 2.8 million civilian employees. Needless to say, not all these civil servants are based in Washington DC. The city isn't big enough — only 11% of federal civil servants work in the Washington area. The federal bureaucracy is spread throughout the length and breadth of the United States. This was most dramatically brought home to ordinary people when the *federal* government building in Oklahoma City was blown up in 1995. Almost every respectable-sized city in America contains such a building. These facts of size and geographic dispersal throughout America bring significant managerial problems.

The federal bureaucracy can be divided into four broad categories. First, there are the executive departments, which might be thought of as the 'giants' of the federal bureaucracy. Initially, there were only three — State, War and the Treasury. Today there are 15 (see Table 6.6), with a great range in size, both of personnel and budget. The heads of these executive departments are designated as the 'secretary' — secretary of state, secretary of defense and so on — with the exception of the head of the Justice Department, who has the title of attorney general. As we shall see shortly, these 15 heads of the executive departments are ex officio members of the president's cabinet. Within these executive departments, there are two 'tiers' — the first tier made up of State, Treasury, Defense and Justice; the second tier comprising all the rest. The first-tier departments are regarded as the most prestigious and important parts of the federal bureaucracy.

The second category is made up of the executive agencies, which are almost indistinguishable from the executive departments, except that their heads — known usually as 'directors' — are not ex officio members of the cabinet. Like the heads of the executive departments, they are appointed by the president with the advice and consent of the Senate. A number of executive agencies — such as housing and veterans' affairs — have, over the years, been upgraded into executive departments.

The Environmental Protection Agency (EPA) was created by President Nixon in 1970. It regulates air and water pollution controls, deals with the clean-up and disposal of hazardous wastes and toxic substances, and regulates drinking water, noise and radiation. The Federal Reserve Board — known colloquially as 'the Fed' — conducts the monetary policy of the federal government, oversees the supervision of banks and enforces the

Table 6.6 Creation of executive departments

Department	Created
State	1789
Treasury	1789
Defense[a]	1949
Interior	1849
Justice	1870
Agriculture	1889
Commerce[b]	1903
Labor[b]	1903
Health and Human Services[c]	1953
Housing and Urban Development	1965
Transportation	1966
Energy	1977
Education[d]	1979
Veterans' Affairs	1989
Homeland Security	2002

[a] Formerly War Department (created 1789); amalgamated with Navy (1798) and Air Force (1947). [b] Commerce and Labor created as a joint department (1903); separated in 1913. [c] Formerly Health, Education and Welfare; Education separated in 1979. [d] Formerly part of Health, Education and Welfare (created 1953); separated in 1979.

laws to protect consumers in financial dealings. The Fed was for many years closely associated with the name of its chairman Alan Greenspan, appointed in 1987 by President Reagan and reappointed by Presidents Clinton and George W. Bush. He eventually stepped down in 2006 to be succeeded by Ben Bernanke. The National Aeronautics and Space Administration (NASA) conducts space exploration and aeronautic research. After the heady days of the moon programme in the 1960s and 1970s it was seen during the 1980s and 1990s as something of a falling star. The loss of the *Challenger* (1986) and *Columbia* (2003) missions led to further questioning of its efficiency and viability. The space station project is now struggling to obtain adequate funds from Congress.

The third category is made up of the independent regulatory commissions (IRCs), which occupy a special status in the federal bureaucracy, for they are administratively independent of all three branches of the federal government. They operate behind barriers created by Congress to shield them from direct presidential control. In practice, however, they are subject to pressures not only from the White House, but also from Congress and the industries and groups they are meant to regulate. An IRC might regulate railways, airlines, radio and television, banks, Wall Street, labour unions, business corporations or federal elections.

Finally, there are the government corporations. Beginning in the 1930s, the federal government established various corporations, some quite high profile, to perform principally commercial functions that might otherwise have been carried out by the private sector. The United States Postal Service was created in 1970 out of the former Post Office Department. The Federal Deposit Insurance Corporation (FDIC) insures savings deposits in commercial banks; outside every bank in the USA is a sign that reads simply: 'Member FDIC'. If you take a passenger train from, say, Washington DC to New York or Boston, your journey will be on AMTRAK, the corporation that runs the nationwide passenger train system.

Functions of the federal bureaucracy

The federal bureaucracy has three principal functions: executing laws, creating rules and adjudication.

Executing laws

The Constitution states in Article II Section 2 that the president shall 'take care that the laws be faithfully executed'. This is the main reason why the president needs the federal bureaucracy. It is also one of the reasons why, as Congress has legislated in more and more policy areas over the decades, the federal bureaucracy has of necessity become larger. Congress passes bills; the president signs them into law. The federal bureaucracy must then see that they are carried out: that mail is delivered (the United States Postal Service); taxes are collected (the Internal Revenue Service: IRS); planes are inspected (the Federal Aviation Administration); the country protected (the Pentagon); and the national parks preserved (the Department of the Interior). This is the principal function of the executive departments — carrying out the laws within their own policy areas.

Creating rules

Legislators usually establish only the broad principles of policy. It is the bureaucrats who are required to write the specific rules that decide how the laws will be executed. The more complex society has become, the greater the need for specialist bureaucrats to create specific rules. It is in this function that the regulatory commissions of the federal government play a significant role.

Adjudication

In executing laws and creating rules, disputes inevitably arise. One party will consider that a law is not being applied rigorously, while another will consider that its application has been partial or unfair. It is a function of the federal bureaucracy to adjudicate in such disputes.

Personnel of the federal bureaucracy

It is a widely accepted belief that recruitment to and promotion within the federal bureaucracy should be on the basis of merit, not political favouritism. Thus, the Civil Service Reform Act (1978) established the Office of Personnel Management (OPM) to manage those who work within the federal bureaucracy. The OPM develops the rules, regulations and policies for federal personnel management. It oversees recruitment,

evaluation, investigation, training and retirement programmes. It also supervises affirmative action programmes and the requirements of the Ethics in Government Act (1978) as it pertains to federal employees.

However, federal civil service recruitment is more decentralised and politicised than these basic rules of thumb seem to imply. First, in recent years, the OPM has offloaded many of its recruitment responsibilities to individual agency heads. Second, recruitment to upper- and middle-level jobs is more political than appears at first glance.

At the upper level, some posts — comprising some 3% of the federal bureaucracy — are appointed on grounds of politics rather than purely on merit. First and foremost are those appointments, authorised by the Constitution and by law, that the president can make of cabinet and sub-cabinet officials, attorneys, ambassadors and various members of boards and commissions. These appointments are subject to confirmation by the Senate. In addition, 'Schedule C' appointments to jobs in the departments and agencies, described as being of a 'confidential or policy-determining character', are available to an incoming president to fill with so-called political appointees. In 1961, President Kennedy had 451 such posts to fill. President Clinton in 1993 had well over 2,000.

Even in the middle-level appointments, there is a certain degree of political appointment in what is known as the 'buddy system'. This is based on what is called the 'name-request job'. This process is similar to one used by most private businesses or organisations. A person learns of a job from someone who already has one, or the head of an agency decides in advance whom they wish to recruit to a certain post. The agency must still send a form describing the job to the OPM, but it also names the person whom it wishes to appoint.

The overwhelming majority of people who work in the federal bureaucracy are career civil servants recruited on the basis of competitive examinations and for the particular skills that they possess, be they economists, nuclear physicists, statisticians or computer programmers. This has been the case ever since the old '**spoils system**' was replaced by a merit system in the Civil Service Reform Act of 1883, known as the Pendleton Act. The Act was a direct result of the assassination of President James Garfield in 1881 by someone who would forever be described in history books as 'a disappointed office seeker'.

Key concept

> **Spoils system.** A system by which government jobs are awarded to political supporters and friends rather than on merit. The term derives from the expression, 'to the victor belong the spoils'.

President-elect Bill Clinton claimed in 1992 that he wanted a cabinet that 'looked like America'. Few thought that his initial cabinet looked much 'like America', but what about the federal bureaucracy? By the time Clinton entered the White House, the federal civil service certainly looked much more like America than it had done when President Kennedy arrived in the Oval Office 32 years earlier. In 1961, only 25% of the civil service was female. By 2010, the percentage of women had risen to 44%. In 1961, it would have been hard to find any ethnic minorities in the federal civil service. Kennedy even commented — apparently disapprovingly — on their absence from his inaugural parade. By 2010, ethnic minorities made up just under one-third (33.1%) of the federal civil service. The federal civil service has a recruitment policy to attract significant numbers of disabled people as well as war veterans. By 2010, 7% of the federal civil servants were disabled and 25% were war veterans, of whom just over 40% were Vietnam veterans. Disabled veterans account for 21% of federal civil servants.

Problems of the federal bureaucracy

There are five problems associated with the federal bureaucracy.

First, agencies tend to serve the interests of those whom they are supposed to be overseeing. This 'clientelism', as it is called, is seen as a particular problem with the regulatory commissions, as these watchdog agencies often turn out to be lapdogs. Special interests are protected at the expense of the public interest.

Second, agencies invariably seek to expand their powers and responsibilities at the expense of other agencies, which is often referred to as 'bureaucratic imperialism'. Political interests become paramount, sometimes regardless of the public interest. Imperialism sometimes manifests itself in 'turf battles' between agencies about who has jurisdiction over which policy area. This was seen in the battles that ensued at the time of the creation of the new Department of Homeland Security in the second year of the George W. Bush administration.

Third, agencies tend to be parochial, having a narrow focus on their own goals rather than on the 'big picture' of the administration as a whole, and departmental interest often triumphs at the expense of national interest.

Fourth, most agencies are known for acting slowly and cautiously, with a tendency to resist change. This can make life frustrating for an incoming president who wants to see radical policy changes being made. Agencies are seen as overly conservative, too resistant to change.

Fifth, in applying rules and regulations, agencies often ignore the particular concerns or specific merits of those who will be affected by the rules. Bureaucracy is seen as inhuman and over-committed to form and process.

One can add to these five general problems three more specific problems, those associated with 'iron triangles', of top bureaucrats 'going native,' and of inefficiency.

Iron triangles

The term **iron triangle** is used to describe a strong, resilient relationship between three distinct political bodies: special interests (often represented by interest groups); congressional committees; and the related agency. The triangle is 'iron' because it

is impenetrable. This relationship results in policies being made and executed to the mutual benefit of the three parties involved. Such iron triangles are generally considered to have a negative impact on the policy-making and policy-execution processes. An example is the relationship between defence contractors, the House and Senate Armed Services Committees and the Defense Department, which results in a large national defence budget. As David McKay (2005) concludes: 'The combined political clout of the leading sub-government actors is formidable, with no individual president, public-interest lobby or congressional leader able to break the pattern of distribution and public expenditure which the iron triangle has moulded.'

 Key concept

> **Iron triangle.** A strong relationship between pressure groups, congressional committees and federal agencies in a given policy area for the mutual benefit of these three parties.

'Going native'

There is always a fear in the White House of the political appointees in the federal bureaucracy **'going native'**. This means that, rather than imposing the president's wishes on the bureaucracy, they become advocates of the bureaucracy's wishes to the president and start to resist his policy preferences. The term derives from a comment made by John Ehrlichman, a senior aide in the Nixon administration, who complained that members of Nixon's cabinet had gone off and 'married the natives'. The picture here is perhaps that of Christian missionaries going to foreign countries to 'convert the natives'. Under this scenario, rather than converting them to their beliefs, they marry them and adopt the native customs and ways of looking at the world.

 Key term

> **'Going native'.** A term used to refer to the situation in which political appointees cease to be advocates for the politician who appointed them — in this case, the president — and instead become advocates for the bureaucracies and special interests associated with their policy area.

Richard Fenno likewise noted that the president's influence over the bureaucracy 'becomes splintered and eroded as [members of the bureaucracy] respond to political forces not presidential in origin and direction'. One way round this problem is to appoint close and trusted friends to key posts in the federal bureaucracy. Both presidents George H. W. Bush and George W. Bush adopted this strategy with some success.

Inefficiency

There is a widespread belief that the federal bureaucracy is inefficient. Many think that this is largely due to the fact that the pay of federal civil servants is determined more by length of service than by job performance. In a government-wide survey published in 2007, federal employees were asked to respond to the statement that 'pay rises depend on how well employees perform their jobs'. The response: 45% disagreed with the statement, only 22% agreed while 25% were neutral.

In an attempt to improve bureaucratic efficiency, incoming president Bill Clinton gave his vice-president, Al Gore, the task of reassessing the organisation and efficiency of the federal bureaucracy in his project called 'reinventing government'. In 1991, then Arkansas governor and presidential hopeful Bill Clinton had remarked:

> I want to reinvent government to make it more efficient and more effective. I want to give citizens more choices in the services they get, and empower them to make these choices. In Arkansas, we have balanced the budget every year and improved services. We've treated taxpayers like our customers and our bosses, because they are.

But the success of the Clinton–Gore administration in actually reinventing government — making it more efficient — was exceedingly limited. By the end of his first term, Clinton was claiming that 'the era of big government is over', and there had been some quite significant reductions in the federal workforce. Furthermore, out-sourcing had produced some significant savings, often because workers were paid less in the private sector. But economic efficiencies did not always lead to practical efficiencies.

The inefficiency of the federal bureaucracy was on full view in the response of the Federal Emergency Management Agency (FEMA) to hurricanes Katrina and Rita in 2005. The appointment by President George W. Bush of Michael Brown as Administrator of FEMA was based more on cronyism than on managerial competence. What the federal government's inadequate response to Hurricane Katrina showed up was the muddled and confused answer to the question 'who's in charge?' Was it the President, was it FEMA, was it state governors, was it city mayors? As Richard Katz (2007) concludes: 'the fact that powers are overlapping, shared and contested rather than neatly divided and separated, which are among the central features of American government, simply became more obvious in a crisis.'

New Orleans after Hurricane Katrina. The US government's response posed the question 'who's in charge?'

Checking the power of the federal bureaucracy

The role of Congress

The power of the federal bureaucracy is checked in the main by Congress. It is Congress that has the legislative power to establish, merge or abolish departments and agencies. Congress has reorganised the federal bureaucracy on a number of occasions, as shown in Table 6.6. There was a substantial reorganisation in 2002 when Congress extracted 170,000 current federal government employees from 22 different agencies — including the departments of Justice, Treasury, Agriculture, Transportation, Health, Energy, Defense and Commerce — and merged them to form the new Department of Homeland Security.

Congress can use its appropriations power — the 'power of the purse' — to finance the various departments and agencies within the federal bureaucracy as well as its power of oversight to investigate federal departments and agencies. Such oversight is conducted largely in the policy specialist standing committees of both houses of Congress (see Chapter 5). Here, members build up policy expertise over many years. Given the high rates of incumbency — especially in the House of Representatives — bureaucrats have every reason to fear the spotlight of key members of the relevant congressional committees, who are likely to remain in office long after a president and his entourage have vacated the White House.

The role of the president

In contrast, most modern-day presidents have gone on record as saying that they found it well-nigh impossible to control the federal bureaucracy. In their attempt to control the federal bureaucracy, presidents must rely principally on staff within the Executive Office of the President and members of the cabinet. Harry Truman (1945–53) once commented: 'I thought I was the president, but when it comes to these bureaucracies, I can't make them do a damn thing.' During his 1980 election campaign Ronald Reagan (1981–89) liked to ask his audiences which were the most frightening words in the English language, to which Reagan's answer was 'I'm from the federal government, and I'm here to help!' In his first inaugural address, Reagan had claimed: 'Government isn't the solution: government is the problem.'

President Clinton set about trying to reorganise the federal government and make it more efficient with his 'reinventing government' initiative, of which Vice-President Gore was put in charge. Although Gore undertook the task with his usual thoroughness, the Clinton–Gore administration found it no easier than its predecessors to make significant reforms of such a large organisation as the federal bureaucracy.

When President George W. Bush arrived in the White House in 2001 he proposed a 'competitive out-sourcing' initiative as part of his agenda to control the federal bureaucracy. Simply stated, Bush proposed that federal government employees would have to compete for their jobs against private contractors and that as a result costs would decrease even if the work ultimately remained in-house. 'Bush Plan To Contract Federal Jobs Falls Short', headlined the *Washington Post* (25 April 2008) during Bush's eighth and final year in office. Here's how *Washington Post* reporter Christopher Lee summed up the situation:

> As Bush's presidency winds down, the [out-sourcing] programme's critics say it has had disappointing results and shaken morale among federal civil servants. Private contractors have grown increasingly reluctant to participate in the competitions [for out-sourced services] which federal employees have won 83% of the time. The programme fell short of the President's goals in scope and in cost savings. Between 2003 and 2006, agencies completed competitions for fewer than 50,000 jobs, a fraction of what Bush envisaged. Moreover, the Government Accountability Office found that the administration overstated the savings from some competitions by undercounting the costs of running them.

All this might look like bad news for governmental efficiency, but it might be good news for democracy. A president who really did have total control over the federal bureaucracy might be in a terrifyingly powerful position. After all, it was President Nixon who tried to use the IRS, the FBI and the CIA to destroy those who featured on his 'enemies list' as well as to effect the cover-up of the Watergate scandal. Fortunately, he failed. The problems of control of the federal bureaucracy are therefore matters not only of efficiency, but also of the checks necessary for democratic government.

The cabinet

Historical background

The cabinet is an advice-giving group selected by the president, membership of which is determined by both tradition and presidential discretion. The traditional members are the heads of the executive departments. Originally there were just three — State, War and the Treasury. Now, as we have already seen, there are 15. The president has the discretion to award cabinet rank to other administration officials, too. In January 2012, at the beginning of his fourth year in office, President Obama announced that he was elevating the administrator of the Small Business Administration, Karen Mills, to cabinet status. Ms Mills was introduced as a full member of the cabinet at its next meeting held on 31 January. By doing this, the President was signalling the importance he placed on small businesses in promoting economic recovery in America.

Key concept

> **The cabinet.** The advisory group selected by the president to aid him in making decisions and coordinating the work of the federal government, membership of which is determined by both tradition and presidential discretion.

The cabinet is not mentioned in the Constitution. As we have already seen, the Founding Fathers created a *singular* executive — no councils or cabinets. However, the Constitution does state in Article II that the president 'may require the opinion in writing of the principal officer in each of the executive departments upon any subject relating to the duties of their respective offices'.

Four words or phrases in this brief extract indicate precisely what the president can require from the heads of the executive departments. First, the word 'may' is significant. This means that, whatever the Constitution prescribes in this section is voluntary, not obligatory. Constitutions are usually about 'shall', not 'may'. Second, the president may require 'opinions' — this is a very low-level word. These are not 'decisions' or even 'recommendations', merely 'opinions'. Third, he may require these opinions 'in writing'. No meeting is envisaged. Finally, there is the restriction as to what these 'opinions in writing' may be about: not 'upon any subject', but rather 'upon any subject *relating to the duties of their respective offices*'. In other words, the secretary of the treasury will offer opinions only on Treasury matters; the secretary of state only on State Department matters. This is certainly not the recipe for what students of UK politics understand by a 'cabinet meeting'.

Why, then, do presidents have a 'cabinet'? In 1789, President Washington thought it would be helpful to have a meeting with the secretaries of War, the Treasury and State, plus the attorney general. The press called them 'cabinet meetings'. Every president since then has had a cabinet and held cabinet meetings. According to presidential scholar Richard Fenno (1959), the cabinet is 'institutionalised by usage alone'. In other words, it is used because it is used.

It is important to differentiate between the cabinet as individuals and the cabinet as a group. Failure to see these two different uses of the term can lead to misunderstandings. The answer to the question 'Was President Obama's cabinet important during his first term?' is impossible to answer until we have established in which sense the term is being used. As individuals, cabinet members were important: some, like Secretary of State Hillary Clinton and Treasury Secretary Timothy Geithner, were very important. On the other hand, cabinet meetings were hardly ever held, so, as a group, the cabinet was unimportant.

Recruitment, membership and confirmation

A new president needs to recruit a completely new cabinet. In a presidential system such as in the USA, there is no 'shadow cabinet' waiting to take office. Furthermore, in a 'separated' system, in which members of the legislature cannot at the same time serve in the executive, the president must cast his net more widely for potential cabinet members. There are four major pools of recruitment.

First, the president may try to recruit from Congress. Unfortunately, asking serving members of Congress to give up their seats to take up a cabinet post, where both prestige and job security are often in short supply, is usually unsuccessful. It was widely reported in November 2008 that Congressman Jim Clyburn of North Carolina, the House Majority Whip, turned down an invitation from President-elect Barack Obama to become Secretary of Housing and Urban Development in the new administration. However, the incoming Obama cabinet in 2009 featured three incumbent members of Congress — senators Hillary Clinton of New York as secretary of state, Ken Salazar of Colorado as secretary of the interior, and Representative Hilda Solis of California as secretary of labor. All three left the Obama cabinet at the start of the second term. Usually, however, incoming presidents are more likely to invite former or retiring members of Congress into the cabinet. In 2009, Obama recruited retiring House member Ray LaHood of Illinois as secretary of transportation. In the 40 years from John Kennedy to George W. Bush, however, fewer than one in five cabinet officers had any congressional experience at all.

Second, the president may recruit from among serving or former state governors. In 2009, Governor Janet Napolitano of Arizona was appointed as secretary of homeland security and Governor Kathleen Sebelius of Kansas was appointed as secretary of health and human services. Obama also appointed two ex-governors: Tom Vilsack (Iowa) as secretary of agriculture and Gary Locke (Washington) as secretary of commerce.

A third pool of recruitment is that of big city mayors. Bill Clinton appointed the former Mayor of Denver, Federico Peña, as secretary of transportation. In his first term, Barack Obama appointed the former mayor of Dallas, Ron Kirk, as US Trade Representative, a post which has cabinet rank.

Academia is a fourth possible source of recruitment. Steven Chu, appointed by Barack Obama as secretary of energy in 2009, was Professor of Physics at the University of California. When he departed in 2013, another physics professor, Ernest Moniz of the Massachusetts Institute of Technology, was nominated to replace him.

What the president is really looking for in cabinet officers is policy specialists. In 2001, Bush's education secretary, Rod Paige, was not only a former professor; he had for 6 years been schools superintendent in Houston, Texas. Eight years later, Barack Obama appointed the Chicago schools superintendent, Arne Duncan, to be his education secretary. At the same time, the president of the New York Federal Reserve Bank, Timothy Geithner, was appointed secretary of the treasury, and the New York City housing commissioner Shaun Donovan was appointed secretary of housing and urban development — all policy specialists.

All cabinet appointments are subject to confirmation by the Senate and we considered this in some detail in Chapter 5. It is highly unusual for the Senate to reject cabinet nominations. The last time this occurred was in 1989 when the Senate rejected George H. W. Bush's nomination of John Tower as secretary of defense. In 2009, most of Obama's new cabinet appointments sailed through their confirmations receiving unanimous votes in committee and waved through on a voice vote in the Senate itself. But in February 2013, Chuck Hagel had a difficult time being confirmed by the Senate as secretary of defense, the final vote being 58-41.

A balanced cabinet

Presidents like to have a 'balanced' cabinet. President-elect Clinton in 1992 talked about having a cabinet that 'looked like America'. There are five principal factors that presidents usually consider to balance their cabinet.

Table 6.7 President Barack Obama's cabinet, March 2013

Post	Cabinet officer
Secretary of State	John Kerry
Secretary of Defense	Chuck Hagel
Secretary of the Treasury	Jacob (Jack) Lew
Secretary of Agriculture	Tom Vilsack
Secretary of the Interior	Sally Jewell*
Attorney General	Eric Holder
Secretary of Commerce	†
Secretary of Labor	Thomas Perez*
Secretary of Health and Human Services	Kathleen Sebelius
Secretary of Education	Arne Duncan
Secretary of Housing and Urban Development	Shaun Donovan
Secretary of Transportation	†
Secretary of Energy	Ernest Moniz*
Secretary of Veterans' Affairs	Eric Shinseki
Secretary of Homeland Security	Janet Napolitano

* Subject to Senate confirmation at time of going to press.
† Vacant at time of going to press.

➤ Presidents like to balance their cabinet in terms of region. In Obama's initial cabinet, there was Hilda Solis (Labor) from California, Janet Napolitano (Homeland Security) from Arizona, Ken Salazar (Interior) from Colorado, Arne Duncan (Education) from Illinois, and Shaun Donovan (Housing and Urban Development: HUD) from New York.

➤ Presidents look for balance by race. President Lyndon Johnson was the first president to appoint an African-American to his cabinet when Robert Weaver was appointed as secretary of housing and urban development in 1966. Expectations had therefore been set, and incoming President Richard Nixon was criticised in 1969 when he appointed an all-white cabinet. Every president since Nixon has appointed an ethnically diverse cabinet. George W. Bush's 2001 cabinet included five cabinet officers who were from ethnic minorities, at the time the most ethnically diverse cabinet ever appointed. Furthermore, throughout his presidency, the State Department was headed by an African-American — Colin Powell in the first term and Condoleezza Rice in the second term. Barack Obama's 2009 cabinet included six members of minority race: African-American Eric Holder (Justice); Hispanics Hilda Solis (Labor) and Ken Salazar (Interior); Chinese-Americans Steven Chu (Energy) and Gary Locke (Commerce); Japanese-American Eric Shinseki (Veterans' Affairs); and Lebanese-American Ray LaHood (Transportation). But only Holder and Shinseki served through into Obama's second term. In March 2013, Obama nominated Thomas Perez as his new secretary of labor, thus one Hispanic was replaced by another.

➤ Gender is an important factor in appointing the cabinet. Once Gerald Ford had become the first modern-day president to appoint a woman to the cabinet, with his appointment of Carla Hills as HUD secretary in 1975, successive presidents felt obliged to follow suit. When, in 1981, President Reagan appointed no women as heads of the executive departments, he faced considerable criticism. In 2001, Bush appointed three women as heads of department: Gale Norton (Interior), Elaine Chao (Labor) and Ann Veneman (Agriculture). There having been no woman secretary of state between 1789 and 1997, three of the last four secretaries of state have now been women — Madeline Albright (1997–2001), Condoleezza Rice (2005–09) and Hillary Clinton (2009–13). In 2009, Obama appointed four women as heads of department: Hillary Clinton (State), Hilda Solis (Labor), Kathleen Sebelius (Health and Human Services: HHS) and Janet Napolitano (Homeland Security).

In terms of both race and gender, some would point out that female and ethnic minority nominations rarely head the so-called 'upper-tier' departments — State, Defense, the Treasury and Justice (see Table 6.8). President Clinton broke this trend by appointing Janet Reno at Justice in 1993 and Madeleine Albright at State in 1997. President George W. Bush did likewise by appointing Colin Powell secretary of state in 2001, replacing him with Condoleezza Rice in 2005. As Hillary Clinton had served as secretary of state throughout Barack Obama's first term, it was 16 years since there had been a white man heading up the State Department when John Kerry was appointed in 2013. The last four appointees had all been black, female or both. In 2009, Barack Obama appointed Eric Holder as the first African-American to head the Department of Justice and retired Army General Eric Shinseki as the first Japanese-American to head the Department of Veterans' Affairs.

Table 6.8 Appointments of women and ethnic minority cabinet officers by department, 1961–2013

Department	Women	Ethnic minorities
'Upper-tier' departments		
State	3	2
Treasury	0	0
Defense	0	0
Justice	1	2
'Lower-tier' departments		
Agriculture	1	1
Interior	2	1
Commerce	2	3
Labor	6	3
Health and Human Services	4	2
Education	2	1
Homeland Security	1	0
Housing and Urban Development	2	5
Transportation	2	3
Energy	1	2
Veterans' Affairs	0	3

> Age is yet another factor. As a rule of thumb, the average age of the cabinet usually reflects the age of the president. The youngest ever cabinet was that of President Kennedy — the youngest elected president. Their average age was just 47. However, that rule was broken when George W. Bush appointed the oldest cabinet in modern times — possibly the oldest ever. Its average age was 58. When they were sworn into office in January 2001, six of them (Rumsfeld, Paige, Powell, Mineta, O'Neill and Principi) were over 60, and a seventh (Thompson) was 10 months away from his 60th birthday. Only three — Norton (46), Chao (47) and Abraham (48) — were under 50. In 2009, Barack Obama also appointed six cabinet officers who were over 60 (Clinton, Gates, Sebelius, LaHood, Chu and Shinseki). Three were under 50 including 47-year old Timothy Geithner as secretary of the treasury, the youngest person to hold the post since the Civil War. As secretary of housing and urban development, Obama appointed Shaun Donovan, though at 42 Donovan was not the youngest to hold the post — Andrew Cuomo was just 40 when he was appointed secretary of HUD by President Clinton. The average age of Obama's first cabinet was just over 55.

> A fifth factor is political ideology. Whether it is a Democrat or a Republican cabinet, the president will want to have the different ideological wings of his party represented: liberal Democrats, conservative Democrats and New Democrats; conservative Republicans and moderate Republicans. George W. Bush had campaigned in the 2000 election as a 'compassionate conservative'. His 2001 cabinet looked more 'compassionate' than 'conservative'. The obvious exception was Attorney General John Ashcroft, who had a solid conservative record during both his 8 years as Governor of Missouri and his 6 years in the Senate. Gale Norton at Interior probably fell into the conservative category too. But with the appointments of Colin Powell (State) and Tommy Thompson (HHS) — as well as Christine Todd Whitman, with cabinet rank, to head the Environmental Protection Agency — this certainly did not look like a conservative cabinet. It is not unusual for a president to pick someone from the other party. In his second term, Democrat President Obama appointed former Republican senator Chuck Hagel as secretary of defense, whilst in his first term he had initially retained George W. Bush's secretary of defense Robert Gates, and appointed Republican congressman Ray LaHood as secretary of transportation.

Cabinet meetings

The frequency of cabinet meetings varies from one president to another. During his first year in office, Ronald Reagan held 36 cabinet meetings, while in his first year Bill Clinton held only six. In some administrations there is a trend to hold fewer cabinet meetings the longer the president remains in office. Reagan's 36 meetings in his first year became 21 in the second year and just 12 in each of the third and fourth years. In 8 years, George W. Bush held 49 cabinet meetings, an average of just over six meetings a year. But unlike with his immediate predecessors there was no wild fluctuation in the number of meetings per year. He never held more than nine in any year (2001) and never fewer than four (2007). This was exactly what Bush had in mind when he arrived in Washington at the start of his first administration in January 2001. Just a month into his presidency, I interviewed Bush's secretary to the cabinet, Albert Hawkins, in his West Wing office. Hawkins told me that President Bush envisaged full cabinet meetings being held 'once every couple of months'. And an average of six meetings a year is just about on the nail (see Table 6.9). Hawkins explained that cabinet meetings would be used 'to brief cabinet members on big picture items'.

In his first term, Barack Obama held just 16 cabinet meetings, an average of four meetings a year. This is fewer than George W. Bush and probably more in line with the frequency of cabinet meetings under Bill Clinton. But when compared with presidents such as Carter and Reagan, one can see the very different ways in which presidents use — or do not use — cabinet meetings. Like George W. Bush, Obama tended to schedule meetings just before or immediately after notable political events such as the State of the Union Address or the mid-term elections and use them as an opportunity for him to deliver a team talk to his cabinet on big ticket items. Table 6.10 shows how much the state of the American economy dominated Obama cabinet meetings.

Who attends cabinet meetings and what does the scene look like? All the heads of the executive departments, the vice-president and all other administration officials granted cabinet rank are expected to attend. The cabinet room contains a huge mahogany table which tapers to both ends, allowing the president — seated in the middle of one side — to see all the participants. All regular attendees are assigned places around the table according to the seniority of the department which they head up. Opposite the president sits the vice-president. To the president's right and left are, respectively, the secretary of state and secretary of defense. To the vice-president's right and left are, respectively, the secretary of the treasury and the attorney general. Other attendees —

Table 6.9 Number of cabinet meetings held per year: 2001–12

Year	President	Number of cabinet meetings
2001	George W. Bush	9
2002		5
2003		8
2004		6
2005		5
2006		6
2007		4
2008–09		6
2009	Barack Obama	5
2010		4
2011		4
2012		3

Source: www.whitehouse.gov

Table 6.10 Policy items discussed at selected Obama cabinet meetings

Date	Policy items discussed
2009 20 April	Need for efficiency in government; the economy
2010 22 June 4 November	The economy; Iraq; Gulf of Mexico oil spill; energy policy Mid-term election results; the economy; START Treaty with Russia
2011 3 August	Federal debt ceiling negotiations in Congress; the economy
2012 31 January 26 July 28 November	State of the Union Address; small businesses Middle-class tax cut Post-election thank-yous; Hurricane Sandy recovery; the economy

mostly senior members of the White House staff — sit around the room, looking in towards the cabinet table.

Meetings of the president with the full cabinet tend to get a bad press. Many describe them as 'boring' and 'a waste of time' (see Box 6.2). Part of the trouble is that so many of the people sitting round the table are policy specialists. They have little or nothing to contribute to discussions in other policy areas. As Reagan's labor secretary Bill Brock put it:

> The problem with the cabinet is that it has become too large. We keep adding new departments, so there are too many issues that come up where people have neither jurisdiction nor competence.

Since Brock sat in the cabinet, two more departments have been created — Veterans' Affairs (1989) and Homeland Security (2002).

Box 6.2 Comments from cabinet officers regarding cabinet meetings

'The president listened to the group with thinly disguised impatience.'

J. Edward Day, postmaster general in Kennedy's cabinet

'I always went to cabinet meetings thinking "I wonder how soon I can get away from this so I can get on with all the work I've got to do." And I think most of my colleagues had the same idea.'

A cabinet officer to President Johnson

'Nothing of substance was discussed. There was no disagreement because there was nothing to disagree about. Things over which one might have disagreed were not discussed.'

Elliot Richardson, attorney general in Nixon's cabinet

'Carter cabinet meetings were almost useless. The discussions were desultory. There was no coherent theme to them, and after a while they were held less and less frequently.'

Zbigniew Brzezinski, national security advisor in Carter's cabinet

'Very often they were a waste of time. You could get very bored.'

A cabinet officer to President George H. W. Bush

However, formal meetings held in most organisations are probably described by at least some of the participants in deprecating terms. It does not necessarily mean that such meetings should not be held or that they perform no useful functions. The same is true of the president's cabinet, for the cabinet meeting performs many useful functions, both from the president's perspective and from that of the cabinet officers.

The functions of cabinet meetings for the president

Cabinet meetings can potentially perform several functions from the president's perspective.

➢ They can engender team spirit. This is especially important at the beginning of an administration. Presidents do not have a 'shadow cabinet' waiting to come into office. Many of the president's cabinet officers will be complete strangers to him. Cabinet meetings can help to weld them into *his* team to move forward *his* agenda. Once this has been achieved — probably within the first year — this function ceases. This may partly explain why cabinet meetings decline in number from that point in most administrations.

➢ It is important for presidents to appear collegial and consultative. This is particularly important for presidents post-Nixon. The Nixon administration was notorious for its lack of openness. A political novel written of the era was famously titled *Washington: Behind Closed Doors*. Cartoonists drew Nixon's Oval Office with guards outside dressed in Prussian-style military uniforms holding 'no entry' signs. Cabinet meetings with a media photo opportunity either before or after the meeting are a good way for the president to send reassuring signals that he is running an open administration. To this extent, cabinet meetings can be a public relations exercise and an opportunity for the president to make some comments that will receive coverage in the media.

➢ Cabinet meetings provide opportunities for both information giving and information gathering. The president can make statements at a cabinet meeting and know that every member has heard them, and he can go round the table asking cabinet officers what is going on in their departments. President Carter's cabinet meetings usually took the form of the president going clockwise — the next time, anticlockwise — round the cabinet table, asking each member to give a brief report on current departmental issues and activity. Cabinet meetings can be an efficient method by which the president keeps in touch with what is going on in the vast federal bureaucracy.

➢ Some presidents have liked to use cabinet meetings as a forum in which to debate policy. Reagan's defense secretary, Frank Carlucci, remembered that 'cabinet meetings were often vigorous, such as the one on the pros and cons of building the Russian oil pipeline — it was quite a shouting match'. Michael Jackson, a senior member of President George H. W. Bush's Office of Cabinet Affairs who attended meetings as an observer, stated:

> At the meeting prior to the Malta summit [with Soviet president Gorbachev in December 1989], the President engaged the cabinet in a very significant discussion of foreign policy. It allowed the President to broaden his consultations.

➤ At cabinet meetings the president can present so-called 'big picture items' that affect all cabinet officers: the budget; up-coming elections; a major legislative initiative or foreign trip. For example, President Obama used his cabinet meeting on 31 January 2012 to talk about his State of the Union address initiative regarding small businesses, as can be seen in Box 6.3. Other examples can be seen in Table 6.10.

➤ Some presidents have used cabinet meetings to check up on legislation going through Congress in which they have a particular interest. Willard Wirtz, labor secretary to President Johnson, stated:

> If the Congress was in session, and you knew there was a cabinet meeting coming up in a day or two, you tried to make sure that there was some progress to report to the President. He knew the system so well. He could often embarrass you. Johnson would often pressurise you into making sure things moved quicker.

➤ President George W. Bush used his 24 September 2002 cabinet meeting to push for congressional action on three key issues: authorisation for military action against Iraq; the passage of the Homeland Security Bill; and the budget. On 14 December 2007 the Bush cabinet discussed the business remaining at the end of that year's congressional session.

➤ Finally, cabinet meetings provide an opportunity for the president to see cabinet members whom he would not otherwise be likely to see. Whereas the 'first-tier' cabinet officers — such as the secretary of state and the secretary of defense — are likely to have fairly frequent meetings with the president, this will not be the case for such 'second-tier' cabinet officers as the secretary of veterans' affairs and the secretary of agriculture. Again, whereas the Treasury Department is only half a block from the White House, other departments are situated in far-flung parts of downtown Washington. There is no obvious reason for the president to see many cabinet officers except at a cabinet meeting. The president might even forget who is in the cabinet. HUD Secretary Sam Pierce never lived down the story of when President Reagan spotted him one day at a White House reception for visiting city mayors and mistook Pierce for a visitor: 'How are you, Mr Mayor?' asked the President of his housing secretary. 'How are things in your city?'

The functions of cabinet meetings for cabinet officers

There are good reasons for cabinet officers, too, to see cabinet meetings as potentially useful occasions, despite their frequent critiques of them:

➤ They provide initial get-to-know-you opportunities. Not only will the president not know many of them; they will often not know each other.

Box 6.3	Remarks by the President to members of the White House press corps before the cabinet meeting, 31 January 2012

This is our first cabinet meeting after my State of the Union address, and it gives me an opportunity to share my ideas and initiatives with my Cabinet, but also to get some feedback from them.

One of the top priorities that I mentioned during the State of the Union was the need for us to promote small business. And I'm very pleased that we've got [the head of the Small Business Administration (SBA)] Karen Mills here, who has participated in our meetings before, but is now an official member of the Cabinet. It is a symbol of how important it is for us to spur entrepreneurship, to help start-ups, to move aggressively so that we can assure more companies that create the most jobs in our economy are getting a leg up from the various programmes that we have in our government.

I mentioned at the State of the Union that there have been bipartisan discussions between Republicans and Democrats about a whole set of measures that can accelerate financing to start-up companies; can provide tax breaks to start-ups and small businesses that are interested in either hiring more workers or increasing their wages; that looks at innovative ways for them to raise capital.

And my expectation and hope is that they will get a bill together quickly, that they will pass it and get it on my desk. I will sign it right away, and I would like to see that bill signed this year.

Source: www.whitehouse.gov

➤ Cabinet meetings can be used to resolve interdepartmental disputes. Ford's secretary to the cabinet, James Connor, remembers a cabinet meeting in which a dispute about affirmative action for African-Americans was aired. 'It was one hell of a show,' stated Connor.

➤ Meetings in many organisations are often as useful for what goes on before and after them as for what occurs during them. The same can be true for the president's cabinet meetings. They can prove a useful opportunity to speak with other cabinet officers, and as there are precious few other opportunities to run into one's cabinet colleagues — unlike in a parliamentary system — these can be valuable occasions.

➤ It may even be possible to catch the president after the meeting, should he linger in the cabinet room. However, such situations can present danger for a president who agrees too readily to what may appear to be an innocent, off-the-cuff request from a cabinet officer. George W. Bush's secretary to the cabinet explained how he would be 'hovering [around the president] at the end of a meeting, not exactly eavesdropping, but at a respectful distance' to ensure that no cabinet officer took advantage of the president in such an unscheduled moment.

➤ Finally, attendance at cabinet meetings gives cabinet officers increased standing back at their departments. They have just heard the president. They know what he

wants, today, as opposed to what others might *think* he wanted, yesterday. President George H. W. Bush's agriculture secretary, Clayton Yeutter, summed up a number of these functions this way:

[Cabinet meetings] were useful for being informative. You got an insight on the top stories. It was for some just the thrill to have a meeting with the President. The 'second tier' cabinet officers don't get to see him that often. They would go back to their departments and be able to say: 'I just came from a cabinet meeting.' They would then hold their own staff meetings and the stories would be passed out to sub-cabinet people and so to the rest of the department. They were evangelistic.

Cabinet councils

There is a problem with using full cabinet meetings for policy discussion, because most cabinet members are policy specialists. To overcome this problem, most modern-day presidents have developed a series of policy-specific cabinet councils. These existed during the presidencies of Ronald Reagan, George H. W. Bush, George W. Bush and Barack Obama. In the administration of Barack Obama there are three: the National Economic Council; the Domestic Policy Council; and the National Security Council.

The National Economic Council (NEC), founded in 1993 by President Clinton, has four principal functions: to coordinate policy making for domestic and international economic issues; to coordinate economic policy advice for the president; to ensure that policy decisions and programmes are consistent with the president's economic goals; to monitor implementation of the president's economic policy agenda. The Director of the NEC is assisted by a staff of policy specialists in such policy areas as: commerce, healthcare, agriculture, financial markets and Social Security.

The Domestic Policy Council (DPC) began life in 1970 under President Nixon as the Office of Domestic Policy but has been reorganised by a number of presidents since then. It has five principal functions: to coordinate the domestic policy-making process in the White House; to offer domestic policy advice to the president; to ensure that domestic policy initiatives are consistent throughout federal agencies; to represent the president's domestic policy priorities to other branches of government; to monitor the implementation of the president's domestic policy agenda. Under President Obama, the DPC has four sub-offices: the Office of National AIDS Policy; the Office of Faith-based and Neighborhood Partnerships; the Office of Social Innovation and Civic Participation; the White House Rural Council.

The National Security Council (NSC) was formed in 1947 by President Truman and is discussed in much more detail below in the section concerned with the Executive Office of the President. But like the NEC and the DPC, the NSC's principal role is one of coordination and advice giving.

As a result, full cabinet meetings are held less frequently and tend to be used for 'big picture' items, as discussed above. Commenting on this arrangement, President George W. Bush's secretary to the cabinet Albert Hawkins stated:

> The President is using a series of three cabinet councils which will mean that full cabinet meetings will not get bogged down on the minutiae of policy. Each cabinet council has designated membership but others will be invited to attend as required. The President will attend as necessary.

An assessment of the president's cabinet

How important, then, is the president's cabinet? Individually, its members are very important — they all run large departments and spend large budgets. Some, however, are more important than others. But as Robert Shrum wrote in late 2008: 'No one in a cabinet outshines the president.' Collectively, there are five structural reasons why the president's cabinet can never be of prime importance.

First, the Constitution grants 'all executive power' to the president. Cabinet officers have no executive power vested in them directly. Second, there is no doctrine of collective responsibility. The president is not 'first among equals'. He is simply 'first'. As Professor Anthony King put it: 'He doesn't sum up at the end of the meeting; he *is* the meeting.' Third, cabinet officers are not the president's political rivals. The cabinet is not seen as a stepping stone to the presidency. This is not to say that some former cabinet officers have not harboured presidential ambitions. Lamar Alexander and Jack Kemp, both of whom served in the cabinet of President George H. W. Bush in the early

---

Is the president's cabinet important? DEBATE

Yes
- it contains some of the most important people in the executive branch (e.g. secretary of state, secretary of defense)
- all the heads of the 15 executive departments are automatically members
- the president always chairs the meetings
- cabinet meetings can fulfil a number of important functions, both for the president and for cabinet officers
- some presidents hold frequent meetings (e.g. Carter, Reagan)

No
- Article II of the Constitution vests 'all executive power' in the president
- there is no doctrine of collective responsibility
- the members of the president's cabinet are neither his equals nor his political rivals
- the president often views members of his cabinet with some suspicion because they have divided loyalties
- the Executive Office of the President is the main source of advice giving for the president
- comments from those who have served in the cabinet suggest that the meetings are often boring and do not often cover matters of great substance

1990s, made unsuccessful bids for the presidency. The last person to step from the cabinet directly to the presidency was Herbert Hoover in 1929. Hoover had served as commerce secretary to Presidents Warren Harding and Calvin Coolidge. Fourth, the members of the president's cabinet have loyalties other than to the president. Charles Dawes (Vice-President 1925–29) once remarked that members of the cabinet are 'a president's natural enemies'! They also do not work in the White House. Some of them may see the president rarely.

The fifth significant limit to the cabinet's importance is the existence, since 1939, of the Executive Office of the President (EXOP). In the EXOP, the cabinet has something of a rival, and a rival with a number of key advantages.

The Executive Office of the President (EXOP)

The Executive Office of the President (EXOP) is an umbrella term for an organisation that consists of the top presidential staff agencies that provide help, advice, coordination and administrative support for the president.

Key concept
> **The Executive Office of the President.** The top staff agencies in the White House that give the president help and advice in carrying out the major duties of his office. Its primary functions are coordination, advice giving and personnel management.

In 1939, the Brownlow Committee reported to President Franklin Roosevelt (FDR) that 'the president needs help'. Why did presidents from the mid-20th century 'need help' in running the federal government? First, there had been a huge increase in the size and scale of the federal government, caused mainly by the westward expansion and industrialisation of the 19th century. In 1789, there were just three executive departments of the federal government — State, War and the Treasury. By 1939, a further five had been added: Interior (1849), Justice (1870), Agriculture (1889), Commerce and Labor (both 1903).

Second, when the great depression hit the USA in the late 1920s, the states looked to the federal government for help. FDR responded to this with his 'New Deal' programme — a whole raft of federal government schemes to promote employment, agriculture, industrial expansion and a huge building programme of schools, roads, hydroelectric schemes and the like.

Third, the USA was about to become a major player on the stage of world politics. This added considerably to the president's role as commander-in-chief. The presidents of the second half of the 20th century had to spend much of their time dealing with the consequences of the Cold War — in southeast Asia, eastern Europe and Central America.

> ## Box 6.4 EXOP under President Obama
>
> Under President Obama, the Executive Office of the President (EXOP) is made up of ten offices, as of January 2013:
>
> ➤ Council of Economic Advisers
>
> ➤ Council on Environmental Quality
>
> ➤ National Security Council
>
> ➤ Office of Administration
>
> ➤ Office of Management and Budget
>
> ➤ Office of National Drug Control Policy
>
> ➤ Office of Science and Technology Policy
>
> ➤ Office of the United States Trade Representative
>
> ➤ Office of the Vice-President
>
> ➤ White House Office
>
> Source: www.whitehouse.gov/administration/eop

As a result, presidents found more demands made on them. Overload became a real danger. So EXOP was established to help the president cope with these increased demands. Through the second half of the 20th century, EXOP grew to include around a dozen offices, the most important being the White House Office, the National Security Council and the Office of Management and Budget. By 2009, the Executive Office of President Obama included 15 offices, but President Obama had reduced this number to just ten by the end of his first term (see Box 6.4). Altogether, EXOP came to number over 2,000 staff. The most important EXOP personnel, including the key presidential advisers, work in the West Wing of the White House, which is where the Oval Office is located.

The White House Office

The White House Office includes the president's most trusted and closest aides and advisers. Although the White House Office is only one of the 10 offices which make up the Executive Office of the President, it is itself made up of 16 different offices, such as the Office of Cabinet Liaison and the Office of Legislative Affairs. In charge of running the White House Office is the White House chief of staff. These people's principal function is to provide advice and administrative support for the president on a daily basis. Whether in the White House, travelling within the United States or out of the country, they are never far from the president.

Specifically, the White House Office is responsible for a host of duties. It acts as liaison between the White House and the vast federal bureaucracy. At the beginning of the George W. Bush administration, the secretary to the cabinet — himself a White House Office member — explained that if a cabinet officer wanted to talk one-to-one with the President, then that cabinet officer would first talk either with himself or with

chief of staff Andrew Card. Those who work in the White House Office act as liaison between the White House and Congress, too. The Office of Legislative Affairs is a branch of the White House Office with that sole responsibility. The staff member designated as head of congressional liaison is the person who arranges for members of Congress to meet with the president. Anyone whose job description includes deciding on who has a meeting in the Oval Office with the president of the United States is a potentially important person.

Even telephone calls to the president are screened by the White House Office to decide who should and who should not be put through to the president. The same goes for paperwork. President Eisenhower was known to read only those documents that included the letters 'OK. SA' on them — indicating that his chief of staff, Sherman Adams, had 'okayed' them. Senior members of the White House Office are responsible for drawing up the president's daily schedule, for the day-to-day running of the White House and for personnel management. They ensure that decisions are arrived at in an orderly fashion — that all relevant options, pros and cons have been presented to the president for him to make his decision. They deal with crisis management and act as 'lightning conductors' — taking the blame when things go wrong.

In order to fulfil these important functions, members of the White House Office are meant to act as 'honest brokers', not as policy-makers. They are meant not to be always in the media spotlight, but to have something of what the Brownlow Report called 'a passion for anonymity'. If senior members of the White House Office are thought to be pursuing their own rather than the president's agenda, this can lead to trouble. In President George H. W. Bush's administration, Chief of Staff John Sununu was thought by many to be pursuing his own conservative policy agenda rather than what the President wanted. Sununu's access to the President put him at a significant advantage over other policy players, who came to resent Sununu's role. Bush eventually had to fire him.

The White House chief of staff

There's a scene in *The West Wing* where the President is just about to leave the White House for Capitol Hill to deliver his State of the Union address and the 'designated survivor' — the cabinet officer who does not attend the event, so that he or she survives any terrorist attack on the Capitol whilst the entire administration is there — comes to visit. President Josiah ('Jed') Bartlet (Martin Sheen) asks Secretary of Agriculture Roger Tribbey (Harry Groener) some questions just in case Tribbey should become president. 'You got a best friend?' asks Bartlet. 'Yes, Sir,' replies Tribbey. 'Is he smarter than you?' 'Yes, Sir,' replies Tribbey with a wry smile. 'Would you trust him with your life?' There's a slight pause before Tribbey replies once more, 'Yes, Sir.' 'That's your chief of staff,' responds the President.

The role of the White House chief of staff is the most crucial job of all within the White House staff and the appointment of the chief of staff is probably the most important that a president makes in terms of the executive branch — hence the truth of the anecdote above. Some, like Sherman Adams (Eisenhower), Don Regan (Reagan) and

Table 6.11 White House chiefs of staff, 1981–2013

President	Chief of staff	Dates
Ronald Reagan	James Baker	1981–85
	Donald Regan	1985–87
	Howard Baker	1987–88
	Kenneth Duberstein	1988–89
George H. W. Bush	John Sununu	1989–91
	Sam Skinner	1991–92
	James Baker	1992–93
Bill Clinton	Thomas (Mack) McLarty	1993–94
	Leon Panetta	1994–97
	Erskine Bowles	1997–98
	John Podesta	1998–2001
George W. Bush	Andrew Card	2001–06
	Joshua Bolten	2006–09
Barack Obama	Rahm Emanuel	2009–10
	William Daley	2011–12
	Jacob (Jack) Lew	2012–13
	Denis McDonough	2013–

John Sununu (Bush), became too obtrusive and too powerful — almost a kind of 'deputy president'. A joke which used to circulate during Republican Dwight Eisenhower's presidency imagined two Democrats talking to each other. 'Wouldn't it be terrible,' says one Democrat, 'if Eisenhower died and Vice-President Nixon became president.' Replied the other Democrat, 'Not as bad as if Chief of Staff Sherman Adams died and Eisenhower became president!' But other chiefs of staff, such as Thomas 'Mack' McLarty (Clinton), were simply overwhelmed by the job because of their lack of Washington experience.

The best model is that of someone who always seeks the president's best interests rather than his own, and who protects the president from political harm. President Ford's chief of staff, Dick Cheney, once remarked of his relationship with Ford: 'He takes the credit; I take the blame.' Jack Watson, who served as chief of staff to President Carter, described his job as being like that of a 'javelin catcher' — protecting the president from incoming missiles that could hurt him. Watson continued:

> The chief of staff's role is to see that all the relevant people have a full and fair opportunity to present their views to the president. To act as an honest broker means that I view my role as a fulcrum rather than being a weight on one end. I must ensure that the president hears conflicting views, and not seek to make the judgement for him.

In a May 1993 *Washington Post* article on the role of the White House chief of staff, Lloyd Grove stated:

> It is the hottest seat in town and its occupant is the orchestrator of presidential paper flow, the 'honest broker' of ideas and opinions, the fearsome disciplinarian of wayward staffers, the president's trusted adviser and sounding board, the White House's apologist and occasionally, when necessary, the president's fall guy.

Those who have received high marks for their chief of staff role include Leon Panetta (Clinton: 1994–97), Andrew Card (George W. Bush: 2001–06) and Rahm Emanuel (Barack Obama 2009–10). It was Andrew Card who was famously seen whispering into President George W. Bush's ear on the morning of 11 September 2001, as the President sat in front of an elementary school class in Sarasota, Florida. Card was informing the President of the second plane hitting the World Trade Center in New York. 'America is under attack,' he told the President. Scott McClellan, who served as President George W. Bush's press secretary (2003–06), comments in his recent book, *What Happened* (2008), about Andrew Card:

Chief of staff Andrew Card telling President George W. Bush about the second plane hitting the World Trade Center

> He was a tireless public servant who brought years of experience to his position as chief of staff. His sphere of influence was built on both his position and his closeness to the President. His role was to serve as an honest broker among the staff inside the White House, and help make sure all views were heard.

Ultimately, though, it is the president who largely decides how he wants the White House organised and run. Staff are there essentially to carry out presidential instructions.

Organising the White House

There are fundamentally two different ways of organising the White House, or any organisation, come to that. The first is described as the 'spokes of the wheel' system. In this organisational structure, the president is at the centre — the hub — of the White House with many different advisers — spokes — having direct access to the Oval Office. This system was popularised by President Kennedy and adopted by such presidents as Jimmy Carter and Bill Clinton. The advantage is that the president is accessible. The potential hazard is that he is too accessible and that some advisers take advantage of their access to the president.

The second method of organising the White House is described as the 'pyramid' structure. In this structure, the president sits at the apex of the pyramid. Only a few key advisers — possibly only one or two — have direct access to the president. The others have to pass their views up through the different layers of the pyramid. The advantage is that it leads to a highly disciplined White House. The potential hazard is that the president becomes isolated and hears only what he wants to hear, not what he needs to hear. This system was adopted most notably by President Nixon. His three senior advisers — Henry

Kissinger, Bob Haldeman and John Ehrlichman — were collectively nicknamed 'the Berlin Wall'. Ronald Reagan and George W. Bush used the same basic White House structure.

The clearest indication of the way President Obama wanted to organise the White House came with his initial appointment of Rahm Emanuel as chief of staff. A larger-than-life character, Emanuel came with experience both of the White House — he had served in the Clinton administration — and of Congress, where he had risen to House Democratic whip. The media started to refer to him as 'Rahm-bo' or 'the pseudo-prime minister', 'the uber-press secretary' and 'strategist-in-chief'. The *Financial Times* dubbed Emanuel as one of 'the fearsome foursome' in the initial Obama White House — along with David Axelrod, Valerie Jarrett and Robert Gibbs. Here's how James Pfiffner (2011) summarised Emanuel's role in the early Obama White House:

> Emanuel was the linchpin. He would have to ride herd on the many policy czars, smooth ruffled feathers, corral large egos, guard access to the President, make the trains run on time, negotiate between White House staffers and cabinet officers, and get all of the separate political and policy threads to go through the eye of the needle at the same time.

Emanuel was the opposite of Obama in so many ways, not only in his wide political experience, but also in his personality. James Pfiffner again:

> Where Obama was idealistic, Emanuel was practical; where Obama was restrained, Emanuel was outspoken; where Obama was smooth, Emanuel was brash; where Obama was given to policy analysis, Emanuel was a master of political calculation; where Obama was 'no drama', Emanuel was histrionic.

The National Security Council

The National Security Council (NSC) was established in 1947 to help the president coordinate foreign, security and defence policy. Headed by the national security adviser (NSA), the NSC began life as an in-house think-tank for the president. The NSC would coordinate information coming to the White House from the State Department, the Defense Department, the Central Intelligence Agency (CIA), the Joint Chiefs of Staff and American ambassadors around the world. It would liaise with the relevant congressional committees, too. Like the White House staff, the NSC was designed to operate as an 'honest broker', a 'facilitator', presenting carefully argued options for presidential decision making.

President Nixon changed the way the NSC worked. Distrustful of the State Department, which he saw as too liberal and establishment-orientated, Nixon decided to run foreign policy from the White House. He appointed Henry Kissinger as his national security adviser to act as a roving foreign policy-maker, largely cutting out the State Department's traditional role. But this enhanced and politicised role for the NSC caused grave problems for subsequent presidents.

President Carter's national security adviser, Zbigniew Brzezinski, feuded with Secretary of State Cyrus Vance over a rescue mission to free 52 American hostages held in Iran. The mission — backed by Brzezinski but opposed by Vance — was an utter disaster. Vance resigned in protest at the way Carter had allowed Brzezinski to influence the policy-making process. Then, in the Reagan administration, national security adviser John Poindexter was discovered to be running a secret — and illegal — foreign policy in the so-called Iran–Contra affair. Poindexter was forced to resign.

Subsequently, presidents George H. W. Bush, Bill Clinton and George W. Bush returned the NSC to its 'honest broker' role. In the 1991 Persian Gulf War, George Bush was skilfully served by national security adviser Brent Scowcroft. He acted as a behind-the-scenes coordinator of policy advice arriving from Secretary of State James Baker, Defense Secretary Dick Cheney and Chairman of the Joint Chiefs of Staff Colin Powell. For Bill Clinton, Samuel 'Sandy' Berger played a similar role. Writing in *The New Republic* in April 1998, Jacob Heilbrunn described Berger as 'the chief coordinator and adviser to the President; the glue that holds the foreign policy team together'. For George W. Bush, national security adviser Condoleezza Rice played a similarly important but facilitating role during his first term (see Box 6.5). Bob Woodward (2003) said of Rice:

> She saw her job as twofold: first to coordinate what Defense, State, the CIA and other departments and agencies were doing by making sure the President's orders were carried out; and second, to act as counsellor — to give her private assessment to the President, certainly when he asked, perhaps if he didn't. In other words she was the President's trouble-shooter.

When Condoleezza Rice was moved to be secretary of state in Bush's second term, Rice's number two, Stephen Hadley, took over as national security adviser. But Hadley was more deferential to the President. And that, coupled with Bush's 'no doubt' approach, led to some problems during Bush's second term. Bob Woodward (2008) commented of the relationship between Bush and Hadley:

> A president so certain, so action-orientated, so hero-worshipped by his national security adviser, almost couldn't be halted. The administration lacked a process to examine consequences, alternatives and motives. There was no system to slow down the process so that the right questions were asked and answered, or alternative courses of action seriously considered. The national security adviser has to be a negotiator and an arbiter, someone who tries to consider every angle to a problem. But Hadley had become the lawyer for the president's foreign policy, his unwavering advocate and a cheerleader for his greatness.

During the Obama first term, there was no doubt at all that the lead voices in foreign policy were those of the President and Secretary of State Hillary Clinton. With such a big name at the State Department, the NSC stayed in the background, performing its traditional coordinating role. During these first four years, Obama was served by

Box 6.5 Functions of the National Security Adviser

The differing cultures of the institutions involved in the National Security Council, and the personalities of the heads who represent them, require deft management by the president and the national security adviser. As I see it, there are three main functions of the adviser: to identify where strategic and policy guidance from the president is necessary or desirable; to organise interagency deliberations so the president can make informed decisions and provide the necessary guidance to his administration; and to oversee the implementation of the president's decisions, ensuring they are carried out effectively. Among the core attendees of NSC meetings, only the national security adviser works in the White House and has routine daily access to the president. In that regard, Condoleezza Rice's closeness to President Bush was an asset. She knew the President far better than the rest of us and spent considerably more time with him than all of his other senior advisers on national security combined. Her personal access to and affinity for President Bush gave Rice substantial influence as a national security adviser and an unusually strong voice in matters under the purview of the NSC.

Donald Rumsfeld, *Known and Unknown: A Memoir* (Penguin, 2011), p. 324.

two national security advisers — General James Jones (January 2009 to October 2010) followed by Tom Donilon who had earlier served as Jones's deputy. Both men fitted the 'honest broker' style of working and both had that 'passion for anonymity' which is meant to characterise those who work in the Executive Office of the President. Bob Woodward (2010) reports Jones's views on his number two and his eventual successor.

> Jones praised [Donilon's] substantive and organizational skills, and told Donilon that he was indispensable to the President and the whole NSC staff. But Donilon had made three mistakes. First, he had never gone to Afghanistan or Iraq or really left his office for a serious field trip. Second, he frequently spoke with absolute declarations about places he'd never been, leaders he'd never met, or colleagues he worked with. Third, he had too little feel for the people who worked day and night on the NSC staff, their salaries, their maternity leaves, their promotions, their family troubles, all the things a manager of people has to be tuned into.

EXOP–cabinet rivalries

Presidents must guard against the development of unhealthy rivalries and distrust between those who work in the EXOP, on the one hand, and the heads of the executive departments — the cabinet — on the other. Such rivalries and distrust can inflict serious wounds on a presidency, as Presidents Richard Nixon and Jimmy Carter discovered.

There is a danger that those who work in the White House might come to regard cabinet officers as distant and disloyal. Similarly, cabinet officers might come to regard those who work in the White House as too close and too loyal to the president. Some of these feelings are born of natural circumstances. Cabinet officers are, physically,

distant from the White House. The office of the secretary of state, for example, is on the seventh floor of the State Department building in Foggy Bottom — an area of Washington about seven blocks west of the White House, making it a good 10 minutes away from the Oval Office. The secretary of defense is even further away. The Pentagon — the department's headquarters — is over the other side of the Potomac river, 15–20 minutes away. In comparison, the national security adviser's office is a 30-second walk from the Oval

President Jimmy Carter — victim of cabinet rivalries

Office. It is hardly surprising that the secretaries of state and defense seem — and feel — a bit distant. Those who work in the EXOP have the key advantage of proximity. Daniel Patrick Moynihan, who served in the White House under President Nixon, commented: 'Never underestimate the power of proximity.' Former Secretary of Defense Donald Rumsfeld refers to this in his comments about national security adviser Condoleezza Rice, with whom he worked in the Bush administration (see Box 6.5).

It is understandable to some extent that cabinet officers sometimes appear disloyal. Although they are appointed by the president and serve only at his pleasure, they have other loyalties. They have a loyalty to Congress, whose votes decide their departmental budgets and whose committees can call them to account in person. They have a loyalty to their own departmental bureaucracy, to interest groups with which their department has close links. On the other hand, those who work in the EXOP have only one loyalty — to the president. They are *All the President's Men* — the title of a 1970s book (and a film starring Robert Redford and Dustin Hoffman) about the Nixon White House and the Watergate affair.

Friction between the cabinet and the White House was clearly identifiable in the Nixon administration. Even the nicknames used by each group to refer to the other were revealing. The cabinet referred to senior White House aides as 'the Berlin Wall' and 'the palace guard'. The White House staff showed contempt for cabinet members when referring, for example, to Postmaster General William Blount as 'the postman' and to Transportation Secretary John Volpe as 'the bus driver'.

When President Carter was trying to sort out the sheep from the goats in his cabinet in mid-1979, the two tests of 'breeding' were, first, 'loyalty to the president' and, second, 'ability to work with the White House staff'. He called all the cabinet to the presidential retreat of Camp David. In a rambling statement, the President — his eyes scanning those who were seated at the table — observed: 'There are times when you do not support the White House policy. I need your absolute loyalty.' For their part, the cabinet bitterly resented the powerful White House Office members who had the proximity and access to the President that they clearly did not have. Landon Butler, a senior aide in the Carter White House, pointed out that there is a danger of the White House coming to see cabinet officers as mere dogsbodies and that this poses serious difficulties. Interviewed in 1980, Butler stated:

> I think every [White House] staff can succumb to the temptation to treat cabinet officers as simply a group of people who we trot out to make speeches when we want them to make speeches, to say what we want them to say and then go quietly back to their offices. Whenever this happens, it always results in political disaster. It is the cabinet officer's role to provide leadership on the major issues. It is the staff's job to carry out decisions.

How can these problems be guarded against? First, it is critically important that the president clearly explains to each group what are, and what are not, its functions. Professor Richard Neustadt (2000) stated:

> The president must prepare the cabinet members against the shocking discovery that most of them are not the principal advisers to the president, are not going to be, and never will be.

Similarly, staff must be staff. Helmut Sonnenfeldt, an aide to Henry Kissinger in the Nixon and Ford administrations, identified the problem and the solution thus:

> The staff capability, in order to be credible and accepted by the cabinet, has to be a neutral capability. The cabinet officer has to be certain that the paper he sends to the president gets to the president as he wrote it. If it's doctored, if it's changed, because you have strong policy advocacy in the White House staff, the credibility gets lost and you have chaos.

Second, it is important that the cabinet officers really do think about what the president wants and do not become ensnared by the iron triangle. One-time Transportation Secretary William Coleman put it this way:

> Too many cabinet officers go away and become advocates of their departmental views and wishes. It's very easy to do that. But a cabinet officer should look only at the issues as the president sees them. It is the president who appointed him. Of all the other people President Ford could have had as transportation secretary, he chose me. So I saw it as my first job to do what the President wanted.

Third, it is helpful if the two sides meet regularly and are made to work together. This is why the use of cabinet councils by Reagan and Bush — both George H. W. and George W. — can be helpful. Cabinet councils are made up of both cabinet officers and those from EXOP. The Economic Policy cabinet council had 271 meetings during Reagan's first term — that is almost 70 meetings a year. This can help with the loyalty factor. Martin Anderson, a White House aide to President George H. W. Bush, stated:

Just the act of having to leave their fiefdoms, get into a car, and be driven to the White House, was a powerful reminder to every member of the cabinet that it was the president's business they were about, not theirs or their department's constituents.

The first term of the Obama administration, like pretty much all its predecessors, experienced its tensions between members of the cabinet and those who worked in the White House as part of EXOP. Obama's extensive use of White House policy 'czars' signalled that policy making was going to take place at the White House and not in the 15 executive departments scattered around downtown Washington. The term 'czar' has no generally agreed definition in American politics. The term tends to be used — especially by journalists — to refer to members of the administration who seem to be obviously in charge of a particular policy area. In Obama's first term, for instance, Carol Browner was portrayed as the energy and climate czar; Lawrence Summers was seen as the economic czar; Nancy-Ann DeParle as the health czar. It all sounds well structured and clear, but as James Pfiffner (2011) points out, there are problems:

> The real problem with White House czars (and sometimes even the national security adviser) is that they confuse the chain of command and leave open the question of who is in charge of administration policy. Czars are often frustrated because they lack the authority to carry out their responsibilities. That is, they do not control budgets or appointments, and they cannot order cabinet officers to do their bidding. The other problem with czars is that cabinet officers often resent the dilution of their policy-advising authority. So the biggest problem is who is in charge of a given policy area. Who has the lead in developing policy alternatives for the president's consideration?

Obama's cabinet resented not only the White House czars but also the treatment they received from Chief of Staff Emanuel, who they felt treated them as 'minions' rather than as major administration officials. Emanuel insisted all cabinet officers had to send him weekly reports of what they were doing in their department. The reports would be returned with Emanuel's comments and instructions scribbled on them.

The president's relations with Congress

The late Professor Richard Neustadt famously remarked that 'the president's power is the power to persuade'. On 31 August 2011, President Obama was getting ready to use his persuasive powers. Frustrated by the slow recovery in the nation's economy, he wanted to go on the record to show his support for a major new stimulus package currently before Congress, the American Jobs Act. So the President announced that he would deliver a primetime televised speech to a joint session of Congress. As is customary on such occasions, the President sent a letter to the Speaker of the House of Representatives asking if he would schedule the address for the early evening of 7 September. Before the President could persuade others, he had to persuade the Republican Speaker, John Boehner. The Speaker said no. 'It is my recommendation,' replied Speaker Boehner to the

President, 'that your address be held on the following evening, when we can ensure there will be no parliamentary or logistical impediments that might detract from your remarks.'

To understand the presidential rebuff, one needs to know two further pieces of information. First, 7 September was the evening on which the Republican presidential candidates had scheduled a televised debate at the Reagan Presidential Library in California. The President had hoped to upstage it, but the Speaker was having none of it. Second, 8 September was the evening of the opening game of the NFL American football season. No Speaker of the House had ever before refused a presidential request to address a joint session of Congress. But this Speaker refused to be persuaded despite much back-and-forth between the Speaker's office and the White House. In the end, the President spoke on the 8th. The president's power is, indeed, the power to persuade — except when he can't!

Almost every power that the president possesses is checked by Congress. The president, therefore, needs Congress's agreement. He needs his persuasion to succeed. However, in a system of 'separated institutions sharing powers' this is by no means easy. Party links may not help much. The president and the majority of Congress may well be of different parties, as shown in Table 6.12. Even when the two branches are controlled by the same party, there is no guarantee of success — witness the difficulties experienced by Bill Clinton in his failed attempt to pass healthcare reforms in 1993–94. As Richard Neustadt (1990) stated: 'What the Constitution separates, the political parties do not combine.'

As Table 6.13 shows, the president can do very little without the agreement of Congress. There is an intricate system of checks and balances devised by the Founding Fathers, who wanted it to be difficult for the president to get his way in Congress. As Nelson Polsby (1976) put it: 'Conflict and cooperation between Congress and the president are not merely the result of whim or wilfulness at one end or the other

Table 6.12 Party control of Congress and the presidency, 1993–2013

Years	Party: President	House	Senate
1993–94	**D: Bill Clinton**	**D: 258–176**	**D: 58–42**
1995–96	D: Bill Clinton	R: 230–204	R: 54–46
1997–98	D: Bill Clinton	R: 227–207	R: 55–45
1999–2000	D: Bill Clinton	R: 223–211	R: 55–45
January–May 2001	**R: George W. Bush**	**R: 221–212**	**R: 50–50**
June 2001–2002	R: George W. Bush	R: 221–212	D: 50–49
2003–2004	**R: George W. Bush**	**R: 229–205**	**R: 51–48**
2005–2006	**R: George W. Bush**	**R: 232–202**	**R: 55–44**
2007–08	R: George W. Bush	D: 233–202	D: 51–49
2009–10	**D: Barack Obama**	**D: 257–178**	**D: 59–41**
2011–12	D: Barack Obama	R: 242–193	D: 53–47
2013–	D: Barack Obama	R: 234–201	D: 55–45

Note: **bold** type indicates years during which Congress was controlled by the same party as the president.

Table 6.13 Powers of the president and checks by Congress

Powers of the president	Checks by Congress
Propose legislation	Amend/block legislation
Submit the annual budget	Amend budget
Veto legislation	Override veto
Act as chief executive	Investigation/impeachment/removal
Nominate executive officials	Confirmation (Senate)
Nominate federal judges	Confirmation (Senate)
Negotiate treaties	Ratification (Senate)
Commander-in-chief of the armed forces	Declare war/power of the purse

of Pennsylvania Avenue.' Professor S. E. Finer (1970) has likened the president and Congress to 'two halves of a bank note, each useless without the other'. However, the Founding Fathers' desire for cooperation and compromise between these two branches of government — 'ambition must counteract ambition', as James Madison put it — often leads to inaction and gridlock.

There is a famous story of President Truman sitting at his Oval Office desk in December 1952, contemplating what it would be like for his successor coming into office in just a few weeks' time. His successor was to be Dwight Eisenhower — a former army general, affectionately known as 'Ike'. Truman was contemplating how strange it would be for the general-turned-president.

> He'll sit here and he'll say, 'Do this! Do that!' And nothing will happen. Poor Ike, it won't be a bit like the army. He'll find it very frustrating.

It would be 'not a bit like the army' because in the army Eisenhower could get what he wanted by issuing commands. As president, Eisenhower would learn that little happens as a result of command; most happens as a result of persuasion. Truman knew that. Earlier in his presidency he had remarked:

> I sit here all day trying to persuade people to do the things they ought to have the sense to do without my persuading them. That's all the powers of the president amount to.

When it comes to persuasion, there are essentially two methods: the president can use other people to persuade on his behalf; or he can get involved himself through the use of 'perks' that he can offer.

Dwight Eisenhower — army general who became president

Presidential persuasion through other people

The president, if he is to be a successful persuader, must work through a number of other people. He cannot — nor should he — try to do it all himself. There are four groups of people he can use. First, he can use the vice-president. All of the last six vice-presidents — covering a period of more than 30 years from Walter Mondale to Joe Biden — have been former members of Congress. George W. Bush's vice-president, Dick Cheney, spent 10 years as a member of the House of Representatives, rising to be minority whip — the second most senior House Republican. He was widely liked and respected on both sides of the aisle. Congressman Jerry Lewis (R — California), who was elected to Congress in 1978 with Cheney, put it like this:

> He's a great asset for the administration, especially in dealing with the House. He's always been a really great person to deal with legislators. He knows them well and has their confidence.

As president of the Senate, the vice-president has a foothold in Congress too. He has an office there, where he can meet with members of both houses.

Second, the president uses members of the Office of Legislative Affairs. They are members of the White House Office who work as full-time lobbyists for the president on Capitol Hill. They meet with members of Congress as well as with senior members of their staff. The congressional liaison staff are usually organised in such a way that some work on the House side and others on the Senate side, hoping to build up good relationships with people whom they will get to know well.

Third, the cabinet officers can be deployed by the White House to talk with members of Congress in their own policy areas. George W. Bush used Education Secretary Rod Paige to sell his education reform package to Congress in 2001. The following year, Secretary of State Colin Powell was dispatched to Congress to help persuade members to support the authorisation of use of US troops against Iraq.

Finally, the president can work through the party leadership in Congress: the House Speaker; the majority and minority leaders of both houses; the party whips; the committee chairs and ranking minority members. The importance that the White House places on these people could be seen when, in December 2002, President George W. Bush quickly withdrew his support from the Republican leader in the Senate, Trent Lott, after Lott had made some unfortunate remarks about racial policy in America. Bush did not want to reduce the chances of his policy agenda being passed through the Senate by having Lott as the spokesman for it. The White House was clearly behind the plot to force Lott to resign and have him replaced by Senator Bill Frist, a close friend and political ally of the President.

Presidential persuasion through perks

Any of these people, however, may report back to the president that, in order to secure the vote of a particular member of Congress, the president himself needs to get involved by utilising a range of 'perks' which he has at his disposal. As David Mervin (1993) stated:

The president must bargain, he must make deals, he must negotiate with those with whom he shares power. Bargaining skill is therefore indispensable in a president.

The president may, for example, make a personal phone call to certain members of Congress. In an important budget vote in the House in August 1993, President Clinton phoned Democrat House member Marjorie Margolies-Mezvinsky in a hallway just off the chamber of the House of Representatives. She cast the crucial 218th vote to ensure passage of his budget by 218 votes to 216. When receiving a personal phone call from the president, it is important not to do what Republican congresswoman Ileana Ros-Lehtinen of Florida did when she received a call from President-elect Barack Obama in December 2008. Thinking the call was a hoax, she replied: 'You know, you're a better impersonator than that guy who does Obama on *Saturday Night Live.*' When Obama persevered, asking how he could convince her that he really was the President-elect, Mrs Ros-Lehtinen merely replied: 'Yeah, sure, have a great day' and hung up!

The president might offer help with legislation that benefits that member's state or district. He might offer to look more favourably on a judicial or executive branch appointment of interest to the member. The president might invite members of Congress for an Oval Office meeting — either individually or in a small group. He might even go to Capitol Hill to meet with a selected group of members of Congress there. If a member whose support is sought is of the president's party, the president might offer to campaign for them in the next congressional elections. A popular president can use this perk to great effect. If all else fails, the president might go on national television to appeal over the heads of Congress directly to the people. This is what President Johnson called 'putting Congress's feet to the fire'.

In the run-up to the passage of the Patient Protection and Affordable Care Act in 2010 — popularly known as the healthcare reform bill — President Obama made a number of attempts to persuade members of Congress to support the legislation. During a two-month period between 27 January and 20 March, the President:

➤ delivered the State of the Union Address to Congress (27 January)
➤ addressed the Republican House Issues Conference in Baltimore (29 January)
➤ took part in a televised session with Senate Democrats in Washington DC (3 February)
➤ addressed the Democratic National Committee winter meeting in Washington DC (6 February)
➤ hosted a bipartisan healthcare reform meeting at Blair House, Washington DC (25 February)
➤ met with 11 House Democrats at the White House (4 March)
➤ met with the New Democratic Coalition Leadership in the Oval Office (4 March)
➤ met with Senator Charles Schumer (D — New York) in the Oval Office (4 March)
➤ addressed the House Democratic Caucus on Capitol Hill (20 March)

This was on top of addressing numerous Town Hall meetings around the country including those in Tampa, Florida (28 January), Nashua, New Hampshire (2 February), St Louis, Missouri (10 March) and Strongsville, Ohio (15 March).

However, persuasion needs to be a two-way street. If members of Congress get the idea that the only time they hear from the president — either directly or indirectly — is when he wants them to cast a difficult vote for him, cooperation will soon dry up. Small courtesies from the White House can pay off. An invitation to a bill-signing ceremony, dinner with the president at the White House, a trip on Air Force One — all these small perks can help to make the wheels of cooperation turn more smoothly.

The results of presidential persuasion

David Mervin (1993) described the US president as 'bargainer-in-chief'. Presidents bargain for a purpose: that their legislation is passed, their appointments are confirmed, their budgets are agreed to, their vetoes are sustained and their treaties are ratified. As Mark Peterson (2000) stated: 'Leaders are those who make things happen that otherwise would not come about.' The president's success rate is measured each year in what is called the presidential support score. This annual statistic measures how often the president won in recorded votes in the House and Senate on which he took a clear position, expressed as a percentage of the whole.

Table 6.14, which shows the presidential support score since 1993, reveals some interesting information. Presidential support tends to decline during a presidential term. Having one's party control both houses of Congress usually results in a high support score. Loss of control of Congress means a dip in the president's support score: witness Clinton in 1995, George W. Bush in 2007 and Barack Obama in 2011. The score is a useful guide to presidential success, but it does have certain limitations.

First, the score does not measure the importance of votes. The president might win trivial votes while losing important ones or vice versa. Second, presidents can avoid low scores by simply not taking positions on votes they expect to lose. There has been a significant decline in recent years in the number of votes on which presidents have declared a position. In 1978, President Carter announced a position on 306 votes; and in 2011, President Obama announced a position on just 184 votes, and that was out of nearly 1,200 recorded votes held in Congress that year — over 900 in the House and over 200 in the Senate. Third, the score does not count bills that fail to come to a vote on the floor in either house. President Clinton's high score in 1994 took no account of the failure of his Healthcare Reform Bill even to reach the floor of either house, yet this was his flagship policy.

It is worth keeping in mind that changes in Congress — and more widely in the US political system — make the president's job of trying to build support for his legislation more difficult than was the case in the 1950s or 1960s. There are five possible reasons to consider.

First, recent decades witnessed declining levels of party discipline in Congress, although the mid-1990s did see a return to higher levels of partisanship in Congress. Second, it is less likely these days that the president and a majority of both houses of Congress will be of the same party. Third, members of Congress are now more aware of constituents' wishes — through the effects of such factors as C-SPAN and e-mail — and

Table 6.14 Presidential support score, 1993–2012

Year	President	Support score (%)
1993	Bill Clinton	86.4
1994		86.4
1995		36.2
1996		55.2
1997		53.6
1998		50.6
1999		37.8
2000		55.0
2001	George W. Bush	87.0
2002		87.8
2003		78.7
2004		72.6
2005		78.0
2006		80.9
2007		38.3
2008		47.8
2009	Barack Obama	96.7
2010		86.2
2011		57.1
2012		53.6

Source: *Congressional Quarterly*

therefore are perhaps less willing merely to go along with what the president wants. Fourth, changes in the methods of selecting presidential candidates have resulted in Washington outsiders becoming president — Governors Carter, Reagan, Clinton and George W. Bush. They know less about the workings of Congress than did presidents who had worked in Congress — Truman, Kennedy, Johnson, Nixon and Ford — and do not have the personal ties to members of Congress that presidents such as Truman and Johnson enjoyed. Finally, there has been a significant fragmentation of power within Congress. The power of the leadership has been eroded as Congress has become more democratic and power more diffused.

All this can make life frustrating for presidents. From Congress's perspective, former House Speaker Tom Foley looked back to the system of the 1950s:

It isn't possible any more for the Speaker of the House — then Sam Rayburn — to call up the majority leader in the Senate — then Lyndon Johnson — and say, 'Lyndon, come on over.' And Lyndon would come over to the Speaker's office and they would agree on the legislative programme for the rest of the year. Then they would go down and visit President Eisenhower and tell him which bills would be passed and which would not. And the President would negotiate a bit with them, and they'd make some agreement and go back and it was done. Now, you have to negotiate with literally hundreds of members and this is an infuriating thing for the president to try and deal with.

The situation doesn't look any better from the White House perspective. Former Nixon White House aide John Ehrlichman saw similar frustrations:

Every time President Nixon turned round there were new restraints on what he could do as president — in the conduct of the war in Vietnam, in dealing with domestic violence, in trying to balance the budget and things of that kind. So he was continually building coalitions in the Congress: on every issue that came up a new coalition — a few southerners, some Republicans, some interested Democrats who needed a judge approved in their District, or a bridge built, or a canal dug, or something of this kind — laborious step by step work, like putting together tiles in a great mosaic.

The partisan presidency

Relations with Congress

The above quotation from John Ehrlichman comes from an era when, in order to get legislation passed through Congress, both branches of government — the executive and the legislature — had to compromise. The system was characterised by high levels of bipartisanship and cooperation. Republican presidents like Nixon, Ford and Reagan would hope to attract a number of conservative Democrats to help pass their legislation, whilst Democratic presidents such as Johnson and Carter would woo moderate Republicans. Most pieces of major legislation were passed with cross-party support.

But as we have seen in Chapters 3 and 5, the political parties — especially in Congress — have in recent decades become more ideologically homogeneous. The Republicans have become a more united and distinctly conservative party whilst the Democrats have become a more liberal party. The numbers of conservative Democrats and moderate Republicans have declined significantly during the past two decades. The result has been that compromise, inter-party cooperation and bipartisanship is much less common than it used to be. Major pieces of legislation are increasingly passed with very few or no votes coming from the party not controlling the White House. Presidents increasingly have to rely on the overwhelming support of their own party in Congress and to expect the near-unanimous opposition of the other party.

We saw this during Obama's first term with the passage of the economic stimulus package, the healthcare reforms and financial regulation legislation. As Table 6.15 shows, these three pieces of legislation were passed with almost exclusively Democrat

Table 6.15 Final passage votes on three landmark laws: 2009–10

Legislation	Final passage votes	Democrats Yes–No	Republicans Yes–No
Economic Stimulus Package (2009)	House: 246–183 Senate: 60–38	246–7 57–0	0–176 3–38
Patient Protection and Affordable Care Act (2010)	House: 219–212 Senate: 56–43	219–34 56–3	0–178 0–40
Dodd–Frank Wall Street Reform Act (2010)	House: 237–192 Senate: 60–39	234–19 57–1	3–173 3–38

votes. Only three Republican senators voted for the stimulus package and only three Republican House members plus three Republican senators supported the financial regulation reforms, whilst not a single Republican voted for Obama's healthcare bill. But much the same phenomenon was evident during the presidency of George W. Bush over immigration reform and social security reform, and it was evident even back in the Clinton administration over healthcare reform and the 1993 budget deal.

Voting at elections

The office of the presidency therefore operates today in a far more partisan setting than it did only a few decades ago and this has started to have a significant effect on the way the office is seen by ordinary Americans both at election time and also between elections. In the era of what we might call 'the traditional' presidency — the era of Nixon, Ford and Carter — presidents won votes on Election Day from across party lines and they did not always receive the fulsome support of their own party's voters. In 1976, for example, Democrat Jimmy Carter in winning the election still received the votes of only 80% of Democratic voters, with 20% of Democrats voting for the Republican incumbent Gerald Ford. Four years later, Carter received only 67% of Democratic votes. However, in the four elections from 2000, the Democratic candidate has never received less than 86% of the Democratic vote and the Republican candidate never less than 90% of Republican votes. In 2012, Obama won 92% of the votes of self-identified Democrats, whilst Romney won 93% from self-identified Republicans. These are levels of partisan voting quite unimaginable back in the 1960s and 1970s.

Presidential approval ratings

And much the same thing happens in opinion polls between elections. When pollsters ask people about their approval of the president's job performance, one would of course expect those of the president's own party to give him a higher approval rating than those who voted for or support the other party. It was ever thus. But what has changed is the gap between the approval rating of the president within his own party and those within the other party. Take figures for the second year of a presidency — by which time folk have had a chance to come to some conclusion about the president's job performance. In 1978 — the second year of Carter's presidency — 57% of Democrats

Table 6.16 Largest recorded gaps in presidential approval ratings by party, 1953–2012

President	Year	Date	Average approval rating among		Party gap (% points)
			Republicans (%)	Democrats (%)	
Barack Obama	4	2012	10	86	76
George W. Bush	4	2004	91	15	76
George W. Bush	5	2005	86	14	72
George W. Bush	6	2006	79	9	70
Barack Obama	2	2010	13	81	68
Barack Obama	3	2011	12	80	68
George W. Bush	7	2007	73	7	66
Barack Obama	1	2009	23	88	65
Bill Clinton	4	1996	24	85	61
George W. Bush	8	2008	67	6	61

approved of the President's performance, and so did 28% of Republicans, making a gap of 29 percentage points between the two. Compare that with the corresponding moments in the Clinton and Obama presidencies. In 1994, 73% of Democrats approved of Bill Clinton's job performance, but that view was shared by only 19% of Republicans — a gap of 54 percentage points. And in 2010, 81% of Democrats approved of Barack Obama's job performance, but amongst Republicans his approval rating was just 13% — a massive gap of 68 percentage points. In 2004, the fourth year of George W. Bush's presidency, his average approval rating amongst Republicans was 91%, but just 15% amongst Democrats — a gap of 76 percentage points, the largest ever measured.

Table 6.16 shows that the nine years between 2004 and 2012 recorded nine of the ten largest gaps in presidential approval ratings by party since this polling began 60 years ago. This is the landscape of the partisan presidency. Marmite, the famous UK yeast extract spread, advertises with the line: 'Marmite: you love it or you hate it.' In this sense, the presidencies of Bill Clinton, George W. Bush and Barack Obama have brought us into the era of 'the Marmite presidency' — as far as the individual is concerned, you either love him or you hate him.

The White House staff
Thus the partisan presidency shows itself in relations between the executive and legislative branches as well as in the partisan way people vote for and view their president. But it shows itself in other ways too. In presidencies of an earlier era, presidential aides and advisers were known for their 'neutral competence'. Such White House staffers were said to have 'a passion for anonymity'. They were non-partisan experts, more interested in policy than politics. But today, 'neutral competence' has been replaced by politics and spin. Dick Morris and James Carville under President Clinton, the likes of Karl Rove under President George W. Bush and of Rahm Emanuel under President Obama can be categorised as ideological salesmen rather than as neutral administrators.

Table 6.17 The 'traditional presidency' and the 'partisan presidency' compared

	The traditional presidency	The partisan presidency
Relations with Congress	bipartisanship cooperation cross-party coalitions compromise	partisanship lack of cooperation disciplined party votes unwillingness to compromise
Presidential job approval	attracted some cross-party support in elections some approval gap during presidency was evident	attracts negligible cross-party support in elections huge approval gap during presidency is evident
Presidential aides and advisers	'neutral competence' 'passion for anonymity' more policy than politics non-partisan experts	politicisation in the limelight more politics than policy spin doctors and ideological salesmen
Media	old media (e.g. terrestrial TV) objective widely trusted ideologically neutral non-partisan	new media (e.g. Internet, talk radio) subjective trusted only by some ideologically slanted partisan

The media

The relationship between the presidency and the media has also changed. Presidents in the 1960s and 1970s used the media — principally television — to appeal over the heads of congressional and party leaders, directly to the people. The media were largely objective in their reporting. The epitome of the objective media was Walter Cronkite, the anchorman of the *CBS Evening News* for 19 years, between 1962 and 1981. Known as 'Uncle Walter', he was once named by an opinion poll as 'the most trusted man in America'. But in the era of the partisan presidency, presidents have to work not through the old, objective media but through the new, alternative media. Whilst the objective media were characterised by impartial, non-partisan political reporting, the alternative media — what is sometimes called the 'new media' of cable television, Internet and radio talk shows — are characterised by partisan political reporting. A recent poll conducted by the Pew Research Center found that 34% of Republicans regularly watched *Fox News*, while only 20% of Democrats did, and while 1 in 10 Republicans regularly listened to *The Rush Limbaugh Show*, only 1 in 100 Democrats listened. Meanwhile, Barack Obama prefers to talk with liberal talk show host Ed Schultz or conduct a conversation with the liberal *Huffington Post* website or the African-American magazine *Ebony*.

The effects of the partisan presidency

There seems little doubt that being president in this era of increased partisanship makes life harder for the occupant of the Oval Office. In earlier decades, presidents could have a realistic expectation that, by force of a good argument, folk who were currently your opponents — be they senators, congressmen or ordinary voters — might become your supporters, at least on a particular issue. But today, with dividing lines so sharply drawn, the number of persuadable minds, both in Congress and in the country, has sharply declined. 'Opponents' have now become 'enemies'. Presidents like Bill Clinton, George W. Bush and Barack Obama were never going to win elections by a landslide — like Lyndon Johnson (1964), Richard Nixon (1972) or Ronald Reagan (1984) did. Too many voters are never going to vote for a candidate of the opposing party. That all makes both electioneering — and governing — a much more complicated and difficult business. Clinton, Bush and Obama never had the huge electoral mandate enjoyed by Johnson, Nixon or Reagan, and they had nowhere near the number of centrist members of Congress with whom they might realistically do a deal. This is the era of the partisan presidency and it makes gloomy reading as far as effective government is concerned.

The president and foreign policy

If you want to know who controls crisis foreign policy making, then think of two iconic photographs from the past two decades. The first dates from 11 September 2001, and appeared a few pages back. It is of White House Chief of Staff Andrew Card whispering to President George W. Bush the news of the second plane having hit the World Trade Center in New York that morning. The second dates from 2 May 2011 and shows President Obama — along with other senior members of his administration — in the White House Situations Room watching the events unfold in Abbottabad, Pakistan, which would culminate in the killing of Osama bin Laden. The expressions on each face tell the story of the drama. The President is transfixed; Secretary of State Hillary Clinton is shown with her right hand clasped over her mouth in a look part of disbelief and part of horror. Such photographs tell us quite clearly that, when it comes to conducting foreign policy at a time of crisis, it is the president — not Congress — who is in charge.

The lines of authority are less clear, however, when it comes to non-crisis foreign policy making and the Constitution does not exactly help. In the words of Professor Edward Corwin, the Constitution is 'an invitation to struggle for the privilege of directing American foreign policy'. It gives powers over foreign policy to both branches of government and a number of the constitutional provisions are somewhat vague.

The Constitution and control of foreign policy

As we saw in the section on the powers of the president, the Constitution granted the president two specific powers relating to foreign policy — to act as commander-in-chief of the armed forces and to negotiate treaties. As we also saw, both of these powers are subject to significant powers vested in Congress. The president's commander-in-chief power is checked by Congress's powers to declare war and to control the purse strings. However, the effectiveness of these checks is open to question. Congress has not declared war since 1941 and its power of the purse has often proved to be of questionable use once a president has already committed troops abroad, as was the case once President George W. Bush had sent troops to Iraq.

Extra-constitutional powers

Appointments

But the president has three other powers relating to foreign policy. First, he has the power to make appointments to the executive branch, some of which have foreign policy implications, such as secretary of state, secretary of defense, secretary of homeland security, director of the Central Intelligence Agency, chairman of the joint chiefs of staff, and national security adviser. There are also all the ambassadors whom the president appoints — both those to national states as well as those to international organisations such as the United Nations, the European Union and NATO. Indeed, it is by appointing an ambassador to a country that the United States formally recognises the government of that country as being legitimate. All of these appointments, with the exception of the national security adviser, are subject to Senate confirmation.

Executive agreements

Second, the president can sign executive agreements. An executive agreement is an international agreement reached by the president with one or more foreign heads of state and does not require Senate approval. Executive agreements are concluded under the president's constitutional power as commander-in-chief and his general authority in foreign relations, or under power delegated to him by Congress. Numbers have mushroomed in recent years and currently run to around 300 per year, though most deal with routine matters such as minor trade agreements.

Setting the tone

Third, the president has the ability to set the tone of foreign policy. The president performs this role mainly through set-piece speeches, notably the inaugural address or the State of the Union address. President Kennedy, in his noteworthy inaugural address in 1961, promised that America would 'pay any price, bear any burden, meet any hardship, support any friend, oppose any foe in order to ensure the survival and success of liberty'. This was the tone of foreign policy during these decades of the Cold War, exemplified by American involvement in the wars in south-east Asia.

Following the 9/11 attack on the United States, George W. Bush set the tone of foreign policy when talking about an 'axis of evil' in his 2002 State of the Union address. The events that America had just lived through and the perceived threats that it faced allowed the President to formulate and announce a new foreign policy doctrine — the Bush Doctrine. This grand strategy was formally unveiled in September 2002 and would have implications for America's relations with every country and international organisation.

The Bush Doctrine was based on two fundamental claims — the virtue of American primacy and the nation's right to wage pre-emptive war against perceived threats. The 'virtue of American primacy' was grounded in the idea that by defeating communism and fascism, the USA had left the world with 'a single sustainable model for national success —

freedom, democracy and free enterprise'. America would not impose this model on unwilling nations but would seek to 'shape a balance of power that favours human freedom'. The right to wage pre-emptive war would allow America to strike first against enemies determined to inflict imminent harm on the United States. According to Steven Hook and John Spanier (2013), the Bush administration believed that the rise of terrorist groups such as al Qaeda and the nations which either harboured or sponsored them 'changed the calculus of world politics to such an extent that conventional instruments of coercive foreign policy no longer applied'. The only thing that would work, President Bush had concluded, was America taking the offensive rather than playing defensive. In the view of Hook and Spanier:

> No other document in American history had ever made such bold assumptions or advanced such ambitious claims. Indeed, the scope of the new grand strategy was unprecedented in world history. The fact that it was accepted with little debate or fanfare in Congress, by the press, and among the public provides stark evidence of the hubris that was felt across America even after the September 11 attacks.

But the Bush Doctrine led to the eventually unpopular — and some would say unsuccessful — wars in Iraq and Afghanistan which would outlast the Bush presidency. It also tended to alarm the very governments it was meant to reassure. Instead of increasing goodwill towards Washington, it tended more to increase apprehension.

In his inaugural address on 20 January 2009, Barack Obama clearly set a different tone:

> Recall that earlier generations faced down fascism and communism not just with missiles and tanks, but with sturdy alliances and enduring convictions. They understood that our power alone cannot protect us, nor does it entitle us to do as we please. Instead, they knew that our power grows through its prudent use. Our security emanates from the justice of our cause; the force of our example; the tempering qualities of humility and restraint.

To this end, Obama announced that America would return to a reliance on 'soft power' — what he described as 'the ability to get what you want by attraction rather than coercion'. He announced that his administration would revive diplomacy as a core instrument of foreign policy. 'We will extend a hand if you are willing to unclench your fist,' said Obama in his inaugural address. To what extent the administration's foreign policy lived up to those expectations is debatable. The promised closure of the Guantánamo Bay detention camp never materialised. The largest offensive by coalition forces in Afghanistan was launched in 2010, and in 2011 Obama signed a 4-year extension of the USA PATRIOT Act and significantly increased the use of Drone attacks. There were estimated to have been some 300 such attacks during Obama's first term compared with fewer than 50 during Bush's second term. But 2011 saw the last American troops withdraw from Iraq and a date of 2014 was set for withdrawal from Afghanistan.

Congress and foreign policy

But, as we have already seen in Chapter 5, Congress has powers relating to foreign policy too: to declare war, to agree to budgets, and to investigate, as well as the Senate's powers to confirm appointments and to ratify treaties. Fearing that its power had been usurped by an increasingly imperial presidency, Congress passed a series of laws in the 1970s to try to reassert its foreign policy authority. Most notable was the War Powers Act, passed over President Nixon's veto in 1973. But even this has proved to be largely ineffective and Congress has seen itself being relegated merely to authorising the use of troops abroad, as it did in October 2002 before President Bush's incursion into Iraq. As Gene Healy (2008) comments in his recent study of the US presidency:

> When it comes to matters of war and peace, Congress now occupies a position roughly analogous to that of a student council in university governance. It may be important for the administration to show pro forma respect and deference to it — but there can no longer be any doubt about where the real authority resides.

Even when the Democrats reclaimed control of both houses of Congress in January 2007, they made very little headway in enhancing their real influence in foreign policy against the wishes of the Republican Bush administration. 'Now Congress must use its main power, the power of the purse, to put an end to our involvement in this disastrous war,' thundered Democrat senator Russell Feingold on the Senate floor in 2007. But when the Democratic majority tried to do just that, Bush vetoed the bill and the Democrats did not have the votes to override the veto.

Congress possesses a great deal of expertise in its foreign policy-related committees — the Senate armed services committee, the Senate foreign relations committee, the House armed services committee and the House foreign affairs committee. In the autumn of 2007, these committees were the scenes of congressional investigation into the conduct of the war in Iraq as members of Congress debated the reports authored by Ryan Crocker, the US ambassador to Iraq, and General David Petraeus, commander of the multinational force in Iraq, and questioned the authors in face-to-face hearings. But Congress's ability to change the direction of policy was negligible.

But at a time of crisis, America looks to the president, not Congress, to lead foreign policy. It is the president, not Congress, who has the daily intelligence briefing. It is the president to whom the secretaries of state, defense and homeland security, the chairman of the joint chiefs of staff, the director of Central Intelligence and the national security adviser regularly report. The president has the facts. And he also has 'the football' — the briefcase, carried wherever the president goes by a member of the US military, containing the nuclear codes. At a time of crisis, the president is looked to for leadership. As former president Gerald Ford put it: 'Our forefathers knew you could not have 535 commanders-in-chief and secretaries of state. It just wouldn't work.'

Theories of presidential power

But how powerful an office is the US presidency, if its limits, weaknesses and frustrations are taken into account?

The presidency has evolved significantly since the time of George Washington. Presidential scholars have used various terms to signal this evolution. The 'modern presidency' and the 'institutionalised presidency' both had their birth in the administration of Franklin Roosevelt (FDR). It was during FDR's presidency that the role of the federal government expanded significantly, EXOP was established and the USA took on its full-time world leadership role. The pendulum swung in the direction of presidential power and away from congressional authority. Congress seemed to become more subservient to the president. This trend continued with FDR's Democratic successors — Truman, Kennedy and Johnson — as well as with Republican Richard Nixon, who succeeded them.

The imperial presidency

Critics of this presidential assertiveness soon materialised. The one whose criticism received the widest recognition was Pulitzer prize-winning author and professor, Arthur Schlesinger. In 1973 he published *The Imperial Presidency* and the term became a catchphrase for critics of the growth of presidential power. According to Schlesinger's thesis, 'the **imperial presidency** was essentially the creation of foreign policy'. He traces its origins to the Japanese attack on Pearl Harbor in December 1941 — a crisis that allowed FDR to break free from Congress's conventional ties on the executive.

Key concept

> **Imperial presidency.** A term, popularised by the book of that title written in 1973 by Arthur Schlesinger, used to refer to a presidency characterised by the misuse and abuse of the powers of the presidency. In particular, it referred to excessive secrecy — especially in foreign policy — and high-handedness in dealing with Congress.

To see how quickly presidential power had increased, there is no need to look further back than 1950. When North Korea invaded South Korea that year, President Truman immediately sent US troops to South Korea without any congressional authorisation, and Congress raised barely a murmur. In 1958, President Eisenhower sent 14,000 US troops to Lebanon. Again, there was no congressional authorisation. In 1961, President Kennedy launched the disastrous attack on the Bay of Pigs in Cuba without congressional authorisation. Congress played no role at all in the Cuban missile crisis the following year. In 1964, Congress signed a virtual blank cheque — the Tonkin Gulf Resolution — to allow President Johnson to take 'all necessary measures' to sort out the problems in Vietnam. In 1970, President Nixon bombed Cambodia without even the knowledge, let alone the authorisation, of Congress.

The imperial presidency might have been the creation of foreign policy, but it soon spread to the conduct of domestic policy. President Nixon's policies to clamp down on the anti-Vietnam War protests smacked to some of excessive use of power. Even the way he organised and conducted business in the White House looked to some more like an emperor's court than a presidential office. The Watergate affair, which broke in 1972 and forced Nixon to resign in August 1974, added fuel to the fire. Watergate was about illegal bugging and break-ins, the payment of hush money, secrecy, impoundment of congressional funds and obstruction of justice — all at the very highest levels of the Nixon administration.

Was the 'imperial presidency' a reality or merely something conjured up by Nixon's critics? David Mervin (1990), one of a number of presidential scholars who are sceptical of the Schlesinger thesis, wrote:

> In the wake of Watergate and other scandals, the pejorative connotations of the imperial presidency gained added weight, but the concept was always something of a cliché. The word 'imperial' summons up images of the president as an emperor, a supreme sovereign authority, a master of all he surveys. Roosevelt, at the beginning of the 1930s and at the height of World War II, may have briefly approached such a position of pre-eminence, but none of his successors has come even close to such a situation.

Indeed, one could argue that Nixon's forced resignation was proof that the imperial presidency did *not* exist. In his resignation statement, Nixon said he was resigning because 'I no longer have a strong enough political base in the Congress.' Nixon resigned, forced out by Congress. In his own memoirs, Nixon (1978) stated that he believed that:

> The 'imperial presidency' was a straw man created by defensive congressmen and disillusioned liberals who in the days of FDR and John Kennedy had idolised the ideal of a strong presidency. Now that they had a strong president who was a Republican — and Richard Nixon at that — they were having second thoughts.

In 1986, even Schlesinger recanted his thesis to some extent.

Congress's reaction to the 'imperial presidency' was re-assertiveness. They passed a number of pieces of presidency-curbing legislation, especially in the field of foreign policy. The Case Act (1972) forced presidents to inform Congress of all executive agreements made with foreign states. The War Powers Act (1973) attempted to limit presidents' use of troops unless Congress declared war or gave 'specific statutory authorisation'. Thus, Presidents Ford and Carter — the immediate post-Watergate presidents — found their hands much more tied. In 1975, President Ford found he was impotent when the North Vietnamese communists finally overran the South Vietnamese capital, Saigon, including the US embassy compound in the city. Ford complained of congressional meddling in presidential powers. In an article for *Time* magazine 4 years later, Ford wrote:

Some people used to complain about what they called an 'imperial presidency'. But now the pendulum has swung too far in the opposite direction. We have not an imperial presidency but an imperilled presidency. Under today's rules, which include some misguided 'reforms', the presidency does not operate effectively. That is a very serious development, and it is harmful to our overall national interests.

The post-imperial presidency

Reagan's 8 years in the White House meant that the 'imperilled presidency' thesis had to be rewritten. In contrast to the 'failed', one-term presidents Ford and Carter, Reagan launched an ambitious legislative programme at home, restored America's damaged self-confidence abroad and was re-elected by a landslide in 1984. He even managed to pass on the mantle to his vice-president, George H. W. Bush, in the 1988 election.

At home the economy boomed — though so did the federal budget deficit. It was 'morning again in America',

The fall of the Berlin Wall in 1989, 2 years before the collapse of the Soviet Union

according to Reagan's 1984 television commercials. Abroad, Reagan called the Soviet Union 'the evil empire'. In 1987, Reagan even went to Berlin's Brandenburg Gate and declared: 'Mr Gorbachev, open this gate! Mr Gorbachev, tear down this wall!' His call did not have instant effect, but the Berlin Wall eventually fell. The Soviet Union collapsed. The USA was the world's only superpower. Presidential power was back.

George H. W. Bush's presidency, successful in foreign policy, fell on the economic recession at home in the early 1990s and Americans' growing concerns about the ballooning federal budget deficit. Enter Bill Clinton, under whose stewardship the economy boomed. Clinton's contribution to the presidency, however, was to repeat Nixon's sin and besmirch its aura and compromise its integrity. Monica Lewinsky was not Watergate. Clinton survived his impeachment trial in the Senate and became the first Democrat president to serve two terms since FDR. But the tawdry affair, the lying, the attempts at concealment, the hair-splitting legalisms all served to diminish the office of the presidency. Political commentator Elizabeth Drew (1999) wrote:

> The presidency must have a certain aura of majesty and mystique. Clinton's lack of dignity, not to mention his sexual recklessness, was an assault on the office itself.

It also harmed his ability to work effectively.

Box 6.6　Quotations on presidential power

'Weakness is still what I see; weakness in the sense of a great gap between what is expected of a man (or, some day, a woman) and assured capacity to carry through.'

Richard Neustadt (2000)

'The presidency is not a powerful office…Presidents cannot command obedience to their wishes but must persuade.'

James Pfiffner (2000)

'Leadership is difficult precisely because the framers of the Constitution wanted it to be so… Opportunities to check power abound; opportunities to exercise power are limited.'

Thomas Cronin and Michael Genovese (1998)

'Novelist Somerset Maugham once said, "There are three rules for writing a good novel. Unfortunately, no one knows what they are." We are tempted to conclude that there are three rules to being an effective president, yet no one knows exactly what they are.'

Thomas Cronin and Michael Genovese (1998)

'All the president is is a glorified public relations man who spends his time flattering, kissing and kicking people to get them to do what they are supposed to do anyway.'

President Harry Truman

George W. Bush came to the presidency pledged to be 'a uniter and not a divider'. But the circumstances surrounding his election in 2000 — he lost the popular vote, and won the Electoral College vote only after a controversial ruling by the Supreme Court about the counting of votes in Florida — made him a divisive president from the start. Following the events of 9/11, Bush briefly took on the role of 'unifier-in-chief' as he brought the nation together in the 12 months or so following the attacks on the nation. But once he had committed troops to Iraq, Bush quickly returned to being a divisive figure with an unpopular war, encroachments on civil liberties and enhancements of presidential power. Add to that mix perceived incompetence over the federal government's response to Hurricane Katrina, a collapsing economy and a ballooning federal budget deficit, and Bush's revival of what some regarded as an imperial presidency quickly reverted to the more usual talk of a lame-duck presidency.

In Lewis Carroll's *Alice Through the Looking-Glass,* Humpty Dumpty claims that 'when I use a word, it means what I choose it to mean'. The problem with the whole concept of 'the imperial presidency' is that many writers have opted for the Humpty Dumpty theory of language. It means different things to different people. According to David Mervin (1993), the imperial presidency 'was always something of a cliché' as it 'summons up images of the president as an emperor, a supreme sovereign authority, a master of all he surveys', which is clearly not an accurate description of the American presidency. Sam Tannenhaus (2002) put it this way:

The imperial presidency is not a useful idea. It is an epithet, dredged up whenever a president combines strength with imagination. Presidents are, in sum, leaders not rulers — which means, of course, they are not imperial at all.

What we can say is that presidential power is limited — the Founding Fathers intended it to be so. All this makes being a successful and effective president exceedingly difficult.

Limits on presidential power

There are limits on the president's powers, which fall into seven broad areas.

Congress

The checks and balances that Congress has on the president are highly significant. As we saw in both Chapters 1 and 5, Congress may:

➤ amend, delay or reject the president's legislative proposals
➤ override the president's veto
➤ amend his budgetary requests through the power of the purse
➤ check his commander-in-chief power, also through the power of the purse as well as through the power to declare war
➤ refuse to ratify treaties negotiated by the president (Senate only)
➤ reject nominations made by the president (Senate only)
➤ investigate the president's actions and policies
➤ impeach and try the president with possible removal from office if found guilty

The Supreme Court

The Supreme Court (see Chapter 7) can declare the actions of any member of the executive branch, including the president, to be unconstitutional. Nixon felt this in *United States v. Richard M. Nixon* (1974), the court judgement that led within days to his resignation. Clinton felt it in *William Jefferson Clinton v. Paula Corbin Jones* (1997), the judgement that resulted in President Clinton having to answer questions from Ms Jones's lawyers. They asked about a certain Monica Lewinsky, and the rest, as they say, is history.

In the case of *Rasul v. Bush* (2004), the Supreme Court ruled that the detainees at Guantánamo Bay did have access to the US federal courts to challenge their detention, thereby striking down an important part of the Bush administration's legal policy regarding the war on terror. In *Hamdan v. Rumsfeld* (2006), the Court declared unconstitutional the military commissions which the Bush administration had set up to try Guantánamo Bay detainees.

Congress and the Supreme Court provide the constitutional limits on presidential power, but there are extra-constitutional limitations too.

Public opinion

Public opinion is a limitation. President Clinton discovered how important public approval was to his continuing in the White House. He survived his many scandals mainly because his public opinion ratings remained high. President Nixon saw the other side of the coin. President George W. Bush's approval rating rose from 51% in the first week of September 2001 to 86% in the second week. When the 2002 mid-term elections came round, he enjoyed the highest public opinion rating of any president at that point in his term of office since polling began, and saw gains for his party in both houses of Congress in those elections. But Bush's approval ratings soon fell away and by 2008 they were down in the low 30% range, and sometimes lower.

Pressure groups

Pressure groups can mobilise public opinion either for or against the president himself or his policies (see Chapter 4). President Clinton experienced this in 1993–94 over his proposed healthcare reforms. It was the Health Insurance Association of America that aired the highly effective series of 'Harry and Louise' commercials which went a long way to scuppering the President's proposals by turning public opinion — and thereby congressional opinion — against them. President Obama will experience much the same thing from the National Rifle Association in the attempts he has announced to move forward with gun control measures during his second term.

The media

The media have a role to play here too. Presidents today live in an era of the 24-hour news cycle. As a result, what the media report and say can profoundly limit what presidents can do: examples are Johnson in Vietnam, Carter in Iran and Clinton in the area of healthcare reform.

Box 6.7 What factors can make for an effective president?

➤ A large popular vote mandate at the last election

➤ High public approval ratings between elections

➤ Party control of both houses of Congress

➤ An understanding of Washington politics

➤ An understanding of international politics

➤ Moral authority

➤ Oratorical skills/good on television

➤ Competent senior White House staff (especially chief of staff)

➤ First term rather than second term (may become lame duck in last two years)

➤ Ability to persuade

The federal bureaucracy

The federal bureaucracy limits the president's powers. The president is only one person in an executive branch made up of 15 executive departments and around 60 other federal government agencies, boards and commissions employing some 3 million civil servants. Getting the federal bureaucracy to *do* something can be a challenge to any president. Moreover, it is not just the federal government that limits the president. Many federal government programmes are implemented — or not — by state and local governments across the USA. Some southern state governors were able to frustrate presidents Eisenhower, Kennedy and Johnson over civil rights reforms.

Other factors

As if these were not enough, there are other potential limitations on the president's power. The level of unity displayed by the president's party is important. President Clinton would have got his healthcare reforms through Congress, had his party been united behind them. Equally, he would not have survived impeachment had the Democrats deserted him.

Crises can limit what a president can do. What might President Carter have achieved, had not the last 14 months of his presidency been given over to trying to solve the Iranian hostage crisis? Even luck can take a hand. It was surely bad lack that the American hostages were taken prisoner by the Iranians on 4 November 1979. It just so happened that 4 November 1980 — the day marking the hostages' full year in captivity — was Election Day. It is not hard to guess what the media spent their time talking about, just as people were going to the polls. The role that crises can play in the success or failure of a presidency was most vividly shown during the presidency of George W. Bush. Immediately after the attacks on New York and Washington DC on 11 September 2001, the President's popularity sky-rocketed and his ability to get things done increased significantly. The same held true through the initial military successes in Afghanistan as well as the removing of Saddam Hussein in Iraq. But as the military operations in Iraq took a dramatic turn for the worse, so did the President's approval ratings and likewise his ability to get things done.

The test for any president is both to work within these limitations and to ensure that they do not shackle him. He needs to persuade Congress, to woo public opinion, to use the media to his advantage, to control the federal bureaucracy and to unite his party even as he works to divide the opposition. The electorate does not want to hear that the president could not deliver his promises because of the limits upon his office. As David Mervin (1993) stated: 'Given the plethora of potential obstacles that stand in their way, it sometimes seems almost miraculous that presidents accomplish anything at all.'

Activity

Go to the Gallup website at **www.gallup.com** then towards the bottom of the home page under 'Interactive Features' click on 'Job Approval Center'. This will bring up data on presidential approval ratings going back over six decades and a dozen presidents. Using these data, try to discover similar patterns in presidential approval ratings over presidents' first and second terms. Try to account for significant changes in approval ratings.

Using the detailed data on President Obama's current approval ratings, find out which groups give the president his highest and lowest approval ratings. How does the President's approval rating amongst Democrats compare with his approval rating amongst Republicans? How does this fit with what you read in this chapter about 'the partisan presidency'?

UK/US comparison

The US president and the UK prime minister

There are six basic characteristics of the US presidency:

➤ The president is elected in a national election.

➤ The Constitution grants the president a number of important powers.

➤ The president's cabinet is a relatively unimportant body. Members are drawn from a number of pools of recruitment. There is no doctrine of collective responsibility. The president is not 'first among equals'.

➤ The Executive Office of the President is a large and highly influential organisation to help the president in his role as chief executive.

➤ In his relationship with Congress (of which he is not a member), the president has some formal powers but must rely largely on 'the power to persuade'.

➤ There has been a move over recent decades towards what some commentators call an 'imperial presidency'. But the president is also limited by significant checks and balances exercised by both Congress and the courts.

There are six basic characteristics of the office of the UK prime minister:

➤ The prime minister comes to office through an internal party leadership election and through his/her party being the largest single party in the House of Commons.

➤ The prime minister has a number of formal powers.

➤ The cabinet operates under the doctrine of collective responsibility, in which the prime minister has traditionally been regarded as 'first among equals'.

➤ There is no real UK equivalent to the Oval Office, the West Wing or the Executive Office of the President. The prime minister has a small Number 10 staff of political and policy advisers.

➤ In his/her relationship with parliament (of which he is a member), the prime minister can rely largely on his/her party's majority status in the House of Commons, control of the parliamentary agenda and high levels of party discipline.

➤ There has been a move over recent decades towards what some commentators have seen as a 'presidentialised' office of the UK prime minister. But the prime minister is also limited by the powers of parliament, the cabinet, his/her party and the electorate.

Exam focus

Short-answer questions

1 How extensive are the constitutional powers of the president?
2 Why has the size and scope of the federal bureaucracy grown so much in recent years?
3 What are the most significant problems concerning the federal bureaucracy?
4 What checks exist on the power of the federal bureaucracy?
5 How important is the president's cabinet?
6 Assess the importance of the role of the vice-president.
7 How much influence does the president have over the legislative process?
8 Explain the meaning and discuss the importance of the 'imperial presidency'.

Essay questions

1 Does the president's cabinet fulfil any useful functions?
2 Examine the importance of the Executive Office of the President.
3 How can a president successfully coordinate the work of his administration?
4 Assess the difficulties that presidents face in their dealings with Congress.
5 How accurate is it to describe the president as 'bargainer-in-chief'?
6 Examine the claim that 'the president's power is the power to persuade'.
7 To what extent do presidents control foreign policy?
8 'There are no effective checks on presidential power.' Discuss.

Further reading

Bennett, A. J., 'The US presidential veto', *Politics Review*, Vol. 18, No. 2, November 2008.

Bennett, A. J., *US Government & Politics: Annual Update 2012*, Chapter 1, Philip Allan Updates.

Edwards, G. C., *The Strategic President: Persuasion and Opportunity in Presidential Leadership,* Princeton University Press, 2009.

Edwards, G. C., *Overreach: Leadership in the Obama Presidency*, Princeton University Press, 2012.

Chapter 7

The Supreme Court, and the protection of rights and liberties

On the northwest corner of Capitol Hill in Washington DC stands the ornate building which for nearly 80 years has been the home of the United States Supreme Court. While the Capitol — which stands just across the road — houses the 535 members of Congress, the Supreme Court is home to only nine people, the total membership of the USA's highest court. The building is imposing and does justice to the importance of the decisions handed down by the members of the Supreme Court, which plays an extremely significant political role in the life of the USA. Many of the Court's decisions in recent decades have affected US society profoundly.

This chapter looks at the institution itself, as well as the Court's important role as defender of the laws, the Constitution and the very rights and liberties of US citizens.

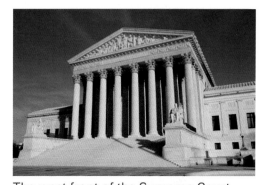

The west front of the Supreme Court

Key questions answered in this chapter

➤ What is the structure of the federal courts in the USA?
➤ What is the membership of the Supreme Court?
➤ How does the appointment process work?
➤ What is the power of judicial review?

➢ What have been the recent landmark decisions of the Supreme Court?

➢ How might the Roberts Court differ from the Rehnquist Court?

➢ What checks exist on the Court's power?

➢ Is the Court now the 'Roberts Court'?

Links to follow up

The place to start for electronic sources on the US Supreme Court is the Court's own website at **www.supremecourtus.gov**. The 'About the Supreme Court' button is the best one to use from the home page. You can also research Supreme Court decisions by going to the button marked 'Opinions' but be aware that these are the actual opinions and hence highly detailed and not easy for the layperson/student to readily understand. There is also **www.scotusblog.com** which has some impressive but very accessible statistics on each recent term of the Court. You can also use this site to keep up to date on cases currently before the Court. For each case it has a short paragraph entitled 'Plain English' with a brief explanation of the case in 'plain English'. There is also a website, **www.law.cornell.edu**, which gives a brief commentary on Supreme Court decisions, and which makes them much easier to follow than the full opinion. Another useful site is **www.uscourts.gov**, which gives clear explanations of the Court's procedure as well as simulations of Court decision making. More widely on the federal judiciary, the website of the Federal Judicial Center is quite helpful at **www.fjc.gov**. Media sites such as **www.washingtonpost.com** and **www.nytimes.com** give regular reports on matters relating to the Supreme Court.

The website of the Senate Judiciary Committee will have details of any judicial confirmation hearings that may take place. Go to **www.senate.gov** and click on 'Committees' and then on 'Judiciary'.

You might also want to consult websites relating to some of the specific rights and liberties discussed in this chapter. These might include:

www.aclu.org

www.freespeechcoalition.com

www.nra.org

www.bradycenter.org

www.deathpenaltyinfo.org

www.naacp.org

www.affirmativeaction.org

www.nrlc.org

www.plannedparenthood.org

www.now.org

The structure of the federal courts

The United States Supreme Court sits at the top of the federal judiciary. According to the original Constitution, the Supreme Court was to be the only federal court. Article III Section 1 begins:

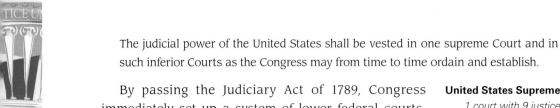

The judicial power of the United States shall be vested in one supreme Court and in such inferior Courts as the Congress may from time to time ordain and establish.

By passing the Judiciary Act of 1789, Congress immediately set up a system of lower federal courts. Below the Supreme Court are 13 Courts of Appeals, known as Circuit Courts, and below those are the 94 trial courts known as District Courts (see Figure 7.1). The vast majority of federal cases begin in the District Courts. Once the case has been decided there, it may be appealed to one of the Circuit Courts and from there to the United States Supreme Court. Cases may also arrive at the United States Supreme Court from the state Supreme Courts, if questions involving the federal government are raised. The United States Supreme Court hears only those cases that it wishes to hear. There is no automatic right to have one's case heard before the United States Supreme Court. The Court rejects over 96% of cases that seek to be heard there. It hears only those cases that it believes are of major constitutional significance.

United States Supreme Court
1 court with 9 justices

United States Court of Appeals
1 in each of 11 'circuits' (regions)
plus 1 in Washington DC
plus 1 in federal Circuit Court

United States District Courts
1 in each of if 94 districts

Figure 7.1 The structure of the federal courts

Membership of the Supreme Court

Today there are nine members of the Supreme Court — one chief justice and eight associate justices. The number is fixed by Congress and has remained unchanged since 1869. They are appointed by the president and must be confirmed by a simple majority vote in the Senate. Once appointed and confirmed, they hold office for life — 'during good behaviour', as Article III Section 1 of the Constitution puts it. This means that members of the Court can be removed only through the impeachment process. The House must impeach a justice by a simple majority and the Senate must then try that justice. If found guilty by the Senate by a two-thirds majority, the justice is removed from office. However, no Supreme Court justice has ever been impeached, although Associate Justice Abe Fortas resigned from the Supreme Court in 1968 rather than face impeachment. Thus, barring impeachment, justices leave the Court only as a consequence of voluntary retirement or death.

When the Supreme Court is sitting, the justices sit along a bench in high-back chairs with a backdrop of a plush red curtain. Sitting in the middle of the nine justices is the chief justice. Although his powers are in most respects the same as those of his colleagues, the chief justice has the opportunity to set the tone of the Court. The current chief justice, John Roberts, is only the 16th person to hold the office in over 210 years. His predecessors include a number of illustrious names, such as John Marshall (1801–35), Roger Taney (1836–64), William Howard Taft (1921–30) and Charles Evans Hughes (1930–41), but students need

Table 7.1 Supreme Court membership, 2013

Justice	Date appointed	President appointing
Chief Justice John Roberts	2005	George W. Bush (R)
Associate Justices Antonin Scalia	1986	Ronald Reagan (R)
Anthony Kennedy	1988	Ronald Reagan (R)
Clarence Thomas	1991	George H. W. Bush (R)
Ruth Bader Ginsburg	1993	Bill Clinton (D)
Stephen Breyer	1994	Bill Clinton (D)
Samuel Alito	2006	George W. Bush (R)
Sonia Sotomayor	2009	Barack Obama (D)
Elena Kagan	2010	Barack Obama (D)

to be familiar only with Chief Justice Roberts and his three immediate predecessors — Earl Warren (1953–69), Warren Earl Burger (1969–86) and William Rehnquist (1986–2005). Commentators often use the name of the chief justice to denote an era in the Court's history. Thus, we talk of the 'Warren Court', the 'Burger Court' and the 'Rehnquist Court'. The membership of the Supreme Court in January 2013 is set out in Table 7.1.

Philosophy of the justices

Strict and loose constructionists

It is often suggested that presidents wish to appoint justices who share their judicial philosophy. From a philosophical perspective, justices can be classified as 'conservatives' or 'liberals'. Another classification used is that of **strict constructionists** and **loose constructionists**.

Key concepts

> **Strict constructionist.** A justice of the Supreme Court who interprets the Constitution in a strict, literal or conservative fashion, and who tends to stress the retention of as much power as possible by the governments of the individual states.
> **Loose constructionist.** A justice of the Supreme Court who interprets the Constitution in a loose or liberal fashion, and who tends to stress the broad grants of power to the federal government.

Strict constructionist judges are usually conservative in outlook. In their decisions they tend to interpret the Constitution in a strict or literal fashion — they look at the original intent of the Founding Fathers and hence are often referred to as 'originalists'. They often favour states' rights over the power of the federal government, and they tend to be appointed by Republican presidents. Chief Justice Roberts and associate justices Scalia, Thomas and Alito fall into this category. Strict constructionist judges focus on *the text* of the Constitution. For them, the language is supreme and the Court's job is to

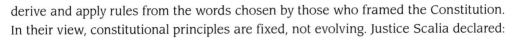

derive and apply rules from the words chosen by those who framed the Constitution. In their view, constitutional principles are fixed, not evolving. Justice Scalia declared:

> The Constitution that I interpret and apply is not living but dead. Our first responsibility is not to make sense of the law — our first responsibility is to follow the text of the law.

In a recent interview on the CBS News programme *60 Minutes*, Justice Scalia put it this way:

> You think there ought to be a right to abortion? No problem. The Constitution says nothing about it. Create it the way most rights are created in a democratic society. Pass a law. A Constitution is not meant to facilitate change. It is meant to impede change, to make change difficult.

Loose constructionist judges, on the other hand, are usually liberal in outlook. Their decisions tend to interpret the Constitution in a loose fashion — reading elements into the document that they think the framers of the Constitution would approve. They tend to favour the power of the federal government over states' rights, and they are usually appointed by Democratic presidents. At the time of writing, associate justices Ginsburg, Breyer, Sotomayor and Kagan fell into this category — the first two appointed by President Clinton, the latter two by President Obama.

In contrast to Justice Scalia, a loose constructionist such as Justice Breyer would say that he looks at *the context* of the Constitution. The language of the text is only the starting point of an inquiry in which a law's purpose and a decision's likely consequence are the more important elements. He sees Scalia's approach as 'too legalistic' and one that 'places too much weight upon language, history, tradition and precedent alone'.

This leaves Associate Justice Anthony Kennedy as what is called the 'swing' justice. In recent years, when the Court has decided cases by 5–4, the decision of Justice Kennedy has often been the deciding factor. In the Court's 2006–07 term, of the 24 cases which were decided by a 5–4 majority, Justice Kennedy was in the majority in all 24 of them, making him the justice most frequently in the majority during that term. Indeed, Kennedy was in the majority in 66 of the 68 opinions (97%) decided by the Court in that term. According to Steven Calabresi, professor at Northwestern University School of Law: 'Kennedy is very much the median justice now, as Justice Sandra O'Connor was.'

Judicial activism and restraint

Another way in which the Supreme Court makes its decisions can be analysed through the terms **judicial activism** and **judicial restraint**. An activist Court is said to be one which sees itself as leading the way in the reform of American society. Thus we shall see that the Court under Earl Warren was said to be activist in the 1950s and 1960s in such decisions as *Brown v. Board of Education of Topeka* (1954) and *Miranda v. Arizona* (1966) in trying to move society along in the areas of black civil rights and the rights of arrested persons. The Court under Warren Burger was probably being activist in *Roe v. Wade*

Key concepts

➤ **Judicial activism.** An approach to judicial decision making which holds that a judge should use his or her position to promote desirable social ends.

➤ **Judicial restraint.** An approach to judicial decision making which holds that a judge should defer to the legislative and executive branches, which are politically accountable to the voters, and should put great stress on the precedent established in previous Court decisions.

(1973), announcing that the right of a woman to have an abortion was a constitutionally protected one. Judicial activism also sees the Court as an equal partner with the legislative and executive branches of government and therefore there is no need for the Court in any way to be deferential to the other two branches of government. Professor Lino Graglia has defined judicial activism as 'the practice by judges of disallowing policy choices by other governmental officials or institutions that the Constitution does not clearly prohibit'. In other words, activist judges are not inclined to be deferential to the other branches of government. In this sense, according to T. R. van Geel (2009), judicial activism can be understood as a judicial attitude which says: 'I'm in charge, and I will seek to be a player equal to the other branches in shaping policy.'

'Judicial restraint' describes the Court when it is more inclined to accept what has gone before, more inclined to leave things as they are, and is more associated with justices who could be described as strict constructionists. The Court exhibiting 'judicial restraint' puts a good deal of importance on what is called *stare decisis* — best translated from the Latin as 'to stand by that which is decided'. Under this principle, once a matter has been decided in a case, it forms a precedent that should not be overturned except under pressing and changed circumstances. Under the principle of judicial restraint, we shall see that having, for example, announced a woman's right to abortion in *Roe v. Wade*, the Court has been willing to see limits put on that right but not to overturn the 1973 decision completely. Judicial restraint also sees the Court as somewhat deferential to the legislative and executive branches of government, as they — unlike the judiciary — are directly accountable to the voters. The Court following the approach of judicial restraint is therefore less likely to declare acts of Congress, or the state legislatures, unconstitutional. For this reason, some writers prefer the term 'judicial deference' to 'judicial restraint' as the opposite of 'judicial activism'.

One problem, however, with these terms is that they are often used judgementally, especially the term 'judicial activism'. Another phrase that is sometimes used by critics of the Court is that the justices are 'legislating from the bench', thus being judicial activists. As Kermit Roosevelt comments in his scholarly book, *The Myth of Judicial Activism* (2006): 'perceptions of appropriate judicial behaviour are invariably affected by ideology'. In other words, people will all too often label as 'judicial activism' those decisions of the Supreme Court of which they disapprove. Roosevelt concludes:

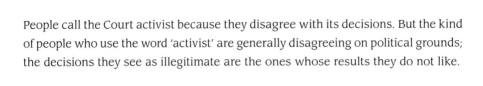

People call the Court activist because they disagree with its decisions. But the kind of people who use the word 'activist' are generally disagreeing on political grounds; the decisions they see as illegitimate are the ones whose results they do not like.

The appointment and confirmation process

The vacancy

First, the president must wait for a vacancy to occur. There have been 118 vacancies to fill on the Supreme Court since 1789 — which is around one every 2 years. Thus, a president might expect to make two such appointments in a 4-year term, and three or four appointments in two terms. Bill Clinton and George W. Bush made only two appointments in each of their 8 years whilst Barack Obama made two appointments during his first 2 years in office. However, some presidents are not so fortunate. Carter made none at all in his 4 years. No vacancies occurred on the Court for just short of 11 years between August 1994 and July 2005 — the longest period since the Court remained unchanged for 12 years between 1812 and 1824.

Second, because of the life tenure that the justices enjoy and the great importance of the Supreme Court, presidents regard Supreme Court appointments as the most important of their entire presidency. Most other appointments that presidents make last only for as long as the president remains in office. Cabinet officers, for example, are lucky to serve more than 2 or 3 years, and all of them will almost certainly leave office the moment the president departs. The same goes for most other appointees — ambassadors, agency heads and Executive Office personnel. But Supreme Court justices will, politically speaking, almost certainly outlive the president. Indeed, they may even outlive him physically. President Eisenhower left office in 1961 and died in 1969. Justice William J. Brennan, whom Eisenhower appointed to the Supreme Court in 1956, retired only in 1990. President Nixon left office in 1974 and died in 1994, but Justice William Rehnquist, whom Nixon appointed to the Supreme Court in January 1972, served until his death in September 2005 — a period of nearly 34 years. Rehnquist thus served on the Supreme Court for 11 years after Nixon's own death. In this sense, the Supreme Court can often appear to be something of an 'echo chamber', through which the voices and views of earlier decades can still be heard to speak.

Box 7.1 **The appointment process of Supreme Court justices**

1 A vacancy occurs through voluntary retirement, death or impeachment.

2 The president instigates a search for possible nominees and interviews short-listed candidates.

3 The president announces his nominee.

4 The Senate confirmation process begins in the Senate Judiciary Committee and ends on the floor of the Senate.

Table 7.2 Supreme Court appointments, 1961–2013

President	Years in office	Number of Supreme Court appointments
John Kennedy (D)	2½	2
Lyndon Johnson (D)	5½	2
Richard Nixon (R)	5½	4
Gerald Ford (R)	2½	1
Jimmy Carter (D)	4	0
Ronald Reagan (R)	8	3
George H. W. Bush (R)	4	2
Bill Clinton (D)	8	2
George W. Bush (R)	8	2
Barack Obama (D)	4 (to January 2013)	2

The search and pools of recruitment

Once a vacancy has occurred, the president commissions a search for suitable candidates. Of course, if a vacancy has been anticipated, this search might have been going on surreptitiously for some time. The president seeks advice from different sources. First, he asks his political advisers — senior White House aides and top officials in the Justice Department — for possible nominees. In addition, he might hear some names being mentioned by key members of Congress of his own party — possibly from members of the influential Senate Judiciary Committee, who have a more formal role to play later in the process. Second, the president — especially Democrats — might seek advice from professional groups such as the American Bar Association (ABA). Third, the president might turn to personal friends and confidants.

The most likely pool of recruitment for Supreme Court justices is the federal Courts of Appeals — the courts one tier below the Supreme Court and the courts that will usually have heard cases before they arrive at the Supreme Court. This has become an increasing trend in the last three decades. Of the current Court membership, eight of the justices were recruited from the federal Courts of Appeals, Elena Kagan being the one exception.

Alternatively, the president might look to the state courts. When President Reagan had his first opportunity to fill a vacancy on the Supreme Court back in 1981, he nominated Sandra Day O'Connor, who was then a judge on the Arizona state Court of Appeals. David Souter, nominated by President Bush in 1990, had been on a federal Court of Appeals for only 3 months. Before that he was a member of the New Hampshire state Supreme Court.

Another possible pool of recruitment is the Department of Justice. In 2010, when President Obama nominated Elena Kagan to the Supreme Court, Kagan was serving as Solicitor General at the Department of Justice.

The announcement

Once a shortlist has been drawn up, FBI background checks are conducted on all the possible nominees and the president personally interviews two or three finalists. Having decided on the nominee, the president makes the formal announcement (before the identity of the nominee is leaked to the press). The public announcement is a major political event attended by the nominee, members of his or her family, key members of Congress and the executive branch, as well as members of the press.

There then follows a part of the appointment process that is entirely unofficial but has become accepted by tradition: this is the rating by the ABA Standing Committee on the Federal Judiciary. Nominees are given one of three ratings: 'well qualified'; 'qualified'; 'not qualified'. As this is a nomination to the USA's highest court, a 'well qualified' rating would be expected. Not to gain that rating would be a significant problem. The only recent Supreme Court nominee to be given a rating other than 'well qualified' was Clarence Thomas, who, when nominated by George H. W. Bush in 1991, was awarded a rating of 'qualified' by the majority of the ABA committee, but a minority submitted a 'not qualified' rating.

The confirmation process

The focus moves to Capitol Hill for the confirmation process. The nominee first has to appear before the Senate Judiciary Committee. Hearings are held at which the witnesses include not only the nominee but also supporters, and maybe critics, of the nominee. Witnesses might be individuals with close knowledge of the nominee or representatives of interest groups who support or oppose the nomination.

If the process goes badly for the nominee, they might be tempted to withdraw. Alternatively, the president might be tempted to call a halt to the nomination to save

Table 7.3 Jobs held by Supreme Court nominees at the time they were nominated since 1789

Job held previously	Most recent example (date)	Number of nominees holding this position
Federal judge	Sonia Sotomayor (2009)	33
Practising attorney	Lewis Powell (1971)	22
State court judge	Sandra Day O'Connor (1981)	18
Cabinet member	Arthur Goldberg (1962)	14
Senator	Harold Burton of Ohio (1945)	7
Solicitor General	Elena Kagan (2010)	3
State governor	Earl Warren of California (1953)	3
Law professor	Felix Frankfurter (1939)	2
State legislator	Benjamin Curtis of Massachusetts (1851)	2

further embarrassment and a possible defeat on the Senate floor. In October 2005 Bush nominee Harriet Miers withdrew after conservative Republican senators were unconvinced as to her ideological credentials. What was extraordinary about Miers' withdrawal was that it came as a result of hostility from members of the President's own party.

Once the hearings have concluded, the committee votes on whether or not to recommend further action. This is therefore only a recommendatory, not a decisive, vote. However, the committee vote is a clear pointer to the likely outcome when the full Senate makes the final decision. If the Senate Judiciary Committee votes unanimously or overwhelmingly in favour of a nominee, the nomination is near certain to be confirmed. If, however, the committee vote is close or is lost, defeat on the floor is a near certainty. The 1987 defeat of the nomination of Robert Bork in the Judiciary Committee was a prelude to his defeat on the Senate floor (see Table 7.4). When the committee voted 7–7 on the nomination of Clarence Thomas, it was clear that he was in for a fight on the Senate floor. The Senate did eventually confirm Thomas, but only by a margin of four votes. However, Ruth Bader Ginsburg (1993) followed her unanimous approval by the committee with a 96–3 vote on the Senate floor. A simple majority is required for confirmation.

The Senate has rejected 12 nominations since 1789 (see Table 7.6), the most recent example being the rejection in 1987 of Reagan nominee Robert Bork by 42 votes to 58. Bork's critics regarded him as being both too conservative and too closely associated with former president Richard Nixon. Bork had played a role in the Watergate affair when, at the orders of President Nixon, he had fired the independent prosecutor, Archibald Cox, who was investigating the Watergate cover-up.

The two other modern-day examples of rejections were both nominees of President Nixon: Clement Haynesworth (1969) by 45 votes to 55 and Harrold Carswell (1970) by 45 votes to 51. Both Haynesworth and Carswell were regarded by a Democrat-controlled Senate as too conservative. It is no coincidence that all three rejections occurred when the president faced a Senate controlled by the opposing party.

Table 7.4 ABA ratings and Senate votes on selected Supreme Court nominees

Nominee	Year	ABA rating	Senate Judiciary Committee vote	Senate vote
Robert Bork	1987	Well qualified	5–9	Rejected 42–58
Clarence Thomas	1991	Qualified	7–7	Confirmed 52–48
Ruth Bader Ginsburg	1993	Well qualified	18–0	Confirmed 96–3
John Roberts	2005	Well qualified	13–5	Confirmed 78–22
Elena Kagan	2010	Well qualified	13–6	Confirmed 63–37

Table 7.5 Senate action on Supreme Court nominees since 1986

Nominee	President	Date	Result	Vote
William Rehnquist*	Ronald Reagan (R)	1986	Confirmed	65–33
Antonin Scalia	Ronald Reagan (R)	1986	Confirmed	98–0
Robert Bork	Ronald Reagan (R)	1987	Rejected	42–58
Douglas Ginsburg	Ronald Reagan (R)	1987	Withdrawn	–
Anthony Kennedy	Ronald Reagan (R)	1988	Confirmed	97–0
David Souter	George H. W. Bush (R)	1990	Confirmed	90–9
Clarence Thomas	George H. W. Bush (R)	1991	Confirmed	52–48
Ruth Bader Ginsburg	Bill Clinton (D)	1993	Confirmed	96–3
Stephen Breyer	Bill Clinton (D)	1994	Confirmed	87–9
John Roberts*	George W. Bush (R)	2005	Confirmed	78–22
Harriet Miers	George W. Bush (R)	2005	Withdrawn	–
Samuel Alito	George W. Bush (R)	2006	Confirmed	58–42
Sonia Sotomayor	Barack Obama (D)	2009	Confirmed	68–31
Elena Kagan	Barack Obama (D)	2010	Confirmed	63–37

* As Chief Justice

Table 7.6 Supreme Court nominations withdrawn or rejected: 1789–2012

President	Dates	Number of Supreme Court nominees	
		Withdrawn	Rejected
George Washington	1789–97	0	1
James Madison	1809–17	0	1
John Quincy Adams	1825–29	1	0
John Tyler	1841–45	3	1
James Polk	1845–49	0	1
Millard Fillmore	1850–53	3	0
James Buchanan	1857–61	0	1
Andrew Johnson	1865–69	1	0
Ulysses Grant	1869–77	2	1
Grover Cleveland	1893–97	0	2
Herbert Hoover	1929–33	0	1
Lyndon Johnson	1963–69	2	0
Richard Nixon	1969–74	0	2
Ronald Reagan	1981–89	1	1
George W. Bush	2001–09	1	0

Obama's Supreme Court nominees

Sonia Sotomayor

President George W. Bush had to wait over 4 years to make his first nomination to the United States Supreme Court. President Obama had to wait only 4 months. On 1 May 2009, Associate Justice David Souter wrote a brief letter to the President indicating his intention to retire from the Supreme Court at the end of its 2008–09 session. Appointed to the Court in 1990 by President George H.

President Obama announcing his nomination of Judge Sonia Sotomayor with Vice President Joe Biden

W. Bush, Souter had thus served just short of 19 years. Just over 3 weeks later, President Obama announced that he was nominating Judge Sonia Sotomayor (pronounced *So-toe-my-yore*) of New York, a Hispanic federal appeal court judge, to replace Justice Souter. The nomination was generally well received — certainly by Democrats and also by a number of prominent Republicans. Indeed, Republicans were eager not to be seen as being anti-Hispanic — Hispanics being a critically important ethnic group whose support George W. Bush had done much to woo during his presidency. Republicans also realised that having been designated by most neutral commentators as a moderate liberal, Sotomayor was unlikely to change the philosophical balance of the Court to any significant extent, as the justice she was to replace — David Souter — could also be described as a moderate liberal. In this sense, like the Roberts-for-Rehnquist nomination back in 2005, the Sotomayor-for-Souter nomination was also being portrayed as a like-for-like replacement, hence less controversial.

The Senate Judiciary Committee hearings opened with introductory statements from the senators and the nominee. Such controversy as there was surrounding Judge Sotomayor's nomination centred mostly upon a remark she had made in a lecture in 2001, in which she had stated:

> I would hope that a wise Latina woman with the richness of her experiences would more often than not reach a better conclusion than a white male who hasn't lived that life.

Democrats were concerned enough about the remark to give her an opportunity early in the hearings to step away from it. In reply to a question from the committee chairman, Patrick Leahy, Judge Sotomayor stated:

No words I have ever spoken or written have received so much attention. I want to state up front, unequivocally and without doubt: I do not believe that any ethnic, racial or gender group has an advantage in sound judging.

Indeed, in asking his question, Senator Leahy misquoted Judge Sotomayor's 'wise Latina woman' comment by omitting the words 'a better conclusion than a white male' and inserting in their place the much more neutral phrase 'wise decisions'. Judge Sotomayor went on in answer to other questions to suggest that her 'wise Latina woman' remark had been 'a poor choice of words' and 'a verbal flourish that had fallen flat', adding that 'the context of the words [had] created a misunderstanding'.

In one of the few moments of genuine interest during the hearings, Judge Sotomayor distanced herself from President Obama's oft-stated philosophy that Supreme Court justices should be guided by 'empathy' and their 'hearts' in deciding cases. But according to Judge Sotomayor:

I wouldn't approach the issue of judging the way the President does. Judges can't rely on what's in their heart. The job of a judge is to apply the law.

Here was another possible nail in the coffin for the oft-repeated argument that suggests that Supreme Court justices are merely echo chambers of the presidents who appoint them. The committee voted to recommend Judge Sotomayor for appointment to the Supreme Court by a vote of 13–6. Republican senator Lindsey Graham joined all 12 committee Democrats to vote in favour, while the remaining 6 Republicans voted 'no'. A few weeks later the full Senate debated and voted on Judge Sotomayor's nomination, approving her by a vote of 68–31. The whole process — from nomination to confirmation — had taken 66 days, not far off the average of 60 days in the period since 1975.

Elena Kagan

On 9 April 2010, Associate Justice John Paul Stevens wrote a brief letter to the President indicating his intention to retire from the Supreme Court at the end of its 2009–10 term. Appointed to the Court in 1975 by President Gerald Ford, Stevens had thus served just short of 35 years. Three weeks later, President Obama announced that he was nominating Solicitor General Elena Kagan of New York to replace Justice Stevens. Aged 50, Kagan would become the youngest member of the current Court and its third woman — the first time in its history that the Court had included three female justices.

It was towards the end of June when the Senate Judiciary Committee hearings opened on the Kagan nomination. To Democrats, Kagan was 'unassailable', 'refreshing' and 'brilliant'; to Republicans she was 'a political lawyer', 'unqualified' and someone who 'seems to bemoan the demise of socialism'. To misquote Dickens, it was a tale of two Kagans: she was (pretty much) the best of nominees and (almost) the worst of nominees. When Kagan finally got to say something herself, she promised, if confirmed, to show the 'even-handedness and impartiality' the Constitution demands and also proper deference to Congress and the laws it passes. She resorted to the motherhood and apple pie generalities that have served previous nominees so well, assuring her audience:

> I will listen hard to every party before the Court and to each of my colleagues. I will work hard. And I will do my best to consider each case impartially, modestly, with commitment to principle and in accordance to law. The Supreme Court is a wondrous institution. But the time I spent in the other branches of government remind me that it must also be a modest one.

Nothing too controversial there. It may have been bland, but it certainly was not dull, enlivened as it was by Kagan's wry sense of humour. Asked by Democrat senator Arlen Specter if she thought the deliberations of the Supreme Court should be televised, she agreed with the suggestion before adding, 'It means I'd have to get my hair done more often!' Another Democrat, Herb Kohl, asked the nominee if she could 'tell us the names of a few current justices with whom you identify', craftily trying to illicit something about her judicial philosophy. 'I think it would be just a bad idea for me to talk about current justices,' Kagan replied with a smile. After just 3 days, the committee voted to recommend Kagan for appointment to the Supreme Court by a vote of 13–6 — a carbon-copy vote of the one on Justice Sotomayor almost exactly a year earlier. And on 5 August 2010, the full Senate voted by 63 votes to 37 to confirm Kagan as the 112th justice of the Supreme Court.

What is wrong with the appointment and confirmation process?

Most modern-day criticism of the appointment and confirmation process centres on accusations of politicisation — by the president, by the Senate and by the media that cover the process.

Politicisation by the president

Although presidents always deny any political consideration in the appointment process, it seems nonetheless to underlie the choosing of Supreme Court justices. Presidents are tempted to choose a justice whose political and judicial philosophy reflect their own. Republican presidents want to pick a justice who is conservative and takes a strict and literal view of the Constitution. Democrat presidents, on the other hand, want to choose a justice who is liberal and takes a looser, adaptive view of the Constitution. There is always the danger that presidents use a 'litmus test' on Court nominees, often scrutinising their previous judgements on controversial cases, such as those regarding affirmative action, capital punishment or abortion.

When President Bush announced his nomination of David Souter to the Supreme Court in 1990, the first question he was asked by the press after he had delivered his introductory statement was: 'Did you ask Judge Souter his views on abortion?' Bush said that he had not, stating: 'It would have been inappropriate to ask him his views on specific issues.' Then, for good measure, the President added:

> What I am certain of is that he will interpret the Constitution and not legislate from the federal bench...You might think the whole nomination had to do with abortion...I have too much respect for the Supreme Court than to look at one specific issue.

On this occasion, however, the President might indeed have been right to deny any political considerations in his choice. Justice Souter, in almost two decades on the Supreme Court, made decisions which would find little favour with President Bush in particular or conservative Republicans in general. He proved to be one of the most consistently *liberal* members of the Court.

Most presidents pick politically, and it is no coincidence that the two Clinton appointees on the Court deliver opinions that are consistently of a liberal position. It is no coincidence either that the most conservative members of the Court are appointees of Ronald Reagan and George W. Bush. Given the opportunity to choose a member of the nation's highest court and thereby have the chance to shape the Court's thinking for the next 15–20 years or more, most presidents understandably take it.

Politicisation by the Senate

The Senate, too, has been accused of politicising the confirmation process. The defeat of Robert Bork, one of the most outstanding jurists and scholars of his generation, is a case in point. Democrat opponents on the Senate Judiciary Committee mobilised an array of liberal interest groups against Bork's nomination. The National Abortion Rights Action League and the National Organization for Women, to name but two, weighed in against Bork. Even a television advertising campaign was mounted against his nomination, costing in the region of $15 million. Conservative groups mounted a counter-attack, but to little avail.

A similar situation arose when President Bush nominated another conservative, Clarence Thomas, in 1991. In this case, the Senate could justifiably have questioned Thomas's nomination on his lacklustre qualifications. It chose instead to concentrate on his conservative philosophy and the allegations of sexual harassment brought against him by a black female work colleague. Thomas was unimpressed by the confirmation process, issuing a forthright denunciation of the Senate's work:

> This is a circus. It's a national disgrace. From my standpoint as a black American, it is a high-tech lynching for uppity blacks who in any way think for themselves... No job is worth what I've been through — no job. No horror in my life has been so debilitating. Confirm me if you want. Don't confirm me if you have been so led. But let this process end. Let me and my family regain our lives.

When the process ended and the Senate finally voted on Thomas's nomination, the vote was almost entirely along party lines. Only 11 Democrats — mostly southern conservatives — voted in favour, and only two Republicans voted against. This does little to rebut the allegation that Thomas's nomination was considered in a partisan fashion by both sides.

In 2006, the *Washington Post* reported that over a 3-month period of the nomination debate concerning Samuel Alito, 'hundreds of advocacy groups on both sides of the battle aggressively competed to shape public opinion, spending more than $2 million in advertising and blanketing the country with millions of e-mails'.

As we also saw with the Alito nomination, senators from the president's party tend to use the occasion to throw soft questions at the nominee, not really trying to probe them for answers that might reveal whether or not they are suitably qualified for the job. This means that, provided a president has party control of the Senate, he can just about get anyone he wants confirmed by the Senate. That is not a recipe for effective checks and balances.

Meanwhile, senators from the opposition party tend to look for opportunities to attack and embarrass the nominee. They are often more interested in scandal, innuendo and gossip than in competence. This happened in the Clarence Thomas hearings in 1991 and, to a lesser extent, in the Alito hearings in 2006. A few years ago, Calvin Mackenzie published a book with the title *Innocent Until Nominated: The Breakdown of the Presidential Appointment Process* (2001). His conclusion was that the confirmation process is characterised by 'invasive scrutiny' and 'cruel and punishing publicity' for the nominee, which discourages qualified people from being prepared to be nominated for high office and thereby 'hinders the president's ability to govern'. A former solicitor general, Theodore Olson, claimed in 2007 that the Senate had abandoned its role of 'advise and consent' for a policy of 'search and destroy'.

Justices are now frequently confirmed on party-line votes, another indicator of a politicised process. In January 2006 an editorial in the *Washington Post* — a left-of-centre newspaper — described Samuel Alito as 'superbly qualified'. An editorial was headed simply 'Confirm Samuel Alito'. The editorial stated:

> Supreme Court nominations have never been free of politics, but neither has their history generally been one of party-line votes or of ideology as the determining factor. To go down that road is to believe that there is a Democrat law and a Republican law, which is repugnant to the ideal of the rule of law. No president should be denied the prerogative of putting a person as qualified as Judge Alito on the Supreme Court.

Yet not a single Democrat in the Senate Judiciary Committee voted to recommend Alito's confirmation, and on the Senate floor only four Democrats voted to confirm him.

> ## Box 7.2 Criticisms of the appointment and confirmation processes
>
> ➤ Presidents have tended to politicise the nominations by attempting to choose justices who share their political views and judicial philosophy.
>
> ➤ Senate has tended to politicise the confirmation process by focusing more on litmus test issues (e.g. abortion) rather than on qualifications and suitability for the job.
>
> ➤ Members of the Senate Judiciary Committee from the president's party tend to ask soft questions of the nominee.
>
> ➤ Members of the Senate Judiciary Committee from the opposition party attempt through their questions to attack or embarrass the nominee rather than elicit helpful information. 'Advise and consent' has been replaced by 'search and destroy'.
>
> ➤ Justices are now frequently confirmed on party-line votes.
>
> ➤ The media conduct a 'feeding frenzy' often concerned with matters of little relevance to the nominee's judicial qualifications.

Politicisation by the media

The media came out of the Thomas hearings with little credit. Their 'feeding frenzy' on the allegations made against Thomas was liberally interspersed with sexual details that bordered on the prurient. Rather than have an informed debate about judicial philosophy and qualification, much of the media chose to compete over who could come up with the most lurid allegations and the most tasteless details. Thomas's use of the word 'lynching' was intended to have racist overtones. According to Edward Lazarus (1999):

> The Thomas affair powerfully reinforced the idea that Supreme Court confirmations were not occasions for seriously evaluating the nominee's legal thinking and qualifications but rather election campaigns for political control of the Court, to be waged by any means necessary.

With the Court so finely balanced between conservatives and liberals — witness the large number of 5–4 decisions in recent years — it is unlikely that either the president or the Senate of either party is going to give up on trying to get its own way.

Why are Supreme Court nominations so important?

There are five reasons why the president's nominations to the Supreme Court are so important. First, they occur infrequently. Whereas appointments to the cabinet, for example, can come up two or three times a year — and there are a whole new set at the beginning of each new administration — appointments to the Supreme Court come up on average only once every 2 years, and sometimes there can be a long period with no vacancies at all, as between 1994 and 2005.

Second, these appointments are for life. When George W. Bush nominated Condoleezza Rice to be Secretary of State in 2005, everyone knew that the longest she would remain in office would be 4 years — until the end of Bush's second term. But when later that year Bush nominated the 50-year old John Roberts to the Supreme Court, it was clear that Roberts was going to be on the Court for much longer than 4 years — possibly 20 or even 30 years and more.

Third, there are only nine members of the Supreme Court, so in appointing a new justice a president is replacing one-ninth of the Court's membership. A member of the House of Representatives is one of 435, a senator is one of 100 — you need respectively 217 and 50 other people to agree with you to get something done. But as a member of the Supreme Court you are one of nine — with four others you are a majority. If the Supreme Court had, say, 50 members then replacing just one of them would not be a big deal. But replacing one of nine is.

The last two reasons why Supreme Court appointments are important concern what we are about to study — the power of the Court. Thus, fourthly, Supreme Court appointments are so important because of the Court's power of judicial review. As we will see, this is an extraordinarily important and significant power. Fifth and finally, the nominations to the Court are important because, through its power of judicial review, the Court can profoundly affect the lives of ordinary Americans as the Court makes decisions in such areas as abortion, affirmative action, gun control and freedom of speech. It is this power of judicial review and these effects on American society to which we now turn.

The power of judicial review

Judicial review is the power of the Supreme Court to declare acts of Congress, or actions of the executive — or acts or actions of state governments — unconstitutional, and thereby null and void. The power is not mentioned in the Constitution; it might be said that the Supreme Court 'found' the power for itself in the 1803 case of *Marbury v. Madison*. This was the first time that the Supreme Court declared an act of Congress unconstitutional.

Key concept

➤ **Judicial review.** The power of the Supreme Court to declare acts of Congress, or actions of the executive — or acts or actions of state governments — unconstitutional, and thereby null and void.

By using its power of judicial review the Court can, in effect, update the meaning of the words of the Constitution, most of which were written over two centuries ago. Hence, the Court decides what the phrase in the 8th Amendment (written in 1791)

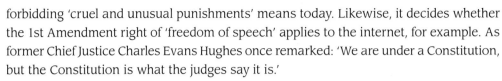
forbidding 'cruel and unusual punishments' means today. Likewise, it decides whether the 1st Amendment right of 'freedom of speech' applies to the internet, for example. As former Chief Justice Charles Evans Hughes once remarked: 'We are under a Constitution, but the Constitution is what the judges say it is.'

Using its power of judicial review, the Supreme Court has involved itself in a host of political issues, not least in acting as a guarantor of fundamental **civil rights and liberties**. It is this that helps give the Court its political importance, because many of the issues dealt with by the Court are the key political issues of the day — matters over which political parties disagree and elections are fought. For example, political commentator Mark Shields has been quoted as saying that America's two major parties are 'separated [only] by the issue of abortion'. Which branch of government decides women's rights concerning abortion? The answer is the Supreme Court. In addition, the Supreme Court has handed down landmark decisions in recent years on such politically contentious issues as the rights of racial minorities, capital punishment, gun control and freedom of speech.

Key concept

➤ **Civil rights.** Civil rights are positive acts of government designed to protect persons against arbitrary or discriminatory treatment by government or individuals. Linked to civil rights are **civil liberties**, which are those liberties, mostly spelt out in the Constitution, that guarantee the protection of persons, expression and property from arbitrary interference by the government.

The political importance of the Court is demonstrated in the case of *George W. Bush v. Albert Gore Jr* (2000). Five weeks after the presidential election, on 11 December 2000, the Supreme Court ruled that the manual recount scheme devised by the Florida state Supreme Court was unconstitutional because it violated the 'equal protection' clause of the Constitution's 14th Amendment. In the same decision, the Court also ruled that because of the time constraints, 'it is evident that any recount seeking to meet the December 12 [deadline] will be unconstitutional'. The Court was seen by some to be handing the election to George W. Bush.

The power of judicial review not only gives the Court political importance, but is also said to turn it into a quasi-legislative body. This is because the decisions that the Court hands down have almost the effect of a law having been passed by Congress. So, for example, when in its 1973 decision in *Roe v. Wade* the Court stated that women have a constitutional right to choose an abortion, the effect was comparable to an abortion rights law having been passed by Congress. In this sense, the Court has been described as 'a third house of the legislature'. So, as we study some of the recent landmark decisions of the Supreme Court, we need to be aware of the ways in which such decisions:

> enable the Court to interpret the Constitution
> turn the Court into a political institution
> give the Court a quasi-legislative power

The constitutional basis for the Court's actions

At the time of its ratification, many Americans expressed concerns that the Constitution provided the new federal government with overly broad powers that could be used against the states and individuals. Partly to allay those fears, the first Congress proposed the Bill of Rights — the first ten Amendments to the Constitution. Initially, these Amendments were intended to restrict the powers of the federal government, not the state governments. For example, the 1st Amendment, arguably the most important provision of the Bill of Rights, begins: 'Congress shall make no law respecting an establishment of religion, or prohibiting the free exercise thereof...' In fact, this provision was intended not only to prevent the federal government from establishing an official religion but — less well known — to prevent the federal government from interfering with existing state government-sanctioned religion in the few states where this still existed.

Not until the passage of the 14th Amendment in 1868, shortly after the end of the Civil War, did the Constitution explicitly begin to restrict the actions that states could take against individual citizens. The Supreme Court has mostly relied on two provisions of the 14th Amendment to protect individuals' rights and liberties. First, as will be seen in some of the decisions discussed below, the Court frequently employs the Amendment's 'equal protection' provision to, among other things, end school segregation and promote affirmative action programmes.

Second, although enveloped in complex legal reasoning, the Court has used the other important provision of the 14th Amendment — the **due process** clause — to 'incorporate' the Bill of Rights' restrictions imposed originally only on the federal government, thereby applying those provisions to the states as well. The Supreme Court's use of the 'due process' provision — preventing states from depriving persons of 'life, liberty, or property without due process of law' — has enabled the Court to review and invalidate a wide range of state legislation. We shall discuss several examples in the section below, including state laws on abortion, school prayers and flag desecration.

Key concept

> **Due process.** The term more fully is 'due process of law' and, although no precise legal definition of the term has been made, it is understood to refer to the principle of limited government. There are two types of due process referred to by the courts. Substantive due process demands that the substance of the law must not be arbitrary, unreasonable or unconstitutional; procedural due process demands that the process of the law must be fair.

The tension involved in the American system of federalism is in play each time the Court rules in these areas. As we know, the laws subjected to the Court's review have been approved by a majority of the relevant state legislature, which, in turn, was elected by a majority of that state's voters. The question becomes one of balancing fundamental and competing considerations: on the one hand, the right of the majority to rule as they see fit and, on the other, the protection of fundamental civil rights and liberties for individual Americans.

The Supreme Court and the protection of rights and liberties

First Amendment: freedom of religion, speech and expression

Freedom of religion

The 1st Amendment begins with this statement: 'Congress shall make no law respecting an establishment of religion, or prohibiting the free exercise thereof.' It is a right that is grounded in the wish of the 18th-century framers of the Constitution to preserve a level of religious freedom within the United States which had been noticeably lacking in those countries from which many of their forebears had come. However, these opening 16 words of the 1st Amendment contain something of a conundrum: how to ensure that there is no established religion while preserving citizens' rights to practise their religion freely. It has posed a seemingly insuperable problem for the Court in its attempts to protect religious freedoms. Critics of the Court — these days mainly evangelical Christians — believe that the Court has been too attentive to the first half of this opening phrase while ignoring the second half.

Prayer in public schools

For a long time, the Supreme Court declined to enter this particular area of civil liberties. But in 1962, in *Engel v. Vitale*, the Court declared (6–1) a New York state law to be unconstitutional because it provided for a prayer written by the New York Board of Regents to be used in the state's public (i.e. state-run) schools. In the Court's view, this violated the 1st Amendment clause against 'an establishment of religion'. Reasoning that they could not write special prayers, states resorted to the use of the Lord's Prayer or the recitation of passages from the Bible, yet these too were declared unconstitutional in *School District of Abington Township v. Schempp* (1963).

The next strategy adopted by schools in certain states, especially in the South, was to set aside a short period of the school day for 'silent reflection' by students. But in *Wallace v. Jaffree* (1985), the Court declared unconstitutional (6–3) an Alabama state law which provided for such a period. Then, in 1992, in *Lee v. Weisman*, the Court declared prayers recited at public school graduation ceremonies to be unconstitutional, even if these prayers were chosen and recited by students. It was a 5–4 decision with conservative justices Rehnquist, Scalia and Thomas amongst the four dissenters.

Table 7.7 Recent landmark decisions on rights and liberties

1st Amendment: Freedom of religion	*Engel v. Vitale* (1962) *School District of Abington Township v. Schempp* (1963) *Wallace v. Jaffree* (1985) *Lee v. Weisman* (1992) *Zelman v. Simmons-Harris* (2002)
1st Amendment: Freedom of speech and expression	*Buckley v. Valeo* (1976) *McConnell v. Federal Election Commission* (2004) *Citizens United v. Federal Election Commission* (2010) *Reno v. American Civil Liberties Union* (1997) *Texas v. Johnson* (1989) *United States v. Eichman* (1990) *United States v. Lopez* (1995)
2nd Amendment: Right to bear arms	*District of Columbia v. Heller* (2008) *McDonald v. City of Chicago* (2010)
5th Amendment: Right to silence	*Miranda v. Arizona* (1966) *Dickerson v. United States* (2000)
8th Amendment: Freedom from 'cruel and unusual punishments'	*Furman v. Georgia* (1972) *Ring v. Arizona* (2002) *Atkins v. Virginia* (2002) *Roper v. Simmons* (2005) *Baze v. Rees* (2008) *Jackson v. Hobbs* and *Miller v. Alabama* (2012)

14th Amendment:
Rights of racial minorities
	Brown v. Board of Education of Topeka (1954)
	Swann v. Charlotte-Mecklenburg Board of Education (1971)
	Adarand Constructors v. Peña (1995)
	Gratz v. Bollinger (2003)
	Grutter v. Bollinger (2003)
	*Parents Involved in Community Schools Inc. v. Seattle School
	  District* (2007)
	Meredith v. Jefferson County (Kentucky) Board of Education
	  (2007)

14th Amendment: Abortion	*Roe v. Wade* (1973) *Planned Parenthood of Southeastern Pennsylvania v. Casey* (1992) *Gonzales v. Carhart* (2007)

School vouchers and religious schools

In what some saw as a change of emphasis, in *Zelman v. Simmons-Harris* (2002), the Court upheld a programme in Ohio giving financial aid to parents to allow them to send their children to religious or private schools. In a 5–4 decision, the Court upheld the so-called 'school voucher' programme being run in the state of Ohio, and so appeared to breach the wall of separation between Church and state. In this case, the four liberal members of the Court — Justices Stevens, Souter, Ginsburg and Breyer — all dissented. The programme was supported by the Bush administration, the Republican Party and ideological conservatives. They saw the voucher programme as the best way to help poor people whose children would otherwise have to attend failing inner-city schools. The opponents were the Democratic Party, the teachers' unions and ideological liberals. They saw the programme as a threat to the state-run school system.

The case was of particular interest because it involved not only issues of religious freedom but also issues of race, as most of the children involved in the voucher programme were African-Americans. Under the programme in Cleveland, Ohio, the parents of some 3,700 children had been given vouchers worth up to $2,250 to send them to private schools rather than the free, state-run, local school. Of these 3,700, around 96% had opted to send their children to religious schools.

In December 2000, the Federal Court of Appeals had declared that the programme had the 'impermissible effect of promoting sectarian schools' and thereby violated the 1st Amendment's prohibition against 'the establishment of religion'. The majority of the Supreme Court disagreed. The majority opinion authored by Justice Thomas was most striking. Justice Thomas is the Court's only African-American and he often credits his own rise from poverty to the rigorous education that he received in a Roman Catholic school in Savannah, Georgia. He wrote:

> The promise of public school [i.e. state-run] education has failed poor inner-city blacks. If society cannot end racial discrimination, at least it can arm minorities with the education to defend themselves from some of discrimination's effects.

Chief Justice Rehnquist wrote in this case for the majority, too, stating that the key issue was not that almost all of the students who used vouchers went to religious schools, but rather that the vouchers were just one part of an array of alternatives to the state-run schools. Rehnquist concluded:

> The question is whether Ohio is coercing parents into sending their children to religious schools, and that question must be answered evaluating all options Ohio provides Cleveland school children, only one of which is to obtain a [voucher] and then choose a religious school.

In other words, it didn't matter that 96% of these children with vouchers happened to enrol in religious schools. That was a choice made by their parents, not the government.

The dissenting minority were unimpressed by this logic. Justice Souter called the Court's decision a 'potentially tragic' mistake that could 'force citizens to subsidise faiths they do not share even as it corrupts religion by making it dependent on government'. Justice Breyer said that the Court 'risks creating a form of religious conflict potentially harmful to the nation's social fabric'. Justice Stevens claimed that the Court had 'removed a brick from the wall that was once designed to separate religion from government, increasing the risk of religious strife and weakening the foundation of democracy'.

Freedom of speech

The 1st Amendment talks about more than just freedom of religion. It goes on to state: 'Congress shall make no law...abridging the freedom of speech, or of the press.' Here again, the Supreme Court has played an important role in protecting these fundamental rights. In *Buckley v. Valeo* (1976) the Court declared unconstitutional part of the Federal

Election Campaign Act (1974) that limited expenditure by presidential candidates. The Court claimed that such limits infringed the 'freedom of speech' provision of the 1st Amendment. The Court made another important judgement on freedom of speech as it affects political campaigning in its 2004 decision in *McConnell v. Federal Election Commission*. In this decision, the Supreme Court upheld the provisions of the Bipartisan Campaign Reform Act (BCRA), commonly known as the McCain–Feingold Act after its two Senate sponsors — Republican John McCain and Democrat Russell Feingold. In upholding the statute, the Court rejected the argument of its opponents that in banning soft money the law stifled free speech and was therefore contrary to the provisions of the 1st Amendment. In the 2010 decision of *Citizens United v. Federal Election Commission*, the Court ruled that when it comes to rights of political speech, business corporations and labour unions have the same rights as individuals, a decision which overturned federal laws and Court decisions going back to 1947 and which had a significant effect on campaign finance during the 2012 elections.

In 1997, the Supreme Court had to decide how the freedom of speech rights guaranteed in the 1st Amendment applied to the world of the internet. In *Reno v. American Civil Liberties Union*, the Court struck down as unconstitutional the Communications Decency Act (1996). The Act had made it a crime to make 'indecent' or 'patently offensive' material available to minors on the internet. In the view of the Court, this infringed the 1st Amendment. In particular, the Court objected to the imprecision of 'indecent' and 'patently offensive', calling them 'vague contours'. The Court claimed that, in attempting to protect minors, the Act had infringed the constitutional rights of adults. Writing for the seven-member majority in this case, Justice Stevens stated:

> The Communications Decency Act (CDA) lacks the precision that the 1st Amendment requires when a statute regulates the content of speech. In order to deny minors access to potentially harmful speech, the CDA effectively suppresses a large amount of speech that adults have a constitutional right to receive and to address to one another.

Civil rights groups, such as the American Civil Liberties Union that had brought the case, hailed the decision as 'the Bill of Rights for the 21st century'. The *Washington Post* headlined the decision: 'The 1st Amendment Goes Digital'. The two dissenters in this case were William Rehnquist and Sandra Day O'Connor, though they agreed with their seven colleagues in part. It is clear to see the difficulty that the Court faced in balancing competing rights. Senator Patrick Leahy (D —Vermont), aware of the interpretations that could be put on the Court's ruling, commented: 'I hope that nobody thinks this is a victory for child pornographers.' Senator Dan Coats (R — Indiana) did not like the judgement at all, saying that it showed the Court as 'out of touch with the American people'.

In these 'freedom of speech' and 'freedom of expression' cases, the Court can be seen trying to balance competing rights and freedoms. The Court in essence is saying: we cannot protect the rights of one group in society by limiting the rights of another

group. The rights of children to be protected from pornography on the internet must be set against the rights of those adults who wish to view pornography. The rights of people wishing to visit door-to-door must be set against the rights of people to be safe in their homes.

Freedom of expression

The Court has extended the 1st Amendment right of freedom of speech to freedom of expression — none more controversial than the 'expression' made by protesters of burning an American flag. In 1984, Gregory Lee Johnson was arrested outside the Republican National Convention in Dallas, Texas, for burning an American flag. Texas, along with 47 other states, had a state law forbidding the desecration of the US flag. In *Texas v. Johnson* (1989), the Supreme Court declared (5–4) that such laws were unconstitutional, as they infringed the 1st Amendment rights regarding freedom of expression. When the United States Congress reacted to the Court's decision by passing a federal law banning flag desecration, the Court promptly declared it unconstitutional in the 1990 case of *United States v. Eichman* by the same 5–4 margin.

Second Amendment: the right to 'bear arms' (gun control)

The 2nd Amendment guarantees American citizens' right to 'bear arms'. Thus, the Constitution implies the right of revolution. The Founding Fathers believed that the ultimate check against tyranny was an armed citizenry. However, the assassination of presidents and leading political figures — President John Kennedy (1963), Senator Robert Kennedy (1968) and Martin Luther King (1968), to name but three — not to mention an alarming rise in gun-related crime, aroused nationwide concern over the ease with which Americans can buy guns. On the other side, the National Rifle Association, gun clubs, and other citizens concerned to be able to defend themselves in their own homes, have argued against stricter gun control.

President John Kennedy, assassinated in 1963

In the 1995 case of *United States v. Lopez*, the Supreme Court declared (5–4) the 1990 Gun-Free School Zones Act to be unconstitutional. This widely popular law had made it an offence 'for any individual knowingly to possess a firearm at a place that the individual knows, or has reasonable cause to believe, is a school zone'. But as we shall see in a later section, this decision was based not on the 2nd Amendment, but on Article I of the Constitution and the powers granted to Congress.

But in 2008, the Supreme Court — for the first time in its history — did decide a case relating to the meaning of the 2nd Amendment. In *District of Columbia v. Heller,* the Court declared unconstitutional a law passed by the District of Columbia in 1976 banning the ownership of handguns and requiring that shotguns and rifles be kept unloaded and either disassembled or with the trigger locked. 'We hold that the District's ban on handgun possession in the home violates the 2nd Amendment, as does its prohibition against rendering any lawful firearm in the home operable for the purpose of immediate self-defence,' wrote Justice Antonin Scalia for the five-member majority, in which he was joined by Chief Justice Roberts, and Associate Justices Kennedy, Thomas and Alito. The dissenting minority was exactly the same foursome who had dissented in the *Lopez* decision 13 years earlier — Breyer, Ginsburg, Stevens and Souter.

At issue was the meaning which the Framers intended in writing the 2nd Amendment, which reads:

> A well regulated Militia, being necessary to the security of a free State, the right of the people to keep and bear Arms, shall not be infringed.

There have come to be two interpretations of this Amendment. Some interpret it to guarantee a *collective* right to own guns related only to the formation of state militias. This is the view taken by most liberals, Democrats and supporters of gun control legislation such as the Brady Center to Prevent Gun Violence. But others interpret the Amendment to guarantee an *individual* right to own guns. They argue that just as all the other rights and liberties — of religion, free speech and the like — are contained within the Bill of Rights, so this right, too, is individual, not collective. This is the view taken by most conservatives, Republicans and groups opposing most gun control legislation such as the National Rifle Association. Up until this point, federal courts had never specifically decided whether the rights bestowed in the 2nd Amendment were collective or individual. But in this case, the majority of the Court took the view that 'the right to keep and bear arms' protected by the 2nd Amendment is, indeed, an individual right and thus declared the District's handgun ban unconstitutional. For the dissenting minority, Justice Stevens called the decision 'a strained and unpersuasive reading' of the text. In a follow-up case, *McDonald v. City of Chicago* (2010), the Court declared that the 2nd Amendment gives to Americans a fundamental right to bear arms and that the due process clause of the 14th Amendment means that this right cannot be infringed by state or local governments.

Fifth Amendment: the right to silence

In a 5–4 decision in *Miranda v. Arizona* (1966), the Court interpreted the 5th Amendment right to remain silent as extending to the right to be reminded of that right when arrested. What have become known as 'Miranda rights' have been read to people arrested by state police across America ever since that judgement.

In *Dickerson v. United States* (2000), the Court had an opportunity to reverse its *Miranda* decision. In the 34 years which had passed since the Court's original judgement, the membership of the Supreme Court had changed significantly from a Court appointed mainly by Democrat presidents to one appointed mainly by Republicans.

As a consequence, the prevailing philosophy of the Court had become much more conservative, much more focused on the original intent of the Founding Fathers. During questioning about a robbery he was connected to, Charles Dickerson made statements admitting that he was the getaway driver in a series of bank robberies. Dickerson was then placed under arrest. But later, Dickerson claimed that he had not been read his Miranda rights. The government argued that even if the Miranda warning was not read, because Dickerson's statement was voluntary it was therefore admissible in court. In a 7–2 opinion delivered by Chief Justice Rehnquist, the Court held that:

> *Miranda* has become embedded in routine police practice to the point where the warnings have become part of our national culture. Whether or not we would agree with *Miranda*'s reasoning and its resulting rule, were we addressing the issue in the first instance, the principles of *stare decisis* weigh heavily against overruling it now.

As we saw earlier, the principle of *stare decisis* (the phrase means 'to stand by that which is decided') is an important principle of the Supreme Court and makes many justices reluctant to overturn previous Court decisions. Justices Scalia and Thomas disagreed. They wanted to overturn *Miranda,* writing in their dissenting opinion that 'today's judgement converts *Miranda* from a milestone of judicial overreaching' into a piece of 'judicial arrogance'.

Eighth Amendment: freedom from 'cruel and unusual punishments'

Linked to these rights are those guaranteed by the 8th Amendment against 'cruel and unusual punishments'. In the case of *Furman v. Georgia* (1972), the Court decided (5–4) that the death penalty, as it was then imposed, was a 'cruel and unusual punishment' and thereby violated the 8th Amendment. The Court made its decision based on the methods used for executing convicted criminals and the arbitrary and unfair way in which, the Court believed, the punishment was handed down. The consequences of this case included the more widespread use of lethal injection and of the two-stage trial. The latter was meant to try to reverse the trend by which the death penalty was more likely to be given to poor members of racial minorities than to more wealthy whites. During a second stage of the trial, mitigating circumstances are considered before the sentence is decided.

In *Ring v. Arizona* (2002) the Court declared (7–2) that death sentences imposed by judges, rather than by juries, were unconstitutional because they infringed the 6th Amendment right to trial by jury. Chief Justice Rehnquist was joined by Justice O'Connor in the dissenting opinion. In *Atkins v. Virginia* (2002) the court decided (6–3) that the execution of mentally retarded criminals infringed the 8th Amendment ban on 'cruel and unusual punishments'. Of the 38 states permitting capital punishment in 2002, 20 of them — including Virginia — still allowed the execution of the mentally retarded. Rehnquist, Scalia and Thomas — the Court's three most conservative justices —

dissented in this opinion. In *Roper v. Simmons* (2005) the Court decided (5–4) that it is unconstitutional to sentence anyone to death for a crime he or she committed when younger than 18. Rehnquist, Scalia and Thomas were joined by O'Connor in the dissenting minority.

In the 2008 case of *Baze v. Rees,* the Court decided that lethal injection — the method used by the federal government and 35 states to execute criminals — did not constitute a 'cruel and unusual punishment' and therefore did not violate the 8th Amendment. 'Simply because an execution method may result in pain, either by accident or as an inescapable consequence of death, does not establish the sort of "objectively intolerable risk of harm" that qualifies as cruel and unusual,' wrote Chief Justice John Roberts. Although seven justices agreed that the procedure used in Kentucky was constitutional, they could not agree on the standard by which execution methods should be judged. Thus this decision is unlikely to be last word on the matter. The two dissenting justices in this decision — Antonin Scalia and Clarence Thomas — believed that the debate about 'standards' was irrelevant. In their view, an execution method would be unconstitutional 'only if it is deliberately designed to inflict pain', which this method was clearly not.

In 2012, in the cases of *Jackson v. Hobbs* and *Miller v. Alabama*, the Court ruled by 5 votes to 4 that a mandatory life sentence without chance of parole when given to a juvenile murderer infringed the provision of the 8th Amendment. This was seen as an extension of the Court's 2005 decision in *Roper v. Simmons*. Again, it was the Court's conservative quartet — by this time made up of Chief Justice Roberts along with justices Scalia, Thomas and Alito — who made up the dissenting minority.

Fourteenth Amendment: the rights of racial minorities

Since the 1950s, the Supreme Court has been at the centre of attempts to protect the rights of racial minorities. The early cases centred upon the rights of black Americans, but as US society has become more diverse, cases relating to other racial minorities have been heard too.

Segregation

In 1954, the Supreme Court handed down one of the most important decisions of the 20th century. In the case of *Brown v. Board of Education of Topeka*, the Court ruled unanimously that a law of the state of Kansas was unconstitutional because it transgressed the 'equal protection' clause of the 14th Amendment. In so doing, the Court ruled that schools — and, by implication, other public facilities such as railway carriages, parks and restaurants — could not be segregated by race. The case overturned the Court's 1896 decision, which had set in place what became known as the 'separate but equal' doctrine. For the previous 60 years, many facilities — including schools — had been designated as being only for whites. The potential implications of the 1954 decision were huge. The case was sponsored by the National Association for the Advancement of Colored People (NAACP), which believed that poor schooling opportunities for black people lay at the root of black poverty and disadvantage.

This case dealt with *de jure* segregation — segregation that resulted from laws passed usually by state legislatures in the South — but it did nothing about *de facto* segregation — segregation that resulted from neighbourhood schooling, mainly in the cities of the northeast. In cities such as Boston, New York, Newark, Philadelphia and Washington DC, there were schools that were attended exclusively or mostly by pupils of only one race. In predominantly black inner-city neighbourhoods, schools were mainly black. The opposite was true in white suburban neighbourhoods. In the 1971 case of *Swann v. Charlotte-Mecklenburg Board of Education*, the Court decided, again unanimously, that *de facto* segregation was unconstitutional too. This led to the introduction of school busing programmes to provide racially mixed schools in all areas.

Affirmative action

In *Adarand Constructors v. Peña* (1995), the Court struck down a federal government affirmative action programme on the employment of minority workers. The federal Department of Transportation had a policy that gave road-building contractors a bonus if they hired subcontractors which employed minority workers. In Colorado, a firm employing white workers put in a bid to erect road safety barriers. However, despite putting in the lower bid, they lost out to a firm employing minority workers. In its decision, the Supreme Court refused to say whether such an affirmative action programme was constitutional. Associate Justice O'Connor, writing for the 5–4 majority, stated that in order to survive a court challenge, such affirmative action programmes must be 'narrowly tailored measures that further compelling governmental interests'. The use of the words 'narrowly' and 'compelling' were meant as signals that the Court would not sanction affirmative action programmes *per se*. The case was much debated during the 1996 presidential election, with President Clinton stating in his re-election campaign that it was his opinion that affirmative action programmes should be 'mended, not ended'.

At the heart of the *Adarand* decision were three fundamental questions about civil rights. First, should racial advancement be on the basis of merit alone? Second, how can the conflict between 'individual rights' on the one hand and 'group rights' on the other be reconciled? And third, is there a moral difference between 'advantageous discrimination', such as affirmative action programmes, and 'invidious discrimination', such as the old segregation laws? Put another way, is affirmative action just a form of 'racial paternalism'? The latter question was debated in this judgement by the conservative Justice Thomas on the one hand and the liberal Justice Stevens on the other. Writing for the majority, Justice Thomas stated:

> I believe that there is a moral and constitutional equivalence between laws designed to subjugate a race and those that distribute benefits on the basis of race in order to foster some current notion of equality. Government cannot make us equal. It can only recognise, respect and protect us as equal before the law. That these [affirmative action] programmes may have been motivated, in part, by good intentions cannot provide refuge from the principle that under our Constitution, the Government may not make distinctions on the basis of race. As far as the Constitution is concerned, it

is irrelevant whether a government's racial classifications are drawn by those who wish to oppress a race or by those who have a sincere desire to help those thought to be disadvantaged. There can be no doubt that the paternalism that appears to lie at the heart of this programme is at war with the principle of inherent equality that underlies and infuses our Constitution.

For Justice Thomas, the Constitution is 'colour-blind'. Writing for the dissenting minority, though, Justice Stevens argued quite the opposite:

> The consistency that the Court espouses would disregard the difference between a 'No Trespassing' sign and a welcome mat. It would equate a law that made black citizens ineligible for military service with a programme aimed at recruiting black soldiers...It is one thing to question the wisdom of affirmative action programmes; there are many responsible arguments against them. It is another thing altogether to equate the many well-meaning and intelligent lawmakers and their constituents, whether members of majority or minority races, who have supported affirmative action over many years, with segregationists and bigots.

In *Gratz v. Bollinger* (2003) the Court ruled (6–3) that the University of Michigan's affirmative action-based admissions programme for its undergraduate students was unconstitutional because it was too 'mechanistic'. All black, Hispanic, and American-Indian applicants were automatically awarded 20 of the 150 points required for admission. But in *Grutter v. Bollinger* (2003), the Court ruled (5–4) that the University Law School's admissions programme was constitutional because it used a more 'individualised' approach in considering the racial profile of its applicants.

The net effect of these two rulings will be to permit universities to continue to use race as a 'plus factor' in evaluating applicants, provided they take sufficient care to evaluate each applicant's ability individually. A majority of the Court also signed up to the idea that affirmative action programmes should not be seen as a permanent fixture of US society, urging universities to prepare for the time when it should no longer be necessary. The Court suggested that this might occur within the next 25 years. It was 25 years previously in *Regents of the University of California v. Bakke* (1978) that the Supreme Court ruled out racial quotas in university admissions programmes but left the door open to race being considered in admissions procedures.

At the centre of the debate in these cases was swing justice Sandra Day O'Connor. It was O'Connor who announced the majority opinion in the Law School case, describing for a hushed audience the grounds of the majority opinion thus:

> Effective participation by members of all racial and ethnic groups in the civic life of our nation is essential if the dream of one nation, indivisible, is to be realised. Moreover, universities, and in particular law schools, represent the training ground for a large number of our nation's leaders. In order to cultivate a set of leaders with legitimacy in the eyes of the citizenry, it is necessary that the path to leadership be visibly open to talented and qualified individuals of every race and ethnicity.

In his dissenting opinion, Chief Justice Rehnquist, joined by Justices Scalia, Thomas and Kennedy, denounced the law school admissions plan as a 'sham' and a 'naked effort to achieve racial balancing', seeing it as 'a carefully managed programme designed to ensure proportionate representation of applicants from selected minority groups'. Justice Clarence Thomas, the only black member of the Court, reverted to his typically colourful language in denouncing racial diversity programmes as 'the faddish slogan of the cognoscenti' that do 'nothing for those too poor or uneducated to participate in elite higher education'.

Racial quotas

In another pair of related cases in 2007 — *Parents Involved in Community Schools Inc. v. Seattle School District* and *Meredith v. Jefferson County (Kentucky) Board of Education* — the Court declared it unconstitutional to assign students to public (i.e. state-run) schools solely for the purpose of achieving racial balance. Both school systems centred upon racial quotas of white and minority representation in schools that would not otherwise be achieved because of racially segregated housing patterns in Seattle, Washington, and Louisville, Kentucky. Both sides of the Court in the 5–4 ruling saw themselves as protecting the equal protection rights announced in the landmark 1954 *Brown* decision. Writing for the majority, Chief Justice Roberts stated that:

> Before *Brown*, school children were told where they could and could not go to school based on the colour of their skin. The school districts in these cases have not carried the heavy burden of demonstrating that we should allow this once again — even for different reasons. The way to stop discrimination on the basis of race is to stop discriminating on the basis of race.

The Chief Justice also made it clear that he and his conservative colleagues on the Court — Scalia, Thomas and Alito, joined by Anthony Kennedy — had a concern that allocating students to schools on the basis of racial quotas violates the equal protection clause of the Constitution's 14th Amendment. 'Simply because the school districts may seek a worthy goal does not mean that they are free to discriminate on the basis of race to achieve it,' Roberts declared. Justice Clarence Thomas wrote waspishly that what the dissenting minority would really like to do would be to 'constitutionalise today's faddish social theories', adding that 'if our history has taught us anything, it has taught us to beware of elites bearing racial theories'.

Writing for the minority, Justice Breyer said the decisions in the Seattle and Louisville cases were ones which 'the Court and the nation will come to regret'. Also alluding to the 1954 ruling, Breyer continued:

> The lesson of history is not that efforts to continue racial segregation are constitutionally indistinguishable from efforts to achieve racial integration. Indeed, it is a cruel distortion of history to compare Topeka, Kansas, in the 1950s with Louisville and Seattle in the modern day.

As a result of these rulings in 2007, some public school systems across the United States have begun to alter their student allocation programmes. For example, in the vicinity of Washington DC, Montgomery County has now ceased to consider race in assigning students to schools.

Fourteenth Amendment: abortion rights

Supreme Court decisions concerning a woman's right to choose an abortion have dominated the argument about rights and liberties in America for over 30 years.

Roe v. Wade (1973)

In 1973 the Court announced in *Roe v. Wade* that the 14th Amendment right of 'liberty' included 'freedom of personal choice in matters of marriage and family life' and that this right 'necessarily includes the right of a woman to decide whether or not to terminate her pregnancy'. The case centred upon Norma McCorvey — identified in the case only by the alias of 'Jane Roe' — who had been denied an abortion by the state law of Texas. (Henry Wade was a Dallas County district attorney.) The *Roe v. Wade* decision was one of the most politically important decisions of the 20th century. It came at a time when the issue of women's rights was gaining importance and support in the USA. It took on political significance as the 'pro-choice' lobby (those who supported the decision) became closely associated with the Democratic Party, while the 'pro-life' lobby (those who opposed the decision) became closely associated with the Republicans. It was a 7–2 decision by the Court in which the recently appointed William Rehnquist — later to be appointed Chief Justice — was one of the two dissenters.

Further decisions

The issue of abortion did not stand still over the next 30 years. In a complex decision in *Webster v. Reproductive Health Services* (1989), the Court upheld a Missouri state law forbidding the involvement of any 'public employee' or 'public facility' in the performance of an abortion 'not necessary to save the life of the mother'. Pro-choice supporters regarded this as the Court nibbling away at *Roe v. Wade*.

In 1992, in *Planned Parenthood of Southeastern Pennsylvania v. Casey*, the Court upheld a Pennsylvania state law that required a woman to receive counselling on the risks and alternatives, and wait 24 hours after receiving that counselling. Women under 18 also had to have parental consent for an abortion. But the Court struck down the provision in the Pennsylvania law which required a married woman to produce 'a signed statement that she has notified her spouse that she is about to undergo an abortion'. Justice Sandra O'Connor was especially harsh on this provision and managed to put together a five-member majority which included Anthony Kennedy and David Souter. In her majority opinion, O'Connor stated:

> Common sense suggests that in well functioning marriages, spouses discuss important intimate decisions such as whether to bear a child. But there are millions of women in this country who are victims of regular physical and psychological

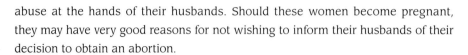

abuse at the hands of their husbands. Should these women become pregnant, they may have very good reasons for not wishing to inform their husbands of their decision to obtain an abortion.

In the light of his later membership of the Supreme Court, it is worth noting that when this particular case had been heard earlier by the Third Circuit Court of Appeals, Judge Samuel Alito had approved of the spouse notification requirement. In 2006, Alito would replace O'Connor on the Supreme Court, evidence that Alito's judicial philosophy was more conservative than that of the justice he replaced.

Partial-birth abortion

Another landmark decision on abortion rights was handed down in *Gonzales v. Carhart* (2007). In a 5–4 decision, the Court upheld the Partial-Birth Abortion Ban Act of 2003. By this time, O'Connor had retired to be replaced by Alito, and the effect was dramatic. On this occasion, Anthony Kennedy wrote the majority opinion, joined by Chief Justice Roberts and Associate Justices Antonin Scalia, Clarence Thomas and Samuel Alito. Here was another instance of the Court chipping away at the right of a woman to an abortion.

First, though, we need some background on this decision. Most abortions — probably well over 90% — are performed within the first 3 months of pregnancy. The procedure ends with the doctor vacuuming out the embryonic tissue. This procedure would be unaffected by this decision. However, if the abortion occurs much later in the pregnancy then some form of surgical operation is required. The woman will be placed under anaesthetic, her cervix dilated and the foetus removed in pieces.

Some doctors use a different procedure for these 'late-term' abortions, to reduce risks to the woman of bleeding, infection and permanent injury. This other procedure involves partly delivering the foetus and then crushing its skull to make removal easier. Opponents say this amounts to infanticide, as the foetus could be viable (able to survive outside the uterus) at the time. It is this procedure that Congress voted to ban in the so-called Partial-Birth Abortion Ban Act of 2003.

Writing for the majority in upholding the legislation, Justice Kennedy announced that 'the government may use its voice and its regulatory authority to show respect for the life within the woman'. He continued: 'While we find no reliable data to measure the phenomenon, it seems unexceptional to conclude some women come to regret their choice to abort the infant life they once created and sustained.' For the minority, Ruth Bader Ginsburg stated that the majority opinion of the Court in this case 'cannot be understood as anything other than an effort to chip away at a right declared again and again in this court — and with increasing comprehension of its centrality to women's lives'. She accused the majority of being paternalistic in its attitude towards women. 'The solution the Court approves,' Ginsburg stated, 'is not to require doctors to inform women adequately of the different procedures they might choose and the risk each entails. Instead the Court shields women by denying them any choice in the matter.'

This was a most significant decision for three reasons. First — and for the first time in its history — the Court declared that a specific abortion procedure could be banned and made no exception for the health of the woman, although it did provide an exception if the life of the woman was threatened. This decision was therefore seen by Democrats and liberal activist groups as a serious inroad into abortion rights.

Second, the decision had a potential political significance in terms of the party political debate on abortion. Conservative interest groups, such as Concerned Women for America, the Eagle Forum and the National Right to Life Committee, were jubilant at the Court's decision. Whereas such groups used to see their goal as getting the Court to overturn *Roe v. Wade*, now they take a much more incremental approach — the 'chipping away' of which Justice Ginsburg spoke in her dissenting opinion.

Third, the decision showed again the significance of the change in membership of the Court with the more conservative Samuel Alito having replaced the more centrist Sandra O'Connor. Back in 2000, in *Stenberg v. Carhart*, the Court had struck down a Nebraska state law prohibiting the same late-term procedure. But in that case, O'Connor had sided with the Court's four liberal justices — Stevens, Souter, Breyer and Ginsburg — to author a majority opinion which, while recognising the procedure could be 'gruesome', nonetheless decided that it was sometimes necessary.

The Supreme Court and congressional power

Not only does the Court rule on the rights and liberties guaranteed in the various amendments to the Constitution, but it also from time to time rules on the powers of the other two branches of government — the Congress and the presidency — and their powers as laid out in Articles I and II of the Constitution, as well as the relationship between the federal government and the states. The particularly relevant parts of the Constitution regarding the powers of Congress are to be found in Article I Section 8 and especially in what are referred to as 'the commerce clause' and 'the necessary and proper clause' which occur in that section. As well as granting very specific powers to Congress — to coin money, to raise and support armies, to declare war, and such like — this section of Article I also grants to Congress the power 'to regulate Commerce...among the several states' and 'to make all Laws which shall be necessary and proper for carrying into Execution the foregoing Powers'. Congress has used such vague clauses as a means of expanding its powers over many decades, and especially since the 1930s, and it has fallen to the Supreme Court from time to time to decide whether or not Congress has exceeded its powers under these provisions.

Gun control

In the 1995 case of *United States v. Lopez*, the Supreme Court declared (5–4) the 1990 Gun-Free School Zones Act to be unconstitutional. This widely popular law had made it an offence 'for any individual knowingly to possess a firearm at a place that the individual

Table 7.8 Landmark decisions on congressional power

Case	Decision
United States v. Lopez (1995)	5–4
National Federation of Independent Business v. Sebelius (2012)	5–4
Arizona v. United States (2012)	5–3*

*Associate Justice Kagan did not participate in this case

knows, or has reasonable cause to believe, is a school zone'. This was Congress's response to the increase in shootings at and in the vicinity of schools in which the lives of pupils had been endangered. In 1992, an 18-year-old Texas high school student had been caught carrying a handgun to school: the Court declared that, by passing the Act, Congress had exceeded its power under the commerce clause. The dissenting minority in this case was made up of the Court's four liberal justices — Stephen Breyer, Ruth Bader Ginsburg, John Paul Stevens and David Souter.

Healthcare reform

But the most recent judgement of the Court in relation to Congress's power under the commerce clause came in the landmark decision on President Obama's healthcare reform — the Affordable Care Act — in June 2012, in the case of *National Federation of Independent Business v. Sebelius*. In this decision the Court, by 5 votes to 4, upheld most of the provisions on the Affordable Care Act with Chief Justice Roberts joining the Court's liberal foursome — justices Ginsburg, Breyer, Sotomayor and Kagan. But the significance of the decision was not so much in the upholding of the Act as in the reasoning of the Chief Justice in writing the majority opinion. Democrats in Congress and the Obama administration had consistently argued that the provisions of the Act were constitutional because of the powers granted to Congress by the commerce clause. Congress therefore, they claimed, could write into the Act the so-called 'individual mandate' requiring every American to get health insurance or pay a 'penalty'. Therefore although this decision was on the surface about the constitutional standing of the Affordable Care Act, much more significantly it was about the power of Congress and the relationship between the federal government and the states within a federal system of government.

Chief Justice Roberts set the scene right at the start of his majority opinion:

> In our federal system, the National Government possesses only limited powers: the States and the people retain the remainder. Nearly two centuries ago, Chief Justice Marshall observed that "the question respecting the extent of the powers actually granted" to the Federal Government 'is perpetually arising, and will probably continue to arise, as long as our system shall exist.' In this case we must again determine whether the Constitution grants Congress powers it now asserts, but which many States and individuals believe it does not possess.

The Chief Justice then rehearsed the arguments put forward by the Act's supporters for an expansive view of the Constitution's commerce clause before declaring in two epoch-making words, 'We disagree.' Roberts argued that the Act was not 'regulating' commerce but the lack of it. Americans were to be penalised for not buying health insurance. This is how Roberts argued the case in his majority opinion:

> The power to *regulate* commerce presupposes the existence of commercial activity to be regulated…The individual mandate, however, does not regulate existing commercial activity. It instead compels individuals to *become* active in commerce by purchasing a product on the grounds that their failure to do so affects interstate commerce…The Framers [of the Constitution] knew the difference between doing something and doing nothing. They gave Congress the power to *regulate* commerce, not to *compel* it. Ignoring that distinction would undermine the principle that the Federal Government is a government of limited and enumerated powers. The individual mandate thus cannot be sustained under Congress's power to 'regulate commerce.'

Indeed, Roberts argued, if the Court allowed Congress to claim the commerce clause power to force people to buy health insurance, Congress might also think that the clause gave them the power to force people to buy cars or broccoli. But rather than declare the individual mandate unconstitutional, the Chief Justice then went on to say that it was constitutional because it was not a 'penalty' but a 'tax' and therefore allowable by the constitutional power granted to Congress in Article I Section 8 to 'lay and collect taxes'. It was a remarkable piece of judicial conjuring.

Immigration

In another landmark decision in 2012, *Arizona v. United States*, the Court struck down three provisions of an Arizona immigration law because they encroached on areas of congressional authority to regulate immigration. Thus the Court can both protect as well as limit the powers of Congress, thereby keeping a balance between the powers of the federal government and those of the individual states.

The Supreme Court and presidential power

Not only does the power of judicial review give to the Supreme Court the power to declare Acts of Congress unconstitutional, but it also includes the power to declare actions of any member of the executive branch unconstitutional, including the president. In some landmark decisions over the past 40 years, the Court has done just that and in doing so has shown itself to be a check on presidential power.

Nixon and Watergate

During the 1972 presidential election, people working for President Nixon's re-election campaign had planned and executed a number of illegal activities, including attempts to bug the headquarters of the Democratic National Committee (DNC) in the Watergate building in Washington DC. On 17 June 1972, five men were arrested in the Watergate building trying to bug the DNC phones. In order to prevent a link being made between these intruders and his re-election committee, President Nixon then instigated an elaborate cover-up over the next 2 years while publicly denying any such thing. However, it became known that the President tape recorded all his conversations in the Oval Office. Congress and the courts then demanded that Nixon hand over the tapes so that they could see whether or not the President had been involved in the Watergate affair or the subsequent cover-up. Nixon refused, claiming executive privilege. But in *United States v. Richard Nixon* (1974) the Supreme Court — in an 8–0 decision — declared that, although executive privilege would apply in matters of defence and national security, it did not apply to the demand for the Watergate-related tapes. On 24 July 1974, Nixon was therefore ordered by the Supreme Court to hand over the tapes. The tapes revealed a 'smoking gun' linking Nixon to the cover-up and obstruction of justice. Sixteen days later, President Nixon resigned.

Clinton and Paula Jones

On 27 May 1997, the Court handed down another president-related decision which would have profound effects upon the occupant of the Oval Office — then Bill Clinton. This case, *William Jefferson Clinton v. Paula Corbin Jones,* arose from an incident alleged to have occurred on the afternoon of 8 May 1991, in a suite at the Excelsior Hotel in Little Rock, Arkansas. Paula Corbin Jones alleged that she was subjected to an improper advance by then Governor Bill Clinton and that this constituted sexual harassment. Ms Jones filed suit against now President Clinton in May 1994, but the lower federal court ruled that the President was immune from prosecution until after he left office, a decision which was overturned in the federal appeal court in January 1996. The Supreme Court — in a unanimous decision — upheld the appeal court's ruling, agreeing that there is 'no support for immunity [from prosecution] for *unofficial* conduct' or from actions committed before the President entered office. Writing the opinion for the Court, Justice John Paul Stevens somewhat ironically stated that dealing with this law suit 'appears

Table 7.9 Landmark decisions on presidential power

Case	Decision
United States v. Richard Nixon (1974)	8–0*
William Jefferson Clinton v. Paula Corbin Jones (1997)	9–0
Rasul v. Bush (2004)	6–3
Hamdan v. Rumsfeld (2006)	5–3**
Boumediene v. Bush (2008)	5–4

*Associate Justice Rehnquist did not participate in this case
**Chief Justice Roberts did not participate in this case

highly unlikely to occupy any substantial amount of [the President's] time'. But it was while dealing with the Jones case that the President found himself being asked questions under oath about a workplace relationship with another woman, Monica Lewinsky. And that led to the President's impeachment by the House of Representatives in 1998.

Bush and Guantánamo Bay

In *Rasul v. Bush* (2004), the Supreme Court struck down some important parts of the Bush administration's legal policy regarding its war on terrorism in general and the detainees at Guantánamo Bay in particular. In its decision (6–3) the Court ruled that the foreign detainees — including some British citizens — held at the US base in Guantánamo Bay on the island of Cuba did have access to the United States federal courts to challenge their detention. While agreeing that it was within President Bush's powers to order the detention of members of al Qaeda or the Taliban as 'enemy combatants', it rejected the administration's view that the detainees were outside the jurisdiction of the federal courts. 'We have long since made it clear that a state of war is not a blank cheque for the president,' stated Justice Sandra O'Connor for the majority. The three dissenting votes in this case were cast by conservatives Rehnquist, Scalia and Thomas.

In the case of *Hamdan v. Rumsfeld* (2006), the Court declared unconstitutional the military commissions set up by President George W. Bush to try people held at Guantánamo Bay. This was a 5–3 decision. Chief Justice Roberts did not participate because he had served on the three-judge Appeal Court panel whose decision to uphold commissions was being reviewed in this case. If Roberts had participated, one can reasonably assume this would have been a 5–4 decision. The majority opinion was written by Justice Stevens, joined by Breyer, Souter, Ginsburg and Kennedy. Scalia, Thomas and Alito dissented. This will go down as another landmark decision of the Supreme Court as it put a significant limit on the commander-in-chief power of the president, even in time of war. The Court seemed to be clipping the wings of a president who had employed not only military commissions that were struck down by this ruling, but also warrantless wiretapping. Thus, the broad assertion of presidential power — which was a hallmark of the George W. Bush administration — was questioned by the Court.

The Supreme Court handed down yet another rebuff to the Bush administration on the Guantánamo Bay detainees in 2008 in the case of *Boumediene v. Bush*. In a 5–4 decision, with Justice Kennedy siding with the liberal members of the Court — Stevens, Souter, Ginsburg and Breyer — the Court held that the procedures set up by the Bush administration and Congress following the *Hamdan* decision in 2006 were inadequate to ensure that the detainees received their day in court. 'The laws and the Constitution are designed to survive, and remain in force, in extraordinary times,' wrote Justice Kennedy for the majority. 'Liberty and security can be reconciled.' Writing for the minority, Justice Scalia called the decision 'a self-invited incursion into military affairs'. Chief Justice Roberts in a separate dissent defended the procedures set up beforehand as 'the most generous set of procedural protections ever afforded to aliens detained by this country as enemy combatants'.

What do these decisions show us about the Supreme Court?

Let us return briefly to the three points of analysis which we mentioned before studying these landmark decisions.

How the Court's power of judicial review enables it to interpret the Constitution

We have seen in these decisions a number of clauses of the Constitution which have been interpreted by the Court. In the death penalty cases, the Court was saying what the phrase 'cruel and unusual punishments' in the 8th Amendment — written in 1791 — means today. In the abortion cases, it was what the word 'liberty' in the 14th Amendment — written in 1865 — means today. The Court has also tried to say what the 1st Amendment phrase forbidding 'an establishment of religion' — another 1791 addition — means in today's America. Or to what extent does the right to 'freedom of speech' granted by the 1st Amendment extend to pornography and political campaign advertising? What does the 2nd Amendment right to 'keep and bear arms' mean in the 21st century? This is what the Court was deciding in the 2008 landmark decision of *District of Columbia v. Heller*. In countless decisions, the Court is, *in effect*, amending the Constitution — not formally by changing the words, but interpretatively, by changing the meaning of those words. Indeed, this is one of the reasons why it is unnecessary to keep passing formal amendments to the Constitution.

How the Court's power of judicial review turns it into a political institution

This is simply because it is making decisions in policy areas which are politically contentious and about which the two major parties fundamentally disagree — affirmative action, the death penalty, abortion, school prayers and gun control, to give but five examples. The Democrats, as a general rule, favour affirmative action, abortion rights for women and gun control, but oppose the death penalty and school prayers. Republicans, as a general rule, oppose affirmative action, abortion rights for women and gun control, but support the death penalty and school prayers. And debate about these policies is the very stuff of American elections, at the national as well as the state level. Any institution which makes decisions in these kinds of areas is bound to be seen as something of a political institution.

How the Court's power of judicial review gives it a quasi-legislative power

This is quite simply because the result of many of the Court's decisions has almost the same effect as if a piece of legislation had been passed. In the UK, policy matters such as abortion rights, the death penalty and gun control, for example, are decided by Parliament. In the USA, they are settled largely by the Supreme Court. The quasi-legislative power of the Court is seen particularly in decisions which are authored by loose constructionist judges — those who read things into the wording of the Constitution, who, in the view of their critics, 'legislate from the bench'. A clear example of this was seen in the 2003 case concerning the affirmative action programme at the University of Michigan. In the majority opinion in the *Grutter v. Bollinger* decision, authored by Justice Sandra O'Connor, the Court laid down a time frame within which such affirmative action programmes would cease to be necessary:

> It has been 25 years since Justice Powell first approved the use of race to further an interest in student body diversity in the context of public higher education…We expect that 25 years from now, the use of racial preferences will no longer be necessary to further the interest approved today.

Jeffrey Toobin (2007) comments thus:

> The imposition of the time limit was O'Connor at her worst — and her best. To be sure, O'Connor was 'legislating from the bench', in the accusatory term that conservatives like [President George W.] Bush use to describe activist judges. From the vague commands of the Constitution, she was extrapolating not just a legal rule but a deadline as well. To originalists like [Justice Antonin] Scalia and [Justice Clarence] Thomas, this was simple judicial arrogance.

Immediately after the *District of Columbia v. Heller* decision was announced by the Court in June 2008, both John McCain and Barack Obama — respectively the presumptive presidential candidates of the Republican and Democrat parties — issued statements regarding their views on the decision. Thus judicial power makes the Supreme Court a hugely influential and significant part of the federal system of government.

Checks on the Supreme Court

Just as the legislature (Congress) and the executive (the president) are subject to the system of checks and balances that pervades the US system of government, so is the judiciary.

Checks by Congress

The Supreme Court is subject to four checks by Congress:

➤ The Senate has the power to confirm or reject appointments to the Court. In having a hand in who does and who does not sit on the Court, Congress therefore acts as a check. This is clearly seen when the Senate rejects nominations as, for example, it did over the nomination of Robert Bork in 1987. In 2005, the opposition of Republican senators to President George W. Bush's nomination of Harriet Miers to the Supreme Court led her to withdraw from the process.

➤ Linked with this is Congress's power to decide how many justices sit on the Court. Congress could, for example, decide to increase the number of justices, thereby obliging the president to make new appointments and potentially altering the philosophical make-up of the Court. Congress refused President Franklin D. Roosevelt's plan to increase the number of Supreme Court judges from nine to 15 for just this reason — that by agreeing to such a plan, the nature of the Court would be altered.

➤ Congress has the power of impeachment. Even the threat of its use can be effective. In 1968 Associate Justice Abe Fortas resigned rather than face almost certain impeachment.

➤ Congress can initiate constitutional amendments that can have the effect of negating a decision by the Court. The clearest example of this was in the Court's 1895 decision of *Pollock v. Farmers' Loan and Trust Company*, when it declared federal income tax to be unconstitutional. Congress then initiated — and the states ratified — the 16th Amendment (1913), which stated: 'The Congress shall have the power to lay and collect taxes on incomes.' However, recent attempts by Congress to initiate constitutional amendments to overturn the Court's decisions on such matters as flag desecration, school prayers, abortion rights and congressional term limits have all failed.

Checks by the president

The president has two important checks on the Court:

➤ The president has the power to nominate justices. By choosing justices of a certain political and judicial philosophy, the president may seek to change the nature of the Court. Between 1968 and 2008 the judicial philosophy of the Court changed significantly as it changed from being one appointed mostly by Democratic presidents — Roosevelt, Truman, Kennedy and Johnson — to one appointed mostly by Republican presidents — Reagan, George H. W. Bush and George W. Bush.

➤ The president can decide either to throw his political weight behind a decision of the Court or to criticise it openly. President Eisenhower gave his political support to the Court's 1954 decision in *Brown v. Board of Education of Topeka*. In this decision, the Court had declared that segregated schools were unconstitutional. In 1957, Eisenhower used his power as commander-in-chief to send federal troops to Arkansas to enforce the desegregation of the Little Rock Central High School. Contrast that with President George H. W. Bush's response to the Court's 1989 decision in *Texas v. Johnson*. In this decision, the Court declared a Texas state law forbidding the burning of the US flag to be unconstitutional. An irate President Bush publicly described the Court's decision as 'wrong, dead wrong'.

President Obama has had a few run-ins with the Supreme Court. In his 2010 State of the Union Address he criticised the Court's judgement in the case of *Citizens United v. Federal Election Commission*. Then in 2012, less than 3 months before the Court was due to hand down its judgement concerning his flagship healthcare reform legislation, the President, answering questions at a White House press conference, made the following remarks about the upcoming decision:

I am confident that the Supreme Court will not take what would be an unprecedented, extraordinary step of overturning a law that was passed by a strong majority of a democratically-elected Congress.

What was certainly unusual — if not 'unprecedented' — was for a president to offer his personal observations on a decision of the Supreme Court before the Court had actually spoken on the matter. Many commentators, and not just conservative ones, pointed out what they regarded as some very obvious factual inaccuracies in the President's remarks. First, it is certainly neither 'unprecedented' nor 'extraordinary' for the Supreme Court to overturn a law that has been 'passed by a strong majority' in Congress. In the 1995 case of *United States v. Lopez*, the Supreme Court declared unconstitutional the Gun-Free School Zones Act (1990), which had received such strong support in Congress that it had passed through most of its legislative stages in both houses by voice votes. The only recorded vote which was held on that bill in the House of Representatives was passed 313–1. Second, the Patient Protection and Affordable Care Act (2010) about which Obama was speaking had passed the House by a vote of 219–212. Most neutral observers would not describe that vote as exhibiting a 'strong majority'. But the President had more to say:

> And I'd just remind conservative commentators that, for years, what we have heard is [that] the biggest problem on the bench was judicial activism, or a lack of judicial restraint, that an unelected group of people would somehow overturn a duly constituted and passed law.

But as we observed earlier, the term 'judicial activism' is often used in a judgemental sense by folk who disagree with a decision of the Court. It furthermore seemed unwise for the President to question the legitimacy of the Court to do its job merely because they are 'an unelected group of people'.

Other checks

➤ The Supreme Court has no power of initiation. It must wait for cases to come before it. Many presidents, politicians and commentators have been of the view that the War Powers Act (1973) may be unconstitutional. However, the Court has been unable to rule on the matter because no case regarding this Act has appeared before it.

➤ The Court does not possess any enforcement powers. The Court is reliant upon either enforcement by other branches of government or majority acceptance by law-abiding Americans. When in 1954 the Court announced in *Brown v. Board of Education of Topeka* that states should desegregate their schools 'with all deliberate speed', there was little the Court could do in practical terms to ensure that this occurred. Some years later the Court complained that desegregation was subject to 'too much deliberation and not enough speed'.

➤ This links with a further potential check on the Court — public opinion. While a judicial body should be thought immune to public opinion, the Court often seems to be mindful that, were the public to view its decisions as lacking credibility, the

Court's legitimacy could be at risk. The Court's attitude towards public opinion seems to vary, however. In some instances, the Court seems to want to mould and lead public opinion: this is what it seemingly wanted to do in its 1954 decision on school desegregation. In other instances, it apparently ignores public opinion altogether, as in the 1989 flag desecration decision. In yet other instances, the Court seems to be careful to try to mirror public opinion, as in its 1992 abortion decision — *Planned Parenthood of Southeastern Pennsylvania v. Casey*. In this case, the Court decided neither that women had no constitutional right to choose an abortion nor that such a right was unlimited. Rather, the Court decided that a woman's right to choose an abortion did exist in the Constitution but could be subjected to reasonable limitations by state legislatures. This decision was actually in line with the views of the majority of Americans.

➤ The Court is also checked by itself, for the Court decisions can amend — even overturn — decisions of earlier Courts. For example, the 1954 *Brown v. Board of Education of Topeka* decision stated that 'separate educational facilities are inherently unequal'. However, the Court's decision in the 1896 *Plessy v. Ferguson* case laid down what became known as the 'separate but equal' doctrine, which was then accepted as law for almost 60 years. More recently, the Court in 1989 (*Stanford v. Kentucky*) had ruled that the states could execute 16- and 17-year-old offenders. But in the 2003 case of *Roper v. Simmons*, the Court decided that such executions were a violation of the 8th Amendment. Antonin Scalia, who had written the majority opinion in *Stanford* in 1989, was still on the Court 14 years later to see his opinion overturned. And as we remarked earlier, in 2000, in the case of *Stenberg v. Carhart*, the Court declared a Nebraska state law prohibiting late-term abortions to be unconstitutional. But just 4 years later in 2007, in *Gonzales v. Carhart*, the Court upheld an almost identical federal law.

➤ Finally, the Constitution is a check on the Supreme Court. Although certain parts of the Constitution are open to interpretation by the Court — such as the 1st Amendment — other parts of the document are unambiguous, allowing little, if any, room for modern-day interpretation by the Court.

The Roberts Court?

It is traditional to prefix the Court with the name of the chief justice, thereby suggesting that he dominates the Court to such an extent that it is, in effect, his Court. Commentators therefore talk of the Warren Court, the Burger Court and the Rehnquist Court, named after Chief Justice Roberts's three immediate predecessors, Earl Warren (1953–69), Warren Earl Burger (1969–86) and William Rehnquist (1986–2005).

During his confirmation hearings in front of the Senate Judiciary Committee in 2005, John Roberts promised that he had 'no agenda' and that he would pursue a 'limited' approach to constitutional interpretation. He famously likened the role of a Supreme Court justice to that of a sports umpire. Said Roberts:

> Justices are servants of the law. They are like umpires. Umpires don't make the rules; they apply them. The role of an umpire and a judge is critical. They make sure everybody plays by the rules. But it is a limited role. Nobody ever went to a ball game to see the umpire. Judges are not politicians who can promise to do certain things in exchange for votes.

But the evidence during the first 7 years of Roberts's tenure as chief justice does not always seem to match with these views. So is there truly a 'Roberts Court' and if there is, what are its principal characteristics?

One way to gauge who dominates the Court is to see which justice is most frequently in the majority in cases that are decided by 5 votes to 4. For all of the first 7 years of Roberts's tenure that distinction has gone to Justice Anthony Kennedy either solely (in 5 of the 7 years) or jointly (see Table 7.10). Even if one broadens this out to the justice who is most frequently in the majority in all cases, this distinction still goes to Kennedy (in 4 of the 7 years), to Roberts in 2005–06 and 2007–08, and jointly between them in 2009–10. Furthermore, in most of the major 5–4 decisions handed down during the first 6 years of Roberts's tenure, such as *Gonzales v. Carhart* (2007), *District of Columbia v. Heller* (2008) and *Citizens United v. Federal Election Commission* (2010), Roberts and his three fellow conservative justices — Antonin Scalia, Clarence Thomas and Samuel Alito — had to rely upon swing justice Anthony Kennedy to give them the fifth vote. Thus by the end of Roberts's sixth term in office — 2011 — many Supreme Court watchers were concluding that what we had was the Kennedy Court rather than the Roberts Court. But Chief Justice Roberts' role in deciding the landmark healthcare reform decision in 2012 changed the view of many Court watchers. What many regarded as a piece of judicial statesmanship by Roberts was widely applauded and as a result many commentators stated their belief that this was now more truly 'the Roberts Court'.

Table 7.10 Membership per term in 5–4 majority decisions: 2006–12 (%)

Justice	2006–07	2007–08	2008–09	2009–10	2010–11	2011–12	Average
Kennedy	100	67	78	69	88	80	80
Thomas	61	67	65	69	75	67	67
Scalia	58	58	70	69	69	60	64
Roberts	67	58	48	56	63	67	60
Alito	71	50	52	63	63	60	60
Sotomayor	–	–	–	43	38	47	44
Breyer	46	45	39	38	31	47	41
Kagan	–	–	–	–	38	40	39
Ginsburg	33	50	52	25	38	33	38

Source: compiled from www.scotusblog.com

Activity

In January 2010, the Supreme Court declined to hear a case in which the US appeal court upheld a high-school dress code which banned students from wearing clothing that featured political comments. High school student Paul Palmer was banned by Waxahachie High School in Texas from wearing various T-shirts including one which had 'Freedom of Speech' on the front and the 1st Amendment printed on the back. By declining to review the case, the Court was in effect agreeing with the lower court's decision.

Here's something interactive for you to try. Go to **www.icivics.org** and click on 'Play Games'. At the bottom of the page under the heading 'The Judicial Branch', click on 'Supreme Decision' and then follow the on-screen instructions. This is a simulation of how Supreme Court justices make decisions about individual rights.

UK/US comparison

The US and UK judiciaries

There are six basic characteristics of the US judiciary:

➢ It operates within a federal system with both federal courts and state courts.

➢ The federal system is structured in three tiers: trial courts; appeal courts; and the US Supreme Court.

➢ The appointment of all federal judges is made by the president but must be confirmed by a simple majority vote in the Senate.

➢ Appointments are for life, subject to the check of impeachment.

➢ The US Supreme Court has the power of judicial review and by this can declare acts of Congress and actions of the executive — at both federal and state levels — unconstitutional.

➢ The federal courts, and especially the US Supreme Court, play a major role in the protection of rights and liberties.

There are seven basic characteristics of the UK judiciary:

➢ It operates within a tripartite system with different structures and procedures for (1) England and Wales, (2) Scotland, and (3) Northern Ireland.

➢ All three legal systems distinguish between criminal and civil law with different courts for each.

➢ Traditionally, the Law Lords (in the House of Lords) have acted as the highest court of appeal in the UK, but the Constitutional Reform Act (2005) established a new UK Supreme Court in 2009.

➢ Candidates for UK judges are now selected by the Judicial Appointments Commission.

➢ The normal retirement age for UK judges is 70.

➢ The UK courts' power of judicial review extends only to interpreting the meaning of Acts of Parliament and the reviewing of actions of members of the executive branch.

> The European Court of Justice and the European Court of Human Rights also play an important role in the UK legal system.

In both the USA and the UK, there are issues regarding the judiciary concerning:

> the appointment process
> the representative nature of judges
> the role of unelected judges in a modern democracy
> the politicisation of the judiciary
> the power of the judiciary
> the role of the judiciary in protecting rights and liberties

Exam focus

Short-answer questions

1 How are Supreme Court justices appointed, and why has the process become so politically controversial?
2 What has been the effect of appointments to the Supreme Court since 2005?
3 What is 'judicial activism' and why is it said to be politically controversial?
4 To what extent have Supreme Court justices reflected the political views of the presidents who nominated them?
5 Using examples, explain the limitations on the Supreme Court's powers.
6 How effective has the Supreme Court been at protecting 1st Amendment rights?

Essay questions

1 Examine the claim that the most important appointments a president makes are to the Supreme Court.
2 Critically analyse the appointment and confirmation process for nominations to the Supreme Court.
3 Discuss the view that the Supreme Court should interpret the Constitution and its amendments by establishing their original meaning when they were adopted.
4 'A political, not a judicial institution.' Discuss this view of the Supreme Court.
5 How effectively have the civil rights and liberties of US citizens been protected by the US Supreme Court?
6 How effective is the Bill of Rights in securing liberty for individual Americans?
7 What effect has the Supreme Court had on the actions of recent presidents?
8 Does the Supreme Court have too much power for an unelected body?

Further reading

Ashbee, E. and Bennett, A. J., 'Is the US Supreme Court too powerful?', *Politics Review*, Vol. 20, No. 2, November 2010.

Bennett, A. J., *US Government & Politics: Annual Update 2012*, Chapters 6 and 7, Philip Allan Updates.

Bennett, A. J., *US Government & Politics: Annual Update 2013*, Chapter 8, Philip Allan Updates.

Biskupic, J., *American Original: The Life and Constitution of Supreme Court Justice Antonin Scalia*, Sarah Crichton Books, 2009.

Singh, R., 'The Roberts Court', *Politics Review*, Vol. 21, No. 3, February 2012.

Chapter 8

Racial and ethnic politics

The United States is a nation of great ethnic diversity. There are American Indians (Native Americans) — nowadays making up a tiny proportion of the US population; WASPS — white, Anglo-Saxon Protestants — who arrived in the New World from the Old from the 17th century onwards; African-Americans, whose initial life of slavery became one of increasing freedom from the 1860s; followed by the great wave of 19th- and 20th-century immigration — initially from Europe, but then increasingly from Central and South America, Asia and Africa. The USA is therefore seen as a 'melting pot' of races, culture, languages and religions.

Many who fled to America over the centuries did so seeking refuge from intolerance and persecution at home: English Puritans, French Huguenots, Jewish exiles from Hitler's Germany, or political exiles from Castro's Cuba. The Declaration of Independence in 1776 was an attempt by suppressed colonists to throw off what they saw as the tyrannical rule of Great Britain. The new nation was not going to exchange one tyranny for another. The Founding Fathers who wrote the Constitution and the Bill of Rights that it eventually contained wanted above everything to devise a system in which government would be limited and citizens' rights — as far as they were understood in the late 18th century — would be protected.

Civil rights are positive acts of government designed to protect people against discriminatory treatment, either by the government or by other individuals or groups within society. Civil liberties are those liberties that guarantee the protection of persons and property from the arbitrary interference of government officials. Restraints on civil liberties are permissible in a free society only in so far as they are imposed to prevent the abuse of such liberties by groups or individuals and to protect public welfare.

This chapter looks at the place of racial and ethnic minorities in the USA, the growth of the civil rights movement and how the US government has adapted to the changes that have taken place in US society, as well as the institutions of government to which racial and ethnic minorities can look to safeguard their rights and liberties.

Key questions answered in this chapter

➤ How ethnically diverse is the USA?

➤ What is affirmative action, how successful has it been and what should be done about it now?

➤ How are minorities represented?

➤ How effectively are rights and liberties protected by the three branches of the federal government?

Links to follow up

Information about the racial and ethnic make-up of the United States can be found at the website of the US Census Bureau — **www.census.gov**.

To follow up on the US civil rights movement, one of the best sites is **www.loc.gov/exhibits/civilrights,** which includes personal stories, oral histories and photographs. Specifically on affirmative action, the website **www.affirmativeaction.org** is probably the place to start.

You can follow up minority representation in Congress through the website of the Congressional Black Caucus at **www.cbcfinc.org**. You can also go to the website of the US Senate — **www.senate.gov** — click on 'Reference' and then click on 'Virtual Reference Desk'. You will then be able to click on 'Minorities'. Alternatively, you can go to the website of the Congressional Research Service (CRS), which can be found at **www.digital.library.unt.edu/govdocs/crs**, where you will find statistics on the make-up of both the House and the Senate. Regarding Hispanics, go to the website of the Library of Congress — **www.loc.gov** — and type 'Hispanic Americans in Congress' into the search window. One can also go to the website of the Congressional Hispanic Caucus by going to **www.house.gov** and then to the website of Congressman Xavier Becerra (D — California) — or any other Hispanic House member — and clicking on the 'Congressional Hispanic Caucus' button.

Ethnic diversity and minority representation

In the beginning, the USA was a creation of white European Protestants. Black people were, in most cases, slaves; American Indians were not regarded as citizens either. The story of westward expansion — as depicted in Hollywood 'westerns' — was the story of the white 'Cowboys' depriving the 'Indians' of their land, livelihood and women. Catholics and Jews were initially a tiny minority and were often persecuted.

However, the 19th and 20th centuries changed all that. The end of the Civil War (1861–65) brought emancipation for the slaves and a slow march towards equality in politics, at home, at school and in the workplace. Immigration brought a flood of new settlers — including Irish Catholics fleeing from the potato famines of the mid-19th

Table 8.1 US population by ethnic groups, 1980–2010 (%)

Ethnic group	1980	1990	2000	2010
White	79.6	75.7	69.1	63.7
Hispanic	6.4	9.0	12.6	16.3
Black	11.5	11.8	12.3	12.6
Asian/Indian	2.1	3.5	4.5	5.7

century, and European Jews fleeing from religious persecution in the mid-20th century. Then came the political and economic Hispanic migrants from Mexico and other Central American countries, and refugees from Africa, the Middle East and Asia. Not all were legal, and certainly not all were white Protestants. Buddhists and Muslims arrived along with people of many other faiths and cultures.

During the 1990s, the combined population of African-Americans, Native Americans, Asians, Pacific Islanders and Hispanics/Latinos grew at 13 times the rate of the non-Hispanic white population. The 2000 census was the first to show Hispanics as a larger proportion of the US population than black people (see Table 8.1). It was also the first to allow Americans to indicate their belonging to more than one ethnic group — what Tiger Woods calls 'Cablinasian'. It was after Woods' 1997 Golf Masters win that he first used the term in public to denote his white, black, Thai, Chinese and American Indian heritage.

The 2010 census showed that the population of the USA had increased by 9.7% since 2000 and that most of this increase was amongst those who reported their race as something other than White and specifically amongst those who called themselves Hispanic or Latino. By 2010 there were 50.5 million Hispanics in the United States, comprising over 16% of the total population. Between 2000 and 2010, the Hispanic population grew by 43%. Indeed, more than half the growth in the total population of the United States between 2000 and 2010 was due to the increase in the Hispanic population. Figure 8.1 shows that the Hispanic population is estimated to be approaching one-third of the population of the United States by 2050. This will have important implications for American politics in the coming decades. That said, how diverse the local population is varies hugely from state to state. In New Mexico, for example, Hispanics and Latinos already make up 46.3% of the population, whereas in West Virginia they account for just 1.2%. In Mississippi, African-Americans make up 37% of the population whilst in Montana the figure is just 0.4%.

Ethnic diversity itself is a challenge to any society. Diversity needs both protection and adequate representation; so do minorities. How to move US society from one that was 'half slave and half free' to one in which the interests of minorities are both protected and represented has raised many problems. As this chapter explains, there has been a role for all three branches of the federal government in this. Over the past half-century, many different policies and approaches have been adopted. Some have been more successful than others. Some have stirred up controversy among both minority and majority groups. Some have been favoured by the right; others by the left.

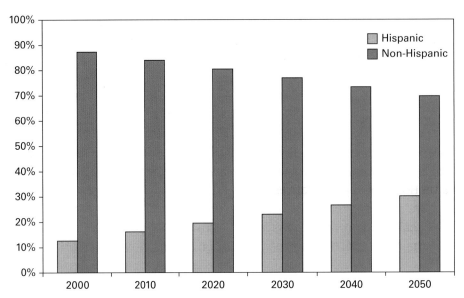

Figure 8.1 Hispanics and non-Hispanics as a percentage of the US population to 2050 (estimated)

Source: Congressional Research Service

The civil rights movement

Early developments

The 19th century had seen attempts to use the Constitution to guarantee rights and representation for racial minorities. The 13th, 14th and 15th Amendments, passed immediately after the Civil War, were meant to put right the wrongs of slavery. For almost a century, however, little changed in practice. Segregation remained rife, especially in the Deep South. The 20th century brought another type of segregation — what might be called 'residential segregation'. With the onset of the Great Depression in the 1930s, black people moved increasingly to the big cities — and especially those of the northeast — to seek work. Cities such as Chicago, Philadelphia and Washington DC saw the arrival of large numbers of ethnic minorities, which tended to congregate in inner-city regions, leaving the suburbs still largely — if not exclusively — white. The result was to create two Americas — metropolitan America, which is multiracial and suburban, and rural America, which is largely white or, in the case of the southeast, biracial.

Minority rights and representation in the 20th century

The 20th century brought two further developments regarding minority rights and representation. From the 1950s, the Supreme Court saw itself as having a major role to play in this area. From the 1960s, Congress too plunged into the area of civil rights. For the Supreme Court, the watershed came in 1954 with its landmark decision in *Brown v. Board of Education of Topeka*. For Congress, it came with the passage of the major civil rights legislation from 1964.

The 20th century also saw an on-going argument between what has been called 'equality of opportunity' on the one hand and 'equality of results' on the other. From the middle of the century, many civil rights advocates — whether in the areas of ethnicity or gender — came to believe that minority rights and representation could not be guaranteed solely by 'giving' rights to people — 'equality of opportunity'. This would merely give the *theory* of rights and equality. If people wanted to see the *practice* of rights and equality, they had to work towards 'equality of results'. The only way to overcome racial *disadvantage* was by introducing racial *advantage* through such policies as **busing**, **quotas**, **affirmative action** and majority-minority districts for elections to the US House of Representatives.

Key concepts

➤ **Busing.** The mandated movement of schoolchildren between racially homogeneous neighbourhoods — white suburbs and black inner cities — to create racially mixed schools in all neighbourhoods.

➤ **Quotas.** A set-aside programme to benefit previously disadvantaged minorities in such areas as higher education and employment. A certain percentage — quota — of places is reserved for people of the previously disadvantaged group. The Supreme Court found quotas unconstitutional in a number of decisions during the 1980s and 1990s.

➤ **Affirmative action.** A programme that entails giving those members of a previously disadvantaged minority group a headstart in such areas as higher education and employment. The term is often regarded as being synonymous with 'positive discrimination'. Affirmative action is now required by law for all federal government agencies and for those organisations in receipt of federal funds.

The Second World War played its part in moving the nation towards desegregation with moves to outlaw racial discrimination in the defence industries in 1941 and in the US armed forces in 1948. But it was the Supreme Court's 1954 decision in *Brown v. Board of Education of Topeka* which was the real catalyst. By this decision, the Court overturned the 'separate but equal' doctrine with the startling conclusion that 'separate educational facilities are inherently unequal'. And what was true in schools would also be true for parks, lunch counters and buses.

'I have a dream'

On 1 December 1955, Rosa Parks — a black woman — was arrested for refusing to move to the 'black' section of a bus in Montgomery, Alabama, following which black people staged a one-day boycott of local buses in protest at her arrest. It was this incident which grew into a much larger programme of civil disobedience orchestrated by Baptist minister Martin Luther King and his Southern Christian Leadership Conference. Picketing, boycotts and sit-ins became the most used forms of protest, modelled on the non-violent methods of the Indian leader Mohandas Ghandi.

In May 1961, the Congress of Racial Equality (CORE) sent 'freedom riders' of both races across the southern states and elsewhere to challenge the segregated seating arrangements on interstate transport. During the next 4 months it was estimated that more than 70,000 people had participated in the protest with approximately 3,600 being arrested. The protests had spread to more than 100 cities in 20 states. All this climaxed in August 1963 with a huge march in Washington DC — the March for Jobs and Freedom — to protest against racial discrimination and show support for civil rights legislation that was being debated in Congress. This was the setting for King's 'I have a dream' speech, delivered on 28 August 1963, from the steps of the Lincoln Memorial, a defining moment in the civil rights movement in America.

Martin Luther King Jnr (1929–68), American black civil rights campaigner

Campaigners for civil rights

Civil rights legislation in Congress was eventually passed, but only after a southerner — Texan Lyndon Johnson — pushed it through, appealing for passage as a tribute to the assassinated John F. Kennedy. The subsequent decades of the black civil rights movement in the USA have seen a struggle between those espousing peaceful protest and working through the established political processes, and those espousing a more radical and even violent response to racial injustice and discrimination. Each group has had, and still has today, its iconic leaders. The first group is associated with such names as Shirley Chisholm, Jesse Jackson, Kweisi Mfume and, more recently, Barack Obama. The second group includes names such as Malcolm X and Louis Farrakhan — both, in their time, leaders of the radical Nation of Islam movement. Straddling the two groups are names like Al Sharpton and, more recently, Jeremiah Wright.

Shirley Chisholm became the first African-American woman elected to Congress in 1968, and 4 years later she ran unsuccessfully for the presidential nomination of the Democratic Party. She remained in the House of Representatives for 14 years, retiring in 1982. Jesse Jackson and Kweisi Mfume also worked through elective politics. In 1984, Jackson established the National Rainbow Coalition — the same year as he made his first of two unsuccessful bids for the Democratic presidential nomination. In 1989, Jackson became what he called a 'shadow senator' for Washington DC to lobby Congress for statehood for the District of Columbia. In 1997, President Clinton named Jackson as a special envoy to Africa. Jackson probably achieved more than any other person during the last two decades of the 20th century to ensure that issues of concern to black people were given prominence within the Democratic Party. Kweisi Mfume was elected to the House of Representatives from Maryland's Seventh District in 1986, where he served just short of five terms, resigning in February 1996 to take up the presidency of the National Association for the Advancement of Coloured People (NAACP), a post he held until 2004. Mfume's politics were characterised by a mixture of progressive ideology and an ability to compromise.

In contrast to these, Malcolm X of the Nation of Islam espoused a far more radical approach to black civil rights. He criticised the mainstream civil rights movement and disagreed with its policies of integration and non-violent protest. He advocated that blacks should pursue their goals 'by any means necessary' and that those goals were more than just the right to sit in a restaurant or vote, but were about black identity and racial pride. To him, the 1963 march on Washington was 'a farce' — a demonstration 'run by whites in front of a statue of a president who has been dead for a hundred years and who didn't like us when he was alive'. Malcolm X was assassinated in February 1965 at the age of 39, having broken with the Nation of Islam the previous year.

In the 1980s and 1990s the name of Louis Farrakhan became synonymous with the Nation of Islam. Farrakhan combined colourful rhetoric with an organisational ability that peaked with the Million Man March in Washington DC in 1995 — a march that was to promote African-American unity and family values. Under his leadership, the Nation of Islam has taken on work to promote AIDS clinics and to force drug dealers out of public housing projects in Washington DC as well as work among black gang members in Los Angeles. But Farrakhan's rhetoric has often landed him in trouble, especially with the American Jewish community. He has also at times claimed that AIDS and drug addiction were both part of a white conspiracy to destroy black people.

Obama's 2008 presidential campaign

The tussle between the Martin Luther King and Louis Farrakhan wings of the civil rights movement — if one can call them that — were played out once again most publicly in the disagreements between Senator Barack Obama and the Reverend Jeremiah Wright — the pastor of the church that Obama attended — during the spring of 2008 as Obama fought for the Democratic Party's presidential nomination. Wright was on record as telling his congregation just 5 days after the attacks on America on 9/11:

> We bombed Hiroshima, we bombed Nagasaki, and we nuked far more than the thousands in New York and the Pentagon, and we never batted an eye. We have supported state terrorism against Palestinians and black South Africans, and now we are indignant because the stuff we have done overseas is now brought right back to our own front yards. America's chickens are coming home to roost.

Obama tried initially to play down the remarks when they were first reported in the media. He said he disagreed with some of Wright's views but still respected him

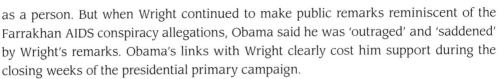

as a person. But when Wright continued to make public remarks reminiscent of the Farrakhan AIDS conspiracy allegations, Obama said he was 'outraged' and 'saddened' by Wright's remarks. Obama's links with Wright clearly cost him support during the closing weeks of the presidential primary campaign.

The election of Barack Obama will doubtless be seen as a milestone in the story of African-American history. His election marked a cultural shift in the political history of the United States. After a list of presidents with first names such as Richard, George, John and Bill, the 44th president is called Barack. Forty-five years to the day after Martin Luther King's 'I have a dream' speech, Barack Obama was giving his acceptance speech to a packed football stadium in Denver, Colorado, accepting the Democratic Party's nomination as president of the United States.

Affirmative action

Given how disadvantaged African-Americans had been during the 100 years after the Civil War, many Democrat politicians began to believe that the government needed to discriminate positively in favour of African-Americans in such areas as housing, education and employment, in what became known as affirmative action programmes.

This takes us back to the 'equality of results' versus the 'equality of opportunity' debate. Many civil rights organisations had become convinced, and Democrat politicians had tended to agree, that the burdens of racism could be overcome only by taking race into account in designing suitable remedies. Groups which had been disadvantaged were now to be advantaged, what in Britain is often referred to as 'positive discrimination'. Rights in themselves would not deliver changes to society; benefits had to be added. This in American parlance is 'affirmative action'. Affirmative action in education meant busing and racial quotas. Affirmative action in employment meant preferential hiring practices for minority groups. And affirmative action was meant to lead to diversity and **multiculturalism** — the view that the school, the college, the firm, the workplace should reflect the racial diversity of the nation. This is 'equality of results'.

Key concept

> **Multiculturalism.** The existence within a nation state, in this case the United States, of people from many different cultures whose own learned patterns of behaviour lead to a diversity of culture in such matters as lifestyle, belief, custom, values and language. Multiculturalism can lead to competition and conflict between different cultural groups. Those from minority cultures or groups may be torn between those who seek to live in the majority national culture and those who wish to remain with their own subculture.

But what is affirmative action to some is merely reverse discrimination to others. More conservative groups, and many Republican politicians, came to believe that affirmative action programmes were both patronising to minorities and unfair to majorities. They believed that the Constitution and both federal and state laws should be 'colour blind'. Children of minority families should certainly be given equal opportunity to attend the school of their choice, but busing or quotas to achieve an artificial racial balance was, in their view, wrong. In employment, by all means open up all jobs for all applicants regardless of race, but numerical targets, goals and quotas were off-limits. This is 'equality of opportunity'. As we shall see, it would be largely up to the Supreme Court to umpire between these two views of American society.

The development of affirmative action

In March 1961, President John F. Kennedy created the Equal Employment Opportunity Commission (EEOC). The Executive Order which created the EEOC also required that projects financed with federal funds 'take affirmative action' to ensure that hiring and employment practices would be free from racial bias. In 1965, President Johnson issued an Executive Order requiring federal government contractors to 'take affirmative action' toward prospective minority employees in all aspects of hiring and employment. President Richard Nixon (1969–74) also played a significant role in pressing ahead with affirmative action programmes. It was the Nixon administration that instituted 'set aside' policies to reserve a certain percentage of jobs for minorities on federally funded construction projects. He also substantially increased the funding for the EEOC and, although he opposed schooling busing programmes, oversaw a substantial reduction in the percentage of African-American students attending all-black schools.

The Supreme Court and affirmative action

But affirmative action programmes soon came in for some criticism from the US Supreme Court. In the first such case — *Regents of the University of California v. Bakke* (1978) — the Supreme Court imposed limitations on affirmative action to ensure that providing greater opportunities for minorities did not come at the expense of the rights of the majority. The case involved the University of California's Medical School in Davis. The School reserved 16 of its 100 places each year for minority students. Allan Bakke, a white applicant, was rejected twice even though minority students who had significantly lower test scores than him were admitted. In a 5–4 decision, the Court ruled that this constituted a violation of the equal protection clause of the 14th Amendment.

Another landmark decision by the Supreme Court on affirmative action programmes came in the 1995 case of *Adarand Constructors v. Peña*, discussed in some detail in Chapter 7. In response to this case, President Clinton in a speech on 19 July 1995, asserted that while *Adarand* set 'stricter standards to mandate reform of affirmative action, it actually reaffirmed the need for affirmative action and reaffirmed the continuing existence of systematic discrimination in the United States'. In a White House memorandum the same day, Clinton called for the elimination of any affirmative action programme that '(a) creates a quota; (b) creates preferences for unqualified individuals; (c) creates reverse discrimination; or (d) continues even after its equal opportunity purposes have been achieved'.

Box 8.1 A letter from Barack Obama, *Harvard Law Review*, 1989

I'd like to add a personal note, in response to the letter from Mr Jim Chen which expressed broad objections to affirmative action programmes. I respect Mr Chen's personal concern over the possible stigmatising effects of affirmative action, and do not question the depth or sincerity of his feelings. I must say, however, that as someone who has undoubtedly benefitted from affirmative action programmes during my academic career, I have not personally felt stigmatised. Indeed, my election last year as President of the Review would seem to indicate that at least among Review staff, and hopefully for the majority of professors at Harvard, affirmative action in no way tarnishes the accomplishments of those who are members of historically underrepresented groups.

Source: adapted from David Remnick, *The Bridge: The Life and Rise of Barack Obama*, Picador, 2010, p. 215

On 3 November 1997, voters in California voted in favour of Proposition 209, which banned all forms of affirmative action in the state. The Proposition stated simply:

The state shall not discriminate against, or grant preferential treatment to, any individual or group on the basis of race, sex, colour, ethnicity, or national origin in the operation of public employment, public education, or public contracting.

The United States Supreme Court refused to review the Proposition, thus clearly indicating its belief that such an action was constitutionally permissible. As a result of Proposition 209, the number of black people and Hispanics entering some of the more prestigious universities in the state dropped significantly after 1997. Voters in Washington State passed a similar initiative the following year, and in 2000 Florida took a similar path to end affirmative action programmes in the state under Governor Jeb Bush's 'One Florida' programme.

In 2003, the Supreme Court made two further rulings on affirmative action programmes regarding the admissions procedures at the University of Michigan. As we saw in Chapter 7, the Court struck down a 'mechanistic' — automatic — programme for undergraduate admissions while upholding an 'individualised' programme for admission to the university's Law School. In the oral argument, Justice Sandra Day O'Connor followed up the issue, touched on by President Clinton back in 1995, that affirmative action programmes ought at some point in time to achieve their goals and therefore become unnecessary. In conversation with the university's lead lawyer in the case, Maureen Mahoney, Justice O'Connor asked:

In all programmes which this Court has upheld in the area of what I'll label affirmative action, there's been a fixed time period within which it would operate, you could see an end to it. There is none here, is there? How do we deal with that aspect?

As Jeffrey Toobin (2007) comments:

O'Connor was raising one of the more profound questions in American life. When will race no longer matter? The question captured O'Connor's ambivalence on the issue of affirmative action — and her practical, solution-orientated mind. To her, racial preferences were a dubious and extreme remedy at best, and she wanted to make sure they were not enshrined for all time. So how much longer would they be needed?

Mahoney's answer came up with a clever formula:

> Well, in Bakke, Your Honour, there were five votes to allow the University of California to use a plan which has been in effect for about 25 years. It has reaped extraordinary benefits for this country's educational system.

The comment found its way, via O'Connor, into the final judgement in the case. O'Connor had her law clerk write into the final draft the following passage:

> It has been 25 years since Justice Powell first approved the use of race to further an interest in student body diversity in the context of higher education. Since that time, the number of minority applicants with high grades and test scores has indeed increased. We expect that 25 years from now, the use of racial preferences will no longer be necessary to further the interest approved today.

In 2007, in another pair of cases — *Parents Involved in Community Schools Inc. v. Seattle School District* and *Meredith v. Jefferson County (Kentucky) Board of Education* — the Court struck down affirmative action programmes in Washington state and Kentucky because they assigned students to public (i.e. state-run) schools solely for the purpose of achieving racial balance. Chief Justice Roberts, writing for the majority, stated simply that 'the way to stop discriminating on the basis of race is to stop discriminating on the basis of race'.

The current position

James Q. Wilson and John DiLulio (2001) summarise the position on affirmative action as follows:

- ➤ The courts will subject any quota system created by state or local governments to 'strict scrutiny' and will be looking for a 'compelling' justification for it.
- ➤ Quotas or preference systems cannot be used by state or local governments without first showing that such rules are needed to correct an actual past or present pattern of discrimination.
- ➤ In proving that there has been discrimination, it is not enough to show that African-Americans (or other minorities) are statistically underrepresented among employees, contractors or union members.
- ➤ Quotas or preference systems that are created by *federal* law will be given greater deference, in part because Section 5 of the 14th Amendment gives to Congress powers not given to the states to correct the effects of racial discrimination.

The debate goes on, not only in the courts, but also in the other two branches of government and in academia too. What are the arguments for and against affirmative action?

Arguments for affirmative action

There are six basic arguments put forward in favour of affirmative action. The first is that such programmes lead to greater levels of diversity which would not have been achieved by just leaving things as they were. Second, affirmative action is justified on the basis that it rights previous wrongs. The previously disadvantaged are now advantaged. Third, it opens up areas of education and employment which minorities otherwise would not have considered. Fourth, in education, a diverse student body creates not only a better learning environment but also one in which ethnic and racial tolerance is promoted. Fifth, it is the most meaningful and effective means thus far devised by government for delivering the promise of equal opportunity. Finally, it works. For example, between 1960 and 1995, the percentage of black people aged 25–29 who graduated from university rose from 5% to 15%. As President Clinton remarked in 1995, 'affirmative action has been good for America'.

Arguments against affirmative action

There are six basic arguments against affirmative action. First, advantage or preference for one group leads inevitably to disadvantage for another group. This is the issue of reverse discrimination which the Supreme Court was first asked to address in the *Bakke* case in 1978. As California State Assemblyman Bernie Richter puts it: 'When you deny someone who has earned it and give it to someone else who has not earned it...you create anger and resentment.' Second, it can lead minorities to be admitted to courses or given jobs with which they are ill-equipped to cope. In a study of American law schools in the November 2004 *Stanford Law Review*, Richard Sander found that putting black students into classes with white students who had higher SAT scores and college grades resulted in 'close to half of black students ending up in the bottom tenth of their classes'. Third, affirmative action can be condescending to minorities by implying that they need a helping hand in order to succeed, thereby demeaning their achievement. Fourth, it perpetuates a society based on colour and race, thereby encouraging prejudice. Fifth, affirmative action is no more than a quota system under another name. Finally, it focuses on groups rather than individuals. As David McKay (2005) succinctly explains:

> Affirmative action is inherently problematic because it involves a clash between the liberal notion of what the individual is worth and the collective interests of a group or race.

Richard Kahlenberg (2008) writing in *The Atlantic* 2 days after the 2008 presidential election wrote:

> This election was a stunning triumph for the notion of colour-blindness: don't discriminate against people of colour — or in favour of them. The election of America's first black president was a moving and long overdue affirmation of the civil rights movement's enduring struggle for equal treatment. The candidate never asked Americans to vote for him because he was black.

On Election Day 2008, the president of the Children's Defense Fund, Marian Wright Edelman, wrote: 'This morning, as I stood in line to vote, I was moved by the realisation that finally this is the day on which my fellow Americans are willing to do what Martin Luther King envisioned: vote for a president based on the content of his character rather than the colour of his skin.'

Has affirmative action been a success?

In order to judge whether or not affirmative action has been a success, we must first establish what it was meant to achieve. In the *Bakke* decision in 1978, Justice Harry Blackmun suggested that the legitimacy of affirmative action programmes was to be measured by how fast they moved society towards a time when they would no longer be needed and a society in which race no longer mattered. This was the line of argument which Justice Sandra Day O'Connor took up in her opinion in the *Grutter* decision in 2003 when she announced the 25-year 'limit' to affirmative action programmes. So how successful have affirmative action programmes been by this measure? There is evidence on both sides.

Some politicians and philosophers, however, think that affirmative action is bound to fail by this measure because a programme that is based on race is unlikely to move society to a point where race no longer counts. In the view of philosopher Carl Cohen (1995), 'the moral issue [about affirmative action] comes in the classic form: "important objectives appear to require impermissible means".' In other words, often the only way we can achieve something is by means which are not allowed. Asks Cohen: 'Might we not wink at the Constitution this once and allow [affirmative action programmes] to do their good work?' In other words, can't we just overlook any constitutional defects in such programmes because they achieve so much that is good and worthwhile? But Cohen, along with a majority opinion on the Supreme Court, has said 'no'. 'In the distribution of benefits under the laws, all racial classifications are invidious.' This was Justice Clarence Thomas's conclusion in his majority opinion in the *Adarand* case in 1995 when he stated:

> I believe that there is a moral and constitutional equivalence between laws designed
> to subjugate a race and those that distribute benefits on the basis of race in order to
> foster some notion of equality. Government cannot make us equal.

The Michigan Mandate

The issue of the likelihood of affirmative action programmes being able to achieve their desired and declared aims was also addressed in the two *Bollinger* decisions in 2003. The University of Michigan had stated that the reason for its affirmative action programme was to strive for a reasonable representation of minorities on the campus because it would further its mission to prepare Michigan's future leaders. The argument, referred to as 'the Michigan Mandate', went like this:

1 The leadership of the state ought roughly to represent the state's population, ethnically and racially.

2 As the state's premier training ground for leadership, the university ought to graduate rising generations of future leaders that conform to this representational goal.

3 To graduate such rising generations, it needs to admit racially and ethnically representative classes.

What the university was arguing here could be called the 'integration' rationale for affirmative action, rather than the 'diversity' rationale. In other words, what affirmative action in education is trying to achieve is an integrated society rather than merely a diverse student body. This was an argument picked up by Justice O'Connor in her majority opinion. In her words, the University of Michigan and the Law School 'represent the training ground for our Nation's leaders'. She continued:

> In order to cultivate a set of leaders with legitimacy in the eyes of the citizenry, it is necessary that the path to leadership be visibly open to talented and qualified individuals of every race and ethnicity. All members of our heterogeneous society must have confidence in the openness and integrity of the educational institutions that provide this training. Access…must be inclusive…of every race and ethnicity, so that all members of our heterogeneous society may participate in the educational institutions that provide the training and education necessary to succeed in America.

Many affirmative action programmes seem to have lost sight of their intended goal — that in the end they should become unnecessary. They are meant to be a means to an end, not an end in themselves. Elizabeth Anderson (2002) concludes:

> Current affirmative action debates have lost sight of the ideal of integration as a compelling moral and political goal. Unless disadvantaged racial groups are integrated into mainstream institutions, they will continue to suffer from segregation and discrimination. But the loss is not only theirs. It is a loss suffered by the American public at large in its failure to realise a civil society.

As Robert Fullinwider (2005) points out:

> The legitimacy of state institutions comes under a cloud if important segments of the population remain on the outside looking in. Democratic governance draws nurture from inclusion rather than exclusion. If the leaders who frame the political agenda and shape public opinion remain uniformly white, the common good gets short changed; it isn't really common.

Thus affirmative action is straightforwardly instrumental — a means to an end, the end being a fully integrated society. If that outcome fails to materialise, then the cause of affirmative action is weakened and its programmes might correctly be labelled a failure.

Some would argue that the Michigan Mandate ought to have a fourth point added to it, namely that the gains from achieving an integrated society do not come at too high a cost. If under-prepared blacks are put in academic environments where they cannot succeed, then the cost may be too high and the programme may be a failure. If many Americans refuse to visit a black doctor or dentist because they assume that he/she was admitted both to medical school and to the position he/she now holds through quotas and a lowering of standards — a finding of black researcher Thomas Sowell — then the cost may be too high. If many Americans regard affirmative action as unfair because it may advantage the already advantaged and further disadvantage the already disadvantaged, then the cost may be too high. Christopher Edley, the White House assistant put in charge of President Clinton's review of affirmative action in 1994–95, speaks of how during his review of affirmative action the discussion kept coming back to what he referred to as the 'coal miner's son' question.

> Imagine a college admissions committee trying to decide between the white son of an Appalachian coal miner's family and the African-American son of a successful Pittsburgh neurosurgeon. Why should the black applicant get preference over the white applicant?

Why indeed? In its 2003 *Bollinger* decisions, the Supreme Court suggested that affirmative action programmes should not be seen as a permanent fixture of American society, urging universities to prepare for a time when they should no longer be necessary. The Court suggested that this might occur within the next 25 years. So, has affirmative action been a success? If in 2028 there are no longer any such programmes and American society can rightly be described as fully integrated both racially and ethnically, the undoubted answer will be 'yes'.

In the same election which saw the election of America's first black president, voters in Nebraska voted for a ban on affirmative action programmes.

Affirmative action and public opinion

Trying to assess public opinion towards affirmative action is not easy. It depends very much on what question one asks. When asked 'In order to overcome past discrimination, do you favour or oppose affirmative action programmes?' 63% said they were in favour with only 29% opposed. Likewise, when pollsters asked: 'Do you think affirmative action programmes designed to increase the number of black and minority students on college campuses are a good or a bad thing?' 60% said it was a good thing and just 30% thought it bad. But in both these questions, a specific purpose of the programme was stated — 'to overcome past discrimination' and 'to increase the number of black and minority students on college campuses'. But when one asks about 'fairness', the answers are quite different. To the question, 'Do you think affirmative action programmes designed to increase the number of black and minority students on college campuses are fair or unfair?' whilst 47% thought they were fair, 42% thought them unfair. 'A good thing'

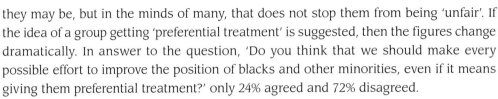

they may be, but in the minds of many, that does not stop them from being 'unfair'. If the idea of a group getting 'preferential treatment' is suggested, then the figures change dramatically. In answer to the question, 'Do you think that we should make every possible effort to improve the position of blacks and other minorities, even if it means giving them preferential treatment?' only 24% agreed and 72% disagreed.

The figures change depending not only on what one asks, but also on whom one asks. Unsurprisingly, African-Americans are more supportive of affirmative action (72%) than Whites (44%). In terms of political ideology, self-identified liberals are more supportive of affirmative action (59%) than self-identified conservatives (32%).

But maybe the most surprising finding of the poll evidence on affirmative action concerns the effect such programmes are perceived to have had. Amongst the white population, just 2% tell pollsters that they have been 'helped' by such a programme and only 13% say they have been 'hurt', leaving 84% saying they were not affected at all. But African-Americans — the group one might expect to have been most affected by affirmative action programmes — were similarly detached. A mere 4% said they had been 'helped' by such a programme whilst 8% said they had been 'hurt', and 87% said that as far as they were concerned the programmes had no effect at all.

What to do with affirmative action?

Put simply, there would seem to be four alternatives as to what to do with affirmative action programmes: abolish them, gradually phase them out, reform them, or keep them as they are. These various options tend to equate with the political ideology of those who support them. Conservatives — found mostly in the Republican Party — tend to favour the abolition of affirmative action programmes. They would argue that society is not about 'equality' but 'equality of opportunity'. They would further suggest that an unequal society has the benefit of providing incentives — to better oneself. Offering 'quotas' is, in their view, a disincentive to hard work and self-improvement. Furthermore, conservatives would point to certain minorities within the USA, such as immigrants from Southeast Asia, who have succeeded without the benefit of affirmative action programmes. To those who argue that affirmative action is necessary to make up for past discrimination, they would argue that today's issues of inequality are not about past discrimination but are rooted in the lifestyle choices — such as those concerned with drugs, alcohol and parenting — that people make for themselves today. Finally, as we have already seen, conservatives argue that affirmative action is based on a false premise — the same false premise upon which the discredited policy of segregation was based, that being racism. As Chief Justice Roberts put it in 2007 (*Parents Involved v. Seattle School District*), 'the way to stop discrimination on the basis of race is to stop discriminating on the basis of race'.

Others of a more moderate persuasion would agree with some of the above but would be more impressed with all that affirmative action programmes have achieved. Their argument would be very much in agreement with that of then associate justice

Sandra Day O'Connor in the *Grutter* decision in 2003 that if affirmative action has achieved all that its supporters claim for it, there must surely come a time when these programmes become unnecessary. Justice O'Connor therefore stated that 'we expect that 25 years from now, the use of racial preferences will no longer be necessary'. In other words, there is an argument for phasing out such programmes. A third argument is that expressed by President Clinton's 'mend it, don't end it' catch phrase, suggesting that such programmes will need tweaking as their effect is more widely felt, and that reform, rather than abolition, is what is called for.

But liberals — found mostly in the Democratic Party — would see affirmative action as something that needs to continue and has much left still to do. For example, they would point out that both African-Americans and Hispanics are under-represented in terms of bachelor degree awards at American universities. Those gained by African-Americans had increased from 5.8% of the total in 1990 to 9.6% by 2006, but that is still below the proportion of this ethnic group within the USA. Likewise Hispanics accounted for only 3.1% of bachelor degrees in 1990 and that had increased to 7.2% by 2006, but there is still some way to go. In January 2012, the national unemployment rate in the USA was 8.3%, but amongst African-Americans it stood at 13.6% and amongst 16–19-year-old African-Americans at a staggering 38.5%. Amongst the similar age group in the white population the figure was 21.1%. Liberals would therefore argue that the vision of an equal society is still a vision of the future.

Minority representation in government

Not only have minorities looked for decisions in government that take their preferences and choices into account but they have looked for adequate representation in government as well — to paraphrase a Bill Clinton phrase, to have a government that 'looks like America'. This is what we call the resemblance model of representation. So to what extent does government in America — at federal, state and local level, as well as in the three different branches of government — resemble the ethnic diversity of the nation?

Minorities and Congress

When Jesse Jackson first ran for the presidency in 1984, there were just 21 African-American members of Congress — all in the House of Representatives. By the time Barack Obama ran in 2008, there were 41 — 40 in the House and Obama himself in the Senate. As we saw in Chapter 2, a late-20th-century innovation was the devising by state governments of congressional districts — electoral districts in which members of the House of Representatives are elected — in which a majority of residents are from a specific racial minority group. These are the so-called 'majority-minority districts'. The adoption in the early 1990s of such strategies for the drawing of electoral boundaries resulted in a significant increase in House members from minority groups in the 1992 congressional elections — the first to be fought under the new boundaries. The 1990s also saw a significant increase in the number of Hispanic members of Congress — from nine in 1992 to 27 by January 2009, including two Hispanic senators.

When the Democrats took over control of the House of Representatives in January 2007, James Clyburn of South Carolina became the first African-American member of Congress to hold a senior leadership post when he was elected as Majority Whip. African-Americans also got to take five House committee chairmanships including John Conyers at Judiciary and Charles Rangel at Ways and Means. This is all a far cry from the early 1970s when Charles Rangel was among the first black members to arrive in Congress. It was in 1971 that Rangel formed the Congressional Black Caucus, still in existence today. But with the Republicans regaining the majority in the House in January 2011, the chairmanships reverted to being all white.

Barack Obama was only the third black person to be elected to the United States Senate — Edward Brooke, a Republican from Massachusetts (1967–79), and Carol Moseley-Braun, a Democrat who held the same Illinois seat as Obama (1993–99), being the first two. Hawaii has elected five Asian-Americans to the Senate including Mazie Hirono elected in 2012. Sam Hayakawa, a Republican from California (1977–83), was the only Asian-American to be elected from the 48 contiguous states. There are currently three Hispanic senators — Democrat Robert Menendez of New Jersey and Republicans Marco Rubio of Florida and Ted Cruz of Texas. New Mexico has elected three Hispanics to the Senate in its history, including Democrat Joseph Montoya who, having served 12 years, was defeated for a third term in 1976. Ben Nighthorse Campbell of Colorado, a member of the Northern Cheyenne tribe, was the most recent Native American-Indian senator. First elected as a Democrat in 1992, Campbell switched parties to become a Republican in 1995 and was re-elected as a Republican in 1998. He retired in 2004 after two terms. At the start of the 113th Congress (2013–14), the House of Representatives included 41 African-American members, 31 Hispanics and 11 Asian-Americans.

Minorities and presidential elections

African-African voters were slow to join the body of the active electorate. Although they had legally been granted the vote after the Civil War, many southern states came up with various devices — literacy tests, the poll tax — to keep blacks from voting. It was not until the 1960s that these practices began to become a thing of the past. Since the 1930s, black people — when they had voted — had voted for the Democratic Party as part of the Roosevelt Coalition. It was FDR's Democratic administration that had tried to address the unemployment which had so blighted them as a result of the great depression of the 1930s and they continued to be a solid Democrat voting bloc.

When black people started to emerge as candidates for federal and state office, they almost always stood as candidates for the Democratic Party. In 1972, Shirley Chisholm became the first major party African-American candidate for the presidency when she competed in that year's primaries. She won 152 delegates to the 1972 Democratic National Convention. Twelve years passed before another black candidate put himself forward for the Democratic presidential nomination — Jesse Jackson in 1984. Jackson won over 3 million votes in the Democratic primaries, finishing third in the number of votes cast behind former Vice-President Walter Mondale (the eventual nominee) and Senator Gary Hart. In April of that year, Jackson became the first African-American candidate to win a major party presidential primary when he won the primary in Washington DC with 67% of the vote. He followed this with victories in Louisiana, South Carolina, Virginia and Mississippi.

Jackson ran again in 1988 and did even better, winning primaries in Alabama, Georgia, Louisiana, Mississippi, Virginia and Washington DC as well as caucuses in Alaska, South Carolina, Michigan, Delaware and Vermont. His most impressive moment came in late March when he won the Michigan caucuses with 55% of the vote and was briefly ahead of all the other major candidates — Michael Dukakis, Dick Gephardt and Al Gore — in the number of pledged delegates. His signature phrase of 'Keep Hope Alive' echoed throughout his speech at the Democratic National Convention in Atlanta, Georgia, in July:

> Wherever you are tonight, you can make it. Suffering breeds character, character breeds faith, in the end faith will not disappoint. You must not surrender. America will get better and better. Keep hope alive. Keep hope alive. Keep hope alive, for tomorrow and beyond.

In that 1988 race, Jackson had frequently remarked that 'hands that picked cotton can now pick a president'. Twenty years later, in 2008, they did just that. Table 8.2 shows that Barack Obama's candidacy increased African-American voting for the Democrats even from the very high numbers seen in the previous four elections: 95% of African-Americans voted for the Obama–Biden ticket, a 7-percentage-point increase on 2004.

Racial and ethnic minorities have traditionally given high levels of support in presidential elections to the Democratic Party. The black vote has been solidly Democrat for decades. What some recent elections have shown is the fluidity of the Hispanic vote (see Table 8.3). And with Hispanics becoming an increasing proportion of the electorate in future years, both parties will continue to battle for their allegiance. Another reason for the importance of the Hispanic vote is that Hispanics are highly significant in such

Table 8.2 Presidential elections and vote by African-Americans: 1992–2012 (%)

	1992	1996	2000	2004	2008	2012
Democrat	83	84	90	88	95	93
Republican	11	12	8	11	4	6

Table 8.3 Presidential elections and vote by Hispanics: 1988–2012 (%)

	1992	1996	2000	2004	2008	2012
Democrat	62	73	67	57	67	71
Republican	24	20	31	43	31	27

swing states as Florida and New Mexico. Having made significant inroads into the Hispanic vote in both 2000 and 2004, increasing their share of the vote by 23 percentage points over those two elections, the Republican Party lost out on the Hispanic vote in 2008 and 2012 with support falling by 12 percentage points in 2008 and a further 4 points in 2012. Clearly the Republicans' strong stance on illegal immigration, and maybe also the fact that they no longer had a presidential candidate who was comfortable to campaign in Spanish, were the major factors.

Research also shows that racial minority voters often have different policy priorities to white voters. In 2004, the most important issue for white voters was terrorism (25%) followed by Iraq (23%). But for both black and Hispanic voters, the most important issue was the economy — the top issue for 33% of black people and 22% of Hispanics. This reflected the difference in the feel-good factor in the different communities. Whereas among white voters 35% of voters felt they were better off than in 2000, only 19% of black voters and 30% of Hispanic voters felt better off.

Minorities and the executive

When Lyndon Johnson appointed Robert Weaver as secretary of the new department of Housing and Urban Development (HUD) in 1966, Weaver became the first African-American to head a federal executive department and thus to be a member of the president's cabinet. Since Weaver's appointment to HUD in 1966, 16 other African-Americans have headed an executive department, with Patricia Roberts Harris holding two posts — HUD and Health and Human Services (HHS) consecutively (see Table 8.4).

The table also shows, however, that the appointment of African-Americans to the president's cabinet has tended to be in second-tier departments such as HUD, HHS and Transportation — these three departments alone counting for half of the appointments. It was not until 2001 that an African-American was appointed to one of the top-tier departments — State, Treasury, Defense, Justice — when Colin Powell was appointed Secretary of State by George W. Bush. He was then succeeded by another African-American, Condoleezza Rice. The most African-Americans in the cabinet at any one time was four — between 1993 and 1996 in Bill Clinton's first term. It was Clinton who had promised during his election campaign to appoint a cabinet that 'looked like America'.

The most racially diverse cabinet to date was the one Barack Obama appointed in January 2009. It included African-American Eric Holder (Justice), two Hispanics — Ken Salazar (Interior) and Hilda Solis (Labor) — as well as two Chinese-Americans — Steven Chu (Energy) and Gary Locke (Commerce) — plus Japanese-American Eric Shinseki (Veterans Affairs) and Lebanese-American Ray LaHood (Transportation). But if African-Americans thought that the election of 'one of us' to the Oval Office in 2008 would result in a number of black cabinet members, they were to be disappointed. Eric Holder was the only African-American to head up an executive department during Obama's first term — no different from the days of Ronald Reagan when Sam Pierce was the only black amongst the departmental heads.

Table 8.4 African-American heads of executive departments (cabinet officers)

Cabinet officers	Department	President	Dates
Robert Weaver	HUD	Johnson	1966–68
William Coleman	Transportation	Ford	1975–77
Patricia Roberts Harris	HUD	Carter	1977–79
Patricia Roberts Harris	HHS	Carter	1979–81
Samuel Pierce	HUD	Reagan	1981–89
Louis Sullivan	HHS	G. H. W. Bush	1989–93
Mike Espy	Agriculture	Clinton	1993–95
Ron Brown	Commerce	Clinton	1993–96
Hazel O'Leary	Energy	Clinton	1993–97
Jesse Brown	Veterans Affairs	Clinton	1993–98
Alexis Herman	Labor	Clinton	1997–2001
Rodney Slater	Transportation	Clinton	1997–2001
Togo West	Veterans Affairs	Clinton	1998–2000
Colin Powell	State	G. W. Bush	2001–05
Rod Paige	Education	G. W. Bush	2001–05
Alphonso Jackson	HUD	G. W. Bush	2004–08
Condoleezza Rice	State	G. W. Bush	2005–09
Eric Holder	Justice	Obama	2009–

Meanwhile, the federal civil service as a whole has become less white during the past two decades. In 1990, 72.7% of the federal civil service were white; by 2010 this had fallen to 65.4% (see Table 8.5). The most significant increase had been among Hispanics: up from 5.4% in 1990 to 7.9% in 2010. But in the Senior Pay Level positions — roughly the top 1% — 83% were white in 2010, just over 7% black and under 4% Hispanic or Latino. In October 2007, a bill was introduced into the House of Representatives, namely the Senior Executive Service Diversity Assurance Act, to 'ensure that, in seeking to achieve a Senior Executive Service reflective of the Nation's diversity, recruitment is from qualified individuals from appropriate sources'. In order to oversee this, the legislation established a Senior Executive Service Resource Office.

Minorities and the judiciary

Not only did President Johnson appoint the first black member of the cabinet, he also appointed the first black member of the US Supreme Court — Thurgood Marshall — in 1967. Marshall, a noted liberal, remained on the Court until his retirement in 1991 when he was replaced by another black judge, Clarence Thomas. Thomas, in contrast, is a solid conservative. In 1986, Antonin Scalia became the first Italian-American to sit on the Supreme Court. In 2006, he was joined by fellow Italian-American Samuel Alito.

Table 8.5 Federal civil service employees, by race: 1990–2010 (%)

Ethnic group	1990	1995	2000	2006	2010
White	72.7	71.1	69.8	67.9	65.4
Black	16.6	16.7	17.0	17.2	17.9
Hispanic	5.4	5.9	6.6	7.5	7.9

Table 8.6 Presidential appointments to the federal courts by race (%)

President	White	Black	Hispanic	Asian
Johnson	93.8	4.3	1.8	–
Nixon	95.9	2.6	0.8	0.4
Ford	90.6	4.6	1.5	3.1
Carter	78.6	14.3	6.2	0.7
Reagan	93.4	1.9	4.0	0.5
George H. W. Bush	89.1	6.4	4.3	–
Clinton	75.4	16.6	6.3	1.4
George W. Bush	82.7	7.1	9.2	1.0
Obama (to July 2012)	64.0	18.0	12.0	7.0

The Court's membership became even more racially diverse in 2009 when Sonia Sotomayor — the Court's first Hispanic justice — was appointed by President Obama.

Research by the American Bar Association following the 2000 census found that 83% of all judges in the United States were white (compared with 75% of the population as a whole), with just short of 9% black and 4.5% Hispanic. The imbalance was even more evident when it came to lawyers, with 89% of all lawyers being white and only 4% black and 3% Hispanic.

As Table 8.6 shows, it was President Carter (1977–81) who made a significant breakthrough in terms of appointing racial minorities to the federal judiciary, with over 20% of his nominees being from racial minorities. And what Jimmy Carter began, Bill Clinton (1993–2001) continued. Right from the start, Bill Clinton had tried to make overtures to the black community. On the morning of his inauguration in January 1993, the Clintons had gone to church, not as tradition had it to St John's Episcopal Church in Lafayette Square, opposite the White House, but to the Metropolitan African Methodist Episcopal Church near Dupont Circle, one of the most influential black churches in the nation's capital. On the same day, Maya Angelou, one of the country's premier black poets, read a poem at the inauguration. By the time he left office, Clinton had appointed 47% of all serving federal judges, and nearly a fifth of those were black. Whilst over 80% of George W. Bush's judicial nominees were white, he did continue the increase in Hispanic judges during his 8-year tenure. But Barack Obama has very much continued where Jimmy Carter and Bill Clinton left off. Up to July 2012 the website **www.judicialnominations.org** reported that Obama's judicial nominees were 18% black, 12% Hispanic and 7% Asian, making them the most diverse appointments thus far.

Box 8.2 'Quiet political shifts as more blacks are elected', by Racel L. Swans

BROOKLINE, New Hampshire.

Melanie Levesque grabbed the campaign signs from her Mercedes SUV and plunged into the white crowd at the fairgrounds here. The cows were lowing, the cider presses churning and Mrs Levesque, a black state legislator, was hunting for votes and a place in history. Blacks account for less than 1% of the population in this small suburban district near the New Hampshire–Massachusetts border. But none of that seemed to matter to the people here. And next month, Mrs Levesque is expected to win re-election to her seat in the New Hampshire House of Representatives, where she represents one of the whitest districts in one of the whitest states in the nation. She is part of a new generation of black elected officials who are wooing white voters and winning local elections in predominantly white districts across the country.

Political analysts say such electoral gains are quietly changing the political landscape, increasing the number of black lawmakers adept at crossing colour lines as well as the ranks of white voters who are familiar, and increasingly comfortable, with black political leadership.

Over the last 10 years, about 200 black politicians have won positions in legislatures and city halls in states like New Hampshire, Iowa, Kentucky, Minnesota, Missouri, North Carolina and Tennessee. In 2007, about 30% of the nation's 622 black state legislators represented predominantly white districts, up from 16% in 2001, according to data collected by the Joint Center for Political and Economic Studies, a research group based in Washington DC that has kept statistics on black elected officials for nearly 40 years. 'There's a fair amount of experience out there among white voters now, and that has lessened the fears about black candidates,' said Dr Zoltan Hajnal, a political scientist at the University of California, San Diego, whose book about white experiences with black mayors, *Changing White Attitudes Toward Black Political Leadership*, was published in 2007 by Cambridge University Press.

Here in New Hampshire, white voters peppered Mrs Levesque with questions about property taxes, repairs to the police station and local zoning rules. No one mentioned race. 'It's a wonderful feeling,' said Mrs Levesque, 51, who in 2006 was the first African-American to be elected to represent her legislative district. 'I just feel like I'm a real part of my community.'

In the 1980s, few black state legislators represented predominantly white districts. By 2001, that number stood at 92 and by 2007, it was 189. But such change, however, does not always come easily. In Tennessee, state Representative Nathan Vaughn, first elected in 2002 from a district that is 97% white, remembers extending his hand to a white man during one of his campaigns. Mr Vaughn said the man refused to take it, uttering a racial epithet and saying he would never vote for a black man.

Source: *New York Times*, 14 October 2008

Minorities and state and local government

Much the same pattern was emerging in state and local government. In 1990, Douglas Wilder became the first African-American to be elected as a state governor when he was elected Governor of Virginia. Subsequent black state governors have been Deval Patrick of Massachusetts, who was elected in 2006, and David Paterson of New York, who became governor in 2008 on the resignation of his predecessor Elliot Spitzer.

Table 8.7 African-American representation in state legislatures in those states with the highest percentage of African-American residents (%), 2012

State	African-American % of state population	African-American % of state legislature
Mississippi	37	21
Louisiana	32	20
Georgia	30	21
Maryland	29	17
South Carolina	28	17
Alabama	26	23
North Carolina	22	18
Delaware	21	8

In 2012, African-Americans made up 8% of state legislators with significant variations in levels of representation across the 50 states. The legislatures of nine states had no African-American members at all — Hawaii, Idaho, Maine, Montana, New Hampshire, North Dakota, South Dakota, Utah and Wyoming. But in only one of these states — Hawaii with 3.1% — did African-Americans make up more than 1% of the population. As Table 8.7 shows, the states with the highest proportion of African-Americans are generally those states with the highest percentage of African-American state legislators, although African-Americans are still significantly under-represented in the state legislatures of such states as Maryland and Delaware.

In 1967, Carl Stokes became the first black mayor of a major city when he was elected Mayor of Cleveland. The number of black mayors rose from 81 in 1970 to 480 by 2000. In 2011, the city of Jacksonville, Florida, elected Alvin Brown as its first black mayor and in 2012 Svante Myrick became the first black mayor of Ithaca, New York.

The protection of the rights and liberties of racial and ethnic minorities

By the Supreme Court

To which institutions of government might racial and ethnic minorities look for the protection of their rights and liberties? The simple answer is that all three branches of the federal government — as well as state governments — have a role to play. However, as has been seen in Chapter 7, in a nation with a written Constitution, which itself includes a Bill of Rights, it is the courts — and in the end the Supreme Court — that is likely to play the most significant role in the protection of rights and liberties.

Most of the Constitution dates from the 18th and 19th centuries and was written at a time when the understanding and public expectations of civil rights and liberties were very different from what they are today. It is the role of the Supreme Court, using its power of judicial review, to interpret the meaning of that document in today's society. The Supreme Court pronounces on what those fundamental rights and liberties enshrined in the Bill of Rights in 1791 mean in practice today. The history of the Supreme Court contains numerous landmark decisions that have had the effect of deciding the extent to which the rights and liberties of racial and ethnic minorities are to be protected. As most have been discussed earlier, we need only a brief summary here.

As was seen in the previous chapter, the Supreme Court began to move the nation towards a more integrated society beginning with the landmark decisions of *Brown v. Board of Education of Topeka* (1954) and *Swann v. Charlotte-Mecklenburg Board of Education* (1971). Then in 1978, in the case of *Regents of the University of California v. Bakke*, the Supreme Court ruled that the University of California medical school could not use an explicit numerical quota in admitting students from racial minorities, but that it could 'take race into account'. But subsequent decisions of the Court have made it far from clear what is and what is not constitutional.

As we also saw in Chapter 7, in *Adarand Constructors v. Peña* (1995), the Court struck down a federal government affirmative action programme on the employment of minority workers, stating that in order to survive a court challenge, such programmes must be 'narrowly tailored measures that further compelling governmental interests'. The Court made a further sortie into this whole area in the two related cases of *Gratz v. Bollinger* and *Grutter v. Bollinger* in 2003. In these opinions, the Court struck down one affirmative action programme but upheld the other. Both cases centred on the admissions procedures at the University of Michigan. In *Gratz*, an affirmative action-based admissions programme for undergraduates was struck down as too 'mechanistic', but in *Grutter*, an affirmative action-based admissions programme for the university's Law School was upheld as it was more 'individualised'.

Then in 2007, in cases involving affirmative action programmes in public (i.e. state-run) schools in Washington State and Kentucky, the Supreme Court struck down the programmes in both states because they assigned students to schools solely for the purpose of achieving racial balance.

By Congress

Although the Supreme Court has often taken the lead in the protection of civil rights and liberties, Congress has frequently been involved as well. This was especially true during the 40-year period between 1955 and 1994, when the Democratic Party controlled the House of Representatives and, with the exception of 6 years (1981–86), the Senate as well. Since the formation of the so-called 'New Deal Coalition' in the 1930s, the Democrats have been the party committed to passing laws to protect the rights of minorities.

As we have already seen, it was the Supreme Court in its 1954 *Brown v. Board of Education of Topeka* decision which gave momentum to black civil rights in the 20th century. Congress was not far behind, passing a raft of civil rights laws during the next four decades.

In 1957, Congress passed a law creating the Civil Rights Commission and making it a federal crime to try to prevent a person from voting in a federal election. The really significant civil rights legislation was passed in 1964 and 1965, following a number of important political developments concerning black civil rights in a number of southern states. These included the bus boycott by blacks in Montgomery, Alabama, the so-called 'freedom rides' in which blacks deliberately travelled in the 'whites only' sections of buses, and the events surrounding the attempt by James Meredith — a black student — to gain admission to an all-white university in Mississippi.

The passage of the 1964 Civil Rights Act was Congress's most far-reaching attempt to improve the civil rights of African-Americans. It dealt with five areas of disadvantage and discrimination: voting, public accommodations, schools, employment and the allocation of federal funds. In voting, it made it more difficult for states to use such ploys as literacy tests and the payment of a poll tax to bar African-Americans from voting. It barred discrimination in public accommodations, whether rooms in hotels or tables in restaurants. It authorised the federal government to take legal action against school districts that failed to desegregate their schools. It established the right to equality of opportunity in employment, for any race or colour. It provided for the withholding of federal government funds from programmes that were administered by state or local governments in a discriminatory fashion. The Senate took 83 days to debate the bill — the longest time in congressional history. The year 1964 also saw the ratification of the 24th Amendment (see Box 8.3).

The following year, Congress passed another major piece of civil rights legislation — the Voting Rights Act (1965). This Act ended the use of literacy and other tests to debar African-American voters and introduced federal officials to register voters. The Act had a profound effect on national elections, as well as elections held in the South, and led not only to thousands of minority voters being added to the electoral registers, but also to the election of an increasing number of office-holders from minority groups.

A third major piece of legislation was the Civil Rights Act of 1968, which dealt principally with discrimination in housing. It banned discrimination, based on race, religion or national origin, in the advertising, financing, sale or rental of houses. It was extended to discrimination on the basis of gender in 1974 and physical handicap in 1988.

In the 1991 Civil Rights Act, Congress effectively overturned the Supreme Court's ruling in *Patterson v. McLean Credit Union*, which limited an employee's ability to sue

Box 8.3 The 24th Amendment

Section 1. The right of citizens of the United States to vote in any primary or other election for President or Vice President, for electors for President or Vice President, or for Senator or Representative in Congress, shall not be denied or abridged by the United States or any State by reason of failure to pay any poll tax or other tax.

Section 2. The Congress shall have the power to enforce this article by appropriate legislation.

for damages if subject to racial harassment at the workplace. The passage of the Act followed a two-year struggle between Republican President George H. W. Bush and the Democrat-controlled Congress. Bush had labelled the first version of the Act a 'quota' bill and had vetoed it in 1990.

By the president

Presidents can play an important role in the protection of rights and liberties in a number of ways. First, through their role as commander-in-chief, they can use troops to enforce legislation as well as judgements of the Supreme Court. President Eisenhower sent federal troops to Little Rock, Arkansas, in 1957 to give weight to the Supreme Court's order to desegregate schools.

Second, presidents can use the office as what Theodore Roosevelt called a 'bully pulpit' — to converse with the American people about important issues such as the rights and freedoms of Americans. Both Kennedy and Johnson used the presidential office to try to lead the country in the direction of civil rights reform during the 1960s. President Clinton conducted a public debate about the role of affirmative action programmes in the USA in the mid-1990s. Presidents can lend their clear and unequivocal support to civil rights legislation being debated in Congress. This was seen most remarkably during 1964 and 1965 with President Johnson's wholehearted support for the civil rights acts of those years. In 2003, President George W. Bush publicly praised the Supreme Court for its decision in *Gratz v. Bollinger*, describing it as 'a careful balance between the goal of campus diversity and the fundamental principle of equal treatment under the law'.

Equally, presidents can use their political clout against developments in rights and freedoms to which they are opposed. President Nixon came out clearly in opposition to the 'busing' decision by the Supreme Court in *Swann v. Charlotte-Mecklenburg Board of Education*. President Reagan opposed the ratification of the Equal Rights Amendment.

Presidents can affect federal government policies on civil rights through the appointments that they make to such groups as the Civil Rights Commission and the Equal Employment Opportunity Commission. In 1983, President Reagan sought to replace members of the Civil Rights Commission who had been openly critical of his administration's civil rights policies. Appointments that the president makes to all federal courts — and especially the United States Supreme Court — affect the way in which civil rights and liberties may, or may not, be protected. The extent to which a president appoints people from a diversity of backgrounds sends clear signals too. President Nixon's cabinet was described as '12 grey-haired guys named George'. President Clinton, on the other hand, said he wanted a cabinet that 'looked like America'.

Since 2008, the Gallup polling organisation has tried to assess Americans' view of the effect of having a black president. On Election Day 2008, 33% of Americans said they thought that Obama's election was 'the most important advance for blacks in the past 100 years'. But by October 2009 that figure had fallen to 20% and by August 2011 to just 15%. Amongst blacks, the figure had fallen from 44% in 2009 to 34% in 2011. When asked whether or not Obama's election had made race relations in the USA better or worse, a majority of respondents thought that it had made no difference at all. This is perhaps largely because, just as Obama did not campaign as a 'black candidate' in 2008, he has not governed as a 'black president'. Therefore neither his election nor his presidency has significantly changed the perception of race in America, at least not in the short term.

Activity

Using an internet search engine, the websites **www.scotusblog.com** and **www.affirmativeaction.org** plus any other resources available to you, research the Supreme Court decision in *Fisher v. University of Texas* (2013). The case was brought by a white student, Abigail Fisher, who alleged that the university's admissions policy, based on the principle of affirmative action, violated her constitutional right of equality on the basis of race. Both the District and Appeal courts of the federal government found in favour of the university. But what did the Supreme Court decide and what are the implications of its decision for the future of affirmative action? It is worth noting that Justice Elena Kagan did not participate in the decision, having been previously involved with the case whilst serving as US solicitor general. Hence only 8 justices participated.

Exam focus

Short-answer questions

1 What are the arguments for and against affirmative action?
2 Has affirmative action in the USA been a success?
3 What is black nationalism and how influential is it still in the USA?
4 How successful has the Supreme Court been at protecting the rights of racial minorities?

Essay questions

1 Assess the impact that the three branches of the federal government have each had on the protection of the rights of ethnic and racial minorities.
2 Discuss the arguments for and against affirmative action.
3 Evaluate the claim that 'affirmative action has been good for America'.
4 'Racial equality in the USA remains a distant dream.' Discuss.
5 How effectively have the civil rights and liberties of ethnic and racial minorities been protected?
6 To what extent is race an important issue in US politics?

Further reading

Johnson, J. W. and Green, R. P., *Affirmative Action*, Greenwood Press, 2009.
Remnick, D., *The Bridge: The Life and Rise of Barack Obama*, Picador, 2010.
Storey, W., 'Affirmative action evaluated', *Politics Review*, Vol. 20, No. 3, February 2011.

Appendix I

Presidents of the USA

1	George Washington	1789–97	(F)
2	John Adams	1797–1801	(F)
3	Thomas Jefferson	1801–09	(D-R)
4	James Madison	1809–17	(D-R)
5	James Monroe	1817–25	(D-R)
6	John Quincy Adams	1825–29	(D-R)
7	Andrew Jackson	1829–37	(D)
8	Martin Van Buren	1837–41	(D)
9	William Harrison	1841	(W)
10	John Tyler	1841–45	(W)
11	James Polk	1845–49	(D)
12	Zachary Taylor	1849–50	(W)
13	Millard Fillmore	1850–53	(W)
14	Franklin Pierce	1853–57	(D)
15	James Buchanan	1857–61	(D)
16	Abraham Lincoln	1861–65	(R)
17	Andrew Johnson	1865–69	(D)
18	Ulysses Grant	1869–77	(R)
19	Rutherford Hayes	1877–81	(R)
20	James Garfield	1881	(R)
21	Chester Arthur	1881–85	(R)
22	Grover Cleveland	1885–89	(D)
23	Benjamin Harrison	1889–93	(R)
24	Grover Cleveland	1893–97	(D)
25	William McKinley	1897–1901	(R)
26	Theodore Roosevelt	1901–09	(R)
27	William Taft	1909–13	(R)
28	Woodrow Wilson	1913–21	(D)
29	Warren Harding	1921–23	(R)
30	Calvin Coolidge	1923–29	(R)
31	Herbert Hoover	1929–33	(R)
32	Franklin Roosevelt	1933–45	(D)
33	Harry Truman	1945–53	(D)
34	Dwight Eisenhower	1953–61	(R)
35	John Kennedy	1961–63	(D)
36	Lyndon Johnson	1963–69	(D)
37	Richard Nixon	1969–74	(R)
38	Gerald Ford	1974–77	(R)
39	Jimmy Carter	1977–81	(D)
40	Ronald Reagan	1981–89	(R)
41	George H. W. Bush	1989–93	(R)
42	Bill Clinton	1993–2001	(D)
43	George W. Bush	2001–09	(R)
44	Barack Obama	2009–	(D)

Appendix II

The Constitution of the USA

We the People of the United States, in Order to form a more perfect Union, establish Justice, insure domestic Tranquility, provide for the common defence, promote the general Welfare, and secure the Blessings of Liberty to ourselves and our Posterity, do ordain and establish this Constitution for the United States of America.

Article I

Section 1

All legislative Powers herein granted shall be vested in a Congress of the United States, which shall consist of a Senate and House of Representatives.

Section 2

The House of Representatives shall be composed of Members chosen every second Year by the People of the several States, and the Electors in each State shall have the Qualifications requisite for Electors of the most numerous Branch of the State Legislature.

No Person shall be a Representative who shall not have attained to the Age of twenty five Years, and been seven Years a Citizen of the United States, and who shall not, when elected, be an Inhabitant of that State in which he shall be chosen.

Representatives and direct Taxes shall be apportioned among the several States which may be included within this Union, according to their respective Numbers, which shall be determined by adding to the whole Number of free Persons, including those bound to Service for a Term of Years, and excluding Indians not taxed, three fifths of all other Persons.

The actual Enumeration shall be made within three Years after the first Meeting of the Congress of the United States, and within every subsequent Term of ten Years, in such Manner as they shall by Law direct. The Number of Representatives shall not exceed one for every thirty Thousand, but each State shall have at Least one Representative; and until such enumeration shall be made, the State of New Hampshire shall be entitled to chuse three, Massachusetts eight, Rhode Island and Providence Plantations one, Connecticut five, New York six, New Jersey four, Pennsylvania eight, Delaware one, Maryland six, Virginia ten, North Carolina five, South Carolina five and Georgia three.

When vacancies happen in the Representation from any State, the Executive Authority thereof shall issue Writs of Election to fill such Vacancies.

The House of Representatives shall chuse their Speaker and other Officers; and shall have the sole Power of Impeachment.

Section 3

The Senate of the United States shall be composed of two Senators from each State, chosen by the Legislature thereof, for six Years; and each Senator shall have one Vote.

Immediately after they shall be assembled in Consequence of the first Election, they shall be divided as equally as may be into three Classes. The Seats of the Senators of the first Class shall be vacated at the Expiration of the second Year, of the second Class at the Expiration of the fourth Year, and of the third Class at the Expiration of the sixth Year, so that one third may be chosen every second Year; and if Vacancies happen by Resignation, or otherwise, during the Recess of the Legislature of any State, the Executive thereof may make temporary Appointments until the next Meeting of the Legislature, which shall then fill such Vacancies.

No person shall be a Senator who shall not have attained to the Age of thirty Years, and been nine Years a Citizen of the United States, and who shall not, when elected, be an Inhabitant of that State for which he shall be chosen.

The Vice President of the United States shall be President of the Senate, but shall have no Vote, unless they be equally divided.

The Senate shall chuse their other Officers, and also a President pro tempore, in the absence of the Vice President, or when he shall exercise the Office of President of the United States.

The Senate shall have the sole Power to try all Impeachments. When sitting for that Purpose, they shall be on Oath or Affirmation. When the President of the United States is tried, the Chief Justice shall preside: And no Person shall be convicted without the Concurrence of two thirds of the Members present.

Judgment in Cases of Impeachment shall not extend further than to removal from Office, and disqualification to hold and enjoy any Office of honor, Trust or Profit under the United States: but the Party convicted shall nevertheless be liable and subject to Indictment, Trial, Judgment and Punishment, according to Law.

Section 4

The Times, Places and Manner of holding Elections for Senators and Representatives, shall be prescribed in each State by the Legislature thereof; but the Congress may at any time by Law make or alter such Regulations, except as to the Place of Chusing Senators.

The Congress shall assemble at least once in every Year, and such Meeting shall be on the first Monday in December, unless they shall by Law appoint a different Day.

Section 5

Each House shall be the Judge of the Elections, Returns and Qualifications of its own Members, and a Majority of each shall constitute a Quorum to do Business; but a smaller number may adjourn from day to day, and may be authorized to compel the Attendance of absent Members, in such Manner, and under such Penalties as each House may provide.

Each House may determine the Rules of its Proceedings, punish its Members for disorderly Behavior, and, with the Concurrence of two thirds, expel a Member.

Each House shall keep a Journal of its Proceedings, and from time to time publish the same, excepting such Parts as may in their Judgment require Secrecy; and the Yeas and Nays of the Members of either House on any question shall, at the Desire of one fifth of those Present, be entered on the Journal.

Neither House, during the Session of Congress, shall, without the Consent of the other, adjourn for more than three days, nor to any other Place than that in which the two Houses shall be sitting.

Section 6

The Senators and Representatives shall receive a Compensation for their Services, to be ascertained by Law, and paid out of the Treasury of the United States. They shall in all Cases, except Treason, Felony and Breach of the Peace, be privileged from Arrest during their Attendance at the Session of their respective Houses, and in going to and returning from the same; and for any Speech or Debate in either House, they shall not be questioned in any other Place.

No Senator or Representative shall, during the Time for which he was elected, be appointed to any civil Office under the Authority of the United States which shall have been created, or the Emoluments whereof shall have been increased during such time; and no Person holding any Office under the United States, shall be a Member of either House during his Continuance in Office.

Section 7

All bills for raising Revenue shall originate in the House of Representatives; but the Senate may propose or concur with Amendments as on other Bills.

Every Bill which shall have passed the House of Representatives and the Senate, shall, before it become a Law, be presented to the President of the United States; If he approve he shall sign it, but if not he shall return it, with his Objections to that House in which it shall have originated, who shall enter the Objections at large on their Journal, and proceed to reconsider it. If after such Reconsideration two thirds of that House shall agree to pass the Bill, it shall be sent, together with the Objections, to the other House, by which it shall likewise be reconsidered, and if approved by two thirds of that House, it shall become a Law. But in all such Cases the Votes of both Houses shall be determined by Yeas and Nays, and the Names of the Persons voting for and against the Bill shall be entered on the Journal of each House respectively. If any Bill shall not be returned by the President within ten Days (Sundays excepted) after it shall have been presented to him, the Same shall be a Law, in like Manner as if he had signed it, unless the Congress by their Adjournment prevent its Return, in which Case it shall not be a Law.

Every Order, Resolution, or Vote to which the Concurrence of the Senate and House of Representatives may be necessary (except on a question of Adjournment) shall be presented to the President of the United States; and before the Same shall take Effect, shall be approved by him, or being disapproved by him, shall be repassed by two thirds of the Senate and House of Representatives, according to the Rules and Limitations prescribed in the Case of a Bill.

Section 8

The Congress shall have Power To lay and collect Taxes, Duties, Imposts and Excises, to pay the Debts and provide for the common Defence and general Welfare of the United States; but all Dutics, Imposts and Excises shall be uniform throughout the United States;

➤ To borrow money on the credit of the United States;

➤ To regulate Commerce with foreign Nations, and among the several States, and with the Indian Tribes;

➤ To establish an uniform Rule of Naturalization, and uniform Laws on the subject of Bankruptcies throughout the United States;

➤ To coin Money, regulate the Value thereof, and of foreign Coin, and fix the Standard of Weights and Measures;

➤ To provide for the Punishment of counterfeiting the Securities and current Coin of the United States;

➤ To establish Post Offices and Post Roads;

➤ To promote the Progress of Science and useful Arts, by securing for limited Times to Authors and Inventors the exclusive Right to their respective Writings and Discoveries;

➤ To constitute Tribunals inferior to the supreme Court;

➤ To define and punish Piracies and Felonies committed on the high Seas, and Offenses against the Law of Nations;

➤ To declare War, grant Letters of Marque and Reprisal, and make Rules concerning Captures on Land and Water;

➤ To raise and support Armies, but no Appropriation of Money to that Use shall be for a longer Term than two Years;

➤ To provide and maintain a Navy;

➤ To make Rules for the Government and Regulation of the land and naval Forces;

➤ To provide for calling forth the Militia to execute the Laws of the Union, suppress Insurrections and repel Invasions;

➤ To provide for organizing, arming, and disciplining the Militia, and for governing such Part of them as may be employed in the Service of the United States, reserving to the States respectively, the Appointment of the Officers, and the Authority of training the Militia according to the discipline prescribed by Congress;

➤ To exercise exclusive Legislation in all Cases whatsoever, over such District (not exceeding ten Miles square) as may, by Cession of particular States, and the acceptance of Congress, become the Seat of the Government of the United States, and to exercise like Authority over all Places purchased by the Consent of the Legislature of the State in which the Same shall be, for the Erection of Forts, Magazines, Arsenals, dock-Yards, and other needful Buildings; And

➤ To make all Laws which shall be necessary and proper for carrying into Execution the foregoing Powers, and all other Powers vested by this Constitution in the Government of the United States, or in any Department or Officer thereof.

Section 9

The Migration or Importation of such Persons as any of the States now existing shall think proper to admit, shall not be prohibited by the Congress prior to the Year one thousand eight hundred and eight, but a tax or duty may be imposed on such Importation, not exceeding ten dollars for each Person.

The privilege of the Writ of Habeas Corpus shall not be suspended, unless when in Cases of Rebellion or Invasion the public Safety may require it.

No Bill of Attainder or ex post facto Law shall be passed.

No capitation, or other direct, Tax shall be laid, unless in Proportion to the Census or Enumeration herein before directed to be taken.

No Tax or Duty shall be laid on Articles exported from any State.

No Preference shall be given by any Regulation of Commerce or Revenue to the Ports of one State over those of another: nor shall Vessels bound to, or from, one State, be obliged to enter, clear, or pay Duties in another.

No Money shall be drawn from the Treasury, but in Consequence of Appropriations made by Law; and a regular Statement and Account of the Receipts and Expenditures of all public Money shall be published from time to time.

No Title of Nobility shall be granted by the United States: And no Person holding any Office of Profit or Trust under them, shall, without the Consent of the Congress, accept of any present, Emolument, Office, or Title, of any kind whatever, from any King, Prince or foreign State.

Section 10

No State shall enter into any Treaty, Alliance, or Confederation; grant Letters of Marque and Reprisal; coin Money; emit Bills of Credit; make any Thing but gold and silver Coin a Tender in Payment of Debts; pass any Bill of Attainder, ex post facto Law, or Law impairing the Obligation of Contracts, or grant any Title of Nobility.

No State shall, without the Consent of the Congress, lay any Imposts or Duties on Imports or Exports, except what may be absolutely necessary for executing its inspection Laws: and the net Produce of all Duties and Imposts, laid by any State on Imports or Exports, shall be for the Use of the Treasury of the United States; and all such Laws shall be subject to the Revision and Controul of the Congress.

No State shall, without the Consent of Congress, lay any duty of Tonnage, keep Troops, or Ships of War in time of Peace, enter into any Agreement or Compact with another State, or with a foreign Power, or engage in War, unless actually invaded, or in such imminent Danger as will not admit of delay.

Article II

Section 1

The executive Power shall be vested in a President of the United States of America. He shall hold his Office during the Term of four Years, and, together with the Vice-President chosen for the same Term, be elected, as follows: Each State shall appoint, in such Manner as the Legislature thereof may direct, a Number of Electors, equal to the whole Number of Senators and Representatives to which the State may be entitled in the Congress: but no Senator or Representative, or Person holding an Office of Trust or Profit under the United States, shall be appointed an Elector.

The Electors shall meet in their respective States, and vote by Ballot for two persons, of whom one at least shall not lie an Inhabitant of the same State with themselves. And they shall make a List of all the Persons voted for, and of the Number of Votes for each; which List they shall sign and certify, and transmit sealed to the Seat of the Government of the United States, directed to the President of the Senate. The President of the Senate shall, in the Presence of the Senate and House of Representatives, open all the Certificates, and the Votes shall then be counted. The Person having the greatest Number of Votes shall be the President, if such Number be a Majority of the whole Number of Electors appointed; and if there be more than one who have such Majority, and have an equal Number of Votes, then the House of Representatives shall immediately chuse by Ballot one of them for President; and if no Person have a Majority, then from the five highest on the List the said House shall in like Manner chuse the President. But in chusing the President, the Votes shall be taken by States, the Representation from each State having one Vote; a quorum for this Purpose shall consist of a Member or Members from two thirds of the States, and a Majority of all the States shall be necessary to a Choice. In every Case, after the Choice of the President, the Person having the greatest Number of Votes of the Electors shall be the Vice President. But if there should remain two or more who have equal Votes, the Senate shall chuse from them by Ballot the Vice-President.

The Congress may determine the Time of chusing the Electors, and the Day on which they shall give their Votes; which Day shall be the same throughout the United States.

No person except a natural born Citizen, or a Citizen of the United States, at the time of the Adoption of this Constitution, shall be eligible to the Office of President; neither shall any Person be eligible to that Office who shall not have attained to the Age of thirty-five Years, and been fourteen Years a Resident within the United States.

In Case of the Removal of the President from Office, or of his Death, Resignation, or Inability to discharge the Powers and Duties of the said Office, the same shall devolve on the Vice President, and the Congress may by Law provide for the Case of Removal, Death, Resignation or Inability, both of the President and Vice President, declaring what Officer shall then act as President, and such Officer shall act accordingly, until the Disability be removed, or a President shall be elected.

The President shall, at stated Times, receive for his Services, a Compensation, which shall neither be increased nor diminished during the Period for which he shall have been elected, and he shall not receive within that Period any other Emolument from the United States, or any of them.

Before he enter on the Execution of his Office, he shall take the following Oath or Affirmation:

"I do solemnly swear (or affirm) that I will faithfully execute the Office of President of the United States, and will to the best of my Ability, preserve, protect and defend the Constitution of the United States."

Section 2

The President shall be Commander in Chief of the Army and Navy of the United States, and of the Militia of the several States, when called into the actual Service of the United States; he may require the Opinion, in writing, of the principal Officer in each of the executive Departments, upon any subject relating to the Duties of their respective Offices, and he shall have Power to Grant Reprieves and Pardons for Offenses against the United States, except in Cases of Impeachment.

He shall have Power, by and with the Advice and Consent of the Senate, to make Treaties, provided two thirds of the Senators present concur; and he shall nominate, and by and with the Advice and Consent of the Senate, shall appoint Ambassadors, other public Ministers and Consuls, Judges of the supreme Court, and all other Officers of the United States, whose Appointments are not herein otherwise provided for, and which shall be established by Law: but the Congress may by Law vest the Appointment of such inferior Officers, as they think proper, in the President alone, in the Courts of Law, or in the Heads of Departments.

The President shall have Power to fill up all Vacancies that may happen during the Recess of the Senate, by granting Commissions which shall expire at the End of their next Session.

Section 3

He shall from time to time give to the Congress Information of the State of the Union, and recommend to their Consideration such Measures as he shall judge necessary and expedient; he may, on extraordinary Occasions, convene both Houses, or either of them, and in Case of Disagreement between them, with Respect to the Time of Adjournment, he may adjourn them to such Time as he shall think proper; he shall receive Ambassadors and other public Ministers; he shall take Care that the Laws be faithfully executed, and shall Commission all the Officers of the United States.

Section 4

The President, Vice President and all civil Officers of the United States, shall be removed from Office on Impeachment for, and Conviction of, Treason, Bribery, or other high Crimes and Misdemeanors.

Article III

Section 1

The judicial Power of the United States, shall be vested in one supreme Court, and in such inferior Courts as the Congress may from time to time ordain and establish. The Judges, both of the supreme and inferior Courts, shall hold their Offices during good Behavior, and shall, at stated Times, receive for their Services a Compensation which shall not be diminished during their Continuance in Office.

Section 2

The judicial Power shall extend to all Cases, in Law and Equity, arising under this Constitution, the Laws of the United States, and Treaties made, or which shall be made, under their Authority; to all Cases affecting Ambassadors, other public Ministers and Consuls; to all Cases of admiralty and maritime Jurisdiction; to Controversies to which the United States shall be a Party; to Controversies between two or more States; between a State and Citizens of another State; between Citizens of different States; between Citizens of the same State claiming Lands under Grants of different States, and between a State, or the Citizens thereof, and foreign States, Citizens or Subjects.

In all Cases affecting Ambassadors, other public Ministers and Consuls, and those in which a State shall be Party, the supreme Court shall have original Jurisdiction. In all the other Cases before mentioned, the supreme Court shall have appellate Jurisdiction, both as to Law and Fact, with such Exceptions, and under such Regulations as the Congress shall make.

The Trial of all Crimes, except in Cases of Impeachment, shall be by Jury; and such Trial shall be held in the State where the said Crimes shall have been committed; but when not committed within any State, the Trial shall be at such Place or Places as the Congress may by Law have directed.

Section 3

Treason against the United States, shall consist only in levying War against them, or in adhering to their Enemies, giving them Aid and Comfort. No Person shall be convicted of Treason unless on the Testimony of two Witnesses to the same overt Act, or on Confession in open Court.

The Congress shall have power to declare the Punishment of Treason, but no Attainder of Treason shall work Corruption of Blood, or Forfeiture except during the Life of the Person attainted.

Article IV

Section 1

Full Faith and Credit shall be given in each State to the public Acts, Records, and judicial Proceedings of every other State. And the Congress may by general Laws prescribe the Manner in which such Acts, Records and Proceedings shall be proved, and the Effect thereof.

Section 2

The Citizens of each State shall be entitled to all Privileges and Immunities of Citizens in the several States.

A Person charged in any State with Treason, Felony, or other Crime, who shall flee from Justice, and be found in another State, shall on demand of the executive Authority of the State from which he fled, be delivered up, to be removed to the State having Jurisdiction of the Crime.

No Person held to Service or Labour in one State, under the Laws thereof, escaping into another, shall, in Consequence of any Law or Regulation therein, be discharged from such Service or Labour, But shall be delivered up on Claim of the Party to whom such Service or Labour may be due.

Section 3

New States may be admitted by the Congress into this Union; but no new States shall be formed or erected within the Jurisdiction of any other State; nor any State be formed by the Junction of two or more States, or parts of States, without the Consent of the Legislatures of the States concerned as well as of the Congress.

The Congress shall have Power to dispose of and make all needful Rules and Regulations respecting the Territory or other Property belonging to the United States; and nothing in this Constitution shall be so construed as to Prejudice any Claims of the United States, or of any particular State.

Section 4

The United States shall guarantee to every State in this Union a Republican Form of Government, and shall protect each of them against Invasion; and on Application of the Legislature, or of the Executive (when the Legislature cannot be convened) against domestic Violence.

Article V

The Congress, whenever two thirds of both Houses shall deem it necessary, shall propose Amendments to this Constitution, or, on the Application of the Legislatures of two thirds of the several States, shall call a Convention for proposing Amendments, which, in either Case, shall be valid to all Intents and Purposes, as part of this Constitution, when ratified by the Legislatures of three fourths of the several States, or by Conventions in three fourths thereof, as the one or the other Mode of Ratification may be proposed by the Congress; Provided that no Amendment which may be made prior to the Year One thousand eight hundred and eight shall in any Manner affect the first and fourth Clauses in the Ninth Section of the first Article; and that no State, without its Consent, shall be deprived of its equal Suffrage in the Senate.

Article VI

All Debts contracted and Engagements entered into, before the Adoption of this Constitution, shall be as valid against the United States under this Constitution, as under the Confederation.

This Constitution, and the Laws of the United States which shall be made in Pursuance thereof; and all Treaties made, or which shall be made, under the Authority of the United States, shall be the supreme Law of the Land; and the Judges in every State shall be bound thereby, any Thing in the Constitution or Laws of any State to the Contrary notwithstanding.

The Senators and Representatives before mentioned, and the Members of the several State Legislatures, and all executive and judicial Officers, both of the United States and of the several States, shall be bound by Oath or Affirmation, to support this Constitution; but no religious Test shall ever be required as a Qualification to any Office or public Trust under the United States.

Article VII

The Ratification of the Conventions of nine States, shall be sufficient for the Establishment of this Constitution between the States so ratifying the Same.

Done in Convention by the Unanimous Consent of the States present the Seventeenth Day of September in the Year of our Lord one thousand seven hundred and Eighty seven and of the Independence of the United States of America the Twelfth.

Amendment I (1791)

Congress shall make no law respecting an establishment of religion, or prohibiting the free exercise thereof; or abridging the freedom of speech, or of the press; or the right of the people peaceably to assemble, and to petition the Government for a redress of grievances.

Amendment II (1791)

A well regulated Militia, being necessary to the security of a free State, the right of the people to keep and bear Arms, shall not be infringed.

Amendment III (1791)

No Soldier shall, in time of peace be quartered in any house, without the consent of the Owner, nor in time of war, but in a manner to be prescribed by law.

Amendment IV (1791)

The right of the people to be secure in their persons, houses, papers, and effects, against unreasonable searches and seizures, shall not be violated, and no Warrants shall issue, but upon probable cause, supported by Oath or affirmation, and particularly describing the place to be searched, and the persons or things to be seized.

Amendment V (1791)

No person shall be held to answer for a capital, or otherwise infamous crime, unless on a presentment or indictment of a Grand Jury, except in cases arising in the land or naval forces, or in the Militia, when in actual service in time of War or public danger; nor shall any person be subject for the same offense to be twice put in jeopardy of life or limb; nor shall be compelled in any criminal case to be a witness against himself, nor be deprived of life, liberty, or property, without due process of law; nor shall private property be taken for public use, without just compensation.

Amendment VI (1791)

In all criminal prosecutions, the accused shall enjoy the right to a speedy and public trial, by an impartial jury of the State and district wherein the crime shall have been committed, which district shall have been previously ascertained by law, and to be informed of the nature and cause of the accusation; to be confronted with the witnesses against him; to have compulsory process for obtaining witnesses in his favor, and to have the Assistance of Counsel for his defence.

Amendment VII (1791)

In Suits at common law, where the value in controversy shall exceed twenty dollars, the right of trial by jury shall be preserved, and no fact tried by a jury, shall be otherwise re-examined in any Court of the United States, than according to the rules of the common law.

Amendment VIII (1791)

Excessive bail shall not be required, nor excessive fines imposed, nor cruel and unusual punishments inflicted.

Amendment IX (1791)

The enumeration in the Constitution, of certain rights, shall not be construed to deny or disparage others retained by the people.

Amendment X (1791)

The powers not delegated to the United States by the Constitution, nor prohibited by it to the States, are reserved to the States respectively, or to the people.

Amendment XI (1798)

The Judicial power of the United States shall not be construed to extend to any suit in law or equity, commenced or prosecuted against one of the United States by Citizens of another State, or by Citizens or Subjects of any Foreign State.

Amendment XII (1804)

The Electors shall meet in their respective states, and vote by ballot for President and Vice-President, one of whom, at least, shall not be an inhabitant of the same state with themselves; they shall name in their ballots the person voted for as President, and in distinct ballots the person voted for as Vice-President, and they shall make distinct lists of all persons voted for as President, and of all persons voted for as Vice-President and of the number of votes for each, which lists they shall sign and certify, and transmit sealed to the seat of the government of the United States, directed to the President of the Senate.

The President of the Senate shall, in the presence of the Senate and House of Representatives, open all the certificates and the votes shall then be counted.

The person having the greatest Number of votes for President, shall be the President, if such number be a majority of the whole number of Electors appointed; and if no person have such majority, then from the persons having the highest numbers not exceeding three on the list of those voted for as President, the House of Representatives shall choose immediately, by ballot, the President. But in choosing the President, the votes shall be taken by states, the representation from each state having one vote; a quorum for this purpose shall consist of a member or members from two-thirds of the states, and a majority of all the states shall be necessary to a choice. And if the House of Representatives shall not choose a President whenever the right of choice shall devolve upon them, before the fourth day of March next following, then the Vice-President shall act as President, as in the case of the death or other constitutional disability of the President.

The person having the greatest number of votes as Vice-President, shall be the Vice-President, if such number be a majority of the whole number of Electors appointed, and if no person have a majority, then from the two highest numbers on the list,

the Senate shall choose the Vice-President; a quorum for the purpose shall consist of two-thirds of the whole number of Senators, and a majority of the whole number shall be necessary to a choice. But no person constitutionally ineligible to the office of President shall be eligible to that of Vice-President of the United States.

Amendment XIII (1865)

1 Neither slavery nor involuntary servitude, except as a punishment for crime whereof the party shall have been duly convicted, shall exist within the United States, or any place subject to their jurisdiction.
2 Congress shall have power to enforce this article by appropriate legislation.

Amendment XIV (1865)

1 All persons born or naturalized in the United States, and subject to the jurisdiction thereof, are citizens of the United States and of the State wherein they reside. No State shall make or enforce any law which shall abridge the privileges or immunities of citizens of the United States; nor shall any State deprive any person of life, liberty, or property, without due process of law; nor deny to any person within its jurisdiction the equal protection of the laws.
2 Representatives shall be apportioned among the several States according to their respective numbers, counting the whole number of persons in each State, excluding Indians not taxed. But when the right to vote at any election for the choice of electors for President and Vice-President of the United States, Representatives in Congress, the Executive and Judicial officers of a State, or the members of the Legislature thereof, is denied to any of the male inhabitants of such State, being twenty-one years of age, and citizens of the United States, or in any way abridged, except for participation in rebellion, or other crime, the basis of representation therein shall be reduced in the proportion which the number of such male citizens shall bear to the whole number of male citizens twenty-one years of age in such State.
3 No person shall be a Senator or Representative in Congress, or elector of President and Vice-President, or hold any office, civil or military, under the United States, or under any State, who, having previously taken an oath, as a member of Congress, or as an officer of the United States, or as a member of any State legislature, or as an executive or judicial officer of any State, to support the Constitution of the United States, shall have engaged in insurrection or rebellion against the same, or given aid or comfort to the enemies thereof. But Congress may by a vote of two-thirds of each House, remove such disability.
4 The validity of the public debt of the United States, authorized by law, including debts incurred for payment of pensions and bounties for services in suppressing insurrection or rebellion, shall not be questioned. But neither the United States nor

any State shall assume or pay any debt or obligation incurred in aid of insurrection or rebellion against the United States, or any claim for the loss or emancipation of any slave; but all such debts, obligations and claims shall be held illegal and void.

5   The Congress shall have power to enforce, by appropriate legislation, the provisions of this article.

Amendment XV (1870)

1   The right of citizens of the United States to vote shall not be denied or abridged by the United States or by any State on account of race, color, or previous condition of servitude.

2   The Congress shall have power to enforce this article by appropriate legislation.

Amendment XVI (1913)

The Congress shall have power to lay and collect taxes on incomes, from whatever source derived, without apportionment among the several States, and without regard to any census or enumeration.

Amendment XVII (1913)

1   The Senate of the United States shall be composed of two Senators from each State, elected by the people thereof, for six years; and each Senator shall have one vote. The electors in each State shall have the qualifications requisite for electors of the most numerous branch of the State legislatures.

2   When vacancies happen in the representation of any State in the Senate, the executive authority of such State shall issue writs of election to fill such vacancies: Provided, That the legislature of any State may empower the executive thereof to make temporary appointments until the people fill the vacancies by election as the legislature may direct.

3   This amendment shall not be so construed as to affect the election or term of any Senator chosen before it becomes valid as part of the Constitution.

Amendment XVIII (1919: Repealed by Amendment XXI, 1933)

1   After one year from the ratification of this article the manufacture, sale, or transportation of intoxicating liquors within, the importation thereof into, or the exportation thereof from the United States and all territory subject to the jurisdiction thereof for beverage purposes is hereby prohibited.

2   The Congress and the several States shall have concurrent power to enforce this article by appropriate legislation.

3   This article shall be inoperative unless it shall have been ratified as an amendment to the Constitution by the legislatures of the several States, as provided in the Constitution, within seven years from the date of the submission hereof to the States by the Congress.

Amendment XIX (1920)

1   The right of citizens of the United States to vote shall not be denied or abridged by the United States or by any State on account of sex.

2   Congress shall have power to enforce this article by appropriate legislation.

Amendment XX (1933)

1   The terms of the President and Vice President shall end at noon on the 20th day of January, and the terms of Senators and Representatives at noon on the 3d day of January, of the years in which such terms would have ended if this article had not been ratified; and the terms of their successors shall then begin.

2   The Congress shall assemble at least once in every year, and such meeting shall begin at noon on the 3d day of January, unless they shall by law appoint a different day.

3   If, at the time fixed for the beginning of the term of the President, the President elect shall have died, the Vice President elect shall become President. If a President shall not have been chosen before the time fixed for the beginning of his term, or if the President elect shall have failed to qualify, then the Vice President elect shall act as President until a President shall have qualified; and the Congress may by law provide for the case wherein neither a President elect nor a Vice President elect shall have qualified, declaring who shall then act as President, or the manner in which one who is to act shall be selected, and such person shall act accordingly until a President or Vice President shall have qualified.

4   The Congress may by law provide for the case of the death of any of the persons from whom the House of Representatives may choose a President whenever the right of choice shall have devolved upon them, and for the case of the death of any of the persons from whom the Senate may choose a Vice President whenever the right of choice shall have devolved upon them.

5   Sections 1 and 2 shall take effect on the 15th day of October following the ratification of this article.

6   This article shall be inoperative unless it shall have been ratified as an amendment to the Constitution by the legislatures of three-fourths of the several States within seven years from the date of its submission.

Amendment XXI (1933)

1   The eighteenth article of amendment to the Constitution of the United States is hereby repealed.

2   The transportation or importation into any State, Territory, or possession of the United States for delivery or use therein of intoxicating liquors, in violation of the laws thereof, is hereby prohibited.

3   The article shall be inoperative unless it shall have been ratified as an amendment to the Constitution by conventions in the several States, as provided in the Constitution, within seven years from the date of the submission hereof to the States by the Congress.

Amendment XXII (1951)

1   No person shall be elected to the office of the President more than twice, and no person who has held the office of President, or acted as President, for more than two years of a term to which some other person was elected President shall be elected to the office of the President more than once. But this Article shall not apply to any person holding the office of President, when this Article was proposed by the Congress, and shall not prevent any person who may be holding the office of President, or acting as President, during the term within which this Article becomes operative from holding the office of President or acting as President during the remainder of such term.

2   This article shall be inoperative unless it shall have been ratified as an amendment to the Constitution by the legislatures of three-fourths of the several States within seven years from the date of its submission to the States by the Congress.

Amendment XXIII (1961)

1   The District constituting the seat of Government of the United States shall appoint in such manner as the Congress may direct: A number of electors of President and Vice President equal to the whole number of Senators and Representatives in Congress to which the District would be entitled if it were a State, but in no event more than the least populous State; they shall be in addition to those appointed by the States, but they shall be considered, for the purposes of the election of President and Vice President, to be electors appointed by a State; and they shall meet in the District and perform such duties as provided by the twelfth article of amendment.

2   The Congress shall have power to enforce this article by appropriate legislation.

Amendment XXIV (1964)

1   The right of citizens of the United States to vote in any primary or other election for President or Vice President, for electors for President or Vice President, or for Senator or Representative in Congress, shall not be denied or abridged by the United States or any State by reason of failure to pay any poll tax or other tax.

2   The Congress shall have power to enforce this article by appropriate legislation.

Amendment XXV (1967)

1   In case of the removal of the President from office or of his death or resignation, the Vice President shall become President.

2   Whenever there is a vacancy in the office of the Vice President, the President shall nominate a Vice President who shall take office upon confirmation by a majority vote of both Houses of Congress.

3   Whenever the President transmits to the President pro tempore of the Senate and the Speaker of the House of Representatives his written declaration that he is unable to discharge the powers and duties of his office, and until he transmits to them a written declaration to the contrary, such powers and duties shall be discharged by the Vice President as Acting President.

4   Whenever the Vice President and a majority of either the principal officers of the executive departments or of such other body as Congress may by law provide, transmit to the President pro tempore of the Senate and the Speaker of the House of Representatives their written declaration that the President is unable to discharge the powers and duties of his office, the Vice President shall immediately assume the powers and duties of the office as Acting President.

Thereafter, when the President transmits to the President pro tempore of the Senate and the Speaker of the House of Representatives his written declaration that no inability exists, he shall resume the powers and duties of his office unless the Vice President and a majority of either the principal officers of the executive department or of such other body as Congress may by law provide, transmit within four days to the President pro tempore of the Senate and the Speaker of the House of Representatives their written declaration that the President is unable to discharge the powers and duties of his office. Thereupon Congress shall decide the issue, assembling within forty eight hours for that purpose if not in session. If the Congress, within twenty one days after receipt of the latter written declaration, or, if Congress is not in session, within twenty one days after Congress is required to assemble, determines by two thirds vote of both Houses that the President is unable to discharge the powers and duties of his office, the Vice President shall continue to discharge the same as Acting President; otherwise, the President shall resume the powers and duties of his office.

Amendment XXVI (1971)

1 The right of citizens of the United States, who are eighteen years of age or older, to vote shall not be denied or abridged by the United States or by any State on account of age.

2 The Congress shall have power to enforce this article by appropriate legislation.

Amendment XXVII (1992)

No law, varying the compensation for the services of the Senators and Representatives, shall take effect, until an election of Representatives shall have intervened.

Appendix III

References

Chapter 1 The Constitution
Finer, S. E., *Comparative Government,* Penguin, 1970.

Grodzins, M., *The American System*, Rand McNally & Co., 1966.

Neustadt, R. E., *Presidential Power*, John Wiley, 1960.

Chapter 2 Elections and voting
Cronin, T. E. and Genovese, M. A., *The Paradoxes of the American Presidency*, Oxford University Press, 1998.

Jacobson, G. C., *The Politics of Congressional Elections*, Longman, 2009.

Loevy, R. D., *The Flawed Path to the Presidency 1992*, State University of New York, 1995.

Wayne, S. J., *The Road to the White House*, Bedford-St Martin's, 2001.

Chapter 3 Political parties
Broder, D., *The Party's Over: The Failure of Politics in America*, Harper & Row, 1972.

Scott, R. K., *Parties in Crisis: Party Politics in America*, Wiley, 1979.

Wattenberg, M. P., *The Decline of American Political Parties*, Harvard University Press, 1984.

Chapter 4 Pressure groups
Ashbee, E. and Ashford, N., *US Politics Today*, Manchester University Press, 1999.

Berry, J. M. and Wilcox, C., *The Interest Group Society*, Pearson Longman, 2007.

Drew, E., *Showdown: The Struggle between the Gingrich Congress and the Clinton White House*, Simon and Schuster, 1996.

Heywood, A., *Essentials of UK Politics*, Palgrave Macmillan, 2011.

Sabato, L., *The Sixth Year Itch: The Rise and Fall of the George W. Bush Presidency*, Pearson Longman, 2008.

Chapter 5 Congress
Brownstein, R., *The Second Civil War: How Extreme Partisanship Has Paralyzed Washington and Polarized America,* Penguin Group, 2007.

Carr, R. K., *Essentials of American Democracy*, Dryden Press, 1974.

Denenberg, R. V., *Understanding American Politics*, Fontana, 1976.

Loomis, B. A., *The Contemporary Congress*, Wadsworth, 2004.

Vile, M. J. C., *Politics in the USA*, Routledge, 1999.

Chapter 6 The presidency

Finer, S. E., *Comparative Government*, Penguin, 1970.

Cronin, T. E. and Genovese, M. A., *The Paradoxes of the American Presidency*, Oxford University Press, 1998.

Drew, E., *The Corruption of American Politics*, Birch Lane Press, 1999.

Fenno, R. F., *The President's Cabinet*, Harvard University Press, 1959.

Finer, S. E., *Comparative Government*, Penguin, 1970.

Healy, G., *The Cult of the Presidency*, Cato Institute, 2008.

Hook, S. W. and Spanier, J., *American Foreign Policy since World War II*, CQ Press, 2013.

Katz, R. S., *Political Institutions in the United States*, Oxford, 2007.

McClellan, S., *What Happened Inside the Bush White House and Washington's Culture of Deception*, Public Affairs, 2008.

McKay, D., *American Politics and Society*, Blackwell, 2005.

Mervin, D., *Ronald Reagan and the American Presidency*, Longman, 1990.

Mervin, D., *The President of the United States*, Harvester-Wheatsheaf, 1993.

Neustadt, R. E., *Presidential Power: The Politics of Leadership from Roosevelt to Reagan*, Free Press, 1990.

Neustadt, R. E., in Felzenberg, A. S. (ed.), *The Keys to a Successful Presidency*, The Heritage Foundation, 2000.

Nixon, R. M., *RN: The Memoirs of Richard Nixon*, Sidgwick and Jackson, 1978.

Peterson, M. A., 'Presidential power and the potential for leadership', in Shapiro, R. Y. et al. (eds), *Presidential Power: Forging the Presidency for the 21st Century*, Columbia University Press, 2000.

Pfiffner, J., *The Modern Presidency*, Bedford-St Martin's, 2000.

Pfiffner, J., 'Organising the Obama White House,' in Thurber, J. A. (ed.), *Obama in Office*, Paradigm Publishers, 2011.

Polsby, N. W., *Congress and the Presidency*, Prentice-Hall, 1976.

Schlesinger, A. M., *The Cycles of American History*, Houghton-Mifflin, 1986.

Shrum, R., 'The Hillary Test', *The Week*, 2 December 2008.

Tannenhaus, S., 'Imperial? No, Presidential. Bush is no "Caesar"', *Wall Street Journal*, 27 December 2002.

Woodward, B., *Bush at War*, Simon and Schuster, 2003.

Woodward, B., *The War Within*, Simon and Schuster, 2008.

Woodward, B., *Obama's Wars*, Simon and Schuster, 2010.

7 The Supreme Court, and the protection of rights and liberties

Lazarus, E., *Closed Chambers: The Rise, Fall and Future of the Modern Supreme Court*, Penguin, 1999.

Mackenzie, G. C., *Innocent Until Nominated: The Breakdown of the Presidential Appointments Process*, Brookings, 2001.

Roosevelt, K., *The Myth of Judicial Activism*, Yale University Press, 2006.

Toobin, J., *The Nine: Inside the Secret World of the Supreme Court*, Doubleday, 2007.

van Geel, T. R., *Understanding Supreme Court Opinions*, Pearson, 2009.

Chapter 8 Racial and ethnic politics

Anderson, E., 'Integration, affirmative action and strict scrutiny', *New York University Law Review*, Vol. 77, November 2002.

Cohen, C., *Naked Racial Preference*, Madison Books, 1995.

Fullinwider, R., in *The Stanford Encyclopaedia of Philosophy* (see entry on Affirmative Action), Spring 2005 edition.

Kahlenberg, R., 'What's next for affirmative action?', *The Atlantic*, 6 November 2008.

McKay, D., *American Society Today*, Blackwell, 2005.

Toobin, J., *The Nine: Inside the Secret World of the Supreme Court*, Doubleday, 2007.

Wilson, J. Q. and DiLulio, J. J., *American Government*, Houghton-Mifflin, 2001.

Index

Page numbers in red type refer to key term terms and concepts.